Subaltern Geographies

GEOGRAPHIES OF JUSTICE AND SOCIAL TRANSFORMATION

SERIES EDITORS

Mathew Coleman, Ohio State University
Sapana Doshi, University of Arizona

FOUNDING EDITOR

Nik Heynen, University of Georgia

ADVISORY BOARD

Deborah Cowen, University of Toronto
Zeynep Gambetti, Boğaziçi University
Geoff Mann, Simon Fraser University
James McCarthy, Clark University
Beverley Mullings, Queen's University
Harvey Neo, National University of Singapore
Geraldine Pratt, University of British Columbia
Ananya Roy, University of California, Los Angeles
Michael Watts, University of California, Berkeley
Ruth Wilson Gilmore, CUNY Graduate Center
Jamie Winders, Syracuse University
Melissa W. Wright, Pennsylvania State University
Brenda S. A. Yeoh, National University of Singapore

Subaltern Geographies

EDITED BY
**TARIQ JAZEEL
AND STEPHEN LEGG**

THE UNIVERSITY OF GEORGIA PRESS
Athens

© 2019 by the University of Georgia Press
Athens, Georgia 30602
www.ugapress.org
All rights reserved
Set in 10/12.5 Minion Pro by Graphic Composition, Inc.

Most University of Georgia Press titles are
available from popular e-book vendors.

Printed digitally

Library of Congress Cataloging-in-Publication Data

Names: Jazeel, Tariq, editor. | Legg, Stephen, editor.
Title: Subaltern geographies / edited by Tariq Jazeel and Stephen Legg.
Description: Athens, Ga. : University of Georgia Press, 2019. |
    Series: Geographies of justice and social transformation |
    Includes bibliographical references and index.
Identifiers: LCCN 2018042679| ISBN 9780820354590 (hard cover : alk. paper) |
    ISBN 9780820354880 (pbk. : alk. paper) | ISBN 9780820354606 (ebook)
Subjects: LCSH: Developing countries—Social conditions |
    Developing countries—Geography. | Postcolonialism—Developing countries.
Classification: LCC HN980 .S79 2019 | DDC 306.09172/4—dc23
    LC record available at https://lccn.loc.gov/2018042679

CONTENTS

Acknowledgments vii

Subaltern Studies, Space, and the Geographical Imagination
TARIQ JAZEEL AND STEPHEN LEGG 1

Subaltern Streets: India, 1870–1947
DAVID ARNOLD 36

Before Subaltern Studies: The Epistemology of Property
MUKUL KUMAR AND ANANYA ROY 58

Practicing Subalternity? Nyerere's Tanzania, the Dar School, and Postcolonial Geopolitical Imaginations
JO SHARP 74

Reading Subaltern Studies Politically: Histories from Below, Spatial Relations, and Subalternity
DAVID FEATHERSTONE 94

Pachamama, Subaltern Geographies, and Decolonial Projects in Andean Ecuador
SARAH A. RADCLIFFE 119

Time, Space, and the Subaltern: The Matter of Labor in Delhi's Grey Economy
VINAY GIDWANI AND SUNIL KUMAR 142

Subaltern Geographies in the Plurinational State of Bolivia: The TIPNIS Conflict
ANNA F. LAING 167

Subaltern Sea? Indian Ocean Errantry against Subalternization
SHARAD CHARI 191

Urban Fragments: A Subaltern Studies Imagination
COLIN MCFARLANE 210

Contributors 231

Index 235

ACKNOWLEDGMENTS

This volume emerges from two sessions co-organized by us at the 2014 annual conference of the Royal Geographical Society (in conjunction with the Institute of British Geographers). While the conference has regularly hosted sessions on colonialism or imperialism, we felt that it had neglected discussions of nonhegemonic understandings of space, descriptions and analyses of subaltern forms of dwelling- and space-making, and examinations of the craft and skill required to engage subaltern archives or groups. We would like to thank all those involved in making those sessions happen, including Thomas Cowan, David Featherstone, Vinay Gidwani, Colin McFarlane, Jenny Robinson, and Jo Sharp, as well as the many who attended those sessions and joined in the subsequent discussions. We would also like to thank the RGS-IBG's Historical Geography Research Group and the History and Philosophy of Geography Research Group for sponsoring these sessions.

David Arnold, Sharad Chari, and Vinay Gidwani gave us valuable feedback on the introductory essay in this book, for which we are both extremely grateful. One of the most valuable lessons we take from subaltern studies is the significance of collaboration, shared learning, and the importance of benefiting from the situated knowledge of others. Our contributors have been, and we know will continue to be, model collaborators. They have taught us much more than we can hope to reciprocate. We thank them sincerely for their patience and diligence.

We would also like thank the editors of the Geographies of Justice and Social Transformation series at the University of Georgia Press, Nik Heynen, Sapana Doshi, and Matthew Coleman, whose enthusiastic support for this project has been crucial and invaluable. Our editor Mick Gusinde-Duffy has helped us see the manuscript through a meticulous review process, and through it all has been kind and available and a pleasure to work with. We also thank the manuscript reviewers for their belief in this manuscript, as well as their critical engagements and provocations to always go just that bit further in our delineations of the intersections between subaltern studies and critical geography. We thank Magnum Photos/Raghu Rai for permission to reproduce the cover image, a section from Rai's photograph of Chawri Bazar in Old Delhi, taken in 1972.

Steve completed much of the work on this volume during a British Academy

Mid-Career Fellowship, for which he is extremely grateful. Tariq has benefited from a period of sabbatical leave from University College London (UCL), which has helped greatly in the production of this book.

Coediting and coauthoring is an exercise of coproduction and coexistence, in this case lasting over five years. Steve would like to thank Tariq for pushing him to read more, think more, and find ever-new perspectives from which to think about his privilege, how he writes, and why. And for making him laugh— a lot. Tariq would like to thank Steve for being a lesson in intellectual care, acuity, and generosity, for his careful yet creative eye, and not least for his warmth, enthusiasm, and compassion through a period in which life, as much as our collective thinking, has taken its course. He would also like to thank Steve for laughing at his jokes.

This is a project born of the best kind of collegiality. Friendship.

Subaltern Geographies

Subaltern Studies, Space, and the Geographical Imagination

TARIQ JAZEEL AND STEPHEN LEGG

> There is no conquest that has only one story to it. It is made up of at least two—one narrated by the conquerors and the other by the conquered. Foil to the story of that steamship sailing into darkness, there is another being told beyond the point where the civilization of hunters, traders, explorers, and colonizers stops and the jungle begins. We have no clue to its content. The most a narratology of the civilized can do, using all the sophistication of its craft, is to acknowledge it by a rhetoric of incomprehension: eyes which glow in the bush as evidence of a numerous but unseen presence; the gathering and dispersal of shadows there after the logic of some mysterious movement; voices which drone like chants, rise like cries, and die back into silence signifying nothing; and the drums: "At night sometimes the roll of distant drums behind the curtain of trees would run up the river and remain sustained faintly, as if hovering in the air high over our heads, till the first break of day. *Whether it meant war, peace or prayer we could not tell*" (HOD, 68; my emphasis).
>
> —Ranajit Guha (2009b, 387)

Joseph Conrad's *Heart of Darkness* (1899) stands as one of the most iconic tributes to, and flawed critiques of, the colonial enterprise. It sits at the center of the founding text of postcolonial studies, quoted as an insignia at the beginning of the final chapter, "Orientalism Now," of Edward Said's landmark book *Orientalism* (1978). It was also the text Said turned to in his influential meditations on the relationships between geography and empire, recalling the narrator Marlow's passion for maps and their potential to dignify conquest with an idea (Said 1978, 216). For Ranajit Guha, the founder of the Subaltern Studies Collective, the *Heart of Darkness* could only be a story of conquest. While Said (1993, 26) later acknowledged the inability of the novel to present what was *outside* the world-conquering attitudes of Kurtz, Marlow, Conrad, or his readership, Guha (2009b, 388) insisted that Conrad's position was "not much help here for those who have been waiting to hear the other story." He spoke explicitly from his "here" of India. This was not a space of nativist authenticity but a space where the pain of conquest and defeat was continually renarrated—a cult of mourning at the heart of Indian nationalism.

More than twenty years prior to Guha's reflection on *Heart of Darkness*, the Nigerian writer Chinua Achebe noted how it was the very elevation of Conrad's novel to the status of "great literature" that facilitated the evisceration of what Guha would refer to as the "other story." Achebe (1977, 791) put it in a way that resonates with Guha's later insistence that the other story is a methodological challenge: "But more important by far is the abundant testimony about Conrad's savages we could gather if we were so inclined from other sources and which might lead us to think that these people must have had other preoccupations besides merging into the evil forest or materializing out of it simply to plague Marlow and his dispirited band."

Guha's own reading of *Heart of Darkness* is characteristically audacious, spanning literary criticism and psychoanalysis, bridging the historical and contemporary "West" and "East." But what is also readily apparent in the quotation at the start of this introduction is the richness of his geographical imagination, the craft with which he could portray the portrayal of a frontier, and his ever-political contrapuntal interrogation of the colonizing gaze and its inability to fully comprehend those who gazed back. Here we find two of Guha's most abiding questions, questions that animated the Subaltern Studies Collective and that continue to provoke subalternist thought today, namely: How should we question and critique the limits of Western thought and representation? And what can we know about the experiences of those non-(colonial, nationalist, or academic) elites who are placed beyond and escape representation, namely, the subaltern?

If these are questions that have been central to the politico-intellectual endeavor of subalternist scholarship since the collective's foundation in the early 1980s, then this volume begins with one quite simple fact that is often overlooked: that these are inherently spatial questions. At least, they are questions that cannot be worked through without due attention to the spatial registers, modalities, locations, trajectories, and imaginary geographies that, as Said has it, were central to the colonial enterprise itself. After all, Conrad's *Heart of Darkness* is a location, a space of dissonant colonial encounter, a set of fleeting trajectories and nodal points situated in dense power-laden networks of trade, commerce, and exploitation that formed the warp and weft of empire, itself a space as much as a project. But if the *Heart of Darkness* depicts a space, as Achebe's (1977) critique reminds us, it is *also* a bourgeois space, a novella with an implied readership both literate and distinctly Anglophone. It is a space of representational encounter, one with its own borders and margins. Thus, when Guha (2009b, 387) describes "eyes which glow in the bush as evidence of a numerous but unseen presence; the gathering and dispersal of shadows there after the logic of some mysterious movement; voices which drone like chants, rise like cries, and die back into silence signifying nothing," he is of course also describing Conrad's reflection on the limits of representation in a contact zone. For signification itself, as both Conrad and Guha well understand, is geographically located. These are eyes, shadows, and noises that allude to the other story, a story of those located at the *borders* and *margins* of the colonizing gaze's ability to represent. The challenge to bring these narratives into representation is thus as spatial as it is historical and anthropological.

Subaltern Geographies takes these provocations around geography, space, and representation seriously. It builds on a rich seam of scholarship in what became known as "postcolonial geography," which dates back roughly to the 1994 publication of Derek Gregory's landmark book *Geographical Imaginations* and David Slater's (1989, 1992) earlier attempts to bring postcolonial theory into dialogue with development and political geography. This work has developed to variously explore such topics as geographical imaginations and representations of colonized (and postcolonial) space, disciplinary geography's complicity in colonialism, the spatial experience and networks of colonialism, colonialism's material cultures, the neocoloniality of theory culture in the contemporary academy, translation and untranslatability, planetary difference, and indigenous geographies (for overviews, see Crush 1994; Nash 2002; Jazeel 2013a; Sidaway, Woon, and Jacobs 2014). Much of this work has, rightly, emphasized colonial domination, violence, and the destructive capacities and afterlives of colonial taxonomies and governmentalities. But as Clayton (2011) warns, particularly in its early incarnations, postcolonial geography risked privileging the abject spaces of colonialism—its plantations, encyclopedias, invasions, and slums. This has implications for how we study the experience of colonialism and opens up a tension with the way in which geographers have used subaltern experience within their pedagogic practice: "In short, geographers treat subaltern space as both a delimited space of oppression and a liminal space of becoming and critical position on the margins" (Clayton 2011, 251).

Nonetheless, part of Derek Gregory's (1994) foundational contribution to what has become "postcolonial geography" has simply been to remind us that postcolonial theory was always already geographical; that is to say, from its early days it was a politico-intellectual endeavor preoccupied with the intersections of coloniality and space. Indeed, the very conceptualization of imaginative geography comes from Said's *Orientalism*, and Gregory is explicit about the debt his own work on "geographical imaginations" (plural, not singular) owes to Said, who he describes as "one of those rare critics for whom a geographical imagination is indispensible" (1995, 447). Though Said was never part of the Subaltern Studies Collective, Gregory's point is important for this book and the conversation between geography and subaltern studies that it precipitates: critical engagements with colonialism and its afterlives are always spatial, even when they are not focused on the abject spaces of colonial domination.

As such, this book makes a concerted attempt to explore the relationships between subaltern studies and geography, both by excavating the embedded spatialities in extant subalternist scholarship and by speculating on what spatialities exist, or can be crafted, beyond the representational capacities of subalternist and formal geographical thought and knowledge production. If the Subaltern Studies Collective attempted to, first, reveal how peasant and worker agency has been effaced from the colonial archive and, second, read those archives against the grain to recover subaltern agency, then this book asks: What are the implications of this for critical geographical theorizations and explorations of what we might call *subaltern spaces*, *spatialities*, and *geographical imaginations*? What methodo-philosophical potential does a rigorously geographical engagement with the concept of subalternity pose for both geographical thought and subalternist scholarship, whether in historical or contemporary contexts? And what types of craft are necessary for us to seek out subaltern spatialities both from the past and in the present? In so doing, this volume acts as a kind of reader for what we are referring to as *subaltern geographies*.

The Space of Subaltern Studies

The Subaltern Studies Collective created profound historiographical innovations (for a detailed history, see Chaturvedi 2000). The collective's co-optation of Gramsci to reconfigure historical narratives and understandings of Indian politics as not simply the achievement of India's political classes but also the result of broader (national and nonnational) peasant agency and political (that is to say, not "prepolitical") organization, has had effects that rippled, globally, across the humanities and social sciences. In the first two decades of the twenty-first century it has been increasingly acknowledged that "theory from the South" (Comaroff and Comaroff 2012; also see Connell 2007), emerging from putatively "developing" regions, holds the key not just to understanding those regions but to better understanding of the supposedly "developed" world. In recent developments of this work, one of the key arguments has been that theorizing from the South should be conceived less as the simple inversion of a more established geography of (theoretical) knowledge production and more as an "epistemological disruption" full with the potential to reworld the conceptual frameworks and methodologies a Eurocentric academy cannot easily escape (Roy 2017, 35, 36–38). During and ever since the last two decades of the twentieth century, the Subaltern Studies Collective has been, repeatedly, making precisely this point. Working against, in, through, and outside of "Northern" or "Western" "theory," the terms "subaltern" and "subalternity" are now watchwords the world over that usefully, and normatively, denote figures, groups, presences, movements, and communities that historical records too easily forget or occlude. And to this extent we would want to retain a sense that the subaltern as a category of analysis is no less useful because of its normative deployment across the academy and beyond. This sensitization to subalternity is just part of a broader awareness across the disciplines of the contingencies of history writing (see White 1973, for example).

But to suggest as we do that the spatial dimensions of what began as an exercise in revisionist history writing are often overlooked is not to imply that subalternist scholarship and the work of the Subaltern Studies Collective was in any sense a-spatial. Indeed, as Mukul Kumar and Ananya Roy argue in their chapter in this volume, as early as 1963 Ranajit Guha began to deconstruct the epistemology of "property" as a form of emergent universal knowledge. As Kumar and Roy show, Guha's book *A Rule of Property for Bengal*, so often overlooked in the history of subaltern studies, in fact prefigured many of the questions and challenges the collective went on to deal with insofar as it rendered "visible the colonial context in which political economy was forged and practiced, with ideas translated and 'bent backward' to accommodate historical difference" (Kumar and Roy, this volume, 61). But key to their argument is the assertion that this text should not just be seen as a prefiguration of subaltern studies but also as imperative to the spatial disciplines (urban and regional planning is their own disciplinary context) insofar as it is a historicization of a key spatial signifier that has today become a more or less ubiquitous signifier of value: property. Likewise, and as we discuss below, Guha's *Elementary Aspects of Peasant Insurgency in Colonial India* (1983a), a more obvious and emblematic subaltern studies text, ceded one entire chapter—one "elementary aspect"—to the spatial category of territory. Thus, in important ways, we suggest subaltern studies was always already spatial.

What, then, do we mean when we stress that geography has been relatively overlooked in the career of subaltern studies? This is as much a disciplinary assertion than anything else, evidenced by the fact that across its twelve-volume formal career (between 1982 and 2005), subaltern studies' disciplinary roll call includes history, political science, anthropology, legal studies, literary theory, legal studies, and feminist studies but not one contribution by a geographer. This is little more than a symptom of the project's lineage in historical scholarship and its subsequent profusion across certain sections of the social sciences in the United Kingdom, the United States, and India. Indeed, it is also difficult to think which geographers might have contributed to the project in the 1980s. And it is not that the project has had no influence in the geographical discipline. As we show below, in disciplinary geography there *has* been a substantial, if fragmented, engagement with the collective's empirical and conceptual provocations. But the time is right for such geographical and spatial thinking to plug back into the key questions that have driven subaltern studies: How should we question and critique the limits of Western thought and representation? And what can we know about the experiences of those beyond the (colonial, nationalist, or academic) elite?

We seek here to respond to those questions by, in part, suggesting how the "we" corralled by such asking might usefully be expanded via the addition of avowedly geographical imaginations and spatial interventions. As Dipesh Chakrabarty (1998, 477) reminds us, "the discipline of history . . . is only one particular way of remembering the past. It is one amongst many." Historians have fully contributed to and reacted to the provocations of subaltern studies (see Chaturvedi 2000; Ludden 2001), and the debate has been taken up across the arts and humanities (Morris 2010), social sciences (Nilsen and Roy 2015), and Latin American studies (Rodriguez et al. 2001). But thinking geographically and spatially about subaltern studies offers opportunities to extend the project's scope, not just historically but more broadly in the task of exploring the spatial invisibilities that power precipitates here and now as well as there and then. This volume collates statements about the intellectual value and radical utility of plugging subaltern studies back into the critical geographical imagination. But before proceeding with this task, we turn first to the collective's own spatial interrogations of territory and territoriality, scale, and the subject itself.

Territoriality and Territory

Rural territoriality was an abiding interest in the early subaltern studies works. The concern here was not territory (that portion of the earth over which sovereignty is exercised; see Elden 2013, 329) but subaltern territorialization of space—living it, knowing it, claiming it, and being restricted *to* it, with all the political *failures* that this entailed. In his reflections on the Gudem-Rampa uprisings during 1839–1924, David Arnold (1982) highlighted the peasant agency and disobedience of the hill people through grounding their "precise forms" in the physical environment of the hills (the Vizagapatam District of Madras Presidency). Whether Indian or British, traders and collectors from the plains were viewed as outsiders who threatened upland territory and ways of life. The local strength of the movements in response, however, restricted their ability to spread to the plains and to foster collaborations with other ethnic or social groups.

As mentioned, territoriality was the last of Guha's (1983a) six *Elementary Aspects of Peasant Insurgency in Colonial India* (the others being negation, ambiguity, modality, solidarity, and transmission). This was not an academic or post-hoc interpretation of peasant uprisings but an analysis of questions that rebel leaders asked themselves: How far could an insurgency spread? What was its natural limit? What was the speed or versatility of its transmission? This stubborn provincialism was the bane of translocal revolutionaries, and it was bemoaned by leftist figures from Leon Trotsky to Mao Tse-tung and Friedrich Engels (Guha 1983a, 278–79). Territoriality was thus a "limiting consciousness" of contiguity (the local bond) and consanguinity (the blood tie), defined against what the Santal tribe in northeast India called the *Diku* (outsiders). As "physical space" and "ethnic space," territory could also, of course, benefit tribal insurgencies. Physically it could demarcate a homeland worth fighting for, containing ancestral rights, plants, routes, and nostalgia. Ethnically, territory could also be a mobile space of ritual, consultation, and preparation for a tribe. Localist tendencies survived the spread of colonial bureaucracies and social modernization, embedding territoriality in geographies of caste solidarity and exclusion or in village networks and particularities of the 1857 uprising ("particles of geography caught in a beam of history"; Guha 1983a, 305–6). Ethnic space could spread over and unite physical space, but primordial loyalties condemned broader movements to failure because they lacked the class or nationalist narrative that would support the mass movements of the twentieth century, whose translocal geographies originated from elite mobilization, not the organic networking of ethnic and physical spaces into a subaltern and insurgent territoriality.

While the Congress Party and other purportedly secular nationalist parties struggled to patch together one type of an "All-India" mass movement in the twentieth century, religious nationalist institutions were busy forging spatial connections and identities that came to be termed "communal." Gyanendra Pandey (1983) focused on the grassroots interests of, and competitions between, northern Indian castes and classes, which, from the late nineteenth to the early twentieth centuries, started to coalesce into sectional religious forms, around demands and symbols, and against neighboring communities. From these local studies, Pandey (2006) produced a sophisticated analysis of discourses that constructed "communalism" as both colonial (essentialist, timeless) *and* nationalist (economic, recent). These discourses were not textualist-ideals but were fully intertextual in the sense of being inseparable from diverse assemblages of symbols (the cow, the crescent), clothing (the veil, the cap, the kurta), bodies (the martial drill, the circumcision, the womb), places (the mosque, the mandir, the ruin, the grave), and cartographies (dual nations). By the late 1930s the territoriality of communal organizations had started to render the geographical imagination of British India in two, attaching Hindu and Muslim sentiments not just to ethnic and physical space alone (territoriality) but also to two territories (India and Pakistan).

For Pandey (1994), understanding this transition was a problem of comprehending violence. Subaltern violence had tended, he argued, to be dismissed as chaotic and excessive in accounts of the colonial state, the Indian ruling class, and the academy, although the question that remained was familiar to earlier subalternist works: "Who is granted agency, whose history we seem to write, and whose pain and suffering therefore matters" (Pandey 1994, 194). Deny the colonial trope that the East *itself* was inherently violent and then a history of types of violence in places called "the East" becomes possible; deny the nationalist trope that the working classes were inherently violent and then a history of types of violence in places *within* "the East" becomes possible. A reflexive approach to violence in the archive allows sequences of events like the Partition to be approached as a question of witnessing, of survival, of bodies, and of territory—all at the same time. This attentiveness to the scale of territory was most evident in Pandey's (2001) breathtaking analysis of three scales of partition: of the subcontinent; of the provinces of Bengal and the Punjab; and of communities, families, and bodies. Sovereignty over territory and sovereign power over bodies here become inseparable, as an exceptionally rich and powerful body of work on the gendered history of partition geographies has made abundantly clear: "the violence of the Partition was unique in the metamorphosis it achieved between the idea of appropriating a territory as nation and appropriating the body of the woman *as* territory" (Das 1997, 82–83; also see Butalia 2000; Menon and Bhasin 1998). As such, the question of scale and, to a lesser extent, gender has been central to subaltern studies, with the former shifting from a (vertically imagined) ontological distinction between elite and subaltern scales to a concern with material and discursive (horizontally imagined) connections between the local and the global.

Scale: Domains and Networks

Much of the agenda set in Guha's (1982) blistering sixteen-paragraph manifesto for subaltern studies continues to drive (or at least latently inform) ongoing subalternist scholarship. It pushes us to understand the following: the shared imperial and bourgeois interpretations of subaltern politics as responsive to state or nationalist stimulation; the politics of the people, in the face of exploitation, and their mobilization; the failure of the bourgeoisie to speak for and integrate the masses; and the failure of the subaltern to develop a unified consciousness and leadership. Where many (including most of the original collective) take their leave from the early work is in the portrayal of the domain of the subaltern and in the sovereignty of its subject (see below).

Many of the early subaltern writings were infused with a vertical ontology (Legg 2009) that imagined laboring populations in town and country as "an *autonomous* domain, for it neither originated from elite politics nor did its existence depend on the latter" (Guha 1988, 40, original emphasis). Their politics was both modern and traditional and had their own logics that worked on the basis of "kinship and territoriality or on class associations," while elite politics relied upon British institutions or semifeudal loyalties: "Mobilisation in the domain of elite politics was achieved vertically whereas in that of subaltern politics this was achieved horizontally" (Guha 1988, 40). The vertical ontology of one scale stacked upon another was also mapped onto typologies of action: the upper elite domain being more legalistic; the lower subaltern domain being more violent, more chaotic, but also more cautious. While Pandey later rejected these typologies, he and fellow authors shared the early depiction of an autonomous, lower subaltern domain. In understanding the emergence of sectarian religious struggles, he explicitly rejected an emphasis solely on elite demands for constitutional or social concessions in favor of studying the substantial "(and I shall argue, autonomous) non-zamind (landowning), Ahirs (agricultural, labouring), castes" (Pandey 1983, 63). Sumit Sarkar (1984, 272–73) defended Guha against early criticisms that perceived a too-simplistic division of society in the elite–subaltern binary. He insisted that the category was just as full of ambiguity as its rough equivalences, such as "popular," "mass," or "lower class," but it had the advantage of emphasizing domination and subordination while being compatible with a class analysis. As such, Sarkar (1984, 277) continued the attack on imperial (neo)historiography, which refused to consider the autonomy of subaltern cultures of mind.

Partha Chatterjee's second contribution to the collective struck, however, an early note of caution. Thinking about political change in terms of institutions, power, and ideology exposed political structures with "relative autonomy" (Chatterjee 1983, 316; for a critique of this Althusserian approach see O' Hanlon 1988, 206–7). But power had many different modes, and Michel Foucault had recently shown that modern power was capillary, touching bodies and lives throughout the social body (also see Arnold 1985). In the India of the early 1980s this modern power was still felt to be qualified by older modes of power, which continued to create possibilities for class domination. But this was a domination connecting elite and subaltern spheres (through what Chatterjee would later call, after Gramsci, "political society"). Similarly, in his study of Gandhi and the connection between the national and the popular, the emphasis was on ideology as a domain of "relative autonomy" (Chatterjee 1984b, 153). Gandhian ideology subverted the structure of elite-nationalist thought but also allowed the masses to be appropriated by an evolving bourgeois Indian state. Here they became the "mob" in need of disciplining; that is, an active and political people who shared more than a little with the orientalist vision of the peasant.

Shahid Amin (2002) has provided a lucid account from within the (ex-)subaltern collective regarding the relationships between the elite and subaltern domains, as negotiated by Chatterjee (1984a) in particular. Combining the urge to locate a domain of politics that was neither new nor a product of elite stimulation with the desire to view those politics as relational, Chatterjee proposed that "the two domains while not *independent* of each other were nevertheless relatively *autonomous*. This is so because while the two interpenetrate, they are in fact structured in wholly different ways" (Amin 2002, 14, emphasis in original). Just as Guha would develop his interest in the interconnections of dominance (coercion and persuasion) and subordination (collaboration and resistance; see Guha 1997), the aim for Chatterjee was to study the interpenetration of these two domains: "Elite/subaltern relations of power thus become articulated into more complex, and rapidly changing, combinatorial forms . . . the principal merit of the elite-subaltern framework is precisely its fluidity, its ability to enter into a complex structure of power relations and break it down into its constituent parts" (Chatterjee 1984a, xlii).

As Sarkar had suggested, the imaginary informing the divided verticality of the elite and the horizontality of the subaltern attracted much criticism, perhaps because the subtle distinction between autonomy and independence had not been made. In his otherwise ringing endorsement of the subaltern studies collective, Said himself insisted that the elite and subaltern must be given overlapping and interdependent histories. A separatist history would mirror the tyranny it opposes, being "as exclusivist, as limited, provincial, and discriminatory in its suppressions and repression as the master discourse of colonialism and elitism" (Said 1988, viii).

Guha's actual research had always, however, emphasized the interrelations of elite and subaltern realms, whether in terms of representations of the subaltern in primary, secondary, or tertiary discourses (Guha 1983b); the structuring of peasant insurgencies (Guha 1983a); or the always partial successes of nationalist elites in disciplining the masses (Guha 1992). Fifteen years after the launch of the project, Guha clarified how it was that power relations could be studied over the elite-subaltern split that he had helped popularize, using a (perhaps not-coincidental) geographical metaphor: "It follows from the notion of a structural split that the domains defined by it are always and inevitably in touch with each other. This does not take away from their autonomy any more than the continuity of two states sharing a common border takes away from the sovereignty of each other" (Guha 2009a, 326).

As the collective developed its interests in the interdependence of the autonomous domains of elite and subaltern politics, the spatial range of these relationships seemed to increase. The interconnections of local and broader scales had always, of course, been acknowledged: from Pandey (1982, 186) noting that "local struggles tended more and more to get caught up in the general wave of anti-imperialism sweeping through India"; to Chatterjee's analysis of the "strategic configurations" by which bourgeois power combined alliances and coalitions with social groups and the state (Chatterjee 1983, 346); the ways in which spaces of modernity and "dispersed disciplines" spread from the colonial to the native quarters, schools, languages, and disciplines of Bengal, seeking out points of equivalence, similarity, adjacency, or substitutability (Chatterjee 1995, 22–23); or those moments when "occasionally, violence occurs on such a scale that it is difficult for the historian to explain in terms of transitional 'dysfunctions' or 'misunderstandings'" (Pandey 1994, 192), which forced historians like Pandey to link the scales of the local, the regional, and the national in the context of imperial cartographies of violence.

But common to many of these studies was a political alertness to the imperatives driving the networking of the local "out" to broader (not higher) scales. What it meant for a place to be named and treated as local within elite networks could be understood alongside what it meant for certain languages and their histories to be termed and treated as "vernacular": "For, the Latin *verna* inheres in the phrase 'vernacular' like memory in a microchip. It is the memory of an ancient subjugation: verna means, among other things, 'a home-born slave'" (Guha 2009c, 474). In the Raj this bondage survived intact within many vernacular histories that, in "native" tongues, reproduced imperial narratives of themselves, many of which were then used by nationalists in an attempt to create a nation-scale narrative that erased the locality of the vernacular source: "The writs of these pasts ran within strictly local jurisdictions beyond the pale of the Raj and the nationalist kingdom-come ... the vernacular pasts went to the ground as an endangered species or simply perished without authorizing either the historian or the nationalist to speak for them" (Guha 2009c, 478).

A great body of subaltern scholarship has focused on the "prose of otherness" (Pandey 1994), attempting to retrieve meaning from minor, vernacular, or popular histories (despite accusations of nihilism, relativism, ignorance of context, and of neo-Orientalism, see Sarkar 2000), while situating these materials in broader scales of production and interpretation. Arnold (2016) has suggested we consider Indian toxicological knowledge of poison as a provincialized and distinct form of knowledge, though one that was and is subject to piracy and profiteering. Chatterjee (2012, xi) explicitly positions a recent book as one that "braids" together two histories, one "little" (a "local" history of Calcutta under the East India Company, Government of India, and nationalist modernities) and one "grand" (a "global" history of modern empires). Empire here is practiced, contingent, and experienced by elite and subaltern alike through place (neighborhoods, buildings, technologies, monuments, statues, theaters, cinemas): "The modern history of empire was thus lived and acted out in these places—places where that history is sometimes still remembered, and at other times, has been erased from memory" (Guha 2009c, xii).

Sovereign Subjects, Essential Subalterns

At the very moment of this assault upon western historicism, the classical figure of western humanism—the self-originating, self-determining individual, who is at once a subject in his possession of sovereign consciousness whose defining quality is reason, and an agent in his

> power of freedom—is readmitted through the back door in the figure of the subaltern himself, as he is restored to history in the reconstructions of the Subaltern project.
> —Rosalind O' Hanlon (1988, 191)

If one set of criticisms of the early subaltern works focused on the notion of autonomous domains, another attack focused on the depiction of the autonomous subaltern subject. "Subject" here refers to the socially and spatially situated individual who inhabits categories and networks that stretch out beyond, and pre-exist, them. These positionings provide the academic, the policy maker, and the storyteller with the materials from which they craft their explanations, their models, and their narratives. Whilst these craftings are often acknowledged as precisely that, it is easy to forget that the materials upon which they worked, imaginings of the subject itself, were also invented.

If the question of domains was partly addressed through clarifying the autonomy-independence question, critical engagements with the question of the subject have been described by various members of the collective as having a pivotal impact on the entire intellectual and political trajectory of the group's work (Chatterjee 2010). Feminist critiques of the collective's project exposed the presumed subaltern subject as uniformly male, which in itself opened a new space of interrogation around the subject of subaltern studies. These profound critiques that we expand upon in the next section effectively questioned how we imagine the agency of the subject, and, in that process of imagining or writing the agency of the subaltern subject, how subalternity becomes essentialized in particular kinds of ways.

Just as forthright claims were made in the early texts about the autonomy of the subaltern domain (via the language of territory and scale), so were claims made about the sovereignty of the subaltern subject. For example, Guha (1983a, 13) suggested of "rebel consciousness" that "we want to emphasize its sovereignty, its consistency and its logic in order to compensate for its absence from the literature on the subject and to act, if possible, as a corrective to the eclecticism on this theme." Peasant consciousness (a rational, planning mind that was self-conscious before nationalist or bourgeois intervention) was presumed in this early work; the challenge was to reconstruct its forms, ideas, and "elementary aspects" that provided the material for political action. This was an approach shared by Arnold (1982) who set out to highlight the "fundamental characteristics" of subalternity in India and possibly of peasant societies more generally. Though there was no intention to rob the peasants of agency, their constitution, for the best of possible reasons, was presumed nevertheless.

This led to accusations that the subaltern studies authors were falling back on colonial stereotypes of the violent and religious peasant or laborer susceptible to rumor and the paternalism of their employer or overseer (Chandavarkar

2000). Rosalind O'Hanlon's (1988) detailed and pathbreaking critique of the early subaltern works had gone further, highlighting the tension between subalternist attempts to reject neocolonial, nationalist, and Marxist forms of history writing whilst attempting to reconstruct a subject of history that was, essentially, familiar to that of liberal, humanist traditions. Whilst the project increasingly drew on poststructuralist literatures that showed how power operated in both elite and subaltern domains to constitute the body and agency of the subject, the subaltern consciousness the collective sought out bore much in common with the classical humanist subject: in history he (he was uniformly a he) was both agent and experiencer; in literature he was the author; in philosophy he was the vessel of sovereign consciousness, thinking, and therefore being (O' Hanlon 1988, 208). This subject has been exposed in post- and antihumanist critiques (from Marx and Nietzsche to Althusser and Foucault) as a myth and a front for inequality, discipline, and subjugation within civil society. Yet the sovereign subject was one which the subaltern collective retained, creating the impression that the collective was letting the subaltern talk for himself.

O'Hanlon acknowledged an earlier, and ultimately more influential, critique along these lines from within: Gayatri Chakravorty Spivak's deconstruction of subaltern historiography in the fourth volume of the collective's work, in which she first advanced a reading of subaltern studies scholarship as deploying "a *strategic* use of positivist essentialism in a scrupulously visible political interest" (Spivak 1985, 342, emphasis in original; for a later, internal critique see Chatterjee 1993, 164, on Guha's historical structuralism and failure to give us a history of peasant consciousness). This was the beginning of Spivak's deconstructive and deeply influential intervention into subaltern studies, which wrenched subaltern subjectivity from its humanist moorings and positioned it, instead, within chains of signs. For Spivak, the humanist subject had unbreakable affinities with the imperial subject, and both antihumanism and subalternism had failed to completely overcome them. This marked subaltern studies' encounter with literary theory—an encounter that has profoundly shaped the path of subalternist scholarship since and necessitated that it is no longer acceptable to be content with normative deployments of the watchwords "subaltern" and "subalternity." If the space of subalternity was once a space read by the academic attuned to the task of discerning the agency, dreams, and desires of the sovereign subaltern subject, after O'Hanlon's and Spivak's interventions subalternity was irretrievably demarcated as an aporetic space of representation (that is to say a conceptual space filled with doubt, perplexity, and impossibility) that cut to the very core of the relationships between knowledge production, ideology, the researcher, and the researched. It is to the crux of this critique, and its implications for thinking geographically about subalternity, that we now turn.

Subalternity and Representation

Subaltern studies always was, of course, a critical engagement with the politics of representation. The collective's work was nothing if not a recognition that history is a form of writing and, further, that its own textuality was utterly dependent upon the discursive structure and power relations that comprise the archives from which historical narratives are pieced together. This was both evident and explicit in the collective's early work. For example, in the second volume Guha stressed that peasant mobilization, debate, petitioning, and planning were all omitted in counterinsurgency discourse through a representational strategy that preferred to naturalize peasant consciousness via environmentally determinist sleights of hand: "The omission is indeed dyed into most narratives by metaphors assimilating peasant revolts to natural phenomena: they break out like thunder storms, heave like earthquakes, spread like wildfires, infect like epidemics. In other words, when the proverbial clod of earth turns, this is a matter to be explained in terms of natural history" (Guha 1983b, 46). Furthermore, *Subaltern Studies IV* included Bernard S. Cohn's (1985) agenda-setting chapter on colonial forms of knowledge and the "language of command." If these early contributions explicitly dealt with history's textuality, Spivak's interventions began to turn the lens back onto subaltern studies scholarship itself, encouraging readers to critically engage not just the archive's textual properties but also the textuality of the theoretical presuppositions of subaltern studies scholarship. If this was subaltern studies' literary theoretical moment, it was also a moment that marked its convergence with postcolonial studies. (Though we would be careful to not make the same mistake as Vivek Chibber [2013] and conflate subaltern studies with postcolonial studies. For critiques, see Featherstone 2016; Spivak 2014.)

Gayatri Spivak's *Can the Subaltern Speak?* (2010 [1988], henceforth *CtSS*) is perhaps the best-known critique of subaltern studies, though it was not published in the subaltern studies volumes. It has, however, indelibly marked subalternist scholarship's subsequent trajectories. Indeed, as Partha Chatterjee (2010, 83) has remarked, after the publication of *CtSS* the question could no longer be "'What is the true form of the subaltern?' The question had become 'How is the subaltern represented?'" At stake for Spivak is the impossible challenge of the transparent representation of difference, the subaltern, by the intellectual in ways that desist from the ideological constitution of the subaltern *as* subaltern. In other words, how can/does the intellectual avoid consolidating a set of liberal assumptions about the subaltern's agency, selfhood, desire, subjectivity, and so on as they bring them into representation? Without due attention to this conceptual problematic, the subaltern subject of the collective's early work becomes what Ritu Birla (2010, 88–92) has referred to as a "prescribed identity-in-difference" (also see Jazeel 2014).

Spivak marshals the tools of deconstructive poststructuralism (Derrida in particular) to set out the textual mechanics of the impossible yet urgent imperative to represent the subaltern on terms true to the singularity of their difference. *CtSS* interpreted imperialism in explicitly gendered terms, specifically by rereading sati (widow immolation) as a historical site wherein subaltern agency was *produced* variously via colonial, Indian social reformist, and Marxist interpretations of the practice but never by widows themselves (Birla 2010, 89). At issue here are the workings of representation, a critical point that Spivak makes by rereading a friendly conversation between Deleuze and Foucault (see Foucault 1977), where both declare that the oppressed subject of history can speak through the intellectual, that is to say without mediation (Birla 2010, 90; Jazeel 2014, 93). In declaring this, Deleuze and Foucault both commit to a conceit that theory is transparent, that it has nothing to do with representation, and that the intellectual's description of the oppressed subject of history's agency is no more than a transparent window onto their subjectivity. Spivak (2010, 242) suggests that, for Deleuze and Foucault, the concrete experience of the oppressed subject of history (the subaltern) "is disclosed through the concrete experience of the intellectual, the one who diagnoses the episteme." This is a negation of theory's own textuality, its own representational qualities and mechanics, which itself is a betrayal of a Derridean faith in the irreducible textuality of the world and its theorization.

Spivak's point is enmeshed with an assertion that at work in representation is a mechanics best understood via the dual meaning of the very word "representation" in German: first, *darstellen*, which denotes the constitutive work of representation (e.g., art or philosophy's capacity to make something present again but interpretively so); and second, *vertreten*, which denotes a more substitutive sense of representation, as in a representative democracy where we elect a representative who speaks on our behalf. The simple point of *CtSS* is that both these overlapping and intersecting processes are always at work in the mechanics of representation. In other words, representations speak for that which they seek to represent. The signifier cannot but signify.

For Spivak, understanding that these representational mechanics are at work in theorizations of the world demands a response from intellectuals; it marks a responsibility incumbent upon the intellectual to attend to the ways that the theoretical work of subaltern studies ideologically constitutes the subaltern subject as it attempts to speak for that subject. The subaltern's actual difference, their real agency, remains epistemologically irretrievable. Hence, *CtSS* advocates for a heuristic move from the collective's assumptive retrieval of subaltern agency, which can only turn out to be the mobilization of a "self-consolidating other," toward the (im)possible effort of making imaginable radical forms of alterity that cannot yet be fully known (Jazeel 2014, 94; Spivak 2010, 265). Once those forms of radical difference become known, subalternity moves elsewhere.

In other words, subalternity is an analytical challenge (not simply an empirical object/subject) always pushing the researcher onward (Legg 2016a).

In the original version of her essay, Spivak's (2010) answer to the question *Can the Subaltern Speak?* was a resounding "no." Vinay Gidwani (2009) has usefully summarized five overlapping readings of the essay that buttress this negative response. First, subaltern speech is disqualified because it is not deemed public and hence not political; second, the subaltern is defiantly other and refuses assimilation; third, the subaltern cannot be known and thus forces us to enter into the relationships of subalternity as interpreters who cannot interpret; fourth, even if subalterns could speak their voices would enter networks of representation, serving the ideologies and politics of others; and fifth, subalterns by definition are those who cannot speak but are spoken for. Hence the answer to the essay's titular question has to be "no."

But this "no" implies a pessimistic silencing of the subaltern as a well as a perpetual misrecognition (not the same as misrepresentation) of the agency of women involved in sati rituals (Mani 1998). Tempering this pessimism and extrapolating on the wider implications of such an emphatically negative response to the question, Spivak herself has in later years been decidedly more ambivalent about whether the subaltern can in fact speak. In her 1999 revision of the essay she wrote how, back in 1988, she "was so unnerved by this failure of communication that, in the first version of this text, I wrote, in the accents of passionate lament: the subaltern cannot speak! It was an inadvisable remark" (Spivak 1999, 308). She never goes as far as admitting the subaltern can in fact speak, but there is an important tension here that might be summed up as follows: yes, the subaltern can speak, but the true cadence of her voice continues to be effaced and dissimulated by the intellectual ("the one who diagnoses the episteme"; Spivak 2010, 242). In this sense, the subaltern exists as an elusive trace; the subaltern is there but ungraspable insofar as just at the moment it is brought into representation by the language or signifying system of power it ceases to be subaltern by virtue of its representational presence. Subalternity then always disappears. It escapes attempts to be representationally fixed, except as trace and methodological challenge to always read for the more-excluded. So although the task of transparently representing subaltern agency remains technically impossible, there is some urgency attached to the task of trying always harder to interpret, listen to, and translate the subaltern's own agency. Even if doomed to fail, doing so exposes the dissimulation of subaltern agency whenever we try to speak for it (Birla 2010, 89; Jazeel 2014, 95). This, as Spivak (1985, 336) remarked in her very first contribution to subaltern studies, remains "the greatest gift of deconstruction: to question the authority of the investigating subject without paralysing him, persistently transforming conditions of impossibility into possibility."

The implication of Spivak's revisioning of subalternity from an empirical (normative) subject/object to an analytical (conceptual) domain does not mean that the latter should necessarily replace the former. There is, we would assert, continued value in holding the empirical subaltern as an analytical, or strategic, tool for the task of rewriting taken-as-given histories (see de Jong and Mascat 2016). In the sphere of geographical thought, as we suggest below, this is equally true. The subaltern challenge for critical geographical scholarship must catalyze work that not only attempts to evoke the geographical imaginations of empirically subaltern actors but also attends to the ways that our taken-as-given geographical-concept metaphors dissimulate "quite other" geographies as a step toward the impossible, but necessary, challenge of bringing into representation heretofore unimagined geographies and spaces. However, given the relationships between geography and the human imagination, this very challenge necessitates the prior existence of an empirical subaltern. Thus, for subaltern geographies as much as subaltern studies, empirical and analytical subalternity remain entwined and deeply implicated in one another (Legg 2016).

Indeed, while Spivak is clear that she works in the register of literary criticism, she has herself criticized the ongoing work of the Subaltern Studies Collective for withdrawing into representational politics and no longer seeking to teach, learn from, or "touch" the subaltern (Spivak 2005, 477). This critique itself asserts the need for a persistent tacking between empirical and analytical subalternity. Dipesh Chakrabarty has also made similar pleas for learning from the subaltern, while acknowledging that he had not practiced what he preached (Chakrabarty 2000, 272). This involves engaging with the subaltern in order to learn to imagine what knowledge might look like if it were to serve histories that were fragmentary and episodic. One way in which the representational work of engaging subaltern subjects and representations has been considered is through exploring the collaborative possibilities of learning and working together (across space in time); another has questioned the nature of the postcolonial archive (tracing time in space). And this attention to a postcolonial archive necessitates a more concerted engagement with Chakrabarty's own interventions into subaltern studies scholarship, which in the context of this volume have had considerable influence in human geography, particularly in the sphere of urban studies.

Eurocentrism

Dipesh Chakrabarty's *Provincializing Europe: Postcolonial Thought and Historical Difference* (2000) and its companion volume *Habitations of Modernity: Essays in the Wake of Subaltern Studies* (2002) took as their critical target European Enlightenment rationalism, not so as to supplant it but to democratize its historiography and to make clear the links between this rationalism and the colonizing violence of state and institutional governmentality (see Chakrabarty 2002, 32; Featherstone, this volume). Together, the books interrogate the relationships among (European) power and knowledge, and Chakrabarty's insight was simply to broaden the Subaltern Studies Collective's critique of the colonial archive of South Asia to encompass a critique of the structural properties of humanistic cultures of knowledge itself. There was a distinctly decolonial imperative to this maneuver insofar as he was highlighting the continuing Eurocentrism of the knowledge structures we all inhabit. As Chakrabarty (2000, 3–4, emphasis in original) boldly put it in the opening pages of *Provincializing Europe*:

> The Europe I seek to provincialize or decenter is an imaginary figure that remains deeply embedded in *clichéd and shorthand forms* in some everyday habits of thought that invariably subtend attempts in the social sciences to address questions of political modernity in South Asia. The phenomenon of "political modernity"—namely, the rule by modern institutions of the state, bureaucracy and capitalist enterprise—is impossible to *think* of anywhere in the world without invoking certain categories and concepts, the genealogies of which go deep into the intellectual and even theological traditions of Europe. Concepts such as citizenship, the state, civil society, public sphere, human rights, equality before the law, the individual, distinctions between public and private, the idea of the subject, democracy, popular sovereignty, social justice, scientific rationality, and so on all bear the burden of European thought and history.

Such supposedly universal notions, theories, and histories—what the geographer David Slater (1992) has referred to as "masked universalisms"—could thus be exposed as provincial and contingent, freeing up spaces for other, subaltern histories, whether these be histories of subaltern groups or of the positioning of the subaltern in mediating discourses. There are clear connections in this popular postcolonial intervention with the broader subaltern studies project: Morris (2010, 10) reads this as an extension of Spivak's provocation to locate the silent antimodern in world history. There are also clear links to Chatterjee's (1986) insistence that colonial governments had to rule racial difference precisely because they were *not* practicing universalism; and there are links to later works on the global framing of laws and exceptions by which colonies, states, and cities were and are governed through the continual definition of who is and is not within the realm of the rational, the enlightened, or the just (Chatterjee 2011).

Chakrabarty's provincialization thesis, however, also takes aim at what Aamir Mufti (2005, 475) capaciously refers to as "theory culture," that is the "*habitus* that regulates 'theory' as a discrete set of practices within departments . . . and the ways that these practices embody Eurocentrism." As such, the decolonial imperative resulting from Chakrabarty's work can be directed to the academy and to the ambit of methodology and craft in relation to academic knowledge production. His work speaks to the ongoing governmentality of academic knowledge production, how "we" as "intellectuals" behave as "we" ought (Jazeel 2009). But as writers from the Latin American Subaltern Studies Collective have recognized, this brings to the table an important sense that subaltern studies must be tied to the task of area studies, "if only because the idea of 'area' itself designates in the metropolitan academy a subalternized space and the corresponding epistemological problem of 'knowing the other.' But, of course, from postcolonial Latin America, Asia, or Africa, the other is (among other things) precisely the metropolitan academy and its information retrieval apparatus" (Beverley 1999, 2). In this sense, and in terms that bear similarities to Spivak's critique of the representational politics of subaltern studies, Latin American modernity/coloniality/decoloniality scholars have noted how any scholarly attempt to decolonize knowledge comes up against a double bind of sorts. For Walter Mignolo (2002), the *geopolitics of knowledge* is such that critique, even in its leftist, postcolonial, and subaltern intellectual variants, always emerges from within a modernist project that itself is inseparable from modernity and thus coloniality (also see Quijano 2007). Latin American decolonialists then argue that subalternity is to be invoked only through a process of delinking the infrastructures that produce and govern the academy from voices positioned beyond and outside it, for example indigenous communities, activists, or even nonhumans (see Asher 2013). The provincialization and decolonial theses then are conscious attempts to straddle the aporetic space between disciplinary knowledge production, with its assortment of specialized axioms (in whichever discipline), and the radically contextual fabric of the real, which is always geographically located (see Jazeel 2016). It makes sense then that the disciplinary enterprise of geography should take this injunction seriously.

Hegemony to Governmentality

As we can track from the above, the mid- to later-period subalternist works were marked by a shift from Gramsci to governmentality (also see Legg 2007, 275–82), although Marx continued to influence many works both explicitly (Chakrabarty 2000) and implicitly (see Nigam 2014). Foucault's 1970s work on discourse and representation was clearly influential in shifting the sense of the subaltern from a preoccupation with consciousness to a discursive position. But his late 1970s to early 1980s work on governmentality has also been influential on subaltern research. In thinking, for instance, about subaltern ethnic conflict Chakrabarty (2002, 80–100) turned to a history of modern state governmentality (measurement, classification, and mapping of the population and its effects on community formation and violence). This work did not mark a turning away from discourse or representation; rather, it examined how governmental rationalities composed of thoughts; diagrams; texts; buildings; bodily regulations; senses of self; and imaginings of population, economy, and society came to supplement older, more violent, and more centralized sovereign powers of the state. Studies of such South Asian governmentalities have become incredibly influential both within subaltern studies and without (see Legg and Heath 2018). However, as with Foucauldian studies more broadly, the archival materials and theoretical interests that adhere to abstract ideals like the state, government, and power have pushed such studies to emphasize the *success* of governmentalities and their rationalities rather than their practices, failings, and resistance to them. As such, (post)colonial governmentality studies could very easily lapse back into both elitist historiography and the denial of political subaltern agency.

Foucault's lectures and publications after 1979 focused on the experience of governmentalities and the use of truth claims to create ethical subjects (see Legg 2016b). Without drawing explicitly on these materials, Partha Chatterjee's early and incredibly influential intervention into the use of governmentality in studying Indian society helped (partly) redirect our attention back to the experience of governmentalities and to the colonial rule of difference through them. Just as Said had hybridized Foucault (discourse) and Gramsci (hegemony) in his study of Orientalism, so Chatterjee repeated the feat in hybridizing Foucault (governmentality) and Gramsci (civil and political society) in his *The Politics of the Governed* (Chatterjee 2004). In the colonial context, civil society was that established by colonial and, later, nationalist elites to replicate Western modernity based on families and civil institutions. From Gramsci, Chatterjee took the notion of political society to represent the rest of the population, the nonelite, envisaged not through families and institutions but as a "population" that could experience interventions through policy (Chatterjee 2001). While attentive to its colonial origins, Chatterjee focused his interest on how political society *functioned* in postcolonial India: framing questions of democracy, structured by new forms of globalized capital, and mobilizing around violations of the law by population groups to meet communities' welfare needs. Multiple governmental agencies interact with the subjects, not citizens, of political society.

Fitting this (mostly) postcolonial analysis into its historiographical lineage, Chatterjee (2004, 39) was explicit that political society marked the recent penetration of the subaltern by the elite through new governmental concerns with the welfare or protection of the population or mobilizations during electioneering. He later made clear that this urge to consider how governmentalities penetrated the subaltern was driven by a feeling that, in the early subaltern studies works, peasant life was external to government or the state (Goswami 2013, 182). From relative autonomy (Chatterjee 1983, 316) in the colonial period we come to the affective political mobilization of the subaltern (Chatterjee in Nigam 2014, 1064). Whilst this could lead us back to a pessimistic tale of failure (the subaltern) and docile normalization (governmentality), Chatterjee focuses on the recrudescence of subaltern agency through political society: on demands to have biological needs serviced through paralegal infrastructures; on kinship claims made around temporary community formations; and on (possibly violent) refusals of policy interventions.

Subaltern Studies and Geography

Disciplinary geography has, thus far, had an at best fragmentary relationship with the twists and turns of subaltern studies scholarship outlined above (see Clayton 2011; Gidwani 2009; McEwan 2009). As we have shown in this chapter, despite the spatialities implied and engaged by early subalternist scholarship, the debates it has precipitated have been most keenly felt in a particular cluster of disciplines (history, anthropology, political science). Geography has been somewhat at a remove from these debates, which is not to suggest that geographers have not productively, creatively, and provocatively used the tools of subaltern studies to advance their scholarship (as we show below). Nonetheless, the *disciplinary* implications of thinking through those questions we have identified as key to subaltern studies—how to question and critique the limits of Western thinking and representation, and what can be known about the experience of those beyond the elite?—have, until this volume, not been pushed in concerted and collective ways resonant with the collective's work. As a result, and perhaps more importantly, the specific contributions of critical geographical thought have not been marshaled and offered back to subaltern studies' continuing historical, anthropological, and political preoccupations. In the latter respect we would identify a number of pathways that the disparate field of subaltern geographical scholarship has pursued that, we suggest, are poised to make valuable contributions to the broader and ongoing scope and legacy of subaltern studies.

The challenge to think beyond isolated spaces, and particularly the national form, has preoccupied a number of geographers who have worked hard to emphasize the stretched, relational, and "transnational" geographies of subaltern lives—geographies both produced by the precarity of subalternity and productive of the forms of organization and political solidarities that the Subaltern Studies Collective has insisted we take seriously. Part of the work of this critical geographical labor has been to think beyond the national form and intellectually plough the interstitial nonnationed geographies that are only made visible once the spatial autonomy of the national form is itself provincialized (Chari, this volume; Featherstone, this volume). To this extent, the very term "transnational" becomes inadequate as it retroactively and conceptually reinstantiates at least two autonomous spatial entities (nations) that dissimulate and fragment the wholeness of longer, more fluid, topological spatialities, the likes of which Paul Gilroy's "Black Atlantic" so vividly brings to mind (also see McKitrrick 2006). For example, David Featherstone has produced a series of important writings that document and craft historical narratives about the stretched and relational spaces and imaginations of political activism forged by disparate subaltern and working-class groups. Working creatively across far-flung archives, tracing court proceedings, ephemera, and newspaper articles, his work not only reveals these disparate subaltern networks (for example, of the London Corresponding Society's international and networked spatialities in the 1790s [2007], and of black internationalism in the 1930s [2013]) but also shows the time-consuming, expensive, and geographically diffuse methodological labor required to bring these geographies into representation.

Understanding these practical challenges to Featherstone's craft is an important step to understanding why these networked and relational subaltern geographies remain relatively occluded against the hegemonic specter of the nation-form. As his contribution to this volume also reveals, a similar relational geographical story can be told about the intellectual provenance of subaltern studies scholarship itself. Likewise, Sharad Chari's contribution to this volume cuts across nationed, territorial spatiality by focusing on the Indian Ocean and transoceanic space as a subaltern composition. Taking the sea itself, its often occluded eventfulness and patinas seriously, he shows, can reconfigure our understandings of a maritime globe, whose surface (and historical depth we would add) is overwhelmingly oceanic. Ultimately, as Featherstone and Chari show us, attending to oceanic histories makes of us a very geographical demand, which is to write space differently. If these fluid oceanic spatialities necessarily implicate subaltern figures and geographical imaginations, they also signal an emerging conversation between black geographies and subaltern studies that, though beyond the scope of this volume, is one particular configuration where terms like "south," "blackness," and "subalternity" are beginning to reconfigure the discipline in epistemologically productive ways (see McKittrick and Woods 2007; Roy 2017).

The attention to thinking beyond the methodological reproduction of the nation-form has been taken up in theoretical terms by Matthew Sparke, whose 2005 book *In the Space of Theory* demonstrated how nation-state geographies are, over and again, not just assumed but also reinstantiated in the writings of critical and social theorists, including Hardt, Negri, Laclau, Mouffe, and Appadurai. Whilst his direct engagement with subaltern studies scholarship is minimal, in important ways Spivak's critique of ideological subject constitution in the collective's work is an important touchstone for Sparke's argument about the ideological nature of the nation-state form. To this extent, one area in critical geographical scholarship that has marshaled the tools and elan of subaltern studies in order to countermap geographies that intersect the nation-state is indigenous geography. For example, Sarah A. Radcliffe's (2011) work on subaltern cartography in Ecuador has shown how indigenous groups have adopted GIS techniques and, through the Indigenous Development Council, redrawn and resignified national cartographic templates by inscribing on them distributions of indigenous groups, land claims, and indigenous language keys. As she ultimately recognizes, however, and with recourse to Sparke's work, the radical potential of such indigenous cartographies is curtailed by the ways that the reappropriation of "national" maps ultimately reinscribes colonial cartographic authority.

In her contribution to this volume, Radcliffe pushes the cartographic metaphor further via Latin Americanist subaltern and modernity/coloniality/decoloniality scholarship in order to creatively reread indigenous Pachamama practices and socioenvironmental knowledges as forms of subaltern political ontology (Radcliffe, this volume). At stake in her chapter is the challenge to know (subaltern) difference in Ecuador on terms true to the singularity of its difference, along with embracing the ethnographic craft required for this difficult task of delinking academic protocols from writing through and with colonial difference. Similiarly, in her analysis of indigenous land politics in the light of Bolivia's historic plurinational constitution of 2009, Anna F. Laing's contribution to this volume also marshals Latin Americanist decolonial scholarship alongside subaltern studies to argue the enduring coloniality of ethnicity as register of difference. As she shows, it is not enough for a government that claims an indigenous provenance and mandate to continue to operate under the taxonomies and watchwords of liberal governance, "ethnicity" being one of them.

One area of geographical research in which empirical subalternity has been normatively apparent over the last few years is development geography. For example, recent turns toward postdevelopment thinking have been premised on a recognition of, as McEwan (2009, 63) has put it, "the continued power of Western conceptualizations of development and modernization and a continued deference to the power of Western discourse." Though the "West" remains a curiously Manichean spatial signifier here, McEwan references work that usefully recognizes a particular kind of subdisciplinary hegemony (also see Simon 2006; Yeboah 2006). But it is a normatively empirical kind of subaltern that crops up most frequently in development geography to always, and usefully, remind us that the subject *of* development is never passive nor without voice. Furthermore, political economists working in the broad terrain of critical geography and development studies have persistently pushed on this point, showing how subaltern voice and agency make differential use of economic systems, "provincializing capital" (Chari 2004a) in the process. For example, Sharad Chari (2004b) has referred to the unique forms of social capital generated by Gounder-caste men in Tiruppur, South India, as subaltern forms of agency and organization. And Vinay Gidwani's (2008, 2015) series of writings on informal waste economies in urban India have enlivened our understandings of the varied spatial constitution of terms like waste, value, labor, skill, and class in sites and assemblages at a distance from the European wellsprings of political economy. In their contribution to this volume, Gidwani and Kumar engage with Indian political economy and Dalit studies to argue the difference that caste (specifically untouchability) makes in readings of labor and the laboring body in India's waste economy. The specifically geographical contribution here is a rereading of commodity, supply chain, and waste networks.

For Gidwani, the subaltern has posed a persistent politico-intellectual challenge, both empirically and analytically. Indeed, his 2006 article "What's Left? Subaltern Cosmopolitanism as Politics" mobilized the worldly geographical and political imagination of a onetime maid in the employ of his family, Connie, positioning her voice as a mode of "subaltern cosmopolitanism." In doing so, this brief article precipitated a more concerted engagement with subaltern forms of cosmopolitanism wrenched from an exclusive focus on "business elites, tourists, corporate networks, and the Western metropolis" (Jeffrey and McFarlane 2008, 420). These intellectual maneuvers tended to deploy the subaltern as an empirical figure, such as the cosmopolitan imaginations of *bahurupiyas*, young lower-caste men in Uttar Pradesh working as street performers (Jeffrey 2008). In the wake of this literature, geographers have also mobilized subalternity as an intellectual and representational challenge to the spatial registers and taken-as-given geographical propaedeutics that inhere in the "cosmopolitan" imagination, liberal or subaltern (see Jazeel 2011). This kind of critical geographical engagement with the subaltern cosmopolitanism literature has asked what, in effect, is subaltern about "subaltern cosmopolitanism" if the power of the adjectival challenge to think differently, to enter into the text of the other, is reconstellated by the conceptual parameters of the concept-metaphor "cosmopolitanism" (Jazeel 2011)? As we stress below, this politico-intellectual provocation is not one confined to cosmopolitanism as concept-metaphor but has been taken up across a series of concept-metaphors across the discipline, including "landscape," "nature," and "religion" (Jazeel 2013b, 2013c, 2016) and the geographies of "exile" (see Davies 2016). A subaltern geography thought this way is poised to unmoor taken-as-given lexicons of spatial grammar across the humanities and social sciences, making room for radical spatial alterities positioned beyond our familiar geographical tropes and imaginations.

The trope of subalternity has also in recent years had an impact on critical geopolitical scholarship. For example, Joanne Sharp (2011; also see Harker 2011; Woon 2011) has advanced the notion of "subaltern geopolitics," a formulation used to name geopolitical knowledge production that falls outside traditional geopolitical binaries of political domination and resistance. Of course, the adjectival description of knowledge *as* "geopolitical," subaltern or otherwise, works to formalize knowledge in ways that theoretically at least move it away from the relational methodological imperative that subalternity names. Sharp's contribution to this volume focuses on the establishment of the University of Dar es Salaam in the immediate wake of Tanzanian independence. As she argues, the school was a deliberate geopolitical attempt to enact a kind of provincialization of European political and intellectual modernity, but one whose historical trajectory of becoming hegemonic speaks to the inherent analytical relationality of subalternity.

Other geographical work that takes a cue from this critical rotation in subaltern studies—from hegemony through to the governmentalization of knowledge production, particularly via Chakrabarty's work—includes that which has sought to explore the tensions among theory culture, knowledge production, and responsibility (Jazeel 2009, 2016; Jazeel and McFarlane 2010). But perhaps most significant has been the lasting impact Chakrabarty's imperative has had on the field of urban geography. Jennifer Robinson (2003, 2006, 2011) has productively used Chakrabarty's work to prise open urban theory's structural Eurocentrism, in turn stimulating the vibrant field of comparative urbanism. Much like the critiques of "subaltern cosmopolitanism" mentioned above, this literature productively explores the implicit forms of comparison instantiated when taken-as-given urban theoretical concept domains are blithely used to study non–Euro-American cities, and it has pushed the political potential of exploring cities in the Global South on their own terms (for examples, see Bunnell et al. 2012; McFarlane 2010). And recently, Kate Derickson (2015) has proposed a reading of urban theory that mirrors Chakrabarty's (2000, 47–71) model of *History 1 and History 2* (also see Chari and Featherstone, this volume). For Derickson, if *Urbanization 1* can be used as a shorthand to denote Marxist-inspired, Lefebvrian accounts of the complete urbanization of society (the turn to "planetary urbanization"; see Brenner and Schmidt 2015), then *Urbanization 2* denotes a more diverse set of interventions united only by their common desire to provincialize Eurocentric theoretical explanations of urban phenomena and take cities on terms true to the singularities of their difference.

There is an argument that Derickson's *Urbanization 2* in fact subsumes too much difference, polarizing a debate that must open out rather than close in on itself (see Hart 2016). But what is at stake in this work is an intense and urgent struggle to allow urban voices from, and in, the Global South a form of expression and conceptual amplification that refuses to be sublimated by a theoretical modernity prescribed in the Global North. This is a depressingly necessary maneuver in a field that must constantly guard against the dissimulating effect of universalist political economic, read Marxist, Urban Theoretical (deliberately capitalized here) explanations of cities the world over (for an example, see Scott and Storper 2015). The resonances here between Vivek Chibber's (2013) vituperative attack on subaltern studies (which he mistakenly refers to as "Postcolonial Studies") are stark, and have not been lost, nor unaddressed, by the more subtle and astute postcolonial and feminist voices in the field (see Roy 2016). At its core, however, the challenge remains to make sure that cities, urbanization processes, and most importantly "citizens" of the Global South are not ideologically constituted by the "we" of an urban studies community whose powerhouses remain firmly located in the metropolitan (read "Western") academy (see Roy 2011). As such, the importance of the early subalternist work's critique of hegemony (and ideology), as well as Chakrabarty's engagement with the governmentalization of knowledge production, have remained as important as each other.

If these are the rough outlines of a large and significant debate in urban geography, contributors to those debates featured in this volume stake out some exciting new ground. Colin McFarlane's chapter mobilizes a key, early motif in subalternist scholarship in order to help him think with and through cities in the Global South: the fragment. If the fragment has been variously mobilized by subaltern studies scholars as that which bears a discontinuous relationship to the nation (see Chatterjee 1993), for McFarlane fragments offer abstract pieces of urban life, often untranslatable, often incommensurable with the logic of the city as a whole, but also productively disruptive in terms of our settled understandings of the urban as a complete entity. As we have discussed above, Mukul Kumar and Ananya Roy choose to revisit the prehistory of subaltern studies, paying close attention to Ranajit Guha's 1963 monograph, *A Rule of Property for Bengal*, arguing the pivotal importance of this book for subsequent understandings of value and comparison in urban contexts. Their chapter is an elaboration on how colonial encounter consolidated and stabilized the category of property as a universal unit of value.

While Roy and Kumar's chapter speaks out to urban studies, it is also an expert dissection of a historical text that, itself, drew upon extensive archives to construct a historical mode of thought, form of governance, and practice of partitioning mud, water, and soil. This mode of investigation is familiar to historical geographers, though the study of subaltern subjects and subalternity, which Guha would later instigate, has had a lesser impact. This is not to say, however, that historical geographers have not sought out silenced voices or questioned the effects of their elitist knowledge practices. For instance, Dan Clayton's (2000) work on imperial mapping and trading in colonial Vancouver has explored the archival traces of encounters with "natives" on land and at sea, recording the acquiesce of, appropriations by, and conflicts with the inhabitants of Nootka Sound (for further global examples see Ogborn 2008). Felix Driver has led a project to recognize the agency of indigenous peoples and intermediaries in the history of exploration (guides, interpreters, porters, and pilots) and to reflect upon their portrayal in visual media (Driver and Jones 2009). Caroline Bressey (2011) has explored the photographic archives of a Victorian asylum to expand our understanding of a multicultural yet incarcerated London. Reshaad Durgahee has also pieced together the archival fragments of Indian indentured laborers in Fiji, differentiated into subaltern geographies of native villages, coolie lines, and free Indian settlements (Durgahee 2017).

There have also been reflections on the epistemological consequences of reliance upon colonial archives, which can duplicate the subject position of spying on the "native" (Duncan 1999) and which raise questions regarding our ethical obligations toward the silenced subjects of the archive (Moore 2010). What these historical studies have established is not just the difficulty of recovering silenced voices from the archive but also the historical significance of place-making in subaltern-making and the way in which subaltern labor and resistance made many of the colonial and imperial geographies that structure our historical imaginations.

David Arnold is of course synonymous with the Subaltern Studies Collective and not historical geography per se. Yet his contribution to the book addresses the urban—the subaltern street—as a way of revisiting what he stresses was one of the key lacunae of early subalternist work: its overwhelmingly rural focus. Arnold's thick description of subaltern life on the streets of eighteenth- and nineteenth-century Calcutta (also "fragments" from Delhi, Bombay, and Madras) is not only instructive for its historical craft but revealingly shows the often unremarked rural squint of subaltern studies scholarship. His revelation of the fecundity of subaltern life in the eighteenth- and nineteenth-century Indian city is also a useful corrective to urban age arguments that would have us believe urbanization and its associated challenges to be a new set of conjunctures in the Global South.

Through much of the work we have considered in this last section, geographers have tacked between the deployment of the subaltern designated as a normative figure, on the one hand, and on the other a challenge that necessarily tests the creativity, guile, and craft of the geographical imagination. This tension—between a kind of empirical and analytical subalternity—is, as we have stressed above, key in Spivak's work in particular, and it continually demands that geographers work hard ethnographically and archivally (what Spivak might refer to as the absolute necessity of "close reading") in order to track spatialities occluded by the hegemony of a scalar imagination in which the state and other taken-as-given spatialities remain firmly implanted. In historical research on the abuse of women in 1930s Delhi ashrams (Legg 2016a), for example, it is precisely this attempt to track the empirical subaltern that enables a more speculative and intellectually creative engagement with the spatialities in and through which the nonelite dwells and moves and that are, by definition, occluded in the archive. As we have suggested above, this work connects closely to critical geographical calls for more creative and concerted attempts to bring into representation what Spivak, drawing on Derrida, refers to as "quite other" geographies too often dissimulated by the hegemony of concept metaphors foundational to the discipline of geography (Jazeel 2014).

Conclusion

There is in this book, therefore, something of a challenge to the discipline. More than forty years ago Derek Gregory's (1978) landmark critique of geography's scientific legacy, and its ideological effects in disciplinary knowledge production, looked to poststructural, phenomenological, and hermeneutic approaches as ways out of the ideological reproduction of the analytical geographical imagination. Today, despite the normalization of postpositivist human geography, subaltern studies reminds us that we still need to be aware of the ideological production of geographical knowledge and its proclivity to flatten difference. In this respect it is helpful to turn to Louis Althusser, because if Althusser's reading of ideology was a way of understanding the reproduction of the relations of production, then we should recall that one of his prior questions was the where of the reproduction of the relations of production, or as he put it, "What is a society?" (Althusser 2008, 8). As a discipline, we are indeed something of a society: we meet at annual conferences, publish in disciplinary journals, transact in discourse, and share a common language about space (even if we frequently do not agree with one another). We are a society that has parameters and conceptual normativities, all of which help to reproduce a disciplinary hegemony. This is a book that aims to pose a set of interventions into our collective openness to "quite other," radically different kinds of spatialities—subaltern geographies that remain subaltern because we often do not have an adequate vocabulary for them. It is a book that attempts to marshal subalternity in empirical ways but also, as Dan Clayton (2011, 246) has put it, as a heuristic and bifurcated figure of constraint and release in disciplinary knowledge production. To locate, reflect on, and turn subalternist tools to our own disciplinary community of practice opens the door to a more discursive conception of ideology than Althusser's, putting on the agenda an interrogation of "how we come to speak 'spontaneously,' within the limits of the categories of thought which exist outside us and which can more accurately be said to think us" (Hall 1996, 30). Ideology, as Vinay Gidwani (2008, 7) has put it, exists in the obviousness of our world—in its empirical immediacy. Inspired by the tools of subalternist scholarship, this book is at its core an attempt to defamiliarize, to de-scribe, the spatial immediacy of our world(s). That will be its contribution to subaltern studies.

REFERENCES

Achebe, Chinua. 1977. "An Image of Africa." *Massachusetts Review* 18, no. 4: 782–94.
Althusser, Louis. 2008 [1979]. *On Ideology*. London: Verso.

Amin, Shahid. 2002. *Alternative Histories: A View from India*. Amsterdam; Calcutta: SEPHIS-CSSS.

Arnold, David. 1982. "Rebellious Hillmen: The Gudem-Rampa Risings 1839–1924." In *Subaltern Studies I*, edited by Ranajit Guha, 88–142. Delhi: Oxford University Press.

———. 1985. "Bureaucratic Recruitment and Subordination in Colonial India: The Madras Constabulary, 1859–1947." In *Subaltern Studies IV*, edited by Ranajit Guha, 1–53. Delhi: Oxford University Press.

———. 2016. *Toxic Histories: Poison and Pollution in Modern India*. Cambridge: Cambridge University Press.

Asher, Kiran. 2013. "Latin American Decolonial Thought, or Making the Subaltern Speak." *Geography Compass* 7: 832–42.

Beverley, John. 1999. *Subalternity and Representation: Arguments in Cultural Theory*. Durham, N.C.: Duke University Press.

Birla, Ritu. 2010. "*Postcolonial Studies*: Now That's History." In *Can the Subaltern Speak: Reflections on the History of an Idea*, edited by Rosalind C. Morris, 87–99. New York: Columbia University Press.

Brenner, Neil, and Christian Schmidt. 2015. "Towards a New Epistemology of the Urban?" *City* 19, nos. 2–3: 151–82.

Bressey, Caroline. 2011. "The City of Others: Photographs from the City of London Asylum Archive." *Interdisciplinary Studies in the Long Nineteenth Century* 13: 1–14.

Bunnell, Tim, Daniel Goh, C. K. Lai, and C. P. Pow. 2012. "Introduction: Global Urban Frontiers? Asian Cities in Theory, Practice and Imagination." *Urban Studies* 49, no. 13: 2785–93.

Butalia, Urvashi. 2000. *The Other Side of Silence: Voices from the Partition of India*. London: Hurst and Co.

Chakrabarty, Dipesh. 1998. "Minority Histories, Subaltern Pasts." *Economic and Political Weekly* 33, no. 9: 473–79.

———. 2000a. *Provincializing Europe: Postcolonial Thought and Historical Difference*. Princeton, N.J.: Princeton University Press.

———. 2000b [1995]. "Radical Histories and Question of Enlightenment Rationalism: Some Recent Critiques of *Subaltern Studies*." In *Mapping Subaltern Studies and the Postcolonial*, edited by Vinayak Chaturvedi, 256–79. London; New York: Verso.

———. 2002. *Habitations of Modernity: Essays in the Wake of Subaltern Studies*. Chicago: University of Chicago Press.

Chandavarkar, Rajnarayan. 2000. [1997]. "'The Making of the Working Class': E. P. Thompson and Indian History." In *Mapping Subaltern Studies and the Postcolonial*, edited by Vinayak Chaturvedi, 50–71. London: Verso.

Chari, Sharad. 2004a. "Provincializing Capital: The Work of an Agrarian Past in South Indian Industry." *Comparative Studies in Society and History* 46, no. 4: 760–85.

———. 2004b. *Fraternal Capital: Peasant Workers, Self-Made Men and Globalization in Provincial India*. Stanford, Calif.: Stanford University Press.

Chatterjee, Partha. 1983. "More on Modes of Power and the Peasantry." In *Subaltern Studies II*, edited by Ranajit Guha, 311–49. Delhi: Oxford University Press.

———. 1984a. *Bengal, 1920–1947*. Vol. 1, *The Land Question*. Calcutta: Centre for Studies in Social Sciences.

———. 1984b. "Gandhi and the Critique of Civil Society." In *Subaltern Studies III*, edited by Ranajit Guha, 153–95. Delhi: Oxford University Press.

———. 1986. *Nationalist Thought and the Colonial World: A Derivative Discourse?* London: Zed for the United Nations University.

———. 1993. *The Nation and Its Fragments: Colonial and Postcolonial Histories*. Princeton, N.J.: Princeton University Press.

———. 1995. "The Disciplines in Colonial Bengal." In *Texts of Power: Emerging Disciplines in Colonial Bengal*, edited by Partha Chatterjee, 1–29. Minneapolis: University of Minnesota Press.

———. 2001. "On Civil and Political Society in Postcolonial Democracies." In *Civil Society: History and Possibilities*, edited by Sudipta Kaviraj and Sunil Khilnani, 165–78. Cambridge: Cambridge University Press.

———. 2004. *The Politics of the Governed: Reflections on Popular Politics in Most of the World*. New York: Columbia University Press.

———. 2010. "Reflections on 'Can the Subaltern Speak?' Subaltern Studies after Spivak." In *Can the Subaltern Speak: Reflections on the History of an Idea*, edited by Rosalind C. Morris, 81–86. New York: Columbia University Press.

———. 2011. *Lineages of Political Society: Studies in Postcolonial Democracy*. New York: Columbia University Press.

———. 2012. *The Black Hole of Empire: History of a Global Practice of Power*. Princeton, N.J.: Princeton University Press.

Chaturvedi, Vinayak. 2000. *Mapping Subaltern Studies and the Postcolonial*. London: Verso.

Chibber, Vivek. 2013. *Postcolonial Theory and the Specter of Capital*. London: Verso.

Clayton, Daniel. 2000. *Islands of Truth: The Imperial Fashioning of Vancouver Island*. Vancouver: University of British Columbia Press.

———. 2011. "Subaltern Space." In *Handbook of Geographical Knowledge*, edited by John A. Agnew and David Livingstone, 246–60. London: SAGE.

Cohn, Bernard S. 1985. "The Command of Language and the Language of Command." In *Subaltern Studies IV*, edited by Ranajit Guha, 276–329. New Delhi: Oxford University Press.

Comaroff, Jean, and John L. Comaroff. "Theory from the South: Or, How Euro-America Is Evolving toward Africa." *Anthropological Forum* 22, no. 2 (2012): 113–31.

Crush, Jonathan. 1994. "Post-Colonialism, Decolonization and Geography." In *Geography and Empire*, edited by Anne Godlewska and Neil Smith, 333–50. Oxford: Blackwell.

Das, Veena. 1997. "Language and Body: Transactions in the Construction of Pain." In *Remaking a World: Violence, Social Suffering, and Recovery*, edited by Veena Das, Arthur Kleinman, Margaret Lock, Mamphela Ramphele, and Pamela Reynolds, 67–91. Berkeley: University of California Press.

Davies, Andrew. 2016. "Exile in the Homeland? Anti-Colonialism, Subaltern Geographies and the Politics of Friendship in Early Twentieth Century Pondicherry, India." *Environment and Planning D: Society and Space* 35: 457–77.

De Jong, Sara, and Jamilla M. H. Mascat. 2016. "Relocating Subalternity: Scattered Speculations on the Conundrum of a Concept." *Cultural Studies* 30: 717–29.

Derrickson, Kate D. 2015. "Urban Geography I: Locating Urban Theory in the 'Urban Age.'" *Progress in Human Geography* 39: 647–57.
Driver, Felix, and Lowri Jones. 2009. *Hidden Histories of Exploration: Researching the RGS-IBG Collections*. London: Royal Holloway, University of London.
Duncan, James S. 1999. "Complicity and Resistance in the Colonial Archive: Some Issues of Method and Theory in Historical Geography." *Historical Geography* 27: 119–28.
Durgahee, Reshaad. 2017. "'Native' Villages, 'Coolie' Lines, and 'Free' Indian Settlements: The Geography of Indenture in Fiji." *South Asian Studies* 33: 68–84.
Elden, Stuart. 2013. *The Birth of Territory*. Chicago: University of Chicago Press.
Featherstone, David. 2007. "The Spatial Politics of the Past Unbound: Transnational Networks and the Making of Political Identities." *Global Networks* 7, no. 4: 430–52.
———. 2013. "Black Internationalism, Subaltern Cosmopolitanism and the Spatial Politics of Anti-Fascism." *Annals of the Association of American Geographers* 103, no. 6: 1406–20.
———. 2016. "Space, Subalternity and Critique, or which Subaltern Studies for which Geography?" *Cultural Geographies* 24, no. 2: 341–46.
Foucault, Michel. 1977. "Intellectuals and Power: A Conversation between Michel Foucault and Gilles Deleuze." In *Language, Counter-Memory, Practice: Selected Essays and Interviews*, edited by Donald Bouchard and translated by D. Bouchard and S. Simon, 205–17. Ithaca, N.Y.: Cornell University Press.
Gidwani, Vinay. 2006. "What's Left? Subaltern Cosmopolitanism as Politics." *Antipode* 38: 8–21.
———. 2008. *Capital Interrupted: Agrarian Development and the Politics of Work in India*. Minneapolis: University of Minnesota Press.
———. 2009. "Subalternity." In *International Encyclopedia of Human Geography*, edited by Nigel Thrift and Rob Kitchen, 65–71. Oxford: Elsevier.
———. 2015. "The Work of Waste: Inside India's Infra-Economy." *Transactions of the Institute of British Geographers* 40, no. 4: 575–95.
Gilroy, Paul. 1993. *The Black Atlantic: Modernity and Double Consciousness*. Cambridge, Mass.: Harvard University Press.
Goswami, Manu. 2013. "Partha Chatterjee." *Public Culture* 25, no. 1: 177–89.
Gregory, Derek. 1978. *Ideology, Science and Human Geography*. London: Hutchinson.
———. 1994. *Geographical Imaginations*. Oxford: Blackwell.
———. 1995. "Imaginative Geographies." *Progress in Human Geography* 19, no. 4: 447–85.
Guha, Ranajit. 1963. *A Rule of Property for Bengal: An Essay on the Idea of Permanent Settlement*. Paris: Mouton & Co.
———. 1982. "On Some Aspects of the Historiography of Colonial India." In *Subaltern Studies I*, edited by Ranajit Guha, 1–8. Delhi: Oxford University Press.
———. 1983a. *Elementary Aspects of Peasant Insurgency in Colonial India*. New Delhi: Oxford University Press.
———. 1983b. "The Prose of Counter-Insurgency." In *Subaltern Studies II*, edited by Ranajit Guha, 1–42. Delhi: Oxford University Press.
———. 1988 [1982]. "On Some Aspects of the Historiography of Colonial India." In *Selected Subaltern Studies*, edited by Ranajit Guha and Gayatri Chakravorty Spivak, 37–44. New York; London: Oxford University Press.

———. 1992. "Discipline and Mobilize." In *Subaltern Studies VII*, edited by Partha Chatterjee and Gyanendra Pandey, 69–120. New Delhi: Oxford University Press.

———. 1997. *Dominance without Hegemony: History and Power in Colonial India*. Cambridge, Mass.: Harvard University Press.

———. 2009a [1997]. "Introduction to the *Subaltern Studies Reader*." In *The Small Voice of History: Collected Essays*, edited by Partha Chatterjee, 318–32. New Delhi: Permanent Black.

———. 2009b [1998]. "A Conquest Foretold " In *The Small Voice of History: Collected Essays*, edited by Partha Chatterjee, 373–90. New Delhi: Permanent Black.

———. 2009c [1991]. "The Authority of Vernacular Pasts." In *The Small Voice of History: Collected Essays*, edited by Partha Chatterjee, 474–78. New Delhi: Permanent Black.

Guha, Ranajit, and Gayatri Chakravorty Spivak. 1988. *Selected Subaltern Studies*. New York; London: Oxford University Press.

Hall, Stuart. 1996. "The Problem of Ideology: Marxism without Guarantees." In *Stuart Hall: Critical Dialogues in Cultural Studies*, edited by David Morley and Kuan-Hsing Chen, 25–46. London: Routledge.

Harker, Chris. 2011. "Geopolitics and Family in Palestine." *Geoforum* 42, no. 3: 306–15.

Hart, Gill. 2016. "Relational Comparison Revisited: Marxist Postcolonial Geographies in Practice." *Progress in Human Geography* 42: 371–94.

Jazeel, Tariq. 2009. "Governmentality." *Social Text* 100: 136–40.

———. 2011. "Spatializing Difference beyond Cosmopolitanism: Rethinking Planetary Futures." *Theory Culture and Society* 28, no. 5: 75–97.

———. 2013a. "Postcolonialism." In *A New Companion to Cultural Geography*, edited by Nuala Johnson, Richard Schein, and Jamie Winders, 17–22. Oxford: Wiley-Blackwell.

———. 2013b. "Dissimulated Landscapes: Postcolonial Method and the Politics of Space in Southern Sri Lanka." *Environment and Planning D: Society and Space* 31, no. 1: 61–79.

———. 2013c. *Sacred Modernity: Nature, Environment and the Postcolonial Geographies of Sri Lankan Nationhood*. Liverpool: Liverpool University Press.

———. 2014. "Subaltern Geographies: Geographical Knowledge and Postcolonial Strategy." *Singapore Journal of Tropical Geography* 35: 88–103.

———. 2016. "Between Area and Discipline: Progress, Knowledge Production and the Geographies of Geography." *Progress in Human Geography* 40: 649–69.

Jazeel, Tariq, and Colin McFarlane. 2010. "The Limits of Responsibility: A Postcolonial Politics of Academic Knowledge Production." *Transactions, Institute of British Geographers* 35, no. 1: 109–24.

Jeffrey, Craig. 2008. "Kicking Away the Ladder: Student Politics and the Making of an Indian Middle Class." *Environment and Planning D: Society and Space* 26: 517–36.

Jeffrey, Craig, and Colin McFarlane. 2008. "Guest Editorial: Performing Cosmopolitanism." *Environment and Planning D: Society and Space* 26: 420–27.

Legg, Stephen. 2007. "Beyond the European Province: Foucault and Postcolonialism." In *Space, Knowledge, and Power: Foucault and Geography*, edited by Jeremy Crampton and Stuart Elden, 265–88. Aldershot: Ashgate.

———. 2009. "Of Scales, Networks and Assemblages: The League of Nations Apparatus and the Scalar Sovereignty of the Government of India." *Transactions of the Institute of British Geographers NS* 34, no. 2: 234–53.

———. 2016a. "Empirical and Analytical Subaltern Space? Ashrams, Brothels and Trafficking in Colonial Delhi." *Cultural Studies* 30: 793–815.

———. 2016b. "Subject to Truth: Before and after Governmentality in Foucault's 1970s." *Environment and Planning D: Society and Space* 34: 858–76.

Legg, Stephen, and Deana Heath. 2018. *South Asian Governmentalities: Michel Foucault and the Question of Postcolonial Orderings*. New Delhi: Cambridge University Press.

Ludden, David. Ed. 2001. *Reading Subaltern Studies: Critical History, Contested Meaning, and the Globalisation of South Asia*. Delhi: Permanent Black.

McEwan, Cheryl. 2009. "Subaltern." In *International Encyclopedia of Human Geography*, edited by Nigel Thrift and Rob Kitchen, 59–64. London: Elsevier.

McFarlane, Colin. 2010. "The Comparative City: Knowledge, Learning, Urbanism." *International Journal of Urban and Regional Research* 34: 725–42.

McKittrick, Katherine. 2006. *Demonic Grounds: Black Women and the Cartographies of Struggle*. Minneapolis: University of Minnesota Press.

McKittrick, Katherine, and Clyde Woods. Eds. 2007. *Black Geographies and the Politics of Place*. Cambridge, Mass.: South End Press

Menon, Ritu, and Kamla Bhasin. 1998. *Borders and Boundaries: How Women Experienced the Partition of India*. New Brunswick, N.J.: Rutgers University Press.

Mignolo, Walter D. 2002. "The Geopolitics of Knowledge and the Colonial Difference." *South Atlantic Quarterly* 101, no. 1: 57–96.

Moore, Francesca. 2010. "Tales from the Archive: Methodological and Ethical Issues in Historical Geography Research." *Area* 42: 262–70.

Morris, Rosalind C. 2010. "Introduction." In *Can the Subaltern Speak: Reflections on the History of an Idea*, edited by Rosalind C. Morris, 1–20. New York: Columbia University Press.

Nash, Catherine. 2002. "Cultural Geography: Postcolonial Cultural Geographies." *Progress in Human Geography* 26: 219–30.

Nigam, Aditya. 2014. "Reflections: Partha Chatterjee." *Development and Change* 45, no. 5: 1059–73.

Nilsen, Alf, and Srila Roy. 2015. *New Subaltern Politics: Reconceptualizing Hegemony and Resistance in Contemporary India*. New Delhi: Oxford University Press.

Ogborn, Miles. 2008. *Global Lives: Britain and the World, 1550–1800*. Cambridge: Cambridge University Press.

O' Hanlon, R. 1988. "Recovering the Subject: Subaltern Studies and Histories of Resistance in Colonial South Asia." *Modern Asian Studies* 22: 189–224.

Pandey, Gyanendra. 1982. "Peasant Revolt and Indian Nationalism: The Peasant Movement in Awadh, 1919–22." In *Subaltern Studies I*, edited by Ranajit Guha, 143–97. Delhi: Oxford University Press.

———. 1983. "Rallying Round the Cow: Sectarian Strife in the Bhojpuri Region, c1888–1917." In *Subaltern Studies II*, edited by Ranajit Guha, 60–129. Delhi: Oxford University Press.

———. 1994. "The Prose of Otherness." In *Subaltern Studies VIII: Essays in Honour of Ranajit Guha*, edited by David Arnold and David Hardiman, 188–221. New Delhi: Oxford University Press.

———. 2001. *Remembering Partition: Violence, Nationalism and History in India*. Cambridge: Cambridge University Press.

———. 2006 [1990]. *The Construction of Communalism in Colonial North India*. Delhi: Oxford University Press.

Quijano, Anibal. 2007. "Coloniality and Modernity/Rationality." *Cultural Studies* 21, nos. 2–3: 168–78.

Radcliffe, Sarah. 2011. "Third Space, Abstract Space and Coloniality: National and Subaltern Cartography in Ecuador." In *Postcolonial Spaces: The Politics of Place in Contemporary Culture*, edited by Andrew Teverson and Sara Upstone, 129–45. New York: Palgrave Macmillan.

Robinson, Jennifer. 2003. "Postcolonialising Geography: Tactics and Pitfalls." *Singapore Journal of Tropical Geography* 24, no. 3: 273–89.

———. 2006. *Ordinary Cities: Between Modernity and Development*. London: Routledge.

———. 2011. "Comparisons: Colonial or Cosmopolitan?" *Singapore Journal of Tropical Geography* 32: 125–40.

Rodriguez, I., M. M. López, S. Saldívar-Hull, and R. Guha. 2001. *The Latin American Subaltern Studies Reader*. Durham, N.C.: Duke University Press.

Roy, Ananya. 2011. "Slumdog Cities: Rethinking Subaltern Urbanism." *International Journal of Urban and Regional Research* 35, no. 2: 223–38.

———. 2016. "What Is Urban about Critical Urban Theory?" *Urban Geography* 37, no. 6: 810–23.

———. 2017. "Urban Studies and the Postcolonial Encounter." In *The Sage Handbook of the 21st Century City*, edited by Suzanne Hall and Ricky Burdett, 32–46. London: Sage.

Said, Edward. 1978. *Orientalism: Western Conceptions of the Orient*. London: Routledge & Kegan Paul.

———. 1988. "Foreword." In *Selected Subaltern Studies*, edited by Ranajit Guha and Gayatri Chakravorty Spivak, i–x. New York; Oxford: Oxford University Press.

———. 1993. *Culture and Imperialism*. London: Chatto & Windus.

Sarkar, Sumit. 1984. "The Condition and Nature of Subaltern Militancy: Bengal from Swadeshi to Non-co-operating c.1905–22." In *Subaltern Studies III*, edited by Ranajit Guha, 271–320. Delhi: Oxford University Press.

———. 2000. [1996]. "Decline of the Subaltern." In *Mapping Subaltern Studies and the Postcolonial*, edited by Vinayak Chaturvedi, 300–323. London; New York: Verso.

Scott, Allen, and Michael Storper. 2015. "The Nature of Cities: The Scope and Limits of Urban Theory." *International Journal of Urban and Regional Research* 39, no. 1: 1–15.

Scott, Heidi. 2004. "Cultural Turns." In *A Companion to Cultural Geography*, edited by James Duncan, Nuala Johnson, and R. Schein, 24–37. Oxford: Blackwell.

Sharp, Joanne. 2011. "Editorial: Subaltern Geopolitics: Introduction." *Geoforum* 42, no. 3: 271–73.

Sidaway, James, Chih-Yuan Woon, and Jane M. Jacobs. 2014. "Planetary Postcolonialism." *Singapore Journal of Tropical Geography* 35: 4–21.

Simon, David. 2006. "Separated by Common Ground? Bringing (Post)development and (Post)colonialism Together." *Geographical Journal* 172, no. 1: 10–21.

Slater, David. 1989. "Peripheral Capitalism and the Regional Problematic." In *New Models in Geography: The Political Economy Perspective*, edited by Richard Peet and Nigel Thrift, 267–94. London; New York: Routledge.

———. 1992. "On the Borders of Social Theory: Learning from Other Regions." *Environment and Planning D: Society and Space* 10: 307–27.

Sparke, Matthew. 2005. *In the Space of Theory: Postfoundational Geographies of the Nation-State*. Minneapolis: University of Minnesota Press.

Spivak, Gayatri Chakravorty. 1985. "Subaltern Studies: Deconstructing Historiography." In *Subaltern Studies IV*, edited by Ranajit Guha, 330–63. Delhi: Oxford University Press.

———. 1999. *A Critique of Postcolonial Reason: Towards a History of the Vanishing Present*. Cambridge, Mass.: Harvard University Press.

———. 2005. "Scattered Speculations on the Subaltern and the Popular." *Postcolonial Studies* 8, no. 4: 475–86.

———. 2010 [1988]. "Can the Subaltern Speak?" In *Can the Subaltern Speak: Reflections on the History of an Idea*, edited by Rosalind C. Morris, 237–92. Chichester, N.Y.: Columbia University Press.

———. 2014. "Book Reviews: Postcolonial Theory and the Spectre of Capital." *Cambridge Review of International Affairs* 27, no. 1: 184–98.

White, Haydn. 1974. *Metahistory: The Historical Imagination in Nineteenth Century Europe*. Baltimore, Md.: Johns Hopkins University Press.

Woon, Chih-Yuan. 2011. "Undoing Violence, Unbounding Precarity: Beyond the Frames of Terror in the Philippines." *Geoforum* 42, no. 3: 285–96.

Yeboah, Ian. 2006. "Subaltern Strategies and Development Practice." *Geographical Journal* 172, no. 1: 50–65.

Subaltern Streets

India, 1870–1947

DAVID ARNOLD

In focusing on the street, this chapter addresses a generic site of subaltern spatiality within the parameters of a single location and time—urban India under British rule. It considers some connections between the subaltern geographies of rural and urban India but argues more especially for the city street as having a distinct political and social, as well as physical, character of its own, one that evolved rapidly across the period of high and late colonialism. The street is used as a heuristic device by which to frame urban subalternity but is used, still more, as a means of understanding its subaltern properties. Concentrating on the street allows us to move away from an excessive emphasis (at least for South Asia) on subalterns as rural subjects. It further enables us to identify the importance of urban subalterns who lived and worked outside the productive and disciplinary space of the factory and so did not form part of the organized industrial workforce about which so much has been written. Apart from what is specific about urban India and its colonial governance, this chapter seeks to pose—even if it cannot fully answer—the more general question: How does the street inform and advance our understanding of subaltern geography?

Subaltern Spatiality

In almost forty years of subaltern scholarship on South Asia, the overwhelming emphasis has been on India's rural society, a trend that has led to the relative neglect of urban subalternity. This observation is not intended to deny that urban society has played *some* part in subaltern writings or to ignore the ongoing importance of peasant politics in the Indian countryside and the centrality of rural issues to contemporary subaltern mobilization and politicization (Chatterjee 2012; Nilsen and Roy 2015). But there has been a general reticence on the part of subaltern scholars to afford equivalent weight to the urban, as to the rural, subaltern. In his *Elementary Aspects of Peasant Insurgency in Colonial India*, Ranajit

Guha surveyed the period from the late eighteenth century to around 1900, but in this pioneering and influential work subaltern consciousness and insurgent action were identified almost exclusively with the "physical" and "ethnic" space of rural society (Guha 1983, 285–86). India's subalterns were seen as belonging essentially to the peasantry, a category sufficiently inclusive to embrace poor peasants, landless laborers, and *adivasi*s or tribals (see also Hardiman 1987, 1996). Subalterns were not primarily identified with urban society, which was taken by Guha to represent an external, oppositional force marked by cultural difference and social distance; by exploitation; and by a dominance exercised through usury, landlordism, and a coercive state. Only exceptionally in Guha's discussion, as in relation to the Indian rebellion of 1857–58, did the insurgent subaltern intrude, as looter, arsonist, and avenger, on urban life (Guha 1983, 25, 138). Just as the peasantry stood for the authentic subaltern, so the "natural" spatial parameters for Guha's subalterns were the rural settlements in which they lived or the broader "territoriality" associated with such activities as marketing, pilgrimage, and hunting. Across this wider terrain a more expansive sense of subaltern solidarity prevailed, the transmission of rumor (as a vital expression of common consciousness) was made possible, and rebellion found its place.

In actuality, many of the elements of rural insurgency that Guha discussed in his *Elementary Aspects*, including the terms "territoriality," "transmission," "ambiguity," and "solidarity," could be applied, with only modest emendation, to India's urban subalterns, and this chapter does, in part, seek to do so. But Guha did not himself speculate on the possibility of using identical or closely related concepts to analyze both urban and rural subaltern groups. Moreover, while to some degree sensitive to rural spatiality, in *Elementary Aspects* there was an almost timeless quality about subaltern temporality. The growth of a British Indian empire—with its attendant roads, railways, telegraph and postal systems, army, and bureaucracy, along with the force of Western science and education—scarcely impinge in this work on the livelihoods and mentalities of rural subalterns, who remain cocooned within a largely autonomous domain of cultural life and political action (Guha 1983, 287). The modern city is understood as being largely detached from rural life, leaving the peasant subaltern moored to precolonial temporalities (Guha 2008). This view of rural India is itself questionable, but certainly any attempt to engage with urban subalternity has to acknowledge a far more dynamic process of historical change and social transformation.

Most of the contributions to the *Subaltern Studies* volumes published under Guha's editorship from 1982 to 1989 followed his lead in situating subalternity primarily in rural India. Only exceptionally were cities afforded subaltern representativeness as sites of communal conflict, working-class agitation, or nationalist mobilization (Chakrabarty 1983; Pandey 1984). To be fair, the historiographical terrain from which subaltern studies emerged in the late 1970s and early 1980s was already well populated with spatially aware accounts of urban riots and street-level conflicts (Kumar 1971). There was, though, also a countervailing historiographical tendency to regard the cities of colonial India as intrinsically alien spaces. Sunil Khilnani (1998, 108) sought to capture nationalist ambivalence toward the city by remarking that it was, "after all, the theatre where India's subjection to the British was most graphically and regularly enacted," adding that India's colonial cities were places where "the British Raj governed public space according to its own quite alien concepts" (Khilnani 1998, 110). If for many Britons the city failed to represent the "real" India, it likewise failed to satisfy the expectations of nationalists, like Gandhi, who saw in the village India's epitome and salvation and of scholars in search of an authentic subaltern identity. The problem was compounded by the way in which many of the academic studies of Indian cities produced in the 1970s and 1980s paid excessive attention to the outward form and function of "colonial cites" but proved largely inattentive to their subaltern populations (Harrison 1980; King 1976).

Of late, South Asian scholarship has sought to move away from the exaggerated dichotomies of the earlier "colonial cities" literature, with its overly segregated "white" and "black" towns (Haynes and Rao 2013). And yet a conceptual space is often created less for subaltern identity and action than for middle-class imaginings of the city and attempts by "colonial modernism" to reform and reconfigure the city (Hazareesingh 2001; Kidambi 2001). Subalterns appear through the critical lens of the urban elite and the municipal authorities rather than in their own right. It remains stubbornly difficult to make the city subaltern "speak," even though, as this chapter attempts to suggest, the urban archive, including municipal records and sanitary and police reports, augmented by newspapers and other contemporary sources, is rich and revealing. Few works of historical scholarship have treated subaltern street life comprehensively enough or gone far beyond the industrial working class to consider other urban subalterns. Nandini Gooptu's (2001) study of the urban poor of early twentieth-century north India remains an exemplary exception. Even in Sumanta Banerjee's well-crafted account of nineteenth-century Calcutta (Kolkata), "the street" remains something of an abstraction, less a physical and social space than a means by which to differentiate popular culture from the "parlor" life of Bengal's *bhadralok* elite (the high-caste Hindu intelligentsia of Bengal) (Banerjee 1989). When some subaltern scholars have written about the street, it has been in ways that seem to affirm its alien and exterior character—a place consigned to garbage and disease, to the turmoil and disturbance that threaten the health, integrity, and conviviality of the *bhadralok* home (Chakrabarty 1991; Kaviraj 1997).

Guha's own limited engagement with subaltern spatiality highlights a lacuna in the writings of Antonio Gramsci, whose prison notebooks provide one of the intellectual underpinnings for subaltern scholarship. Gramsci's analysis of the political history of the Italian city and the subordination of the backward, feudal South to the industrial, capitalist North suggest, but regrettably do not develop, the ways in which hegemony and coercion have historically been articulated across space as well as through time (Gramsci 1971). Thinking spatially about subalternity has received greater stimulus from the writings of Michel Foucault. His "spatialized thinking" and his "appeal to space," with "its transformations and displacements" (Flynn 1994, 40–43), along with his reflections on governmentality (Legg 2007), have been a potent influence in opening up for investigation corporeal and carceral spatiality and the relationship of space to the construction of knowledge and the exercise of power. Partly as a result, the new "urban turn" in South Asian studies has seized the "opportunity to revise the history of Indian modernity, to bring into view spaces of power and difference suppressed by the historicist discourse of the nation" (Prakash 2002, 6).

However, part of the residual value of Guha's *Elementary Aspects* is as a constructive point of departure for thinking about the specific forms of urban, as well as rural, subalternity. In addition, following Gramsci, it frees us from too dogmatic a notion of how the subordinate classes, both rural and urban, were constituted and from teleological assumptions about how a working class came into being. Where, in studies of India, industrial capitalism and its relationship with urban labor has been the principal field of inquiry, the tendency has been to concentrate exclusively on the factory and on organized labor rather than to reflect on other, often intersecting, spatial locations and social arenas (Basu 2004; compare Chandavarkar 1994, 1998). This conventional making-of-the-working-class narrative violates the heterogeneous nature of urban subalternity and overlooks the motley composition of urban subaltern groups, many of whom were not factory workers, and the spatial, as much as social, diversity and mobility of the subaltern city. Recent essays on more contemporary events have signaled the importance of the "urban subaltern" and "subaltern urbanism" outside India and across the Global South (Bayat 2000; Ismail 2013; Roy 2011), but little of this literature has, so far, addressed colonial India. And yet the historical argument for the street as a site of subaltern lives and subaltern politics can only be enhanced by awareness of its present-day manifestations.

The Existential Street

As a site of perception and analysis, the street can be configured in many different ways, even, perhaps especially, in relation to the non-Western world. During the colonial era, the street was often the first point of observation and contact for the arriving European, the place where he or she, within hours of landing in Cairo or Bombay or Colombo, felt confirmed in exotic preconceptions of "Oriental" life or empowered to pronounce on the evils and afflictions of "native" society (e.g., Low 1907, 6–7, 23–24). Conversely, for the "native" or the empathetic Orientalist, the street, as in the Hindu holy city of Benares (Varanasi), might suggest a bustling vitality, a colorful diversity, and a historical connectedness between people, place, and culture (Dutt 1895, 1–10; Havell 1905). Then again, the street—the Indian street, the Arab street—might be the bearer of more overtly political connotations for those who seek in it an "authentic" expression of public opinion or evidence of an underworld of criminality and popular discontent (for the distinctive meaning given to the "Arab street," see Lynch 2003; Regier and Khalidi 2009). All of these have some bearing on the hegemonic construction of the street and its ideological usages. This essay, however, is an attempt to move away from those external perspectives to an analysis grounded, so far as that is possible, in the spatiality of subalterns themselves.

Guha's analysis of consciousness and insurgency presents a model of social collectivity rooted in the village and a peasantry only periodically impelled to revolt (though the countryside also had itinerant artisans and traders, pastoralists, and peasants seeking new land to colonize). By contrast, urban subalternity calls for a more fluid and quotidian understanding of subaltern experience and consciousness (or at least a more heterogeneous way of thinking about subalternity than has commonly been adopted in relation to rural subalterns). In the long history of India's cities, we must assume that subordinate groups, such as servants, craftsmen, entertainers, and laborers, were always present. But if one takes the mid- to late nineteenth century as a critical point of departure in the making of the modern city in South Asia, we can see ways in which various subaltern groups moved into, through, and sometimes out of the urban arena and so began to coalesce into the making of a new, if still highly varied and divided, urban subalternity.

Displacement, both physical and social, was a core ingredient in urban subalternity. Rural migrants, drawn to the city by the need to find work or propelled there for want of employment and subsistence, commonly had their first encounters with the city through the physical spaces and social environs of its streets. Banerjee (1989) gives a good description of how individuals and families from rural backgrounds moved into eighteenth- and nineteenth-century Calcutta, and similar patterns of in-migration apply to Indian cities well into the twentieth century, with city dwellers often retaining active links with the countryside (*Royal Commission on Labour* 1931, 12–16). Marxist historians have been wary of the representation of India's industrial proletariat as an "uncommitted" workforce, consisting of precapitalist transients whose real home lay in the village and who brought to the city a crude communal awareness rather than a developed class consciousness (Basu 2004, 12–13). Yet the fact remains that most of those who came to reside in the city had relatively recent origins in the countryside and might return there whenever family commitments, unemployment, ill health, or agricultural necessity required them to do so.

The movement from countryside to town frequently had calamitous beginnings. It might originate in oppression, exploitation, and failed resistance but gained further impetus from "natural disasters"—the droughts, epidemics, famines, earthquakes, and floods—whose dislocating and impoverishing impact on the rural poor was accentuated by the greed of landlords and moneylenders and by officials' indifference or neglect (Kingsbury 2015). Here was a form of displacement and involuntary mobility that resulted not so much in an intensification of rural subordination, or even in revolt, than with peasants being wrenched from their rural homes and driven to the cities in search of food and shelter. Such surges in urban in-migration not only changed the social composition of the city but also reconfigured, often to lasting effect, the physical environment of city streets, parks, and open spaces. Thus, as famine began to ravage the rural hinterland in late 1876 and early 1877, more than 10,000 poor migrants flocked into Bombay (Mumbai), a city of almost 700,000 people, crowding onto its streets and threatening to overwhelm its already precarious social and sanitary order. By the end of September 1877 more than 36,000 "destitute paupers" had entered the city, and one response of the municipal authorities was to try to segregate and confine them in specially created camps so as to minimize their adverse impact on the rest of the city (*Bombay* 1878, 2–6, 16, 21). Famine had a similar impact on the streets of Madras (Chennai) during the same famine episode (Digby 1878), as it did, still more visibly, in Calcutta in 1943 (Mukherjee 2015).

On each of these occasions, city spaces became flooded with famine sufferers, subverting the seemingly ordered spatiality of the colonial city and transforming it into a scene of confusion, suffering, and death. The effect of this wholesale displacement might prove only temporary, as migrants drifted back to the countryside once the worst of the famine had passed, but some of the immigrant population stayed and settled down in city slums, the *chawls* and *bustees* that became a permanent feature of the urban landscape. In the short term, famine might transform some areas of the city, especially near temples, mosques, and churches where aid was sought; charitable institutions and state depots where relief was distributed; and grain markets, warehouses, and railway yards where hopes of finding food still lingered. Famine in the countryside and the inflow of impoverished migrants also brought disease to the city, redrawing the map of mortality from smallpox, cholera, and fevers. The rise of municipal government coincided with an enhanced sanitary awareness on the part of the colonial authorities; thus the municipal reports and records of the period are sources of some of the most informative accounts of how poverty, locality, and occupation reflected, and in turn impacted on, the lives of city subalterns. Death and disease helped make the lives of city subalterns visible—on the street and in the archive.

Famine exacted an exceptional toll of misery and mortality, yet even in "normal" years significant numbers of city dwellers died on the streets or perished soon after their removal to hospital. The police picked up the destitute and dying and many were taken to Calcutta's Pauper Hospital, where more than a thousand people died each year and the mortality rate hovered between 25 to 30 percent of those admitted (*Report on the Calcutta Medical Institutions* 1873, 92–93). Even in death subalternity manifested itself spatially through physical displacement or differential treatment. Rather than being interred or cremated, the bodies of those who died or were killed on the street were taken to the morgue and subjected to a postmortem investigation (an indignity most Indians, even the very poor, keenly opposed and stubbornly resisted) or were transferred to the local teaching hospital for dissection. Such was the fate of the "feeble old woman" who died in a tramcar accident in Calcutta and whose dissected corpse was used to provide data for calculating the average size and weight of the female Bengali brain (Buchanan and Daly 1902). Urban necrogeography told its own story. While high-caste Hindus in Bombay were cremated, a prestigious if costly rite, the low-caste dead, whether from poverty or by convention, were interred in separate burial grounds, like that on the city's Haines Road, or their unclaimed bodies dispatched to municipal crematoria.

Many subalterns lived on the street, on the pavements, or in makeshift roadside encampments. In 1931 in Madras (Chennai), more than four hundred families, mostly casual workers and unskilled laborers, were said to be squatting on the streets in the Harbour and Esplanade areas of the city or sleeping on warehouse verandas (*Royal Commission on Labour: Madras* 1931, 10). Other subalterns dwelt on the outskirts of the city, traveling daily to their place of work. As early as 1822, it was estimated that 100,000 artisans and "coolies" entered Calcutta every day from the suburbs and, across the river, from Howrah (Sandeman 1869, 473). The development of modern transport links—tram and bus services—facilitated this daily migration. But these services had a price that few subalterns could afford, so many continued to trek in and out of the city on foot or by bicycle and rickshaw.

But subaltern mobility was not solely into, or around, the city. Subaltern mobility and displacement were evident, too, in the existential crises that periodically engulfed the modern city. The outbreak of bubonic plague in Bombay in 1896 and the draconian state measures that accompanied it impelled thousands of workers to flee to the countryside, crowding the roads and railway stations and causing widespread disruption to textile mills and municipal services. It was estimated that nearly 400,000 people—close to half the city's population at the time—left Bombay between October 1896 and February 1897 (Arnold 1993, 200–239; Chandavarkar 1998, 234–65). To the municipal authorities (Snow 1897, 4) this might be "a wild, unreasoning panic," but it was also a rational response to the threat of deadly disease and the coercive state measures designed to contain and suppress it. By 1902, some 38,000 residents, who had not quit the city and were too poor to find other means of escape, were crowded into plague camps (*Bombay* 1902, 153). The flight of Bombay's subaltern population in 1896–97 was replicated in many other industrial towns and cities across northern India. The influenza pandemic of 1918–19 had a similar effect on Bombay, with thousands again leaving the city, but with the probability, as in the plague exodus, that they carried the disease with them into the countryside, and thus human migration fueled the spatial mobility of the pathogen. In Calcutta, too, influenza struck at the poorest, but also the most mobile, among the subaltern population, including postal and tramway workers, bringing transport, communications, and commercial activity to a virtual standstill (*Calcutta* 1919, 81–85). In other words, subordination was only one marker of urban subalternity. We need to recognize, too, the physical mobility of the subaltern population and the vulnerability this represented.

To a greater extent than the village, the subalterns' city was a place fraught with danger, uncertainty, and risk. The hazards might simply lie in the rural immigrant's unfamiliarity with the noise and confusion of city traffic or the ease with which he or she might be swindled, duped, drugged, or coerced into unpaid labor or the unwitting surrender of scant possessions. Exploitation took different forms in the city with tricksters, con men, and counterfeiters at almost every street corner. There were perennial risks from passing traffic to the blind, disabled, and aged, or those too negligent, slow, or encumbered to avoid wayward carts, trams, trucks, and buses. As street dwellers and street users, subalterns were made vulnerable by sleeping out on the streets at night and being run over or, as in the case of one sixty-year-old beggar in Calcutta, being knocked down and killed by a car (*Statesman*, February 15, 1933, 4). In the wake of World War II, army trucks (or trucks previously belonging to the army but now sold into private hands) sped through the streets of Calcutta, causing numerous accidents and fatalities. City subalterns retaliated by stoning trucks and trying to assault their drivers (*Statesman*, July 10, 1946, 5; *Statesman*, July 21, 1946, 3). Even workers employed by the municipalities were not immune to hazard. For instance, sanitary workers sent to clear blocked drains risked fatal attacks of sewer gas (Arnold 2016, 183). Much of the precariousness that governed urban subalterns' existence was acted out on, or even under, the street.

The Economic Street

The street was a place where many urban subalterns worked or sought employment. With the help of a foreman-jobber from their own caste or community, or by waiting at the gates, rural migrants might find work in factories and mills, but even there employment might not be long-term or secure. A decline in the demand for cotton, jute, and other goods might lead to the abrupt laying off of workers, especially the less skilled. Factories processing foodstuffs, such as rice and oilseeds, tended to operate sporadically, taking on workers with the harvest and then shedding them in the off-season. In the 1920s and 1930s a large part of the workforce employed in India's rice mills consisted of seasonal hands (Adarkar 1946, 1). Women were especially likely to be casually employed, poorly paid, and exposed to industrial accidents.

Apart from those left out on the street due to unreliable factory employment—men and women for whom the street represented exclusion from stable employment—other subalterns found work and a hard-earned subsistence on the street. Banerjee (1989, 55) cited the low-caste palanquin-bearers, originally from Orissa, who formed part of the "floating population" that entered Calcutta daily from the suburbs to work on its streets; others included flower- and fruit-sellers, water-carriers, coachmen, and entertainers. By the early twentieth century palanquins were fast disappearing from Indian streets to be replaced not only by trams, buses, and cars but also by hand-pulled rickshaws. Still a novelty in the 1890s, by 1917–18 there were 2,330 rickshaws on the streets of Madras and, by 1924–25, 3,838, with an even greater number of rickshaw-*wallah*s (the men who pulled rickshaws), few of whom owned the vehicles they operated (*Madras* 1918, appendix 1, 89; *Madras* 1925, appendix 1, 122). Here were men who lived, as well as worked, on the street, hunkering down beside or under their rickshaws, vulnerable to all the incidents of street life, including being maimed or killed in traffic accidents or having their vehicles—their livelihood—smashed up in street riots and communal clashes (*Statesman*, September 12, 1946, 6).

As studies of other Asian cities have shown (Strand 1989; Warren 1986), employment as a rickshaw puller was arduous and dangerous: rates of sickness, injury, and death were extremely high. This was work that only the most low-status and impoverished of rural migrants were willing to take. In Madras they were mostly agricultural laborers from the Tamil hinterland, and in Calcutta they were migrants from rural Bihar and the United Provinces (Uttar Pradesh) (Mukhtar 1946, 18, 35). Even among subaltern groups, rickshaw-*wallah*s were exceptionally poor, transient, and vulnerable. And yet, even though they worked alone, dispersed around the city, in conditions very different from the collective enterprise of the factory floor, that did not prevent them showing some capacity for combined action and a sense of shared interests. In other words, what was "subaltern" about the street was not just the impoverished, physically arduous, and socially marginalized lives of those who lived and worked there but also the conditions the street itself created as a space conducive to a degree of subaltern solidarity, even if the effect of their self-interested action might be only to perpetuate their exploitation. In May 1913 there was a strike of rickshaw-pullers in Madras protesting against regulations that required two men to push or pull any rickshaw containing more than one passenger. When the deputy police commissioner intervened to rescind this unpopular rule, the strike quickly ended (*Madras Mail*, May 13, 1913, 5). Twenty-five years later, in July 1938, three thousand rickshaw-*wallah*s again went on strike in Madras to protest over new regulations prohibiting them from carrying more than one passenger (*Bombay Chronicle*, July 2, 1938, 9).

Other street occupations might be less conducive to solidarity or less literally lived on the streets, but rickshaw-*wallah*s were not altogether exceptional. The *halalkhor*s and *bigari*s, the sweepers and garbage collectors of Bombay, lived in purpose-built, segregated "lines," located close to the noxious sites where urban waste was dumped, buried, or burned (*Bombay* 1914, 168; Pradhan 1938). These low-ranking municipal employees spent their working day on the streets and in the back lanes of the city, the *halalkhor*s gathering up human excrement from households and tipping it into bullock-carts, the *bigari*s sweeping up litter from streets and gutters. This almost incessant circulation through the city streets provides one demonstration of the physical movement that characterized many urban subalterns and demonstrates how, at least for work purposes, they were not restricted to a few spatially segregated low-caste or "black town" ghettos.

About six thousand municipal sweepers were employed in Bombay in the late 1890s in a city of close to three-quarters of a million people. They were recruited from some of the lowest "untouchable" communities, the *halalkhor*s coming principally from the Mahars of the Deccan and the *bigari*s from the sweeper castes of rural Gujarat; they were attracted to Bombay by pay of between 10 and 20 rupees a month (*Gujarat Population* 1901, 338). Despite the degrading nature of their work, the poverty of their living conditions, and the "imported" character of their labor, there were occasions when city rubbish collectors and scavengers went on strike in protest against changes to their work regime or in pursuit of higher wages and better working conditions—in effect, holding the city to ransom through its very streets. In the "great *halalkhor* strike" of 1866, 480 men stopped work, causing "an inconceivable amount of danger and nuisance," before returning ten days later (Snow 1897, 5). In August 1889 the *bigari*s took strike action; in June 1913 and again in August 1920 the *halalkhor*s struck, demanding increased pay to counter steep rises in living costs. In 1913 the strikers returned after only two days, but in 1920 they held out for a week before being forced back to work without any significant gains. Even so, it is indicative of caste and occupational differences among conservancy workers that the demands of the 4,000 sweepers and cartmen in 1920 were not supported by the *halalkhor*s who instead kept aloof from the protest (*Bombay* 1914, 38; *Bombay* 1920, 38–39).

In a caste-divided society, working alongside each other on the street was no guarantee of occupational solidarity. And yet, as Bombay's municipal commissioner, P. C. H. Snow, wrote of the municipal sweepers during the plague crisis in 1897: "Scattered as they are through every portion of the city in large numbers, any unrest or tendency to strike among them immediately affects other numerous low-caste natives, and any development of panic or alarm straightway spreads to their immediate surroundings" (Snow 1897, 5). The concern at the time was that "panic" among the *bigari*s and *halalkhor*s would spread to the rest of the municipal workers on whom the regime's antiplague measures so heavily depended. As Snow put it, "On their presence or absence . . . depended the safety or ruin of this vast and important city." Without them, "Bombay would be converted into a vast dunghill of putrescent ordure" (Snow 1897, 5). Many street-working subalterns were aware of the power they could potentially exercise over labor relations and municipal governance. But the fact they were municipal employees deepens the ambiguity (to invoke another of Guha's terms) of urban subalternity: How far did such groups identify with the authorities who employed them or were they closer to the subaltern communities from which they were recruited? How and when, if ever, did they switch roles and assume a more overtly anticolonial or anticapitalist stance? Caste and religion might be a barrier to urban solidarity, but what of race? For among those who worked on the street were relatively poor European, and more especially Anglo-Indian, tram drivers, conductors, and chauffeurs. In the eyes of the white elite and high-status Indians, these workers were among the more lowly of the urban population but when, during strikes, lockouts, or political demonstrations, violence erupted on the streets, stones were thrown, and traffic was disrupted, Anglo-Indians were among those commonly targeted and abused.

While we can gain only limited access to the consciousness of the urban subalterns, by reading their reported statements and interpreting their demands and actions we can note that one of the ways in which elite/state knowledge about subalterns was constituted was through the emergence of an urban ethnographic literature. Historians are familiar with the gazetteers, manuals, and handbooks produced about India's rural population—the "criminal tribes and castes," "martial races," plantation "coolies," and so on—most of which were compiled before 1914. Urban ethnographies, by contrast, had a later provenance and constitute a more fragmented body of knowledge. Some of the more academic works were sociological or socioeconomic studies of groups like the "untouchable" workers of Bombay (Mann 1967; Pradhan 1938). Others, embedded in police files, concentrated on the urban equivalent of rural "criminal tribes"—the "rowdies" and "goondas." From the 1880s onward, these amorphous elements were seen as constituting a violent, criminal underclass, periodically caught up (or instrumental) in political episodes like the disturbances during the Simon Commission's visit to Madras in February 1928 (Dhareshwar and Srivatsan 1996; Home (Political), 418, 1922, NAI; Madras, Public, GO 166, February 23, 1928, IOR). There were also investigations into specific occupations, such as rice-mill workers and rickshaw pullers (Adarkar 1946; Muhktar 1946) and surveys of urban diets and household incomes that also shed light on subaltern lives more generally (Aykroyd 1939; Burnett-Hurst 1925). If less comprehensive than its rural counterpart, this urban literature constituted a new knowledge grid within which city subalterns could be categorized and (in theory) contained. Here, too, it was frequently nonfactory labor that was the object of attention or the lives of millworkers and their families outside the disciplinary space of the factory.

Men toiled on the streets as day laborers and as cart and carriage drivers, negotiating the narrow, congested lanes of the inner city, crisscrossing its industrial, commercial, and residential districts (Gooptu 2001, 56–60). Prostitutes and entertainers frequented streets where they might hope to find customers or attract a crowd (Legg 2009). Even the indigenous oculists who removed eye cataracts (or, more exactly, depressed them), and so almost magically restored their clients' sight, relied on the theatrical possibilities of the street to attract onlookers and boost their trade (Ratnakar 1941, 28–29). Like the sale of hazardous drugs and toxic substances (Arnold 2016), the oculists' activities underscored the role of the street as an uncolonized site of medical activity and a showplace for rival or informal systems of medical and surgical knowledge. Carpenters, masons, and other artisans gathered at roadside locations in cities like Lahore and Cawnpore (Kanpur) to advertise themselves for hire (Gooptu 2001, 88–89), often displaying the tools of their trade, as they still do on the streets of Old Delhi.

The street provided many of the diverse ecological niches in which the city's lowliest, and often most arduous, trades subsisted. Barbers, tailors, and tinkers worked on the pavement, almost under the feet of passersby, while in adjacent yards, men and boys toiled in "offensive" trades and sweatshops—tanning hides, parboiling rice, making tallow, rolling bidis. Spinners, weavers, and dyers treated the street as their workplace, stretching yarn or drying cloth in the open air. Betel-nut sellers, cycle repairmen, ice-cream and soft-drink vendors, astrologers, sadhus, and beggars, even typists and sewing machinists, took up temporary residence on the street outside temples, cinemas, and railway stations or in proximity to post offices and marketplaces. Messenger boys and government peons sauntered past or sped by on bicycles, and a small army of municipal rat-catchers went about their work. Indian cities had a cast of characters as colorful and as varied as a Dickens novel or *Mayhew's London* (*Bombay* 1867, 23–32; Mayhew 2010).

Living in the Subaltern City

Humans were not the only subaltern occupants of the street, for subaltern cities were invariably animal cities as well. Pigs, goats, buffaloes, and cows, owned or tended by the city's poorer inhabitants, were not confined to squalid pens and fetid stables; they roamed the streets foraging for food from gutters, waste bins, and food stalls, in return providing the city with part of its food and drink (*Bombay* 1867, 4–5). In 1914 there were an estimated 20,000 milk-yielding animals in Bombay, located in 86 licensed stalls. There were also 45 dairies and nearly 800 milk shops, but large quantities of milk were bought directly from street hawkers (*Bombay* 1915, 124–25). Milk gives a further practical demonstration of patterns of spatial circulation within the city. Taken from animals that practically lived on the street, it was sold to customers on or from the street, but since milk was commonly adulterated with untreated water to increase its profitability it was not only milk that circulated in this way but also waterborne diseases. The spatial distribution of cows and buffaloes in Bombay showed a close correlation, too, with the poorest, most insalubrious wards, just as, until determined efforts were made by the municipal authorities to remove them, many slaughterhouses were situated in inner-city areas, with blood and entrails spilling out onto adjacent roadways (*Bombay* 1868, 7).

Sanitation (or its imperilment) apart, Western medicine also made its appearance on, or in close proximity to, the street. In addition to vaccinators, inoculators, and midwives, dispensaries treated the sick who arrived off the street and would not consent to stay in a hospital. As with the routine operations and venal exactions of the urban constabulary, who similarly had a more conspicuous presence in the city than in rural India, this degree of urban surveillance and governance shows the greater degree of exposure of urban subalterns to contact with state agencies, and hence the constant need to be wary of, but also to engage with—and, where necessary, negotiate with—the "everyday state." This was a politicizing process, one that might instill an enhanced sense of grievance and oppression, but it was also a familiarizing, educating process in which the opportunities, as well as the hazards, presented by urban life also became apparent.

Accounts of rural revolt, like that given by Guha in *Elementary Aspects*, emphasize the importance of orality in subaltern communication and mobilization, implying a contrast between illiterate subaltern groups and the power of the written and printed word among Indian elites and state agencies. But the subaltern street was also defined by its visibility—by the power of ocular perception and the governing gaze. For those who could read, or who simply absorbed the visual message of posters and advertisements plastered on walls and buildings, the street provided an education in the desirability of consumer goods, in political creeds and public heroes, in cinema entertainment and religious iconography. The city street was a learning experience in a way that a village lane was not. In colonial discourse, too, what was visible in, and known from, the street served to typify Indian society at large—its criminality and communalism as well as its poverty, instability, and disease. The street was a highly visible space, which is one reason a whole range of subaltern activities, from prostitution to street trading, increasingly came under the censorious eye of the colonial state and the municipal authorities. But the street, as an enabling, facilitating space, also allowed for transmission and communication by, and among, subalterns themselves. The streetwise subaltern learned by watching how to avoid passing traffic or to evade the unwelcome attentions of the policeman, the sanitary inspector, and the vaccinator. He (but also she) acquired skills by observing on the street how to use a sewing machine or repair a bicycle.

As places for living and working, the streets acquired a territorial identity of their own—defined, as in the village, by occupation and trade, religion, caste, and ethnicity—but also spatially delineated by main roads, railroad tracks, canals, creeks, and culverts and by the institutional sites and recreational spaces already appropriated by European and Indian elites. In some city areas, as in Madras and Bombay, erstwhile villages were incorporated into the urban sprawl and municipal jurisdiction and yet still retained elements of vernacular building styles or occupational pursuits, like weaving and pot-making, that might appear better suited to village life. If the countryside could engender territoriality and solidarity, so might the streets and lanes of the modern city. The sense of locality was reinforced by cultural practices and "bonds of community" (Joshi 1985) as powerful as any in the countryside—through the celebration of births and marriages, through worship at roadside shrines, and through street processions and the annual cycle of festivals, themselves largely acted out on the streets. No less than in Europe, India's streets were a site for the generation and dissemination of popular culture, such as the bawdy songs and satirical ballads that circulated in the streets of Calcutta (Ghosh 2013) and articulated a subaltern view of the world, long before loudspeakers began to blare out Bollywood songs and puncture the air with political slogans.

And yet there was always—to echo Guha once more—an element of ambiguity as well as danger about the subaltern street. At times, and not just during sporadic moments of riot and insurrection, subalterns might seem to command the streets and through their occupancy and occupations make such spaces their own. But this sense of possession was seldom secure, never complete. Policemen demanded bribes from street vendors or for alleged traffic violations. Roadside shanties were summarily demolished; smallpox vaccinators or plague inoculators suddenly seized their victims from the street and sanitary officers whisked them away to hospitals or detention camps. The decision to hold a strike or call a *hartal* (the closure of shops and cessation of work) might engulf the denizens of the street or render them the unwitting victims of police *lathi*-charges and firing. Industrial disputes might originate within the factory, but when the gates were closed and protest spilled over onto the streets, it was often there that violence ensued (Basu 1998, 959). There was an enduring precariousness, an abiding unsettledness, about subaltern street-life.

The Political Street

The urban street was an evolving political space, part enabling, part constraining, and in this regard Guha's notion of "transmission" has particular utility. There are perhaps two ways in which that idea might usefully be applied. The first relates to the constant circulation and communication of news, gossip, and rumor—the "bazaar *gup*" of which the colonial authorities spoke with a mixture of alarm and contempt and which constituted one of the weak points of the "colonial information order" (Bayly 1996). The subject of this largely oral transmission might vary widely—from reports of imminent invasion to more routine (if no less alarming) concerns about escalating food prices, the "poisoning" of food and drink sold in the bazaar, or the onset of epidemics and coercive state responses. Rumor spread rapidly through the streets, less hampered by distance than in the countryside. It raced through the bazaars and on to other places of subaltern protest and assembly outside temples, mosques, railway stations, hospitals, law courts, and police stations. The second aspect of transmission was its mobilizing power. If suspicion and rumor could excite rural subalterns to revolt, so could they, with still greater rapidity, arouse urban subalterns, often in ways that transcended individual occupational groups and religious or caste communities.

The opening phases of the Bombay plague epidemic in 1896–98 created a number of incidents in which rumor and report played their part, mobilizing millworkers and other subaltern groups to gather on the streets and take action against what they saw as individuals they suspected of malevolent intentions or institutions that, due to a policy of segregation and hospitalization, seemed menacing and injurious. As the municipal commissioner reported of the attack on the Arthur Road Hospital for contagious diseases on October 10, 1896, in which millworkers threatened violence against the staff and even seemed bent on demolishing the building: "The incident was a grave one, not so much in itself, but as an indication of general feeling, and the secret intelligence which I received from time to time showed that our sanitary staff were almost in open sympathy with the rioters owing to the fear of forcible segregation" (Snow 1897, 6). In his view millhands were an "ever-present source of danger," especially so when they quit their factories and poured out onto the street (Snow 1897, 7).

A further illustration of urban transmission and mobilization among subaltern groups comes from food riots, such as those that erupted in Madras city on several occasions during the nineteenth century and as late as 1918. These, too, were largely street-level events, facilitated by the street as a site of subaltern contact and communication but also by the exposed nature and vulnerable location of bazaars selling food, cloth, and other essential commodities. Crowds, particularly those that gathered in the evening after work, complained loudly about unaffordable prices or unavailable items of everyday subsistence.

Sometimes they took their protests to the local magistrate, but, when he declined to act, and united by a shared sense of need and indignation, they looted stalls or broke into warehouses. Reports of what was happening "spread like wildfire" as people were caught up in "the fever of excitement" (Arnold 1979, 125). Participants in these episodes typically included women and children as well as adult men. They came from the lower castes, such as fishermen, boatmen, "coolies," domestic servants, and transport workers, but they might also be joined, as in the Madras food riots of September 1918, by other subaltern groups—millhands and laborers from the railway workshops (Arnold 1979). But, as we have already seen, the street was not necessarily conducive to such displays of collective action and also witnessed episodes when conflict occurred between subaltern groups, albeit aided, on one side or the other, by employers, magistrates, and the police. Such, for example, was the case during a protracted and bitter strike in Madras in July 1921, when Adi-Dravida ("untouchable") textile workers clashed in the streets and outside the factory gates with striking caste Hindus and Muslims from the Buckingham and Carnatic mills and a nearby slaughterhouse (Madras, Public, GO 671, October 7, 1921, TNA; Murphy 1977).

In many instances, the street was more a site of the emerging political hegemony of the Indian middle class than of autonomous subaltern protest, reminding us of Gramsci's dictum that subaltern groups "are always subject to the activity of ruling groups, even when they rebel and rise up" (Gramsci 1971, 55). Roadside philanthropy and religious institutions, charitable libraries and dispensaries, even sympathetic merchants reached out to the subaltern public, empathizing with their plight, nurturing their social awareness, and cultivating their political imagination (Madras, Public, GO 342, April 18, 1918, TNA). Among the early trade union leaders and organizers in Madras were several conspicuous "outsiders," including B. P. Wadia, a Parsi "home ruler" from Bombay, who helped organize tramway and rickshaw workers as well as factory hands (Veeraraghavan 2013, 84–92). The colonization of the street by elite politicians is further instanced by the Ganapati festival promoted by the Hindu nationalist B. G. Tilak in western India in the mid-1890s. Before this time, the annual celebration of the god Ganapati was held privately in individual households. In order to create a Hindu alternative to the Muslim Muharram, which itself had a lively street presence, Tilak began in Poona (Pune) to encourage local *melas* (festivals) in which streets and city wards would club together to raise subscriptions for processions, religious songs, and dancing. Although a central committee was formed to oversee these events, a large measure of local, even street-level, autonomy remained (Cashman 1970, 352–56). However, when the Ganapati festival became a means not just for raising Hindu awareness and communal consciousness but also, after 1905, for propagating *swadeshi* (the manufacture and purchase of Indian-made goods) and promoting Indian patriotism, the government began to intervene and by 1910 had virtually stifled the movement (Cashman 1970, 358–63).

Like the plague disturbances in Bombay and the food riots in Madras, the Ganapati festival testified to a growing awareness by both the colonial authorities and the Indian elite of the restive energy and public prominence of the subaltern street and the desirability of finding ways either to contain or to exploit it. From the Rowlatt Satyagraha of 1919 onward (Kumar 1971), Gandhi's noncooperation and civil disobedience campaigns paid particular attention to the street as a site of anticolonial protest and nationalist demonstration. Many of the movements with which he was associated began as, or rapidly became, street satyagrahas. Activists took to picketing on the street against shops that sold foreign cloth and liquor; organized processions with chanting, flag waving, and singing to arouse or revive public support; collected funds for the nationalist cause; and courted arrest by defying government orders banning meetings. The very public clashes between protesters and police that ensued underscored the value of the street as a site of political propaganda and recruitment, especially when unarmed men, women, and youths were savagely attacked by *lathi*-wielding policemen (Arnold 1986, 191–204). The street, to adopt another of Guha's formulae, was thus a site of emerging nationalist hegemony, a place where India's nationalist leadership sought to discipline as well as to educate and mobilize the masses (Arnold 1997, 100–151). This disciplinary intent was not always successfully realized, especially when, as in Bombay in November 1921, street violence broke out and for a while almost took over the city, but the desire to command and control was clearly present (Krishnadas 1951, 122–51).

But if these events show the street as an enabling space, whether for subalterns themselves or for those who aspired to direct them, two contrary, constraining aspects of the street need to be reckoned with. One was the increased ability of the state to mobilize the evolving technologies of urban governance and street control. In the case of the city police this was evident in the deployment of armed police units, backed up by motor vans, telephones, and radios that aided intelligence gathering, mobility, and the capacity to respond quickly to events (Arnold 2013). Second, alongside this expansion of the coercive and controlling mechanisms of the state was a pronounced change in the nature of urban governance. In the wake of the plague crisis in the late 1890s, and the growing evidence of the physical and political presence of the industrial working class, municipal government in India became a more active and interventionist force. Just as one can date changes in urban governance back to the creation of a reformed police establishment in the early 1860s, so from about that time onward there had been a marked growth in the regulatory powers assigned to, or assumed by, India's municipal authorities as they claimed, or sought, greater control over housing, sanitation, the water supply, and street trading. The creation of urban "improvement trusts" in the wake of the plague epidemic marked a further stage in the intensification of municipal governance, as slum areas were cleared, new roads created, and residential areas reassigned in the name of improved sanitation and urban well-being. By the 1920s municipal governments possessed far-reaching powers to tax or prohibit street vendors, regulate the sale of food and drink, and remove and resite "offensive" or "dangerous" trades. Many of these changes bore down, with particular weight, on subaltern street life. The social geography of Indian cities and their subaltern population was being radically reconfigured (Gooptu 2001, 66–109).

Conclusion

The street is a conceptual space as much as a physical entity. In colonial India, as elsewhere, what was seen or heard on the street was made to stand for urban society at large or for the country or nation in which the street was seen as a microcosm. In formal governance, in elite politics, even in fiction, the street became emblematic of a wider domain of social activity and political engagement. As a site of observation, inspection, and surveillance, the street might create an illusion of orderliness and omnipotence, even though the reality was actually very different. But while recognizing the value of the street as an idea, we should not be blind to its stark materiality, especially for those who lived and worked there, nor to the historical processes by which the street and its denizens were in a state of almost perpetual uncertainty and constant change. This chapter has argued for the importance of the city street rather than for the village or the factory; so much has been written about South Asia as a crucial, in many ways distinctive, site of subalternity. As an existential, residential, and political space, the street was mobile, unpredictable, and dangerous. The street might provide the urban subaltern with opportunities—for food, shelter, work, sociability, and collective self-expression. It might be socially enabling and politically empowering. But it could also be a site of troubling exposure—to surveillance, violence, and destitution as well as to exploitation, forced displacement, and interventions of the "everyday state." As in the countryside, there were moments of defiance and revolt, but there was also a more constant need for organization, protest, and negotiation. In the city street, in its evolving history, as in its contemporary politics, we can see a primary example of what subaltern geography might mean.

ARCHIVAL ABBREVIATIONS

GO   Government Order
IOR India Office Records, British Library, London
NAI National Archives of India, New Delhi
TNA Tamil Nadu Archives, Chennai

REFERENCES

Adarkar, B. P. 1946. *Report on Labour Conditions in the Rice Mills.* Delhi: Manager of Publications, Government of India.
Arnold, D. 1979. "Looting, Grain Riots and Government Policy in South India 1918." *Past & Present* 84: 111–45.
———. 1986. *Police Power and Colonial Rule: Madras, 1859–1947.* Delhi: Oxford University Press.
———. 1993. *Colonizing the Body: State Medicine and Epidemic Disease in Nineteenth-Century India.* Berkeley: University of California Press.
———. 2016. *Toxic Histories: Poison and Pollution in Modern India.* Cambridge: Cambridge University Press.
Aykroyd, W. R. 1939. *Note on the Results of Diet Surveys in India.* New Delhi: Indian Research Fund Association.
Banerjee, S. 1989. *The Parlour and the Streets: Elite and Popular Culture in Nineteenth Century Calcutta.* Calcutta: Seagull Books.
Basu, S. 1998. "Strikes and 'Communal' Riots in Calcutta in the 1890s: Industrial Workers, Bhadralok Nationalist Leadership and the Colonial State." *Modern Asian Studies* 32, no. 4: 949–83.
———. 2004. *Does Class Matter? Colonial Capital and Workers' Resistance in Bengal, 1890–1937.* New Delhi: Oxford University Press.
Bayat, A. 2000. "From 'Dangerous Classes' to 'Quiet Rebels': Politics of the Urban Subaltern in the Global South." *International Sociology* 15, no. 3: 533–57.
Bayly, C. A. 1996. *Empire and Information: Intelligence Gathering and Social Communication in India, 1780–1870.* Cambridge: Cambridge University Press.
Bombay. 1867. *Bombay Municipality: Health Officer's Report, 1866.* Bombay: n.p.
———. 1868. *Annual Report of the Municipal Commissioner of Bombay, 1867.* Bombay: Times of India Press.
———. 1878. *Annual Report of the Municipal Commissioner of Bombay, 1877.* Bombay: Times of India Steam Press.
———. 1902. *Administrative Report of the Municipal Commissioner, Bombay, 1901.* Bombay: Times of India Press.
———. 1914. *Administrative Report of the Municipal Commissioner, Bombay, 1913.* Bombay: Times of India Press.
———. 1915. *Administrative Report of the Municipal Commissioner, Bombay, 1914.* Bombay: Times of India Press.
———. 1920. *Administrative Report of the Municipal Commissioner, Bombay, 1913.* Bombay: Times of India Press.
Buchanan, W. J., and F. J. Daly. 1902. "Weights of Human Viscera (in Natives of Bengal)." *Indian Medical Gazette* 37, no. 2: 56
Burnett-Hurst, A. R. 1925. *Labour and Housing in Bombay: A Study in the Economic Conditions of the Wage-earning Classes in Bombay.* London: P. S. King & Son.
Cashman, R. 1970. "Political Recruitment of God Ganapati." *Indian Economic and Social History Review* 7, no. 3: 347–73.
Chakrabarty, D. 1983. "Conditions for Knowledge of Working-Class Conditions: Employers, Government and the Jute Workers of Calcutta, 1890–1940." In *Subaltern Studies II,* edited by R. Guha, 259–310. Delhi: Oxford University Press.

———. 1991. "Open Space/Public Space: Garbage, Modernity and India." *South Asia* 14, no. 1: 15–31.

Chandavarkar, R. 1994. *The Origins of Industrial Capitalism in India: Business Strategies and the Working Classes in Bombay, 1900–1940*. Cambridge: Cambridge University Press

———. 1998. *Imperial Power and Popular Politics: Class, Resistance and the State in India, c. 1850–1950*. Cambridge: Cambridge University Press

Chatterjee, P. 2012. "Gramsci in the Twenty-First Century." In *The Postcolonial Gramsci*, edited by N. Srivastava and B. Bhattacharya, 119–36. New York: Routledge.

Dhareshwar, V., and R. Srivatsan. 1996. "'Rowdy-Sheeters': An Essay on Subalternity and Politics." In *Subaltern Studies IX*, edited by S. Amin and D. Chakrabarty, 201–31. Delhi: Oxford University Press.

Digby, W. 1878. *The Famine Campaign in Southern India, 1876–1878*. 2 vols. London: Longmans, Green.

Dutt, R. C. 1895. *Rambles in India during Twenty-Four Years, 1871 to 1895*. Calcutta: S. K. Lahiri.

Flynn, T. 1994. "Foucault's Mapping of History." In *The Cambridge Companion to Foucault*, edited by G. Gutting, 28–46. Cambridge: Cambridge University Press.

Ghosh, A. 2013. "Singing in a New World: Street Songs and Urban Experience in Colonial Calcutta." *History Workshop Journal* 76: 111–36.

Gooptu, N. 2001. *The Politics of the Urban Poor in Early Twentieth-Century India*. Cambridge: Cambridge University Press.

Gramsci, A. 1971. "Notes on Italian History." In *Selections from the Prison Notebooks of Antonio Gramsci*, edited and translated by Q. Hoare and G. N. Smith, 52–120. London: Lawrence & Wishart.

Guha, R. 1983. *Elementary Aspects of Peasant Insurgency in Colonial India*. Delhi: Oxford University Press.

———. 1997. *Dominance without Hegemony: History and Power in Colonial India*. Cambridge, Mass.: Harvard University Press.

———. 2008. "A Colonial City and Its Time(s)." *Indian Economic and Social History Review* 45, no. 3: 329–51.

Gujarat Population: Hindus. 1901. Gazetteer of the Bombay Presidency IX: 1. Bombay: Government Central Press.

Hardiman, D. 1987. *The Coming of the Devi: Adivasi Assertion in Western India*. Delhi: Oxford University Press.

———. 1996. *Feeding the Baniya: Peasants and Usurers in Western India*. Delhi: Oxford University Press.

Harrison, J. B. 1980. "Allahabad: A Sanitary History." In *The City in South Asia*, edited by K. Ballhatchet and J. B. Harrison, 166–95. London: Curzon Press.

Havell, E. B. 1905. *Benares: The Sacred City*. London: Blackie.

Haynes, D. E., and N. Rao. 2013. "Beyond the Colonial City: Re-evaluating the Urban History of India, ca. 1920–1970." *South Asia* 36, no. 3: 317–35.

Hazareesingh, S. 2001. "Colonial Modernism and the Flawed Paradigms of Urban Renewal: Uneven Development in Bombay, 1900–25." *Urban History* 28, no. 2: 235–55.

Ismail, S. 2013. "Urban Subalterns in the Arab Revolutions: Cairo and Damascus in Comparative Perspective." *Comparative Studies in Society and History* 55, no. 4: 1865–94.

Joshi, C. 1985. "Bonds of Community, Ties of Religion: Kanpur Textile Workers in

the Early Twentieth Century." *Indian Economic and Social History Review* 22, no. 3: 251–80.
Kaviraj, S. 1997. "Filth and the Public Sphere: Concepts and Practices about Space in Calcutta." *Public Culture* 10, 1: 83–113.
Khilnani, S. 1998. *The Idea of India*. London: Penguin.
Kidambi, P. 2001. "Housing the Poor in a Colonial City: The Bombay Improvement Trust, 1898–1918." *Studies in History* 17, no. 1: 57–79.
King, A. D. 1976. *Colonial Urban Development: Culture, Social Power and Environment*. London: Routledge & Kegan Paul.
Kingsbury, B. 2015. "An Imperial Disaster: The Bengal Cyclone of 1876." Unpublished PhD diss., University of Wellington.
Krishnadas. 1951. *Seven Months with Mahatma Gandhi*. Ahmedabad: Navajivan Trust.
Kumar, R. Ed. 1971. *Essays on Gandhian Politics: The Rowlatt Satyagraha of 1919*. Oxford: Clarendon Press.
Legg, S. 2007. *Spaces of Colonialism: Delhi's Urban Governmentalities*. Oxford: Wiley-Blackwell.
———. 2009. "Governing Prostitution in Colonial Delhi: From Cantonment Regulations to International Hygiene, 1864–1939." *Social History* 34, no. 4: 447–67.
Low, S. 1907. *A Vision of India*. 2nd ed. London: Smith, Elder.
Lynch, M. 2003. "Beyond the Arab Street: Iraq and the Arab Public Sphere." *Politics and Society* 31, no, 1: 55–91.
Madras. 1918. *Administration Report of the Corporation of Madras, 1917*. Madras: Government Press.
———. 1925. *Administration Report of the Corporation of Madras, 1924*. Madras: Government Press.
Mann, H. H. 1967 [1912]. "The Untouchable Classes of an India City." In *Harold H. Mann: The Social Framework of Agriculture*, edited by D. Thorner, 75–91. Bombay: Vora.
Mayhew, H. 2010 [1861]. *London Labour and the London Poor*. Edited by R. Douglas-Fairhurst. Oxford: Oxford University Press.
Mukherjee, J. 2015. *Hungry Bengal: War, Famine and the End of Empire*. London: Hurst.
Mukhtar, A. 1946. *Report on Rickshaw Pullers*. New Delhi: Manager of Publications, Government of India.
Murphy, E. D. 1977. "Class and Community in India: The Madras Labour Union, 1918–21." *Indian Economic and Social History Review* 14, no. 3: 291–321.
Nilsen, A. G., and S. Roy. Eds. 2015. *New Subaltern Politics: Reconceptualizing Hegemony and Resistance in Contemporary India*. New Delhi: Oxford University Press.
Pandey, G. 1984. "'Encounters and Calamities': The History of a North Indian *Gasba* in the Nineteenth Century." In *Subaltern Studies III*, edited by R. Guha, 231–70. Delhi: Oxford University Press.
Pradhan, G. R. 1938. *Untouchable Workers of Bombay City*. Bombay: Karnatak Publishing House.
———. 2002. "The Urban Turn." In *Sarai Reader 2: The Cities of Everyday Life*, edited by R. S. Vasudevan et al., 2–7. Delhi: Sarai.
Ratnakar, R. P. 1941. "Presidential Address." *Indian Journal of Ophthalmology* 2, no. 1: 25–29.
Report on the Calcutta Medical Institutions, 1872. 1873. Calcutta: Central Press.

Regier, T., and M. A. Khalidi. 2009. "The 'Arab Street': Tracking a Political Metaphor." *Middle East Journal* 63, no. 1: 11–29.

Roy, A. 2011. "Slum Dog Cities: Rethinking Subaltern Urbanism." *International Journal of Urban and Regional Research* 35, no. 2: 223–38.

Royal Commission on Labour in India: A Report. 1931. London: HMSO.

Royal Commission on Labour in India: Evidence. 1931. Vol. 7, Part 1. Madras. London: HMSO Office.

Sandeman, H. D. Ed. 1869. *Selections from Calcutta Gazettes, 1816–1823*. 5 vols. Vol. 5. Calcutta: Superintendent of Government Printing.

Snow, P. C. H. 1897. *Report on the Outbreak of Bubonic Plague in Bombay, 1896–97*. Bombay: Times of India Steam Press.

Strand, D. 1989. *Rickshaw Beijing: City People and Politics in the 1920s*. Berkeley: University of California Press.

Veeraraghavan, D. 2013. *The Making of the Madras Working Class*. New Delhi: LeftWord Books.

Warren, J. F. 1986. *Rickshaw Coolie: A People's History of Singapore, 1880–1940*. Singapore: Oxford University Press.

Before Subaltern Studies

The Epistemology of Property

MUKUL KUMAR AND ANANYA ROY

> How was it that the quasi-feudal land settlement of 1793 had originated from the ideas of a man who was a great admirer of the French Revolution?
> —Ranajit Guha (1996, xv)

In his essay "After Subaltern Studies," Partha Chatterjee (2012) revisits and shifts some of the key analytical questions that have animated subaltern studies since its inception. Instead of the figure of the insurgent peasant, which has been central to subaltern historiography, Chatterjee draws our attention to the "ordinary stuff of democratic politics," which he conceptualizes as "constant tussles of different population groups with the authorities over the distribution of governmental services" (2012, 47). Chatterjee's essay is significant for many reasons, including it being an example of the revisable, even autocritical, nature of the project that is subaltern studies. In homage to Chatterjee's essay, we enact a similar revisiting but this time by excavating the prehistories of subaltern studies. By undertaking an analysis that we call "before subaltern studies," we foreground historiographical moves and methods that are more expansive than conventional readings of subaltern studies. While Ranajit Guha's *Elementary Aspects of Peasant Insurgency in Colonial India* is one of the iconic texts of subaltern studies, we undertake a close reading of a preceding text, *A Rule of Property for Bengal*, published in 1963. *A Rule of Property for Bengal* follows the establishment, in 1793, of the Permanent Settlement in Bengal, instituted by the East India Company and arguably the most important land law introduced by the British in India. We take up Guha's call to grapple with the category of "property," particularly with the making of property in the context of empire. In doing so, we argue that Guha's early work prefigures many of the epistemological moves, such as the critique of Eurocentrism and its universal categories, associated with subaltern studies. Indeed, we find its methodologies to be especially sophisticated and nuanced with important implications for spatial disciplines such as urban planning and political geography.

Our interest in the question of property as framed by Guha is threefold. First, we argue that Guha provides us with what we call "an epistemology of property." As Amartya Sen (1996, x) notes in his foreword, *A Rule of Property for Bengal* is a "significant departure . . . from standard works on British colonial policy in India [given] its focus on ideas as opposed to interests." But Guha's emphasis on ideas is distinctive, showing how the discipline of political economy was reconfigured in order to confront the dilemmas of colonial governance. Property, a universal category of rule, was thus forged through historical difference. Citing Guha's work, Timothy Mitchell (2008, n.p.), in an essay titled "The Properties of Markets," thus notes, "Much of modern European thinking about the nature and importance of private property was worked out in the context of colonial rule, whether by the British in Ireland, India, Egypt, and Australia or the French in North Africa and other territories. What was different in the colonies was the outcome." We will return to this question of outcome later in the essay. For now, we wish to emphasize that although *A Rule of Property for Bengal* and the subsequent texts of subaltern studies have seemingly divergent objects of inquiry—the intellectual history of the idea of landed property and the question of peasant rebellion and revolt—they share a common epistemological project. This includes an understanding of political economy as a form of knowledge produced and honed through colonial rule; a recognition that colonial power relations are thoroughly modern and political; and a critique of hegemonic historiographies, be they colonial, nationalist, liberal, or Marxist (Chakrabarty 2002). These of course are key elements of postcolonial thought, and our interest in *A Rule of Property for Bengal* is that it provides an early and rigorous figuration of such themes.

Second, we argue that property is an especially useful idea for the conduct of postcolonial historiography. The intent of the Permanent Settlement was "to ensure the right of private property in land" (Guha 1996, 2). The purpose was to ensure a steady stream of revenue for the colonial government and, more important, to "establish 'the permanence of dominion'" through the entrustment of property "to the care of a class of native entrepreneurs" (Guha 1996, 9). But the Permanent Settlement must be read not just as a colonial policy but instead as an effort to test and apply key tenets of an emerging European philosophy of land, value, and revenue in a context that permitted experimentation. In Guha's (1996, 99) words, it was an endeavor "to try out the formula in Bengal." That formula hinged on a theory of value based in land. But at its heart was a paradox: How did physiocratic thought—defined as a critique of feudalism within the context of Europe—produce and reinforce neofeudal relations in colonial India? We argue that this paradox, foregrounded in *A Rule of Property for Bengal*, not only allows us to understand the role of colonialism as a constitutive force in modernity but also connects to later discussions in subaltern studies about theories of value and more broadly with a critique of political economy at the present historical juncture.

Third, while not immediately evident, *A Rule of Property for Bengal* speaks in important ways to a central concern of subaltern studies: the mass-political subject. As we have already noted, we draw inspiration from Chatterjee's (2012, 46) essay, which outlines a "deepening and widening of the apparatuses of governmentality" and marks a realignment of subaltern studies from "subject to citizen." *A Rule of Property for Bengal* is an even more significant realignment, organized around a quite different epistemological operation and political gesture. Rather than naming who (or what) constitutes the subject of history, it seeks to understand the ways in which forms of knowledge and power individuate the subject through the rule of property—yet resolutely fails to do so as a consequence of certain epistemic and political limits. But we argue that Guha's line of inquiry is closely connected to the problematic of subject/citizen raised by Chatterjee. In what ways are the subject of colonial rule and the citizen of postcolonial democracy constituted through the rule of property?

By engendering such questions, *A Rule of Property for Bengal* provides invaluable methodological direction for postcolonial thought. While Gayatri Chakravorty Spivak's decisive intervention recast subalternity as the limits of archival and ethnographic recognition (Roy 2011), we view *A Rule of Property for Bengal* as an interposition of considerable significance. There are at least two methodological opportunities here. Reflecting on Guha's *Elementary Aspects of Peasant Insurgency in Colonial India*, Dipesh Chakrabarty (2013, n.p.) notes that "one day scholars will return . . . not to read the book on Guha's terms but find in it a way, a method, of constructing a genealogy of the mass-political subject in India. This would not be the only genealogy—the very logic of genealogies is multiple—but would be one important way of figuring out how the history of subaltern rebellion has left its imprint on contemporary India." It is our contention that such genealogies would be greatly enriched through a simultaneous reading of *A Rule of Property for Bengal*. In particular, such a reading would speak to the dilemma outlined recently by Andrew Sartori (2014, 2–3, emphasis in original): that contemporary land struggles in Bengal are taking place "*in the name of property*" and as a "defense of petty proprietorship." Sartori notes that the present historical conjuncture must be placed in "a history of arguments about the rights of smallholders that turned on appeals to claims about the property constituting powers of labor." We concur and note that Guha's analysis of the Permanent Settlement as an experiment in physiocratic thought is pivotal to this history.

But also at stake in *A Rule of Property for Bengal* is the question of representation so forcefully posed by Spivak (1988) in her intervention. If the subaltern marks the limits of archival and ethnographic recognition, what histories of subalternity are possible? In *The Land Question*, a text that we see as closely related to *A Rule of Property for Bengal*, Partha Chatterjee (1984, xli) argues that the challenge of an "autonomous history of the subaltern classes" is that "written history is overwhelming the history of the ruling classes." This of course is the challenge that animates postcolonial historiography. But Chatterjee's response to the challenge is interesting and one that may have gone unnoticed. He calls for "the particular reading of the given historical material which record the perceptions and concerns of those who rule in order to infer from it the history of their adversaries, those who are ruled (who will only at certain critical moments like rebellions enter the records as adversaries)" (Chatterjee 1984, xli).[1] We thus interpret both *The Land Question* and *A Rule of Property for Bengal* as tracing the constitution of the subaltern subject through a history of the universal categories of rule, notably property and land.

It is our contention that these early works have important implications for the spatial disciplines. As we note in the following section, Guha deconstructs the epistemologies that constitute property as a form of knowledge. In doing so, he renders visible the colonial context in which political economy was forged and practiced, with ideas translated and "bent backward" to accommodate historical difference. But such analysis also speaks directly to the present historical conjuncture and the ongoing efforts of postcolonial government to govern land. For example, Roy (2014) notes that the project of "inclusive growth," now ascendant in many parts of the Global South, including India, requires a transformation of slum land into property settlements. This complicated task of converting the multiplicity of ownership, occupancy, and tenancy into cadastral property, with legible and discrete rights, rents, and revenue, is reminiscent of the Permanent Settlement and what Guha identifies as the problem of indeterminacy in relation to property. More important, the works we have designated as "before subaltern studies" allow us to interpret the land question in contemporary cities. They invite us to pose the following questions: To what extent does a genealogy of property in the present historical conjuncture require interrogating the relationship between urban property relations, the discipline of urban planning, and the limits of liberal democratic citizenship? In what ways should a genealogy of property that takes the twenty-first-century Indian city as its point of departure draw upon Guha's historiographical and epistemological arguments?

The Epistemology of Property

There are many ways to read Ranajit Guha's path-breaking first monograph. Historians, for example, might seek to situate *A Rule of Property for Bengal* within the voluminous historiography on landed property relations under colonial rule. Literary critics might use Guha's text to track the "operation" of the "Asiatic Mode of Production," as Spivak (1999, 86) has suggested. We propose to read Guha as an epistemologist and *A Rule of Property for Bengal* as a work of epistemological analysis. What makes Guha stand out is not only his creativity as a historian but also the rigor with which he proceeds to deconstruct the epistemologies that constitute property as a form of knowledge. If we read Guha in this way, we argue that Guha's work enables a distinctive conceptualization of property and also demonstrates the uncanny ability of postcolonial thought to render visible the colonial histories of political economy.

Our interest then is not in examining the historical debates that led to the formation of the Permanent Settlement in Bengal, how various schools of political economy defined the concept of property, or how these notions were transposed on the existing zamindari system of landed property relations. Rather, we are interested in the epistemological question of how Guha renders property as his object of study and, in doing so, shows that property must be understood as a particular form of colonial knowledge. Taking cues from not only *A Rule of Property for Bengal* itself but also the preface to the second edition of the book published in 1982, and the recent republication of Guha's essays on property written in the 1950s and 1960s, we read Guha's intervention as an epistemological argument.

Guha (1996, xiii) begins with what he calls an "epistemological paradox," which he frames in the following way. On the one hand, physiocratic thought, the precursor to classical political economy, was an "implacable critique of feudalism" (1996, xiii) within the context of Europe. Yet within the context of Bengal, the colonial state drew upon physiocratic thought in order to "graft" notions of private property onto the heterogeneous social and economic landscape of colonial Bengal. In the process, it established what Guha calls a "neo-feudal organization of landed property" (1996, xiii). How, in other words, did physiocratic thought, a powerful critique of feudalism in Europe, ultimately produce neofeudal relations in colonial Bengal? It is this "epistemological paradox" that Guha seeks to explain in *A Rule of Property* by examining the relationship between "Bengal and its British rulers" (1996, xiii). Guha's framing of the question of property as an epistemological paradox carries with it subtle yet significant implications. He does not dismiss the rationales, premises, and precepts of political economy out of hand as merely elite ideology or the machinations of capital. Guha takes the precepts of classical political economy quite seriously in order to understand how they were "bent backward" in order to produce neofeudal forms of property relations in colonial Bengal. This requires examining the debates among different schools of political and economic thought—mercantilists, physiocrats, and classical political economists—and how they came to agree that the rule of property must constitute the "basic principle of government" (1996, 9).

Guha's notion of "epistemological paradox" suggested that the dilemmas of colonial governance were the crucible in which the purportedly universal categories of political economy, including property, were formed. The radical implications of this argument, as Chatterjee (2010, 10) notes, would be taken up only by "a later generation of scholars." Within the context of historiographical debates in the 1960s, Guha's book was difficult to classify and generated considerable disciplinary anxiety among mainstream nationalist and Marxist historians. A review published in the *Indian Economic and Social History Review*, for example, commented that *A Rule of Property for Bengal* was "not Indian economic and social history, but British intellectual history" (Gopal 1966, 214; see also Gopal 1949). This comment by the eminent historian Sarvepalli Gopal was intended to demarcate the disciplinary boundaries of what constituted a legitimate object of study in the fields of Indian economic and social history. We view Guha's intervention as an attempt to unsettle these boundaries by insisting that an interrogation of the history of the Permanent Settlement required developing a critique of Western forms of knowledge and how they were "bent backward" in order to govern colonial Bengal. For Guha, political economy constituted a "colonialist form of knowledge" (1996, xiv).[2] In the preface to the second edition of his book, Guha responded directly to his critics: "If the historical origins of the concepts and theories relating to the first important—some would say, the most important—land law introduced by the British in India and the economic and political circumstances under which those were used to formulate the statute of permanent proprietary rights are of no relevance to the studies of Indian history, I do not know what is" (1996, xiii).

Guha's emphasis on relations of knowledge and power also constituted a challenge to positivist historiographies of colonialism. *A Rule of Property for Bengal* was an intervention that intended to "redress the one-sided interpretation of British rule in India exclusively in terms of conflicts and coalitions of interests" (1996, xv). Guha's book, like that of Eric Stokes (1959), was classified as a work in the history of ideas. We certainly do not disagree with this characterization given that Guha's book sought to track how the idea of property had been translated and transformed through processes of colonial rule. But Guha's monograph, when read in concert with his early essays on property, are also much more than a history of ideas. These essays demonstrate that Guha was also interested in how particular ideas of property and proprietorship had profoundly material social and economic effects, a subject that we discuss in greater detail below. In this sense, Guha's work on property in the 1950s and 1960s complicates any straightforward distinction between ideas and materialism.[3] These essays also demonstrate that Guha was grappling with the relationship between the archive and the production of historical knowledge (see, e.g., Guha 2010a). This would become one of the defining themes of the subaltern studies project, as Chakrabarty (2002) has argued. More than twenty years before the launch of subaltern studies, Guha was beginning to grapple with the question, "What are the archives, and how are they produced?" (Chakrabarty 2002, 16).

The Principle of Property

In the field of urban political economy, Nicholas Blomley (2004, 15, emphasis in original) has emphasized that the question is not so much "what is property?" as "what is to *count* as property?" It is precisely this latter question that we find at the very heart of *A Rule of Property for Bengal*. Colonial rulers set out to ensure the right of private property in land in Bengal and to vest it in a class of native proprietors. They called this, as Guha (1996, 8) notes, "the principle of property." But the principle of property had to reconcile the question of revenue with that of proprietorship. The Permanent Settlement of 1793 was meant to not only ensure a permanence of dominion for British rule in Bengal but also secure a steady stream of revenue. The physiocrats who advocated for the Permanent Settlement drew a distinction between "Crown-ownership and zamindar-ownership," arguing that the Government of the East India Company had a "right to revenue" but were not proprietors of the soil (Guha 1996, 100–101). Yet, the question of proprietorship was itself a complex one. Philip Francis, the fierce advocate of the Permanent Settlement, believed that zamindars already had proprietary rights and the colonial government "had only to extend legal recognition to make it permanent" (Guha 1996, 35). Francis argued: "With respect to the general propositions, I have yet seen no reason to admit that principles unquestionably true in every other country, should not be applicable in Bengal. It is in the nature of justice and good government to deduce its arrangements from undisputed points of original right. It is in the nature of arbitrary power to make exceptions" (Guha 1996, 135).

Francis's arguments are based on the idea that the principle of property is universal and therefore applicable in *all* countries, as Timothy Mitchell (2002) has argued. Drawing on Guha's work, as well as the passage by Francis quoted above, Mitchell (2002, 56) comments: "The principle of property was presented as the opposite of arbitrary power or coercion, represented by the state ownership of land; but it justified a violent exercise of power, and in fact was established by this violence." Mitchell's argument calls for attention to the often violent processes by which certain forms of knowledge are made universal and mobile while others, such as "land" and "peasants," are made into objects that are "anchored to a specific place and moment" (Mitchell 2002, 58).

But in the debates that unfolded about the Permanent Settlement, critics of the policy noted that the system of landed property onto which the British were grafting a regime of private property rights had considerable ambiguity. Guha (1996, 207) notes that one such critic, John Shore, "shrewdly suspected" that "the idea of proprietary rights . . . was an English notion wrongly applied to the historical circumstances of medieval India. 'A property in the soil,' he said, 'must not be understood to convey the same rights in India as in England; the difference is as great as between a free constitution and arbitrary power.'" Shore's criticism of the Permanent Settlement raises the issue of translation and its role in political economy and its universal categories. While Guha does not explicitly use the concept of translation, we argue that the logic of translation is central to the rule of property. Guha seeks to understand how particular notions of property, developed within the context of Western Europe, were translated in the context of colonial Bengal. This epistemological move entails three operations, as Chakrabarty (2011) has recently argued. First, it requires understanding how the discipline of political economy defined conceptions of property. Second, it requires understanding how the discipline sought to interpret existing forms of property—from the arithmetic of Mughal revenue accounts to the figure of the zamindar—in colonial Bengal. How, for example, did the notion of "zamindar" become equivalent to the British conception of the landlord? Third, it entails understanding how processes of translation are constitutive not only of the rule of property that came to exist in Bengal but also of the very discipline of political economy. Put another way, the principle of property advocated by the physiocrats could only be crafted through practices of translation. This in turn raises the issue of equivalence to which we now turn.

The Equivalence of Property

In his essay on the Burdwan district records, Guha (2010a, 66) observed that the sale of lands after the Permanent Settlement in 1793 far exceeded all previous recorded land sales. "This by itself," he wrote, "shows how unrealistic had been the claim made on behalf of the Permanent Settlement as an excellent guarantee of security of property." He continues: "One might, indeed, throw back the argument by saying that in Burdwan, as elsewhere in Bengal, the Permanent Settlement, at the initial stage, was itself the cause of a great flux: it succeeded in creating a new pattern of proprietorship only at the cost of the old and traditional one. It should be noted, however, that *the transformations took place within the existing framework*" (Guha 2010a, 66, our emphasis). The Permanent Settlement, in other words, did not ensure security of property as its advocates claimed. Nor did it erase existing "traditional" patterns of proprietorship. Instead, Guha emphasizes the need to understand how the transformations inaugurated by the Permanent Settlement "took place within the existing framework." Guha, we suggest, viewed the historical transformations inaugurated by the Permanent Settlement as a process of translation, an argument that would later become fundamental to the project of subaltern studies and postcolonial theory.[4]

Our interest in the question of translation as it relates to the rule of property is this: liberal historiography posits equivalence between different conceptions of property—between Mughal and English landlords and between proprietary rights under a "free constitution" and those under "arbitrary power." The project of subaltern studies has been precisely to call into question such assertions of equivalence and to instead foreground forms of historical difference. Here, subaltern studies also departs from Marxist historiography and its tendency to narrate a universal history of capital. Marxist historiography asserts that the universalizing tendency of capital, as Guha (1997, 16) summarizes, will ultimately "subjugate all antecedent modes of production, and replace all jural and institutional concomitants of such modes and generally the entire edifice of precapitalist cultures by laws, institutions, values and other elements of a culture appropriate to bourgeois rule." Marxist historiographies often presuppose that processes of primitive accumulation—the forcible separation of workers from the land to create bourgeois relations of private property—will necessarily create a waged working class, *the* subject of such historiographies. Thus, whereas liberal historiography solves Guha's epistemological paradox by positing an equivalence between different conceptions of property, Marxist historiography conceptualizes this process as one of subsumption (Chakrabarty 2000). Other histories and socialities are simply subsumed into the universal history of capital. We follow postcolonial thought in arguing that theories of value rely on practices of translation and that *A Rule of Property for Bengal* prefigures such methodologies in vitally important ways.

In an essay titled "Scattered Speculations on the Question of Value," Spivak argues that forms of value require acts of representation. She quotes from Marx's *Grundrisse* to develop her argument: "To compare money with language is erroneous. *Ideas which first have to be translated out of their mother tongue into a foreign language in order to circulate*, in order to become exchange, offer a somewhat better analogy; but the analogy then lies not in language, but in the foreignness of language" (Spivak 1985, 83, our emphasis). Marx, in this remarkable passage, suggests that the circulation of value is analogous to the "foreignness of language." *A Rule of Property for Bengal* documents, quite literally, how the colonial state and political economists sought to learn local languages in order to translate concepts of private property and enable the circulation of value. But following Spivak (1985), we would like to argue that Guha's analysis of the Permanent Settlement introduces a fundamental indeterminacy in the question of how property produces value. In order for property to produce value, it must constantly translate forms of difference outside of itself, as Chakrabarty (2000) argues in his analysis of histories of capital. These processes of translation are never complete. Capital, in other words, can never be fully universalized. There is always a gap between liberal historiography's representation of capital as universalizing and its limits in reality (Guha 1997). The ambivalences that mark the Permanent Settlement indicate such limits.

The Ambivalence of Property

The application of the physiocratic formula to colonial Bengal rested on a theory of value based in land. Yet, various dilemmas haunted the Permanent Settlement, notably those related to rent. In various essays published prior to and alongside *A Rule of Property for Bengal*, Guha shows the confusions that attended the matter of rent for the East India Company, thereby marking the limits of equivalence and indeed of the universal category of property. We quote at length from Guha's (2010b, 94–95, our emphasis) essay, "Rent in Kind and Money Rent in Eastern India under Early British Rule":

> In examining land grants and deeds of transfer among the archives belonging to two of the largest estates for the region, I have been unable to find a single document for the eighteenth century stating the precise amounts of rents charged or paid for any piece of land. . . . This strictly one-sided documentation was apparently inspired by the law which exempted from fiscal demand all those parts of an estate that paid no rent. This administrative generosity, introduced first by the Mohammedans in India and rather reluctantly continued under early British rule, had indeed for decades, even before 1757, been abused by the landlords in a manner as to *omit all quantitative statements from the deed of lease, so that there could be no legal basis for the Government to demand revenues on account for the land granted, nor for the ryot to resist rack-renting*. Thus, there is nothing much in the surviving land deeds to furnish any useful information on the subject of rents.
>
> One, therefore, inevitably falls back on administrative evidence: the reports, letters, and, memoranda prepared by the officials of the East India Company for the Government of Bengal and the Court of Directors. There are two factors limiting the use of this kind of evidence for the study of rents. In many of the records *the words "rent" or "revenue" and "land-tax" are used as synonymous*. The immaturity of the vocabulary of political economy in the pre-Ricardian period, the attempt often made under the influence of the French *economistes* to seek an analogy between agrarian conditions under the *ancien régime* and those of contemporary Bengal and, of course, the still unresolved dilemma about the nature of landed property in the Orient (did it belong to the individual? Did it belong to the State?)—all these contributed in varying degrees to the confusion.

Here we have returned once again to the problem of indeterminacy in the production of property values as well as to the problem of translation. In this passage, Guha is attentive both to the absence of "quantitative statements" in lease deeds and to the ways in which the colonial records conflated categories of "rent," "revenue," and "land tax." For Guha, one of the principal reasons the government could not differentiate between these categories was because its understanding was based upon an analogy—that is, a certain kind of cultural translation and historical comparison—which equated the agrarian conditions in Bengal with the ancien régime in France. Guha draws upon these close and critical readings of colonial archival sources to conceptualize the nature of political relationships among the government, zamindars, and the peasantry under colonial rule. We view these passages as an example of how Guha analyzes "the very textual properties of [archival] documents in order to get at the history of power that produced them" (Chakrabarty 2002, 16).

Guha's early essays on property also return us to the question of subalternity, specifically to the mass-political subject/citizen. In his essay on the Burdwan District records, Guha (2010a, 50, our emphasis) writes:

> While produce rent was officially recognized as a constituent of the Company's revenue, the reports, statements, and accounts of this period make no mention of the existence of labour rent in any form. Even more curious is the fact that the greater part of labour rent originated from the so-called rent-free lands or *baze zamin*. This is of course easily explained by the characteristic confusion in the *economic vocabulary* of the East India Company. By an erroneous identification of revenue and rent, lands which yielded no revenue for the Government were considered rent-free. The fortunes of the Company were by no means affected by this misunderstanding, but, *accepted uncritically by generations of scholars*, this has succeeded so far in *concealing one of the principal forms of exploitation of the peasantry of Bengal in the eighteenth century.*

We are interested in this passage because it provides insights into how Guha develops a critique of contemporary historiographies, which, he argues, "uncritically" accept the meaning of "rent" articulated by colonial records. For Guha, basic categories of political economy—property, land, rent, and revenue—cannot be taken for granted as stable, universal referents. Guha thus draws our attention to the "economic vocabulary" of political economy and its concealment of actually existing forms of exploitation.[5] And the point is that it could not have been otherwise. In his work on the land question in Bengal, Chatterjee (1984, xlvii) notes the "numerous ambiguities, uncertainties, and contradictions in the legal framework of agrarian property" during colonial rule. While the physiocrats had carefully distinguished between Crown ownership and zamindari ownership, between the right to revenue and proprietary rights, the Permanent Settlement soon had to contend with the right of occupation. As Chatterjee (1984, 9) demonstrates, a series of rent and tenancy acts followed in the wake of the Permanent Settlement, identifying and defining various rights of occupation, often conceptualizing them as "customary" rights derived from "tradition." In his recent work, Andrew Sartori (2014, 97) notes that this deployment of "custom" was a response to peasant insurgency and the "normative claims" that emerged from such mobilizations. It is thus that "land use" rather than "state rights over revenue" became the hinge for "new conceptions of property" in Bengal (Sartori 2014, 112).

These shifting conceptions of property, the impossibility of equivalence, the indeterminacy of value, and the tangle of rights—to revenue, to proprietorship, to occupation—are all of interest to us. Together they demand the critique of liberal *and* Marxist historiography that subaltern studies has skillfully and repeatedly undertaken. For us, they also indicate the necessity of a genealogical understanding of the present historical conjuncture. As Sartori (2014, 128) notes, peasant mobilizations in colonial Bengal emphasized "property as the foundation of independence . . . frequently placing the property-constituting powers of labor at the core of such claims." Our own intellectual interests lie in tracing how such claims also inflect contemporary land-based struggles in India and elsewhere in the world. Whether in agrarian or urban settings, we are keenly concerned with how the right of occupation is marshaled in contexts where proprietary rights are indeterminate and unmapped. Interpolated in a discipline—urban planning—that constantly seeks equivalence and that claims universal scope for its ideas and practices, we remain committed to tracing the limits of property. Chatterjee (1984, 12) reminds us that the colonial efforts to recognize the rights of tenancy and occupation had created, by the late nineteenth century in Bengal, a "subdivision and diffusion of the rentier interest," with "a few wealthy zamindars at the top and innumerable fragmented estates and tenures at the bottom." It is in this fragmented terrain, amid subinfeudation, that we conduct our research. Chatterjee's (1984, 190–91) assessment of the colonial state applies quite directly to the postcolonial forms of rule—in city and countryside—that we study:

> In this conflict between contending agrarian classes within the colonial state formation, the colonial state retained a role of ambiguity . . . the government was always careful to use the complexity and ambiguity of its land laws to balance the grant of new legal rights to sections of tenants with compensatory restatements of the "customary" privileges of landlords. It thus attempted to present itself as a neutral arbiter in the developing agrarian class struggle, aiming to protect the "sanctity of private property" against incipient revolutionary movements as well as to help the survival of small peasants against rapacious landlords and moneylenders.

Conclusion

In this essay, we have excavated a text that is seen to exist outside of, and prior to, the ongoing project that is subaltern studies. We have argued that this text not only prefigures but also amplifies key themes of subaltern studies. These themes condense around a central argument that runs through our individual and collective work, namely to undertake a political economy attentive to historical difference as a fundamental and constitutive force in the making of global urbanization (see Roy 2015).

First, we view the task of postcolonial thought not as decoding the non-West but rather as conducting an alternative historiography of the West. Roy's (2015) essay was partly written in response to Vivek Chibber (2013, 213), who views subaltern studies as an effort to narrate how "the history of the non-West has been affected by the incursion of capitalism." Postcolonial thought is in fact animated by a quite different concern. In his response to Chibber, Chatterjee (2013, 69) thus notes that "the historical problem confronted by Subaltern Studies is not intrinsically a difference between west and east." Instead, the task was "intended as a critique of liberal historiography and the liberal ideology it represented." Rather than a "historical sociology of bourgeois revolutions of Europe as Chibber understands it to be" (Chatterjee 2013, 69), subaltern studies demonstrated that liberal historiography claimed this history of Europe as universal. This is the work that *A Rule of Property for Bengal* does, well before Chakrabarty's landmark *Provincializing Europe*, well before Spivak's *A Critique of Postcolonial Reason*, and even before Said's *Orientalism*. For us, it serves not as origin but as model, especially since it demonstrates how political economy had to "bend backward" to find universal application. While we have limited our discussion in this essay to the context of Bengal, it should be obvious that the implications of Guha's analysis are far reaching. They speak directly, for example, to the important questions raised recently by Alyosha Goldstein (2014, 4) in his conceptualization of "United States colonialism": "How might the diversity of colonial pasts, settler claims, territorial annexations, and overseas occupations be understood in relation to one another? How have specific normative forms of jurisprudence, racialization, violence, militarism, politics, property, and propriety served to at once facilitate and delimit the conditions of colonial dispossession? How and why do these formations matter now?"

One of the reasons Guha's intervention continues to speak so powerfully to struggles over the meaning and politics of property in the present historical conjuncture is his attention to the epistemologies through which property is constituted. Guha presciently argued that his monograph "addresses itself to the question of *colonialist knowledge* which Indian historiography and the social sciences will have to consider sooner or later" (1996, xiii, emphasis in original). Guha's work on property in the 1950s and 1960s demonstrated that the colonial project crucially depended on accounts of land tenure in non-European societies.[6] We draw upon Guha's work, and postcolonial theory more generally, in order to better understand how colonialism has shaped the spatial methods and concepts through which property is understood in the discipline of urban planning. For, as Guha wrote, "the formal termination of colonial rule, taken by itself, does little to end the government of colonial knowledge" (1996, xiv).

Our interest in the historiography of colonialism is also part of a broader interest in liberalism itself.[7] While much of the debate around contemporary land struggles pivot on conceptualizations of neoliberalism, we seek to uncover the long history of liberalism. Following Sartori (2014), we find the "ambivalences" of liberalism to be especially important and find these to be especially evident in the idea (and ideal) of property. The history of liberalism, as Sartori notes, cannot be told solely in the West. It requires the history of "vernacular liberalism" but where such history is necessarily global. It is crucial to pay attention to Sartori's (2014, 197) clarification of the term "global": "I don't mean this primarily in the sense of global interconnectedness, but in the sense that liberal ideas have been bound inextricably to practices of social abstraction." For us, Guha's *A Rule of Property for Bengal* provides a crucial point of departure for a rich global history of liberalism with its abstractions, ambivalences, and limits.

Finally, while Chatterjee and Sartori each dwell on the ambivalences and contradictions of colonial agrarian policy, and thus of "liberalism in empire," we wish to go further by considering the "agonism of liberalism." We follow Patrick Joyce (2003, 261; see also Roy 2008) to consider liberalism's "definition of itself as a moral struggle, a struggle in and with the world of the political." This agonism is evident in intellectual as well as in personal histories. *A Rule of Property for Bengal* is an unusual embodiment of these entangled histories and the agonistic reflexivity they can engender. Guha's choice to study the question of property had to do with his own class formation. Guha notes that his own "livelihood was derived from remote estates [he] had never visited; his education was oriented by the needs of the colonial bureaucracy"; and "his world of culture was strictly circumscribed by the values of a middle class living off the fat of the land and divorced from the indigenous culture of its peasant masses" (1996, xv). Guha's book, in other words, was both a radical epistemological and political intervention that sought to better understand the formation of his own class. Twenty years later, Partha Chatterjee's first book, *The Land Question*, echoed Guha's approach to the politics of knowledge: "If one is indeed to talk of the relation between theory and practice, and of vanguardism and political education, the first task is not the 'raising' of the consciousness of 'the masses,' a characteristically elitist project; the first task is to achieve greater self-consciousness of the historical role of one's own class" (Chatterjee 1984, 215).

NOTES

1. See also Guha's "The Prose of Counterinsurgency" (1982) and *Elementary Aspects of Peasant Insurgency in Colonial India* (1983).

2. Stokes (1959) and Cohn (1987, 1996) advanced related arguments in the 1950s and 1960s.

3. Indeed, as postcolonial theory would later emphasize, the very distinction between what counts as ideas and matter is itself shaped by the historical legacies of colonialism. See Mitchell's *Rule of Experts* (2002).

4. See especially Chakrabarty's *Provincializing Europe* (2000).

5. Guha (2010a, 51) describes these forms of exploitation in the following way: "Subsequently, the transformation of zamindars into proprietors and the consequent absorption

of much communal property into their private estates, a considerable amount of the free lands turned into freeholds paying in cash or in crop. At the same time the zamindars regranted a large part of the lands 'free of rent' on the condition that the services of the grantees were now placed at the disposal of the zamindar rather than the community."

6. For a recent discussion of this argument, see Mantena's *Alibis of Empire* (2010).

7. As Mehta (1999) argues in his classic study, *Liberalism and Empire*, the universal ideals of liberalism were premised upon the constitutive exclusions of empire.

REFERENCES

Blomley, Nicholas. 2004. *Unsettling the City: Urban Land and the Politics of Property*. New York: Routledge.

Chakrabarty, Dipesh. 2000. *Provincializing Europe: Postcolonial Thought and Historical Difference*. Princeton, N.J.: Princeton University Press.

——. 2002. *Habitations of Modernity: Essays in the Wake of Subaltern Studies*. Chicago: University of Chicago Press.

——. 2011. "Can Political Economy Be Postcolonial?" In *Postcolonial Economies*, edited by Jane Pollard, Cheryl McEwan, and Alex Hughes, 23–36. London: Zed Books.

——. 2013. "The Peasant, Then and Now: Thirty Years of Ranajit Guha's Elementary Aspects." Lecture delivered at the Centre for the Study of Developing Societies, Delhi. Available at: https://www.youtube.com/watch?v=YXKyxc6pzb4, accessed March 6, 2016.

Chatterjee, Partha. 1984. *Bengal, 1920–1947: The Land Question*. Calcutta: KP Bagchi, Center for the Study of Social Sciences.

——. 2010. "Introduction." In *The Small Voice of History*, edited by Partha Chatterjee, 1–18. Ranikhet: Permanent Black.

——. 2012. "After Subaltern Studies." *Economic and Political Weekly* 47, no. 35: 44–49.

——. 2014. "Subaltern Studies and Capital." *Economic and Political Weekly* 48, no. 73: 69–75.

Chibber, Vivek. 2013. *Postcolonial Theory and the Specter of Capital*. London; New York: Verso.

Cohn, Bernard. 1987. *An Anthropologist among the Historians and Other Essays*. Oxford: Oxford University Press.

——. 1994. *Colonialism as a Form of Knowledge*. Princeton, N.J.: Princeton University Press.

Goldstein, Alyosha. 2014. "Introduction: Toward a Genealogy of the U.S. Colonial Present." In *Formations of United States Colonialism*, edited by Alyosha Goldstein, 1–32. Durham, N.C.: Duke University Press.

Guha, Ranajit. 1982. "The Prose of Counterinsurgency." In *Subaltern Studies II*, edited by Ranajit Guha, 1–42. Delhi: Oxford University Press.

——. 1983. *Elementary Aspects of Peasant Insurgency in Colonial India*. Delhi: Oxford University Press.

——. 1996. *A Rule of Property for Bengal: An Essay on the Idea of Permanent Settlement*. 3rd ed. Durham, N.C.: Duke University Press.

——. 1997. *Dominance without Hegemony*. Cambridge, Mass.: Harvard University Press.

——. 2010a [1956]. "Introduction to the Burdwan District Records 1788–1800." In

The Small Voice of History, edited by Partha Chatterjee, 36–82. Ranikhet: Permanent Black.

———. 2010b [1963]. "Rent in Kind and Money Rent in Eastern India under Early British Rule." In *The Small Voice of History*, edited by Partha Chatterjee, 94–116. Ranikhet: Permanent Black.

Gopal, S. 1949. *The Permanent Settlement and Its Results*. London: Allen & Unwin.

———. 1966. "A Rule of Property for Bengal." *Indian Economic and Social History Review* 3, no. 2: 214–15.

Joyce, Patrick. 2003. *The Rule of Freedom: Liberalism and the Modern City*. London; New York: Verso.

Mantena, Karuna. 2010. *Alibis of Empire: Henry Maine and the Ends of Liberal Imperialism*. Princeton, N.J.: Princeton University Press.

Mehta, Uday. 1999. *Liberalism and Empire*. Chicago: University of Chicago Press.

Mitchell, Timothy. 2002. *Rule of Experts: Egypt, Techno-Politics, and Modernity*. Berkeley: University of California Press.

———. 2008. "The Properties of Markets: Informal Housing and Capitalism's Mystery." Institute for Advanced Studies in Social and Management Sciences, University of Lancaster, Cultural Political Economy Working Paper Series, No. 2.

Roy, Ananya. 2008. "Post-Liberalism: On the Ethico-Politics of Planning." *Planning Theory* 7, no. 1: 92–102.

———. 2011. "Slumdog Cities: Rethinking Subaltern Urbanism." *International Journal of Urban and Regional Research* 35, no. 2: 223–38.

———. 2014. "Slum-Free Cities of the Asian Century: Postcolonial Government and the Project of Inclusive Growth." *Singapore Journal of Tropical Geography* 35, no. 1: 136–50.

———. 2015. "Who's Afraid of Postcolonial Theory?" *International Journal of Urban and Regional Research* 40, no. 1: 200–209.

Said, Edward. 1978. *Orientalism*. New York: Vintage.

Sartori, Andrew. 2014. *Liberalism in Empire: An Alternative History*. Berkeley: University of California Press.

Sen, Amartya. 1996. "Introduction." In *Ranajit Guha, A Rule of Property for Bengal: An Essay on the Idea of Permanent Settlement*. 3rd ed. Durham, N.C.: Duke University Press.

Spivak, Gayatri Chakravorty. 1985. "Scattered Speculations on the Question of Value." *Diacritics* 15, no. 4: 73–93.

———. 1999. *A Critique of Postcolonial Reason*. Cambridge, Mass.: Harvard University Press.

———. 2010 [1988]. "Can the Subaltern Speak?" In *Can the Subaltern Speak? Reflections on the History of an Idea*, edited by Rosalind Morris, 237–92. New York: Columbia University Press.

Stokes, Eric. 1959. *The English Utilitarians in India*. Oxford: Oxford University Press.

Practicing Subalternity?

Nyerere's Tanzania, the Dar School, and Postcolonial Geopolitical Imaginations

JO SHARP

Following Tanganyikan independence in 1961, and especially during the period after the announcement of Tanzania's intention to follow an independent path of African socialism after the Arusha Declaration in 1967, Julius Nyerere challenged the geopolitics of colonialism and the Cold War. Like many other Third World leaders at the time, he sought a voice for those previously marginalized from the imaginings of the world order and proposed an alternative geographical imagination of a united Africa and an alliance of the poor.

This chapter explores the challenges faced by Nyerere in trying to *practice* his postcolonial vision as the leader of a state that came into being on the lower echelons of the postwar world order. Subaltern studies, of course, emerged from scholars in the Indian subcontinent. However, while postcolonial African leaders focused on the neocolonial political and economic entanglements that the new states found themselves caught up in, these were not discussed in isolation from questions of the agency of new states and their people and of the politics of representation and epistemic power, more characteristic of subaltern studies. After all, Nyerere was effectively seeking to find a voice for those marginalized within a world order that actively sought to silence those in the South and that he felt was structured in such a way that it would ensure their continued economic, political, and epistemological marginality. Through the spatial politics of nation-building and pan-African, nonaligned cooperation, he sought to interrupt the system that created such inequalities.

It has been noted that, due to the challenge of enacting postcolonial politics in the postwar order, leaders such as Nyerere tended to a pedagogical style toward their citizens (Chakrabarty 2010). Nyerere emphasized the necessity of educating the Tanzanian population to create citizens able to make the new nation and, significantly, who understood the importance of unity and discipline in achieving this goal. He used a variety of education policies for nation-building, including moving talented students to high schools around the country; using Swahili as a nontribal, non-European language through which to narrate and perform the new nation; and using radio broadcasts to provide adult education. Within this political context, the University of Dar es Salaam (UDSM) was established as a postcolonial site of learning. During this period at UDSM, there were intense debates around the meaning of African knowledge, the role of the postcolonial university, and the most appropriate future for Tanzania, Africa, and the Third World. Drawing on both archival research and interviews undertaken between 2011 and 2015 with Tanzanian and international academics who spent time at UDSM during the 1960s and 1970s, this chapter explores the challenge of bringing subaltern spatialities and imaginations into academic and (geo)political practice. It explores the ways in which, by seeking to represent a geographical imagination from the margins, the examples of both Nyerere and UDSM highlight contradictions inherent to subaltern geographies and the necessarily relational nature of the concept of the subaltern in both temporal and spatial dimensions.

Subaltern Geopolitics

Ferguson (2006, 2) has suggested that "Africa, as a category, enters Western knowledge and imagination first of all, as Mbembe [2001] says, as 'an absent object,' set always in relation to the full presence of the West. Today, for all that has changed, 'Africa' continues to be described through a series of lacks and absences, failings and problems, plagues and catastrophes." What this has meant is that sub-Saharan Africa is more often seen as a place for Western knowledge to explore and explain rather than a source of explanation itself. This has ramifications, of course, for how disciplines have developed. Writing from within a world structured by Cold War geopolitics, Pletsch (1981) highlighted an academic division of labor wherein the Third World provided Western theorists with case studies of societies lacking the characteristics of modernity; theory was made elsewhere. Political science, international relations, and political geography, for instance, have historically drawn on the experiences of dominant European and North American powers for theories of international politics such as realism. This is despite, as Ayoob (2002, 40–41) has highlighted, the fact that it is "the common experience of all human societies that these are the elements that constitute the large majority of any members of any social system." While realism has faced extensive critique in international relations and political geography, Ayoob highlights the significance of realism's state-centrism to newly independent states seeking for the first time the political agency that this institution promised.

Ayoob's concept presents an apparently oxymoronic pairing of terms, tying together a position of structural weakness with a dominant way of seeing, ordering, and organizing the world. It is this tension that is also central to the conceptualization of "subaltern geopolitics," combining the notions of subaltern (a presence of lower-ranking order) and geopolitics (a dominant form of knowledge that has attempted to order and regulate space). The term's internal tensions and contradictions are thus an inevitability due to the *spatial enactment* of any subaltern imagination (Sharp 2011a, 2011b). Choosing to focus on geopolitics rather than realism looks not only to the role of the postcolonial state but also to an awareness of its entanglement in other scalar politics, whether dominant Cold War relations, the more resistant practices of pan-Africanism and nonalignment, or national or local politics.

Using "subaltern" as relational, and therefore shifting from a notion of the subaltern as a preexisting identity toward the concept of "subalternity," refocuses attention on practice. Subalternity is "endlessly (re)constituted through dialectical processes of recognition, within multiple networks of power" (Butler 2004, 44, quoted in Mitchell 2007, 706) and, as such, produces political identities that are "ongoing interventions in social and material relations" (Featherstone 2008, 6). Almost by definition, then, any expression of subaltern identity is a will to power whose very enunciation creates a political identity that can no longer be subaltern. Hence this spatial imagination is always already relational and always already in tension; the enunciation of subalternity moves the subaltern elsewhere.

What this means is that it is important to go beyond the binaries of conventional geopolitics, which are replicated in many critical engagements with it and which split the world into spheres of powerful states and those who represent "an assertion of permanent independence from the state *whoever is in power*" (Routledge 1998, 245, emphasis in original; see Sharp 2011a, 2011b, 2013). This moves the focus toward the entangled and contradictory politics of the middle orders, questioning, as did the subaltern studies group themselves in the late 1980s, "what it means for someone to be in a subaltern position . . . that someone could be from the elite classes, from the middle classes, from the extremely deprived classes; there could be inflections of race and gender and so on" (Chatterjee 2012, n.p.). Leaders of newly independent countries "embodied an ambiguous and shifting relationship to dominant geopolitics, representing both national elites *and* countries marginalized in the international arena" (Craggs 2014, 42, emphasis in original). Such postcolonial hybrids represent a "a way of 'doing' world politics in a seemingly 'similar' yet unexpectedly 'different' way" (Bhabha 1990; Bilgin 2008, 6) within practices that are entangled with forces of both domination and resistance at a variety of often interlocking scales (see Sharp et al. 2000).

Regarding subalternity this way also recognizes the limitations to subaltern studies that Vivek Chibber (2013) has recently outlined in his controversial suggestion that there is an Orientalism in subaltern studies: "Its celebration of the local, the particular—whether as History, or as the 'fragment'—ends up justifying an exoticization of the East. . . . The more marginal, and the more mysterious, the better. The various practices are all construed as ways of being, or better yet, ways of knowing, that have escaped the totalizing grasp of capital, and hence presented as potential escape routes from it. Traditional Orientalism is thereby repackaged as resistance to capital" (Chibber 2013, 289).

Instead, Chibber (2013, 287), like Ayoob, regards nationalism and state building not simply as an internalization of Western knowledge and practice but as "a rational response to economic and geopolitical pressures." Chibber's conflation of postcolonialism with subaltern studies and his suggestion of a latent Orientalism in subaltern studies scholarship is, however, problematic insofar as it overemphasizes processes of similarity. It is unquestionable that the newly emerging states were subject to the same forces of capital as are the more established ones (see also Kuus 2013). Nevertheless, the ways in which subaltern geographical imaginations were brought to bear in political practice have not simply been identical and instead offer a "useful past" through which to imagine alternatives today. Although there has been a tendency to reflect back on the period of decolonization as one of limited success, a number of voices are now insisting on the importance of understanding the significance of this period as one that not only promised a new world order but also did so with Africans, and other subaltern voices, as active agents creating this new order. For instance, as Craggs (2014, 40) has reflected, decolonization is "often seen in retrospect in a cloud of disappointment," and yet, she continues, the experience of the period and its ongoing struggles was "one of overwhelming optimism and opportunity" in which there were attempts to remake the world order. Certainly this was the intention of Nyerere's vision for postcolonial Tanzania, and it was a vision and experience shared by many Tanzanians and people who traveled to the country from around the world. Despite the fact that many of the policies, ideals, and organizations did not last, "to skip over this period—or to suggest colonial logics merely continued without transformation and disruption—excludes a whole range of practices which were invested with substantial value at the time and still have legacies in the present" (Craggs 2014, 40; see also Lee 2010; Sharp 2014).

Creating Postcolonial Tanzania

Julius Nyerere led Tanganyika to independence from Britain in 1961 in a mostly peaceful process of decolonization. Tanzania was created from the union with the islands of Zanzibar in 1964. At first, Tanzania was regarded by the West, and especially Britain, as an ally because of the relatively nonviolent nature of the independence movement and the respect Nyerere attained internationally as a statesman.[1] However, Nyerere made it clear that Tanzania would seek a non-aligned position, attempting to follow a path of self-sufficiency that would avoid political allegiance with either of the Cold War blocs. He was a powerful advocate for an alliance of African states as the only way for the poor to be heard on the international stage. In 1967, Nyerere's vision of a postcolonial African geopolitical imaginary was laid out in the Arusha Declaration, which promoted equality, self-reliance, "traditional" African communal values, and the virtues of education and hard work. Concerned with the growth of a divisive nationalism shaping newly independent African states, while also being cognizant of the neocolonial power relations within which they had emerged, the Arusha Declaration was a stand against the emerging indigenous elite and a statement about a form of development that was independent of existing models promoted by the United States or USSR.

Nyerere wrote extensively about his vision. His writing can be understood to construct a subaltern geopolitical critique of Cold War geopolitics and to posit an alternative geopolitical imagination from the margins (see Sharp 2013). Nyerere was clear that Tanzania would avoid either of the Cold War blocs and was a prominent advocate of both pan-Africanism and the Non-Aligned Movement: "Every possible attempt is made to squeeze African events into the framework of the cold war or other Big Power conflicts.... They imply that Africa has no ideas of its own and no interests of its own.... They are based on the belief that African actions must inevitably be determined by reference to either the Western liberal tradition or to communist theory or practice" (Nyerere 1969, x).

Nyerere's vision of a united pan-Africa challenged the Cold War binary and the zero-sum power-political geopolitics on which it was based, and instead projected a geographical imagination based on issues of international justice and cooperation. To him, the challenge for Africa was to overcome this poverty by developing national economies in such a way that they did not "run the risk of being sucked into the orbit of one or other of the big powers" (Nyerere 1970, 6). The establishment of the Non-Aligned Movement and Nyerere's philosophy of pan-Africanism were based on clear geopolitical principles: "just by the fact of meeting—asserting the independence of either bloc, the member states of that conference were taking an important political action: they were announcing that a refusal to become an ally of either side was not a temporary aberration of a few states! It was an important new international development, which the big powers could not ignore" (Nyerere 1970, 2).

Nyerere recognized that, within the international political system, subaltern states were not heard, and through cooperation and the creation of a transnational collaboration he sought to find a form of geopolitical expression. Nonalignment, he insisted, is not about neutrality; it is, "or certainly ought to be, a policy of involvement in world affairs" (Nyerere 1970, 3). This was a powerful rhetorical device as Nyerere placed himself as mediator between the international elite and his people. Precisely because of his claims for the state's subalternity, then, he was able to claim power through uniting in opposition, thus placing himself alongside the Tanzanian population as a subaltern, despite his elite position within the country.

However, there *were* limitations placed on Nyerere's ability to enact this African-centric imagined geography, not least because he was, as he acknowledged, attempting to achieve the African socialist development of Tanzania in a hurry and from a position of what he considered to be very limited economic and geographical development after years of colonial neglect and within a system of neocolonial subjugation. The title of one book about Nyerere illustrates this well: *We Must Run While They Walk* (Edgett Smith 1971). Prashad (2007, 191) explains: "Hemmed in by pressures from the advanced industrial states, the aristocratic rural classes, and the emergent mercantile classes, the new state had little time. Things had to change in a hurry. But socialism requires imagination and time. It cannot be made in a hurry."

Although usually referred to as *mwalimu* (Swahili for teacher), Nyerere was "not just *mwalimu*" but also "a *mwalimu*-in-power—a moral teacher who [was] also a political leader with a great deal of authority and power" (Pratt 1976, 256). Nyerere's concern that Tanzanians lacked the education needed for full (modern) citizenship led to a pedagogical style of leadership and a system of leadership that put "development ahead of diversity" (Chakrabarty 2010, 55). Just as was the case for Nehru in India, for Nyerere, independence marked a shift from the politics of struggle against the colonizers toward a politics that was shaped around the negotiation of the day-to-day challenges of development (see Chakrabarty 2007, 38). His desire to channel the energy of the postcolonial population toward the common good of the nation was heightened by Nyerere's need to act decisively in the face of changing political contexts within which postcolonial Tanzania found itself.

Educating a Nation

Chakrabarty (2010, 53) noted how Nyerere's (and other postcolonial leaders such as Nehru, Nasser, and Sukarno's) "emphasis on development as a catching-up-with-the-West produced a particular split that marked both the relationship between elite nations and their subaltern counterparts as well as that between elites and subalterns within national boundaries." Nyerere was acutely aware of the limited education previously available to Tanzanians, and this limitation had significant implications for the skills required for developing various sectors of the postcolonial nation's society and economy. However, more than this utilitarian approach to education, there is also a sense that Nyerere felt the need to educate the population to be "good" citizens (Chakrabarty 2010). Nyerere had been a school teacher before he became involved in the independence movement, but the fact that he is commonly referred to in Swahili as *mwalimu* is only partly due to this previous career as a teacher and the respect this profession attracts in East African society. It has often been noted that his leadership style was pedagogic. An academic who had spent time at UDSM in the 1970s described his style as follows:

> I heard Nyerere speak at The Hill [as UDSM was known due to its location] several times, and ... it was fascinating to listen to him to figure out what the message really was, but there was no doubt he was lecturing his children, he was lecturing his flock, including on what was good behaviour and bad behaviour.... I think *mwalimu*, the Catholic notion, ... is deep inside him, of the shepherd and his flock, I mean it just resonates even though it draws on the indigenous ideas as well as the role of the Chief. (interview, July 28, 2013)

The mixture of teacher, chief, and modern leader appeared to be a conscious performance by Nyerere to literally embody the nation and to negotiate the tensions between his elite and subaltern roles noted above. He often carried a staff with him at public events, something that one commentator suggested "provided a way to celebrate his African heritage and assert his identification with traditional African culture. It was also a symbol of his political authority and source of mystique" (Aminzade 2013, 143). Nyerere admired the work ethic of communist China and adopted a Chinese-style suit to embody a sense of frugality, an embodiment reinforced by his own thinness (Aminzade 2013).

This symbolism, drawing on both African and international images of leadership and nation, helped to narrate roles for Tanzania's postcolonial leaders and citizens. Nyerere's promotion of *ujamaa* as a model for his African socialism drew on idealized notions of community and interdependence, bonds of kinship and respect, characteristic of tribal society, and he sought to promote these as central to postcolonial Tanzanian identity:

> The term *ndugu*, used to refer to comrades, actually meant brother/sister/cousin, and *mwanachama*, or child of the party, was used to refer to party members. Politics were also translated into kinship terms when the President was referred to as the father of the nation (*baba wa taifa*). This rhetoric of a founding father trapped into what Ali Mizrui refers to as an "elder tradition" which "carries a heavy preference for consensus in the family" and "a preference for reverence and reaffirmation of loyalty towards party leaders." In using such family metaphors, social leaders referenced traditional age categories by referring to political authorities as "elders" and to citizens as "youth." (Aminzade 2013, 142–43)

Despite this emphasis on traditional values, Nyerere recognized the need for the provision of nation-building through the modern trappings of statehood. The need for an educated workforce was met with policies also intended to transcend tribal difference and build the nation. Literacy was considered vital to this endeavor, and great efforts were put into primary school education and the use of radio broadcasts to deliver adult education to a highly dispersed population. This was very successful, leading to an increase in literacy rates from around 15 percent at independence to nearly universal literacy when Nyerere stood down from office in 1984. His decision to use Swahili, the language of trade, as the national language evidenced Nyerere's desire to unite the country under one language but to avoid the privileging of either the language associated with any one tribal group and tradition or the colonizers' language as the lingua franca of the postcolonial state. Secondary school education reinforced this process. While primary education was to be rolled out to all, initially secondary education had to be more selective due to the lack of qualified teachers (and students) as well as broader financial constraints. Selected students were educated at institutions distant from their homes to ensure that the future leaders would have a sense of Tanzanian-ness rather than being tied to geographical or tribal perspectives, experiences, and loyalties. He also hoped that this would help to instill a sense of loyalty to Tanzania and its citizens—a commitment to a collective effort—rather than a selfish focus on individual careers. Such concerns were magnified in Nyerere's considerations regarding the establishment of tertiary education at the UDSM, an institution that has the country's president as its vice chancellor.

UDSM was established at independence as an affiliate college of the University of London but soon after became part of the independent University of East Africa, with campuses in Uganda and Kenya as well as Tanzania. In 1970, the University of East Africa split into three separate universities. UDSM was established to train local graduates to take their place in the nation's leadership, but it was not simply designed as a training college. In an article in the *Tanzanian Civil Service Magazine* in 1966, Nyerere (1966, 2) insisted that universities in developing countries must not simply receive ideas from elsewhere but "must also make their contributions to the world of knowledge."

The View from the Hill

If Tanzania became known the world over for the humane social vision of its leader, . . . the Hill became renowned for the social critique of that vision. The Hill has seen days of intense intellectual debates—when radical academics from all over the world trekked to the *Ujamaaist* "homeland."
—Issa Shivji (1992, back cover)

There had been a high level of dependence on non-Tanzanian academics in the early years of the university. In some disciplines, especially in the years before the Arusha Declaration, this could be seen as a Westernization of the university curriculum—an intellectual cultural imperialism. However, especially in the period after Nyerere's pronouncement about African socialism, particular types of academics were drawn to Tanzania, not to play their part in bringing "development" to the country or simply to transfer their skills to the next generation of African scholars (although this training component was essential in many areas) but to take part in this new endeavor and to learn from Tanzanians. A number of my respondents talked about "planned obsolescence"—that expats would make themselves irrelevant. The first wave of perhaps more reformist academics would be replaced by a second generation of mainly East Africans. "Educating Tanzanians," was, as one U.S. medical researcher put it, "the most obvious means of putting self-reliance into practice.... Train Tanzanians and then leave; that should be a good credo for expatriates" (Swift 2002, 39). In a letter to then president of UDSM, Cranford Pratt, the History Chair Terrance Ranger explained the need for a Tanzanian to take up the post that he was vacating to relocate to the United States: "Thus although I shall myself in many ways be very sorry to leave Tanzania I think it will work out as the more or less ideal 'de-colonisation' process" (letter from Ranger to Pratt, February 16, 1968).

Most of those I spoke with talked of this process, and all considered it to be effective. One English academic told me that when he had arrived, "a certain, heroic moment of expatriates—big celebrities—had passed" (interview, July 28, 2013) and that the agenda was being set by Tanzanian and other African intellectuals. For many researchers and academics who were drawn to Nyerere's Tanzania, the reasons for going to UDSM went far beyond the requirements for training. Many saw in postcolonial Tanzania a place of knowledge production and vibrant political activity and thus regarded time at UDSM to be an enlivening learning experience, rather than simply a teaching job. For some, there was a belief that a shift in political and ideological leadership was immanent in the postcolonial world order and Tanzania was to be one of the countries at the heart of this change. As one English academic put it to me, "You did really feel that you are at the center of things" (interview, August 16, 2011). One citizen of New Zealand, who had spent time at UDSM in the 1970s, explained the context for his move, an explanation that has been repeated in different words by other respondents:

> Well we were all pretty clear that capitalism was in its death throes at that stage. It's 1968 and everything was changing.... The Americans were definitely going to lose in Vietnam; in Czechoslovakia there was sort of a new form of socialism that might be possible—it didn't happen there either, but students basically took over Paris for a month in May in '68, and,.... So, essentially, these were all signs of the end of capitalism. On the other hand, socialism in Eastern Europe doesn't look incredibly attractive... and Africa was where it was going to be and it was going to be a new way. (interview, August 11, 2011)

In a similar vein, reflecting on his time at UDSM after he had been deported from Rhodesia for political activity, Ranger initially could not imagine that academic life could match the same level of excitement as public life before his move. "But," he continued, "I have found at Dar that the excitement of research and teaching is equal in intensity and in many ways more satisfying in achievement" (Ranger 2014, 172). Marxist theorist Giovanni Arrighi echoed Ranger's words in an interview with David Harvey in 2009:

> It was a very exciting time, both intellectually and politically. When I got to Dar es Salaam in 1966, Tanzania had only been independent for a few years. Nyerere was advocating what he considered to be a form of African socialism. He managed to stay equidistant from both sides during the Sino-Soviet split, and maintained very good relations with the Scandinavians. Dar es Salaam became the outpost of all the exiled national liberation movements of southern Africa—from the Portuguese colonies, Rhodesia and South Africa. I spent three years at the University there, and met all kinds of people: activists from the Black Power movement in the U.S., as well as scholars and intellectuals. (Arrighi 2009, 64–65)

Such examples suggest that Tanzania in the 1970s presented a material provincializing of Europe as intellectuals from the north moved to participate in and learn from Nyerere's Tanzania. In many ways this was a situation that moved beyond intellectual postcolonialism, critiqued as a movement that emerged only from the migration of Third World academics to the north, leaving certain geographies of privilege in place. As Shilliam (2009, n.p.) has suggested:

> Eurocentrism is most evident in the unspoken assumption that we do not need to attempt to travel to the intellectual terrain of the non-West and interrogate its archive of thought in order to problematize the modern experience. It is not just that the non-Western thinker must be added into the existing archive of the Western Academy, but rather, that an engagement with the non-Western thinker might be necessary in order to reveal the boundedness of this Academy and thus open the way for more salient explorations of the making of the modern world order.

The Western academics at UDSM in the 1970s, by definition, were privileged, but this was not straightforward. While some nationalities received expatriate salaries, others were paid at the same rate as local academics, and thus the significant division of wealth did not simply lie between Africans and non-Africans. Indeed, more than one respondent explained to me that their sense of privilege was not financial but instead inhered in their ability to leave should things not work out well. He believed that there was no sense of their either being looked up to, or down upon, by Tanzanians:

> The fact that you were a *mzungu* [Swahili for European, but refers to all white people] didn't really count for, either way actually, didn't count for anything. You

weren't privileged and you weren't ignored. . . . And here at the university, then you were part and parcel of these debates and discussion and . . . there were all sorts of discussions there where you would see groups of whites and blacks, just very comfortable in each other's company and debating all sorts of things. It was actually a really nice time to be here, it was an exciting time. And you did feel part of the debates. Now, I don't think we were part of the struggle here because ultimately we were in a privileged position, and that privileged position was because we were expatriates. It wasn't a white thing. It was just an expatriate thing. At the end of the day, by definition, you don't have a commitment to the country. You are going to go home; this is not home. (interview, August 16, 2011)

In disrupting some of the geographies and epistemologies of the Western domination of knowledge production, this intellectual context allowed for solidarities that created a collaborative and often tentative model of postcolonial politics in the conventional sense. It led to some progressive collaborations, as one Tanzanian participant reflected later: "It was a very, very special time for us in Africa, I would say, not only in Tanzania. The kind of lecturers also who came, . . . they were from the West, but the West which believed in the liberation of South Africa, which believed that this apartheid system must go, it was full of value. . . . In the seventies, Tanzania was at the center of the decolonization movement" (interview, November 29, 2011).

The process of shedding privilege was, of course, not straightforward as one Tanzanian commentator observed of the expatriate staff:

They themselves are often anxious to help in the work of building our nation, but are frightened of appearing to push their own ideas too hard lest their motives be misunderstood. As a Professor said on one occasion—"I am anxious to be drafted for a job, but there are too many Europeans in the world trying to tell Africa what it should do and how. If I am asked to help I will respond with alacrity, but outside my own clear field of responsibility the Tanzanians in Government and [the party] must take the initiative." (Kawawa 1967, 10–11)

Teaching Postcolonial Tanzania

In the establishment of a postcolonial university, staff were only part of the issue. A further challenge was the problem of providing education to a nation that had been systematically exploited through German colonialism and then neglected by Britain under a League of Nations mandate. Very few students had a secondary education, let alone a university education. Nyerere feared the possibility of creating an elite class, cut off from the rest of the country in the rarefied atmosphere of the university campus, or "the College" as it was initially known. He noted that: "The cost of keeping a student at the College will be about £1000 a year. That is to say that it takes the annual per capita income of more than 50 of our people to maintain a single student at this College for one year. It should not be necessary to say more. It is obvious that this disparity can only be justified, morally or politically, if it can be looked upon as an investment by the poor in their own future" (Nyerere 1964, 11).

The symbolism of the campus built on a hill overlooking the center of Dar es Salaam some 10 kilometers away clearly reflects a Western tradition of elevated enlightenment. There were concerns that the university itself might be too luxurious and might start to create the national elites about whom Frantz Fanon (1963) had warned. One expat academic at the time remarked that while they were conducive to creating a focused study environment, the university buildings were not luxurious; "functional but frugal!" (Honeybone 1967, 31). Nevertheless, tension emerged from the very physical form of the new university. Its location on the hill and placement away from the distractions of the city center were designed to enable students to work without distraction and to concentrate on learning and thinking. At first there were very few qualified students. But even when more had passed successfully through the secondary education system UDSM, as the country's only university, still represented a highly selective environment. By its very nature, then, it separated the select few from the society at large. Nyerere (1966, 18) continued to explain, "Anyone who walks off the campus into the nearby villages, or who travels up country—perhaps to Dodoma or into the Pare Hills—will observe the contrast in conditions here and the conditions in which the mass of our people live." Thus, he was keen to ensure that students saw themselves as "servants-in-training" to their fellow countrymen. His words were carefully chosen, as he was determined to instill the right sort of social responsibility in the minds of the students, reinforcing a postcolonial politics where effort should be directed toward the country's future and away from any divisive critical focus: "And this must not be the idea of giving aid to the poor. . . . It must be an attitude of wanting to work, in whatever work there is to do, alongside and within the rest of the community" (Nyerere 1966, 19).

It was a concern that appeared to have been justified. In October 1966 the government introduced a new requirement that after graduation students should do two years' national service before entering the civil service. This required them to spend the first two months "doing nation-building work in rural areas, followed by eighteen months performing skilled labor, mainly as teachers or civil servants, at 40 per cent of the job's regular salary" (Aminzade 2013, 153). The students protested and marched into town in their academic gowns. The students themselves thought that their actions were in line with the egalitarian society being promised by their leaders. One of those who had been involved explained in an interview in 2014: "We had written a long [pause] we had thought it was [a] very exciting and useful letter to government. The core of it was that we refused to go to national service on the grounds that you, government, are cheating us, you are writing budgets but people have no medicines, you are claiming to do socialism but you have big salaries and you are not going to national service. So if you want us to go, you go first!" (interview, April 24, 2014).

The government's interpretation of the protest was very different, painting students as spoilt elites who wanted special treatment. The embodiment of the protest—students walking down the hill into town clothed in their academic gowns—was presented as a performance that highlighted the students' perception of their difference from the rest of the population, a clear violation of Nyerere's goals of a united and equal struggle for the good of postcolonial Tanzania. His anger at their challenge to this vision was intensified by some of the ways in which the students had chosen to express their protest when they arrived in town: "There were a lot of banners, but there was one banner that really made *Mwalimu* go mad. It was written 'Better colonial days' in English. It was written on a very small bit of paper and the media photographed that one: students telling the president that it was better [in] colonial days!" (interview, April 24, 2014).

The students were taken to the State House to meet with Nyerere who was furious at the nature of the protest. After a dressing down from their president, the students were taken back to the university to pick up their things before being "rusticated" (sent home from the university). As one Tanzanian who had been one of the rusticated students explained:

> We were rounded up at gunpoint, brought back here, escorted to our rooms, by gunpoint, to pack things, if we were hungry, go to the cafeteria to eat. We were taken to the bus and then taken home. So, it happened that we were taken to our home. I arrived home, in rural Moshi, the soldier took out his gun and he guided me, he asked me "who's your father?" and I said, "that one there," and he said, "*Mzee* [elder], is this your son?" and he said yes. "Take him from me. The university is closed and he should stay here. And teach him manners!" The soldier left. We were left at home. (interview, April 24, 2014)

Only those for whom their communities spoke up—who bore witness to the students' commitment to Tanzanian society through their hard work during their absence from the university—were allowed to return to UDSM a year later. Letters from the expelled students to the university highlighted the degree of social and economic marginalization they faced. One said that "the 'rebels' are broke and miserable" because people were reluctant to employ them back at home, while another puts a slightly more positive spin on things, explaining that "employment is of course very difficult although there seem to be people in [the] area who do not reject the students entirely" (student letter, November 3, 1966). It should also be noted that immediately after his meeting with the students Nyerere cut his own salary by 20 percent and instructed other members of the government to take cuts of 10–15 percent.

In the end, the majority of the rusticated students were allowed to return to the university. As members of the government noted at the time, the country needed trained graduates. However, there was a great deal of attention focused on ensuring there was no repeat of this confrontation. A conference on the role of the university college was held in March 1967 to discuss the nature of the university in the postcolonial nation, especially in light of the Arusha Declaration presented a month beforehand. The response of some at the university was to seek changes to the curriculum. In 1967, in light of the student rustication and the Arusha Declaration, a group of nine radical academics, including Walter Rodney, John Saul, and Giovanni Arrighi, put forward a proposal for a discussion about the curriculum. It started as follows: "The Arusha Declaration has brought into sharper focus that whole question of the nature and role of our educational institutions. Tanzania is now firmly committed to the course of self-reliance and socialism; yet the implications of this commitment for the organization and curricula of our schools and colleges have scarcely begun to be examined" (Hoskins et al. 1967, 116).

Their proposal was based on a concern that the students "cannot be returned to the university with any confidence of a 'change of heart'—that is, of intellectual and moral conviction—so long as the present organization and assumptions remain unchallenged" (Hoskins et al. 1967, 117). This reflected a wider concern about the role of the university in postcolonial Tanzania. At the conference on the role of the university college, Second Vice President Rashidi Kawawa (1967, 9) stated that "many of our young graduates from Universities, from the Medical School, and from the secondary schools, began work with a conviction that society owes them a high-paying and interesting job. . . . And many of them have scant patience with their uneducated fellow-citizens, and very little interest in the needs and thinking of the men and women in the rural areas—or even those of the back streets of Kariakoo [the local market]."

There followed a proposal for a new course called "Common Course in Social Analysis" as an instruction in "Tanzanian realities." This course—proposed to take up a third of students' time—would be both interdisciplinary and compulsory for students whether they were studying for arts, social science, or science degrees to ensure that all students understood the nature of the communities they would serve after graduation. The first year was to center on social formations in Africa, the second to put this East African system into dynamic context through a focus on social change, and the third year would consider East Africa within the current international system.

This new curriculum represented a conscious decentering of colonial knowledge in two ways. First, instead of starting with Europe and its history and experience, Africa and Tanzania were to be put on a central stage. This was not in any way parochial, however, as this understanding of Africa and Tanzania was firmly related to an examination of the colonial experience and the neocolonial capitalist world order with which the new states were struggling. Second, there was a resolutely interdisciplinary way in which issues were to be addressed. In discussions around the revision to the university syllabus, some argued for a radical interdisciplinarity that did away with disciplines altogether, thus avoiding the "fragmentation of perspectives entailed by separate academic 'disciplines' which provides the main obstacle to the development of an integral and coherent vision of man [sic] in history and society"[2] (Hoskins et al. 1967, 117). This more radical version was not followed in the curriculum (although it was the driving force behind debates and seminars held alongside the formal curriculum), but the Common Course was introduced for all students. Inevitably perhaps, this was more popular with social science students and staff, and many interviewees told me of resistance from the sciences to this approach.

In addition to challenging the content and form of teaching, the debate challenged the privileging of particular academic practices. The proposal also suggested changes in the relationship between staff and students "to remove elements of privileges and servility at the University College," which should include a reduction in senior salaries, dropping of academic titles, and greater support of junior academics, while students should regard their education as going beyond the term and the campus and engage in project work during their vacation, which "should involve the student in activities through which he [sic] comes into contact with the problems and potentialities of his country" (Hoskins et al. 1967, 131).

Famously, the debates were inflected with Marxist analysis. However, while this involved a cosmopolitan collection of academics, the debate had a distinctively East African focus, as one participant explained: "The debates [were] about what kind of capitalism *was* established in East Africa as a result of colonialism . . . of course western Marxism can be highly problematic in many ways but the interesting thing when I was there . . . the debates were being set by East Africans" (interview, July 28, 2013).

UDSM emerged in the late 1960s and early 1970s as a place of intense political debate around the postcolonial condition for Africa. Nyerere took his role as vice chancellor of the university seriously, regularly visiting the Hill to talk with students and staff and hear their views. While there was considerable criticism of Nyerere from some quarters for not following a Marxist path closely enough, there was clear engagement with academic discourse on the nature of the postcolonial country. One U.S. expatriate noted that on one such visit in the early 1970s, the students' "questions were respectful in tenor but reflected a desire to hear their President affirm his commitment to socialism" (Swift 2002, 108). Debates continued about how best to achieve African Socialism with many staff and students feeling that Nyerere was insufficiently rigorous in his application of

Marxist and socialist values. It became clear that, for Nyerere, African Socialism was a moral rather than a structural imperative. In 1969 law students occupied the faculty building because they opposed the number of U.S. staff who they felt had imperialist leanings. They pushed for more staff to be hired from socialist countries and for more Tanzanian leadership. Nyerere responded that the students should not be concerned by the place of origin of people—whether they were from a former colony or defined by race or class location—and instead look at what individuals do. He often warned people of the dangers of racism and xenophobia following the Arusha Declaration, claiming in a newspaper editorial in February 1968 that if these were not rejected, "socialism will become ruthless Fascism and will lose the belief in the oneness of man [sic]. . . . Neither is it sensible for socialists to talk as if all capitalists are devils. . . . To divide up people working for our nation into groups of good and bad according to their skin colour or their national origin, or their tribal origin, is to sabotage the work we have just embarked upon" (quoted in Aminzade 2013, 170).

In his reflections on the intellectual history of UDSM, Blommaert (1997, 131) suggests that, despite attempts at Africanization, "the philosophy of education . . . was still the one left behind by the British, and the products of higher education were still *wazungu weusi*—black-skinned whites." The vision presented by Nyerere, however, attracted many expatriates to become involved, which also meant that it was not a simple case of Westernized knowledge coming to Tanzania and colonizing debates; many of the Western academics and the debates they took back home were profoundly Tanzanian-ized.

Conclusion

In postcolonial Tanzania, and especially in sites of active political theorizing such as was found at UDSM in the 1970s, the "margins" were seen, however briefly, as offering the future "center"; people were drawn to Tanzania from around Africa and from both Western and Eastern superpowers. The kind of "provincializing of Europe" that was witnessed through work undertaken at the UDSM might be thought of perhaps as a less theoretically pure, but more material and experiential, decentering of European (and Western) privilege as intellectuals and political figures from north and south moved to participate in and learn from Nyerere's Tanzania. At the time, the location of agency was clear. Speaking from his post at UDSM, Walter Rodney made it clear that this was something to come from the grassroots of African society—that "every African has a responsibility to understand the system and work for its overthrow" (Rodney 2012, 28). Commentators have highlighted the fact that "Walter dared to say and believe that such a stupendous transformation must be initiated by Africans and other dwellers in the nether regions of exploitation and domination"

(Harding, Hill, and Strickland 2012, xvii). It was an optimistic and powerful moment. As Issa Shivji, a student of Walter Rodney and now one of Tanzania's most prominent critical scholars, explained of the university and of Tanzanian society more generally, "We thought globally. We thought in terms of epochs, not in terms of a tomorrow, not in terms of years, not in terms of decades, but in terms of epochs" (Shivji 1992, cited in Shivji 1993, 204). Tanzania emerged as a site of an African-centered geographical imagination, which was developing a political presence that sought to provincialize Europe.

However, these processes of centering the margins and seeking to challenge the Western dominance of geopolitics and intellectual production cannot be regarded as a narration of the subaltern speaking as, simultaneously, new elitisms formed. In the messy realm of practice, it appears that subalternity can *only* be relational: Nyerere's vision created new forms of subalternity even as it sought to challenge colonial and neocolonial power. As a relational concept, subalternity is significant in exploring the quixotic experiences of the majority of the world, those who are excluded from the centers of power but who seek representation through such potentially emancipatory, but also inherently problematic, institutions of statehood. While he represented Tanzania's subalterns, Nyerere's role as leader made him an elite, and he established a political system that created elites within the country, even as the Tanzanian state languished in the lower echelons of the international system. Indeed, the subalternity of Tanzania's international role has provided a discourse that has helped to support Nyerere (and subsequent presidents) in maintaining consent within the country (see Sharp 2011a, 2011b), as it provides legitimacy for the president's claims for shared subalternity with his population. Similarly, UDSM produced local and national elites, even as it sought to challenge the Western domination of knowledge production and provincialize Europe. Such tensions and contradictions do not in any way diminish the value of the concept of the subaltern; but they do highlight the complexity of any spatial expression of subalternity. Shivji makes a similar point in his reflections back on Nyerere's role in Tanzania's postcolonial history: "As a head of state, it is true he came out against struggles from below. But does that mean that a progressive person should not celebrate Nyerere's progressive legacy and draw lessons from its contradictory character? My friend, a Marxist is not a purist; s/he is political!" (Shivji, n.d.).

NOTES

I would like to thank Steve and Tariq for their insightful comments on an earlier version of this work. The research for this chapter was undertaken as part of an ESRC Mid Career Fellowship (RES-070-27-0039).

1. However the union with Zanzibar to create Tanzania in 1964 saw considerable violence; see, e.g., Shivji (2008) and Myers (2000).

2. While some women were involved in the postcolonial Tanzanian government and at UDSM, and "women's issues" were sometimes discussed, as was the case in most

university environments at the time gender and feminism were not prominent in these debates.

REFERENCES

Aminzade, R. 2013. *Race, Nation, and Citizenship in Post-Colonial Africa: The Case of Tanzania*. Cambridge: Cambridge University Press.

Arrighi, G. 2009. "The Winding Paths of Capital: Interview by David Harvey." *New Left Review* 56 (March–April): 61–94.

Ayoob, M. 2002. "Inequality and Theorising in International Relations: The Case for Subaltern Realism." *International Studies Review* 4, no. 3: 27–48.

Bhabha, H. 1990. *The Location of Culture*. London: Routledge.

Bilgin, P. 2008. "Thinking Past 'Western' IR?" *Third World Quarterly* 29, no. 1: 5–23.

Blommaert, J. 1997. "Intellectuals and Ideological Leadership in Ujamaa Tanzania." *African Languages and Cultures* 10, no. 2: 129–44.

Butler, J. 2004. *Precarious Life: The Powers of Mourning*. London: Verso.

Chakrabarty, D. 2000. *Provincializing Europe: Postcolonial Thought and Historical Difference*. Princeton, N.J.: Princeton University Press.

———. 2007. "'In the Name of Politics': Democracy and Power of the Multitude in India." *Public Culture* 19, no. 1: 35–57.

———. 2010. "The Legacies of Bandung: Decolonization and the Politics of Culture." In *Making a World after Empire: The Bandung Movement and Its Political Afterlives*, edited by C. Lee, 45–68. Athens: Ohio University Press.

Chatterjee, P. 2012. "Reflecting on 30 Years of Subaltern Studies: Conversations with Profs. Gyanendra Pandey and Partha Chatterjee, Interviewer: Chatterjee, M. Curated Collections." *Cultural Anthropology Online*, December 13, 2012. Available at http://www.culanth.org/curated_collections/6-subaltern-studies/discussions/14-reflecting-on-30-years-of-subaltern-studies-conversations-with-profs-gyanendra-pandey-and-partha-chatterjee.

Chibber, V. 2013. *Postcolonial Theory and the Spectre of Capital*. London: Verso.

Craggs, R. 2014. "Postcolonial Geographies, Decolonization, and the Performance of Geopolitics at Commonwealth Conferences." *Singapore Journal of Tropical Geography* 35: 39–55.

Edgett Smith, W. E. 1971. *We Must Run While They Walk: A Portrait of Africa's Julius Nyerere*. New York: Random House.

Fanon, F. 1963. *The Wretched of the Earth*. Translated by C. Farrington. New York: Grove Weidenfeld.

Featherstone, D. 2008. *Resistance, Space and Political Identities: The Making of Counter-Global Networks*. Oxford: Wiley-Blackwell.

Ferguson, J. 2006. *Global Shadows: Africa in the Neoliberal World Order*. London: Duke University Press.

Harding, V., R. Hill, and W. Strickland. 2012. "Introduction 1981." In *How Europe Underdeveloped Africa*, edited by W. Rodney, xv–xxviii. Cape Town: Fahamu Books.

Honeybone, R. 1967. "The Organisation, Operation and Place of the University College, Dar es Salaam." In *Report of the Conference on the Role of the University College, Dar es Salaam, in a Socialist Tanzania*, 29–42. Dar es Salaam: UDSM.

Hoskins, C., F. Livingstone, J. Mellen, S. Picciotto, W. Rodney, J. Saul, H. Shore, G. Arrighi, and G. Kamenju. 1967. "Proposals for Discussion Tabled by a Group of Staff Members: Curriculum." In *Report of the Conference on the Role of the University College, Dar es Salaam, in a Socialist Tanzania*, 116–31. Dar es Salaam: UDSM.

Kawawa, R. 1967. "Speech by the Tanzania Second Vice President, Mr. R. M. Kawawa, at the Opening of the University College Conference on the Role of the University College in a Socialist Tanzania." In *Report of the Conference on the Role of the University College, Dar es Salaam, in a Socialist Tanzania*, 6–13. Dar es Salaam: UDSM.

Kuus, M. 2013. "Places of Lower Rank: Margins in Conversations." *Political Geography* 37: 30–32.

Lee, C. 2010. "Between a Movement and an Era: The Origins and Afterlives of Bandung." In *Making a World after Empire: The Bandung Movement and Its Political Afterlives*, edited by C. Lee, 1–42. Athens: Ohio University Press.

Mbembe, J. 2001. *On the Postcolony*. Berkeley: University of California Press.

Mitchell, K. 2007. "Geographies of Identity: The Intimate Cosmopolitan." *Progress in Human Geography* 31, no. 5: 706–20.

Myers, G. 2000. Narrative Representations of Revolutionary Zanzibar. *Journal of Historical Geography* 26, no. 3: 429–48.

Nyerere, J. 1964. "Address at the opening of the Dar es Salaam University Campus, 21/8/67." In *President Nyerere opens Dar es Salaam University College Campus, 21st August 1964* [Booklet], 9–21. N.p.

———. 1966. "Graduate Members of a Classless Society: 'The University's Role in the Development of the New Countries.'" *Civil Service Magazine* 7: 1–19.

———. 1970. "Stability and Change in Africa (1969)." In *Man and Development*, edited by J. Nyerere. Nairobi: Oxford University Press.

Pletsch, C. 1981. "The Three Worlds, or the Division of Social Scientific Labor, circa 1950–1975." *Comparative Studies in Society and History* 23, no. 4: 565–90.

Prashad, V. 2007. *The Darker Nations: A People's History of the Third World*. New York: New Press.

Pratt, C. 1976. *The Critical Phase in Tanzania, 1945–1968: Nyerere and the Emergence of a Socialist Strategy*. Cambridge: Cambridge University Press.

Ranger, R. 1968. "Letter to Cranford Pratt." *Terence Ranger Archives*, Bodleian Library, Oxford, February 16, 1968.

———. 2014. *Writing Revolt: An Engagement with African Nationalism, 1957–67*. Woodbridge, Suffolk: James Currey.

Rodney, W. 2012 [1972]. *How Europe Underdeveloped Africa*. Cape Town: Fahamu Press.

Routledge, P. 1998. "Anti-Geopolitics: Introduction." In *The Geopolitics Reader*, edited by Ó. Tuathail, G, Dalby, and P. Routledge, 233–48. London: Routledge.

Sharp, J. 2011a. "Subaltern Geopolitics: Introduction." *Geoforum* 42, no. 3: 271–73.

———. 2011b. "A Subaltern Critical Geopolitics of the 'War on Terror': Postcolonial Security in Tanzania." *Geoforum* 42, no. 3: 297–305.

———. 2013. "Geopolitics at the Margins? Reconsidering Genealogies of Critical Geopolitics." *Political Geography* 37: 20–29.

Sharp, J., P. Routledge, C. Philo, and R. Paddison. Eds. 2000. *Entanglements of Power: Geographies of Domination/Resistance*. London: Routledge.

Shilliam, R. 2009. "The Enigmatic Figure of the Non-Western Thinker in International

Relations." *AntePodium: Online Journal of World Affairs*. Available at http://www.victorial.ac.nz/atp/articles/pdf/Shilliam-2009.pdf, accessed November 10, 2015.

Shivji, I. 1992. "What Is Left of the Left Intellectual at 'the Hill.'" In *Intellectuals at the Hill: Essays and Talks 1969–1993*, edited by I. Shivji, 200–219. Dar es Salaam: Dar es Salaam University Press.

———. 2008. *Pan-Africanism or Pragmatism?: Lessons of the Tanganyika-Zanzibar Union*. Dar es Salaam: Mkuki na Nyota Publishers.

———. n.d. "A Life of Critical Engagement: An Interview with Issa Shivji." *Global Dialogue: Newsletter for the International Sociological Association*. Available at http://isa-global-dialogue.net/a-life-of-critical-engagement-an-interview-with-issa-shivji/, accessed June 11, 2015.

Swift, C. 2002. *Dar Days: The Early Years in Tanzania*. Lanham, Md.: University Press of America.

Reading Subaltern Studies Politically

Histories from Below, Spatial Relations, and Subalternity

DAVID FEATHERSTONE

In his essay "Gramsci in India," Ranajit Guha (2009) provides important reflections on the political context that shaped the emergence of the subaltern studies project. He notes, "We started working together in the mid-1970s when the Naxalite upsurge had clearly subsided, although the questions it had provided were still unanswered. We sought to situate these questions in the context of the colonial past. For, the end of colonial rule had done nothing to replace or substantially alter the main apparatus of colonial domination—that is, the state. It was transferred intact to the successor regime" (Guha 2006, 364–65). Guha goes on to argue that the encounter with Antonio Gramsci's work opened up a "vast space" that allowed "our questions and concerns to crystallize around the overlapping themes of state and civil society." He notes that "Gramsci's lessons were of invaluable help to us. However, in order to benefit from these we had to adapt them to the Indian experience which was, of course, significantly different in many ways from the Italian and generally, the Western experience on which Gramsci's own thinking was based" (Guha 2006, 364–65).

Guha's reflections on Gramsci open up two key problematics that are central to this chapter. Firstly, his account of the political context from which the project emerged asserts the importance of reading subaltern studies politically. By this I mean both engaging with the insights of the collective's work to understand diverse articulations of the political and subalternity and tracing the political interventions that stem from projects bearing that mantle. Guha's invocation of Maoism emphasizes how constructions of the political have also shifted through the work of the collective and should caution us against finding an authentic, insurrectionary subaltern studies project prior to its fateful intersection with postcolonial theorizing in the late 1980s.[1]

Secondly, Guha locates subaltern studies in relation to transnational movements of left theorizing and engagement, most notably through the impact of Gramsci's work on dissident left projects in the 1960s and 1970s. There are important, well-recognized similarities and linkages with the intellectual movement that has become known as "histories from below," but the geographies of such linkages and exchanges have seldom been considered in depth. This chapter makes a contribution by developing a critical account of the routes, trajectories, and connections that shaped subaltern studies and histories from below. I argue that doing so can offer significant resources for thinking about the shape a subaltern geographies project might take.

Exploring these routes and connections is of more than arcane historical and intellectual interest. They serve as a reminder of the ineradicably entangled political roots of the Subaltern Studies Collective, which I contend should also be foundational for any subaltern geographies project. This is not to argue that the kind of political imaginary adopted by Guha in his inaugural manifesto for the project can be appealed to as a fixed or unchanging anchor for such an endeavor. Rather I contend that engaging with subaltern agency in different contexts, and tracing the diverse geographies shaped through such agency, opens up important resources for thinking and engaging politically in different situations. Tracing the relations between subaltern studies and diverse articulations of histories from below can be generative. As I suggest in the chapter, both broad traditions offer different ways of thinking about articulations of subaltern politics, and engaging with them in dialogue can offer new ways of thinking about what Burton and Ballantyne (2016) have termed "world histories from below." Such dialogues, especially worked through a geographical lens, can make a distinctive contribution to work on the study of global histories, which has often been better at asserting forms of subaltern agency than specifying situated forms of translocal solidarity, agency, and identity.

To do so, this chapter adopts an account of the relations between subalternity and the political that foreground subaltern agency and presence in shaping the terms on which the political is configured and the relationalities crafted through political activity. I contend that a focus on the geographies of subaltern politics can be central to reasserting the importance of situated geographies of subaltern agency and trajectories. In this vein, as Sharad Chari has argued, far from being an "atavistic space of doubt," subalternity can be refigured as the "active determination of society and space" (Chari 2011, 511). The first section explores the ways subaltern studies intervened in the understandings of the political that structured key texts associated with history from below. The second section of the chapter traces some of the dissident left trajectories that shaped both intellectual traditions and draws out commonalities and intersections between them. The third section serves to unsettle the confining nation-centered spatialities of both subaltern studies and histories from below and by so doing seeks to open up different ways of accounting for and engaging with dynamic subaltern spaces of politics. The final section of the chapter illustrates this argument through engaging some of the routes and trajectories articulated through the "global" Indian seafarers' strikes of 1939.

Subaltern Studies, Histories from Below, and the Political

In his book *Black Pacific*, Robbie Shilliam draws attention to the influence of "E. P. Thompson's approach to 'history from below,' and its Gramscian sensitivities to culture and meaning, as key sites of social struggles" on "the intellectuals of Subaltern Studies" (Shilliam 2015, 4–5). Shilliam's timely invocation of the debt of subaltern studies to E. P. Thompson and the question this raises about the relation of subaltern studies to "histories from below" is significant. Such a lineage has, for example, been largely effaced from one of the most influential critical assessments of the work of the collective: Vivek Chibber's (2013) *Postcolonial Theory and the Specter of Capital*. By failing to give more than a cursory nod to the role of histories from below in the intellectual genealogy of the project, Chibber's book abstracts the work of the collective from the transnational circulations of both histories from below and the related intellectual milieu of the new left.[2]

These intellectual exchanges and engagements, however, were a significant part of the context in which, as Shilliam has argued, subaltern studies "sought to create a cognate space of democratization within the historiography of India, a practice of story-telling that had hitherto therefore been dominated by the 'Cambridge School'" and Marxist nationalist historiography, "both of which had produced elitist accounts wherein the peasantry were rendered an unreasoning or pre-political mass" (Shilliam 2014, 5). In this regard a central contribution of Guha's *Elementary Aspects of Peasant Insurgency* was the direct challenge it made to Eric Hobsbawm's notion of the "pre-political." Hobsbawm's influential conceptualization of "the pre-political" set up peasant movements and early modern artisans as "spontaneous," "primitive rebels" lacking the coherent forms of structure and organization that would be bestowed on them by the formation of trade unions and political parties and their associated intellectuals and leaderships (Hobsbawm 1959; see also Hobsbawm and Rudé 1973). Hobsbawm's writings established a linear sense of the formation of political organization, where such "pre-political peasant rebels" in societies "still to be fully industrialized" would be established into more disciplined forms of organization as industrialization took hold (Guha 1983, 5).

Guha argues that Hobsbawm uses the terms "pre-political people" and "pre-political populations" "again and again" to "describe a state of supposedly absolute or near absence of political consciousness of organization which he believes to have been characteristic of such people" (Guha 1983, 5). By contrast Guha asserts the importance of the politicality of peasant struggle. He argues that there was "*nothing* in the militant movements of [colonial India's] rural masses that was not *political*" (Guha 1983, 6, emphasis added). This argument dislocates the temporalization of political difference at work in Hobsbawm's notions of the "pre-political" and thus has important geographical implications. Rejecting

Hobsbawm's linear framing of the attainment of political consciousness allowed Guha to assert two things. Firstly, it allowed him to engage with the different trajectories of political articulation, that is, to draw attention to the way that there could be different ways of attaining and asserting political consciousness. Secondly, it was attentive to the coexistence of difference in the formation of political identities and practices. Rather than temporalizing such difference, it enabled a focus on the different ways in which militant political identities could be asserted in different contexts.

One of the resources that Guha used in challenging Hobsbawm's account of the "pre-political" was E. P. Thompson's writings in the 1970s on the forms of political struggle in eighteenth-century England that he once memorably described as "class-struggle without class" (Thompson 1978, 133). Thus Sumit Sarkar observes that Ranajit Guha "seems to have often used 'subaltern' somewhat in the way Thompson deployed the term 'plebeian' in his writings on eighteenth-century England" (Sarkar 1998, 83). In particular Guha drew on Thompson's account of the Black Acts in *Whigs and Hunters*. These were draconian statutes designed to repress gangs of poachers who from 1717 onward in Windsor Forest had "hustled the forest officers" and "attacked the forest deer" (Thompson 1975, 54).

Guha used Thompson's account to directly challenge what he describes as Hobsbawm's tendency "to depoliticise this violence," to fall back on "economism" and to "render it impossible for us to understand why 'those who took part in these attacks refused to regard their actions as in the least criminal'" (Guha 1983, 146, citing Thompson 1975, 160–61). Guha directly invoked Thompson's work to challenge such economism. Thus he notes that "Blacking ... in most parts of eighteenth century England could hardly be explained in terms of the poacher's involvement in the illicit venison trade" (Guha 1983, 146). Instead Guha draws on Thompson's contention that "the whole pattern of Black actions—the threatening letters, felling of young trees, blackmail of forest officers—disallows a simple economic explanation" (Thompson cited by Guha 1983, 146). Guha contends that the "dominant motive here is clearly political—that of undermining the authority of the gentry by the demolition of its symbols. This inversive function of popular violence is raised to its highest power by insurgency, and destruction becomes in that context the signifier of a consciousness which is as negative in orientation as it is political in context" (Guha 1983, 146). What is significant here, then, is that by treating such activity as political and generative Guha shows such actors as challenging broader symbolic construction of authority rather than being confined within deferent structures associated with the "moral economy."

Thompson's engagement with tactics such as threatening letters and the felling of young trees speaks to his attentiveness to the materialities and spaces of politics in *Whigs and Hunters*. Across his work, in essays in both *Customs and*

Common (1991) and *Making of the English Working Class* (1963), Thompson is attentive to such spatial relations—even if he rarely theorizes or engages them explicitly (see Featherstone and Griffin 2016; Navickas 2011). Thus Carl Griffin draws attention to the significance of Thompson's engagement with practices such as "tree-maiming," noting that "the Blacks not only embraced incendiarism and the maiming of cattle, dogs and horses as their chosen weapons of rural terror—such acts in part sought to hurt the pockets of forest officers but were primarily deployed to terrorise—but also acts such as the destruction of the heads of fish ponds and the malicious cutting down of trees" (Griffin 2007, 94).

Griffin's engagement with Thompson's account of "the Blacks" usefully troubles the autonomous conception of the political subject that was central to both Guha's *Elementary Aspects of Peasant Insurgency* and his inaugural manifesto of the collective. Guha viewed subaltern politics as produced through an "autonomous" domain rather than positioning subaltern political activity as negotiating crosscutting relations of power (see Moore 1998). His position, paradoxically, tends to close down the agency of marginalized political actors in similar ways to those inherent in the "pre-political" approach. The agency and distinctiveness produced through articulating antagonisms in specific ways is often downplayed in accounts that stress the autonomous character of actors. Guha's account of the coexistence of class and ethnic solidarities in communist-led agrarian uprisings among sharecroppers of Bengal in 1946–47 falls back on accounts of "spontaneity" to explain the strength of the mobilization (Guha 1983, 170).[3]

His focus on the autonomous subaltern subject here downplays the spatial dynamics through which class and ethnicity are articulated together. Thus he argues there was more to these sharecropper struggles "than class consciousness alone; otherwise it would not have erupted with such spontaneity. This apparent spontaneity was nothing but a measure of the displacement of class solidarity by ethnic solidarity" (Guha 1983, 170). If political subjectivities are seen as fully formed before engaging in political action, it becomes difficult to imagine how such activity might be generative of new forms of identities and relations. Thus Spivak argued in her influential critique of the first three volumes of *Subaltern Studies*, "Deconstructing Historiography," that "subaltern consciousness can never be continuous with the subaltern's situational and uneven entry into political (not merely disciplinary, as in the case of the collective) hegemony as the content of an after-the-fact description" (Spivak 1985, 346).

Spivak makes this critique as part of her broader argument that there was a tension in the project between a reification of subaltern consciousness and a more deconstructive practice. Priya Gopal argues, however, that by counterposing the recovery of subaltern consciousness and the methods of deconstruction Spivak makes it difficult to engage with the "possibility that the subaltern may have a mediated . . . relationship" to consciousness and agency (2004, 149). Gopal argues that, as a result, Spivak's approach evades the "work of examining the complicated engagement of selves, societies, bodies, histories, events, memories, interests and desires that goes into the making of both consciousness and action" (Gopal 2004, 148). The remainder of this chapter argues that a focus on the geographies of subaltern politics, particularly one that reasserts situated geographies of subaltern agency and trajectories, can help transcend the binary positions marked out by Spivak.

Dissident Left Political Trajectories and the Emergence of Subaltern Studies

Rajnarayan Chandavarkar argues that, despite the impact of *The Making of the English Working Class*, it was "only in the late 1970s that [Thompson's] influence came to be more directly and tangibly registered in Indian historiography" (2000, 53). He notes that the influence of moral economy, and in particular the more open sense of class antagonism in essays like "Class Struggle without Class," moved more successfully to a South Asian context than *The Making* itself. Thus he notes that "Thompson's argument seemed to be that class struggle and the cultural and historical experience which it encompassed could be studied more extensively in societies where capitalism had manifested itself weakly and unevenly" (Chandavarkar 2000, 54). Thompson's influence on Indian historical writing was facilitated by his election in the 1970s as president of the Indian History Congress. Sarkar notes that Thompson had "a significant impact when he visited India in the winter of 1976–77 and addressed a session of the Indian history congress" (Sarkar 1998, 83).

This visit built on Thompson's long-standing connections with Indian left politics, which were partly shaped by his father, Edward John Thompson, who taught English in Bengal, was an associate of Rabindranath Tagore, and was involved in forging links with key Indian independence leaders in the 1930s and early 1940s. As Priya Satia has recently argued, E. P. Thompson's work, "including its insistent 'Englishness,' romantic outlook and critical view of religion, owed a great deal to his father's ties to India and the Indian nationalist movement" (Satia 2016, 135). Sarkar notes that Thompson's history of India, *The Other Side of the Medal*, embodies the "contradictory, indeed tortured, sensibility" that shaped "liberal British perception about colonial India during the interwar years" (Sarkar 1998, 115). In a similar vein, Scott Hamilton notes that his father "became an active, if sometimes reluctant and equivocal, supporter of Indian independence"; Jawaharlal Nehru and Mahatma Gandhi were both visitors to the Thompsons' home in Oxford, and Nehru gave the young E. P. Thompson batting lessons on "the Thompson's backyard cricket pitch" (Hamilton 2011, 18).

Nehru's advice on Thompson's batting prowess notwithstanding, it is important to recognize that the engagements between Thompson and Guha came out of long-standing geographies of connection between the British and Indian lefts. Thompson forcefully articulated the importance of such connections and solidarities in a 1963 polemic addressed to members of the *New Left Review*'s editorial board. He argued that their particular inflection of "Third Worldism" was unhelpfully dismissive of the long-standing internationalist commitments of the U.K. left. Thompson observed that

> there was a marked interpenetration of ideas between the Indian nationalist movement and British left. The student movement, notably at Oxford and Cambridge, always had a large Asiatic element, whose members were active and prominent (some of us received our first tuition in Marxism from Indian comrades, and vice versa). Already in the Twenties, British agitators (the Meerut prisoners) had assisted the Indian C[ommunist] P[arty] into being; and if one follows the reports of Congress or of Communist and Trotskyist movements in India, Ceylon and Burma, many intellectuals who returned from this British milieu will be found in leading roles. (Thompson 2014, 228)

Further, Thompson recalled seeing "everywhere, indefatigable and uncompromising the saturnine Krishna Menon [of the India League]" (Thompson 1980, 140).[4] By situating this anti-imperial strand within "a deep and authentic tradition in the British labour movement," Thompson, however, refigures a very nationed articulation of internationalism (Thompson 2014, 229; see also Thompson 1978). These relations were also more contested than Thompson's metaphor of interpenetration might imply; M. N. Roy, representing the Communist Party of India (CPI), challenged in the mid-1920s, for example, the Communist Party of Great Britain's "understanding that its own colonial committee had the sole right to conduct colonial work in India" (Datta Gupta 2011, 119).

These exchanges emphasize that the "space of democratization within the historiography of India" that Shilliam writes about had diverse routes. In this regard both Guha and Thompson had been intellectually and politically embedded within the work of Communist parties but broke with them in 1956. Guha had become involved in the CPI as a student at Presidency College in Calcutta and after university "joined the staff of *Swadhinata*, the Communist party daily" (Chatterjee 2009, 8). After representing the CPI in the secretariat of the World Federation of Democratic Youth in 1947, he spent the next six years "based in Paris, organizing events, building networks and travelling, often under false identities, in Eastern Europe, West Asia, and North Africa" (Chatterjee 2009, 8). He returned to India in 1953 and, like Thompson, Guha resigned from the CPI over the Soviet invasion of Hungary (Amin and Bhadra 1994, 223).

Shahid Amin notes that "it was 1968 and more specifically the Indian variant of Maoism associated with the peasant uprising in Naxalbari in North Bengal in

1967 that ... helped shape my intellectual concerns. As with several colleagues who came together in the late 1970s to form the Subaltern Studies collective, even after the political challenge of the Naxalbari movement had been crushed the fundamental question of political power in post-colonial India that it managed to raise had important bearing on our understanding of India's colonial history" (Amin 2003, 93). The collective drew on the pioneering engagement with Gramsci's work by a small number of Indian left intellectuals working in Calcutta, notably Susobhan Sarkar and Asok Sen.

Thus Susobhan Sarkar "began discussing Gramsci's work with his students at Jadavpur University, his ongoing interest in the Italian thinker resulting in publications in the late 1960s and 1970s" (Kaiwar 2015, 82). Guha, who was taught by Sarkar and was later to be his colleague, was strongly influenced by his critical engagements with Gramsci, which were significant intellectual engagements in a context where "mainstream left parties in India were 'lukewarm if not indifferent' to Gramsci" (Kaiwar 2015, 82). Partha Chatterjee notes in his tribute to Asok Sen that his reading of "Gramsci at a time when Indira Gandhi's populist programmes delivered through a centralised bureaucratic state machinery, were being loudly endorsed by intellectuals associated with the Communist Party of India. Sen sharply criticised the abandonment of sustained struggles in the various institutions of civil society to build up the hegemonic foundations of popular consent and instead tagging behind a thoroughly coercive state apparatus working at the behest of a Caesarist leader" (Chatterjee 2016, 30).

The terms on which the colonial past was being engaged with, then, were not depoliticized but part of a broader critique of the ways in which popular consent and agency was elided and repressed by the institutions of postcolonial India. Thus in a 1976 essay Guha located "the present Emergency" not as an exceptional event, related to personalized flaws of Indira Gandhi, but arguing that it represented "no radical break with a democratic past but an aggravation of a chronic denial of elementary freedoms and justice" that were integral to the foundation of postcolonial India (Guha 2010, 580). During the "emergency," Thompson in turn developed a strongly critical position on Indira Gandhi's regime, reserving particular ire for the support of Michael Foot, then a prominent figure on the left of the U.K. Labour Party, for her authoritarian rule (Thompson 1980, 146; see also Hamilton 2011, 161).Thompson's exposure to India's secret police and the resistance to the emergency intersected with his own concerns about U.K. politics, which was becoming increasingly authoritarian; he articulated these concerns in essays such as "Taking Liberties" (Hamilton 2011, 161; Thompson 1980, 136).

The mobilities through which these connections were forged and articulated, then, were not smooth, notwithstanding what Thompson described as the "chores of solidarity" (Thompson 1980, 140). By 1980, Thompson's own travels to India, as with some of his public pronouncements in England, were being "policed" due to his increasingly prominent role as a leading figure in the Campaign for European Nuclear Disarmament (ENDS) (Featherstone 2012, 161–63). In 1986 a group of distinguished Indian historians, including Sumit Sarkar and Irfan Habib, complained in a collective letter to the *Economic and Political Weekly* that a "recent invitation extended to him to visit India on a two- or three-week long lecture tour" had "been summarily and rudely withdrawn by the British Council on the curious ground of a suddenly discovered shortage of funds" (Sharma et al. 1986). A vehement critique of Thompson's work with ENDS, published in the *Economic and Political Weekly* in the early 1980s, emphasizes, however, that Thompson's vision of trans-European solidarities in ENDS was not uniformly welcomed by Indian left activists and intellectuals (see also Davis 1982). Govind Purushottam Deshpande argued in contradistinction to Thompson that any "analysis of international politics which takes a supra-bloc and supra-ideology view is Eurocentric" (GPD 1988).

In a related vein the Englishness that was central to Thompson's left politics became increasingly challenged by postcolonial critics such as Paul Gilroy by the 1980s (see Gilroy 1987, 1993). This commitment to Englishness, albeit a radically inflected one, ultimately came into conflict with the anticolonial political and theoretical commitments of subaltern studies intellectuals. Such concerns came into focus particularly starkly as the project moved to the wider terrain of the critique of universality and epistemologies in the later 1980s and 1990s. Thus Ranajit Guha's essay *Dominance without Hegemony* critiqued the complicity of Thompson's reflections on law in *Whigs and Hunters* with "the pervasive power of the ideology of law in English political thought" (Guha 1997, 67).

Guha argues that this ideology has "acquired the prestige of a code mediating all perceptions of civil conflict" and "stands thus for that universalist urge of bourgeois culture which has realized itself so much and so well in the theory and practice of law under metropolitan conditions as to acquire the aura of 'a cultural achievement of universal significance' in the eyes not only of English liberals and colonists like Dodwell, but also alas, of English radicals like E. P. Thompson from whom these words are taken" (Guha 1997, 67). Interestingly, Thompson is rather more attentive to the uneven spatialities of law than Guha allows. Thompson argued that "transplanted as it was to even more inequitable contexts, this law could become an instrument of imperialism. For this law has found its way to a good many parts of the globe. But even here the rules and the rhetoric have imposed some inhibitions upon the imperial power. If the rhetoric was a mask, it was a mask which Gandhi and Nehru were to borrow, at the head of a million masked supporters" (Thompson 1976, 266).

Nonetheless, Guha's critique of Thompson was part of a broader challenge to the geographical imaginaries of history from below as he makes clear in a passage that only appears in the original version of the essay in *Subaltern Studies VI*. Thus he asked, "Is it possible to find as much as a twinge of self-critical recognition in the pages, say, of the *History Workshop*, to suggest the need to challenge the Mill-Dodwell tradition of writing on India and join issue with the recycling of imperialist historiography in terms of teaching and research at all the major centres of South Asian studies in the United Kingdom?" (Guha 1989, 306).[5] The next section discusses the terms of this broader challenge to the geographical imaginaries of history from below.

Subaltern Agency and Political Trajectories

In the conclusion to *Rethinking Working Class History*, Dipesh Chakrabarty furthers such a concern with the implications of the centering of English articulations of liberty and freedom in the text. He asks, "If the particular notions of 'free born Englishman,' of 'equality before the law' and so on were the most crucial heritages of the English working class in respect of its capacity for developing class consciousness, what about the working classes for instance, the Indian one, whose heritages do not include such as a liberal baggage? Are the latter condemned forever to a state of 'low classness' unless they develop some kind of cultural resemblance to the English?" (Chakrabarty 1989, 223). Chakrabarty's critique of the implied universalism of English articulations of liberty and popular struggle in *The Making of the English Working Class* presaged his later attempt to "provincialize" "western universalisms" (Chakrabarty 2000a).

In Chakrabarty's influential discussion of what he terms "History 1 and History 2," he positions Thompson's essay on "Time, Work-Discipline and Industrial Capitalism" as an exemplar of what he terms "historicist thought" (Chakrabarty 2000a, 48). He notes that Thompson's essay rests on an argument that "the worker in the history of advanced capitalism has no option but to shed precapitalist habits of work and 'internalize' work-discipline. The same fate awaits the worker in the third world. The difference between these two figures of the worker is a matter of the secular historical time that elapses in the global career of capitalism" (Chakrabarty 2000a, 48). There are important resonances here with Doreen Massey's critique of the temporalization of difference. She critiques accounts where differences between political configurations in different places become positioned in temporal terms on a linear pathway, rather than being seen as different trajectories that coexist (Massey 2005). In Thompson's account, the division between workers in advanced capitalist contexts and the Third World is rendered as a temporal rather than a spatial difference. This is problematic as it positions some parts of the world as "ahead" of "others" and views them as part of fundamentally different "problem-spaces" in David Scott's (2004) terms.

To engage with the problems associated with "historicist thought," Chakrabarty suggests a distinction between "History 1" and "History 2." For Chakrabarty, History 1 bears on the universalizing and totalizing logic of capital. It "corresponds to the kinds of histories we would write on the basis of the abstract categories of Marxism" (Rabasa 2010, 274, see also Mezzadra 2016). History 2, on the other hand, are those multiple possibilities or pasts that are "under the institutional domination of the logic of capital and exist in proximate relationship to it, but . . . do not belong to the 'life' process of capital" (Chakrabarty 2000b, 671). The role of History 2, then, becomes to "interrupt" the "totalizing thrusts of History 1." As Chakrabarty argues, the histories in History 2 are "not pasts separate from capital; they inhere in capital and yet interrupt and punctuate the run of capital's own logic" (Chakrabarty 2000a, 64).

Chakrabarty's distinction develops a significant contribution to understandings of the relations between the spatiotemporal construction of capital and subalternity that shape the distinction between History 1 and History 2. This distinction, however, reproduces the kind of binary logic that various critics have argued has been foundational to the work of the collective (Chari, this volume; Moore 1998; Sarkar 1998). Sumit Sarkar has argued that the binary logics that have structured much of the collective's work, from Guha's inaugural statement onward, have tended to close down a focus on the diverse relations shaped through political struggles and organizing. Thus he argues that the "separation of domination and autonomy tended to make absolute and homogenize both within their separate domains" (Sarkar 1988, 90). By sifting out capital and asserting it as prior and existing in "empty homogenous time," this approach still risks positioning subaltern agency and trajectories as secondary to capital, even while Chakrabarty seeks to deconstruct these binary relations. This speaks to a broader tendency in the subaltern studies project to externalize questions of the economic from understandings, and articulations, of subalternity (Chari 2004, 183–84; see also Sarkar 1988, 108).

The relationalities of the political at work in Chakrabarty's account of History 1 and History 2 has been incisively challenged by Jose Rabasa. In contradistinction to writers like Hardt and Negri who would see the "peasantry" as a doomed social formation, Rabasa develops a focus on subaltern political activity as coexisting with, rather than secondary to, colonialism, capital, and/ or the state (Rabasa 2010, 274). For Rabasa to develop this focus on coexistence involves an explicit challenge to Chakrabarty's demarcation between History 1 and History 2, which he contends retains a certain capital-centered framing. Thus, he argues that this distinction redefines the terms for writing "the good history of capital rather than proposing an alternative to history and capital" (Rabasa 2010, 273–74). In similar terms Vivek Chibber warns that separating the logic of capital and contingency risks rendering capital as "an all pervasive force" (Chibber 2013, 221).

Chibber's critique, however, falls back on a sense of universality rooted in "basic needs" with little sense of how political grievances are articulated through specific struggles. This speaks to a flattening logic in his work, such that in the conclusion he notes that the "global economic crisis has brought into relief the basic fact that the entire world is now part of the same universal history, subject to the same underlying forces" (Chibber 2013, 294). There is a key tension here between this flattened "basic needs" kind of argument and understanding political constructions of universality. A key implication of this approach is that it erases an engagement with the practices through which such grievances become politicized and articulated in relation to universal claims.

By contrast, Peter Linebaugh and Marcus Rediker, in their iconoclastic history from below of the early modern Atlantic, *The Many Headed Hydra*, argue that the multiethnic resistances that traversed the Atlantic world in the seventeenth and eighteenth centuries were productive of "multi-ethnic conceptions of humanity" (Linebaugh and Rediker 2001, 352; see also J. Scott 1986). Through a focus on interconnected slave revolts, shipboard mutinies, port city riots, and commoners' struggle, they develop a focus on the coeval, and often conflictual, trajectories through which different notions of democracy, equality, or liberty were articulated. In doing so they make an explicit challenge to some of the foundational spatialities that shaped history from below.

This approach is attentive to the geographies of universality that are effaced in Chibber's work. Further, considering how subaltern activity coexists with and engages with, rather than simply interrupts, capital can illuminate the alternative and competing universalities produced through subaltern politics. This positions subaltern political activity in more generative terms than simply destabilizing the universalizing logics of capital and evokes the multiple geographies through which subaltern political activity is shaped. Such activity can then be seen as bearing on the oppositional forms of agency crafted through subaltern geographies of connection and contestation. This emphasizes that work that has challenged the nation-centered spatialities, which shaped the work of Thompson and other writers associated with "history from below," present resources for enriching understandings of relational geographies of subaltern politics (Featherstone 2008).

The possibilities opened up by attempts to reconfigure histories from below in less nation-centered terms has, however, been rather closed down by accounts that counterpose subaltern studies and history from below. Thus Partha Chatterjee, in his response to Chibber's critique of the subaltern studies project, draws a sharp distinction between the two projects. He avers that

> Subaltern Studies could never have been carried out in the same way as History from Below in Europe. The recounting in the latter body of work of the struggles of peasants and artisans in the period of the ascendancy of capitalism in Europe was inevitably written as tragedy, since the ultimate dissolution of those classes was

already scripted into their history. Should we assume the same trajectory for agrarian societies in other parts of the world? Does a different sequencing of capitalist modernity there not mean ... that the historical outcomes in terms of economic formations, political institutions or cultural practices, might be quite different from those we see in the west? (Chatterjee 2013, 75)

Chatterjee here delineates a bifurcated cartography of the trajectories of subaltern studies and histories from below. Arguably the spatial logic he mobilizes here is not dissimilar to Thompson's (1967) framing of the relations between the West and the Third World in "Time, Work-Discipline and Industrial Capitalism" (1967). Chatterjee comes close to providing a mirror image of Thompson's historicism, which reproduces his sense that the West and Third World are constitutively separate and existing in fundamentally different temporalities. This also positions "the West" in rather homogeneous terms and tends to ignore contestation of capital/empire within the West, often produced through diverse trajectories and solidarities that stretch beyond "the West" (see also Kaiwar 2015, 168–69).

This raises the question of what is at stake in articulating more interconnected sets of relations between diverse articulations of subaltern studies and histories from below. It also raises the question of how this might challenge the spatial imaginaries through which subaltern studies projects have been constituted. This is an important problematic as the spaces of subalternity that have been envisioned through the subaltern studies project have often been rather circumscribed and limited (Ballantyne 2003, 111–12; Clayton 2010; for an exception, see Ghosh 1992, 204). By contrast, recent scholarship, such as Clare Anderson's book *Subaltern Lives,* "moves beyond the national (and for that matter trans-national) to focus on the Indian Ocean as constituted through overlapping spaces of governance, mobility and experience" to produce more routed, networked, and relational performances of subaltern agency (Anderson 2012, 9). As Lakshmi Subramanian has argued, a focus on "maritime politics" offers possibilities of "unravelling the skeins" of distinct modes of "subaltern protest" (Subramanian 2016, 3; see also Chari, this volume).

Such challenges to nationed framings of subalternity have also been central to recent work on South Asian internationalisms. As Raza, Roy, and Zachariah observe in the context of what they term "the internationalist moment" of the 1920s and 1930s, "it is necessary to place South Asia in the history of that internationalist flood, from which subsequently the ubiquitous narrative of 'nationalist movement(s)' has wrested it" (Raza, Roy, and Zachariah 2015, xi). They point to the importance of South Asian seafarers in shaping such internationalist politics, and accordingly the final part of this chapter engages with the trajectories of Indian seafarers who worked in the British merchant marine in the interwar period.

Subaltern Maritime Networks and Contested Articulations of the Political

In his fine essay "Guns, Drugs and Revolutionary Propaganda," Jon Hyslop (2009, 838) engages with the "extensive trans-continental smuggling by Indian sailors of commodities including weaponry and narcotics" in the 1920s. The smuggling routes and practices he engages with include the activities of Indian seafarers, who shipped out of ports such as Antwerp and Hamburg and carried seditious literature for radicals such as M. N. Roy, one of the founders of the Communist Party of India. Hyslop argues, against the grain of both political radicals and colonial officials, that "although some of the sailors did see themselves as revolutionaries and workers, most understood themselves, at least insofar as they engaged in smuggling, as traders" (Hyslop 2009, 839). He asserts that "Civil Servants and Policemen, Revolutionaries and Organisers, Shipping Magnates and Captains all attempted to pin down the sailors to their own projects, but all failed" (Hyslop 2009b, 846).

Hyslop argues against a way of constructing subaltern maritime actors "as victims, overwhelmingly tightly regulated by the British authorities, a pattern broken only by occasional moments of heroic insurgency" (Hyslop 2009b, 839). Some of the ambiguities that are foreclosed by "heroic" readings of subaltern maritime resistance are captured by the interventions made by a Mr. H. Straker during a meeting of the Cardiff branch of the National Union of Seamen (NUS) in 1927. Straker, who is recorded in the branch minutes as a "Coloured men's Representative," argued during a discussion of the nonpolitical policy of the NUS in the face of a challenge from the Communist-affiliated National Minority Movement that the matter "has been referred to the Annual General Meeting [of the NUS]. I don't see why there should be any necessity for this meeting, my advice as a seaman, and as an official for this organisation, is to assist these men to better themselves. I have had to go into the stokehold, and I think of those poor fellows smashed by Bolshevism. . . . There is more at bottom of this than meets the eye. Shinwell and Cook are at the bottom of this."[6]

Straker's critical remarks about Bolshevism, the Glasgow seafarer's leader Emanuel Shinwell, and A. J. Cook, the Communist leader of the Miners' Federation of Great Britain, signal a critical engagement with the terms on which left politics mobilized seafarers' grievances and activity. Straker was also critical of the NUS branch leadership in Cardiff, having clashed earlier in the decade over union officials' attitudes to seafarers of color. In the ensuing encounter with the union hierarchy, the president Havelock Wilson had left Straker in no doubt about his "subaltern" status within the union.[7] As Tim Bunnell has argued in his work on Malay seafarers, "non-white seamen in Britain appear in government records as a problematic if not outright undesirable presence" (Bunnell 2016, 60). "Such conceptions," he observes, "were bound up with broader racist fears about demographic contamination and miscegenation" (Bunnell 2016, 60). Engaging with subaltern actors' articulations of grievances and organizing has the potential to recast understandings of the political.

As Rehana Ahmed has argued in an insightful discussion of the dynamics of the working-class South Asian presence in interwar Britain, it is impossible to reduce Indian workers' struggles in Britain in the 1920s and 1930s "to a singular or universal narrative of anti-colonial resistance" (Ahmed 2011, 79). Drawing on Dipesh Chakrabarty's work, she explores the "dissonance between some Indian workers' representations of their practices in Britain as apolitical" and her own "politicization" of them. Her approach enables a focus on the diverse ways in which seafarers' organizing and anticolonial politics and imaginaries were articulated. As Andy Davies demonstrates in his account of the Royal Indian Navy (RIN) mutiny of 1946, by examining the "ways in which the sailors, through the processes of being a sailor and living in the RIN, created and inhabited a number of open political identities," it is possible to foreground "the processes which created contentious political identities amongst the sailors of the RIN" (Davies 2013, 25). Davies's concern with the ways mutineers' politics were assembled offers an account of political agency that stresses the ongoing constitution of such political practices and grievances. In similar terms, Gopalan Balachandran, in his discussion of the labor practices and organizing of Indian seafarers in the early to mid-twentieth century, has argued that their forms of organizing shaped both "individual and collective" forms of "networked subaltern agency" (Balachandran 2012, 34). The account of "subaltern agency" that emerges here is forged through the fashioning of connections and relations.

A significant episode marked by such agency was the "global" strikes by Indian seafarers, which marked the outbreak of World War II in 1939. Thus Rozina Visram notes that "after decades of racial discrimination, facing the same risks in war, Indian seamen in Britain refused to sail without a wage increase, basic provisions and security for their families. Within weeks, strikes had spread from London, Glasgow, Liverpool and Southampton to countries as far apart as South Africa, Australia and Burma" (Visram 2002, 234). One of the first of these strikes by Indian crews in Britain, as Balachandran notes, was a coordinated one at Tilbury docks in early September on two Clan Line vessels, *Clan Ross* and *Clan MacBrayne* (Balachandran 2012, 259). A key sense of their demands is given in an account of an "interview" between officials from the Board of Trade and the Indian High Commissioner with two representatives of the striking crews.

The report of the discussion in the India Office papers record that, on September 8, 1939, "Atur Miah, of *SS Clan Ross*," and Abdul Majid, of the *SS Clan MacBrayne*, representing the Lascar crews of their respective ships, "interviewed me this morning and put forward the following claims on behalf of the Lascar crews of both ships."[8] The demands included that wages were "to be doubled and these increased wages to be paid right up to the time when the Indian crews of these two ships land back in Calcutta." It also noted that "half the wages [were] to be paid to the High Commissioner for India in London, and he is to send this money to the wives and heirs of the men working on the ships if they so desire. The High Commissioner [is] to send an officer to the ships to take the names and addresses of each member of the Indian crew and their heirs in India who are to receive this money." It was recorded that Messrs. Norman and Justice of the Board of Trade "agreed to the conditions stated above relating to these two vessels, and the representatives of the crews have agreed to go back and resume work immediately" (UK National Archives [hereafter TNA] MT 9/3150). These actions fed into a broader context official anxieties about the unreliability of merchant seamen across the British Empire, which led to the adoption of new "Regulations for the Control of Merchant Seamen."[9]

The geographies of the strike were not just a matter of the impressive reach of this action, which affected ships as far apart as Durban, Bombay, Calcutta, London, and Glasgow. Their spatial politics were also interwoven into the demands raised through the strike action. Thus a central demand was that wages should not just be doubled but that "increased wages" should "be paid right up to the time when the Indian crews of these two ships land back in Calcutta" (MT 9/3150). The strikes intersected with struggles over the terms on which crews were transferred between different routes. Balachandran notes that "customary interpretations" of the "transfer clause in the articles of agreement for Indian seamen" enabled "shipowners to deploy their Indian crews more flexibly, and the latter to prolong their engagements" (Balachandran 2012, 236). This clause (and its customary interpretation, which, despite their best efforts, shipowners failed to incorporate into law even during World War II) opened up possibilities for "Indian crews on British ships who would normally have had an opportunity to consider it at least once during the course of their engagements" (Balachandran 2012, 237). Nonetheless there were struggles over the terms on which transfers were produced and negotiated. The Chief Superintendent (Scotland District) for example, noted on November 2, 1939, that "[the] Lascar deck ratings of the Anchor line 'Cicassia' have refused to transfer to the 'Britannia' and are being prosecuted."[10]

Struggles over the terms on which mobilities were shaped and experienced are foregrounded in the testimony of the Sylheti seafarer Mortuja Ali. Ali recalled to Yousuf Choudhury that he was on a Clan Line vessel in 1941 or 1942 sailing from London to Calcutta when "the ship was returning to India. When it reached halfway in the Middle East, the crew were told by the shipping company that they were going to be released as soon as the ship would reach Cochin in India. The rest of the way, the crew was making plans, we made up our mind to visit our families, we were looking forward to the day when we would be paid up and released. . . . When our ship reached Cochin, the shipping officials changed their mind. They had no excuses ready. So we went on strike" (Ali 1995, 33–34). The consequences of taking strike action were severe. Ali recalls that the "striking crew were punished with three month's hard labour. For the first one and half months they were to beat out coconut husks with a stone and for the last one month and half they were to make rope with beaten coconut fibre" (Ali 1995, 33–34). Ali himself "quietly disappeared from the port" when the next ship he got a job on was docked in Liverpool (Ali 1995, 34).

The repression of Indian seafarers during the 1939 strikes produced particular spatial practices of subalternization. There is evidence, for example, that Tahsil Miah of the All India Seamen's Federation, who acted as a spokesperson for imprisoned seafarers, was deported from Britain to India on the ss *Tribesmen* of the Harrison Line on December 9. It was reported that Krishna Menon "of the India League" was "making every possible effort to prevent TAHSIL Miah's 'deportation' as he realises this action is a preventive one rather than a judicial penalty for ship desertion."[11] Such subalternization also emerges from a *Daily Worker* report of a trial at Southampton Police Court on November 15, 1939. The report of the trial of "a large number of Lascar seamen" for "disobeying the orders of the Captain" noted that the "lines of men completely filled the court and a numbered cloakroom ticket was pinned to each man to assist identification."[12]

The interest that the *Daily Worker* displayed in the case reflects the significant, if decidedly uneven, relations between communism and black and Asian seafarers in British port cities. One of the figures who emerged seeking to broker relations among striking seafarers, shipping companies, and the Board of Trade/India Office was Surat Ali, a Communist who had a strong base among Indian seafarers in the East End of London. Ali had been secretary of the Colonial Seamen's Association (CSA), which was formed in 1935 to contest the National Shipping Assistance Act that sought to exclude black, Arab, and Asian seafarers from the maritime labor market in British port cities (Evans 1995). Surat Ali "was an enterprising individual who combined several roles: owner of a boarding house, ship-chandler, supplier of crews, trade unionist who also founded and ran an Oriental film artistes union, communist activist, war time reservist and air raid warden, and, according to some accounts, police informer" (Balachandran 2012, 195). The chair of the CSA was Chris Braithwaite, the Barbadian seafarers' activist, pan-Africanist, and employee of the shipping federation, in the Colonial Seamen's Association, locating the CSA as produced through overlapping political trajectories that crossed Atlantic and Indian Ocean spaces (Høgsbjerg 2011, 2013).

The multiethnic spaces and organizing practices that were produced at the intersections of anticolonial politics and maritime labor also generated possibilities for the formation of translocal solidarities. Thus activists like Chris Braithwaite and Surat Ali played a key role in challenging the imperial articulations of labor organizing and linked anticolonial politics to labor struggles in important ways. These articulations became contested during the 1939 Indian seafarers' strikes through disputes over who had legitimacy to negotiate with officials on behalf of striking crews. It would appear that there were some contacts between Indian seafaring unions and left organizations in ports like Glasgow immediately prior to the strikes. Thus Aftab Ali of the Indian Seamen's Union and the All India Seamen's Federation, who visited the United Kingdom in the summer of 1939, was in contact with the Glasgow Trades' Council in August 1939. In turn the Glasgow Trades' Council sought to support the striking seafarers through a proposed joint committee involving the Trades' Council, the local branch of the India League, and the NUS. This initiative, however, was stymied by the NUS, who refused to take part.[13]

There were particular struggles between Surat Ali, Aftab Ali, and Krishna Menon of the India League, which was backed by the Indian Congress Party.[14] Official papers suggest that India Office and Board of Trade officials also struggled to read who to engage with and recognize as legitimately representing the seafarers. Thus a Board of Trade "Note on the Representation of the Indian Seamen's Union and the All India Seamen's Federation in the UK" commented that "Surat Ali is a communist and has for some years been in the pay of the CPGB. Tahsil Miah on the other hand, has been receiving backing from V. K. Krishna Menon, of the India League, who has recently established an Indian Social Centre in the East End [of London] as a rival organisation to the Hindustan Social Club, and is anxious to set Tahsil Miah against Surat Ali, whom he cordially dislikes."[15]

The note continues that, when Aftab Ali of the Indian Seamen's Union and the All India Seamen's Federation visited the United Kingdom in the summer of 1939, "he became somewhat suspicious of Surat Ali's communist connections and more or less gave Menon (by whose influential political connections he was obviously impressed) to understand that if he were to form a branch of the Indian League in the East End, he would entrust him with the official representation of the Indian Seamen's Federation." It would appear though that Menon hadn't put down enough organizational roots in the East End to convince Aftab Ali to deal directly with him during the seamen's strike; there is also a suggestion that the India League alienated many of the mainly Muslim seafarers (Adams 1987, 157–58). Further, there was contestation of Menon's failure to make the seafarers' strikes part of the public discourse of the India League. According to correspondence from the India Office, Menon "made no reference whatever to the grievances of Indian seamen" at "a public meeting convened by him under the auspices of the India League to discuss the Indian political situation" at Conway Hall on November 16, 1939. This was "an omission which was much resented by Surat Ali and Tahsil Miah, who were both present at the meeting."[16]

Conclusion

In his lecture on the subaltern studies project at the Gramsci Institute in Rome, Ranajit Guha insisted on the "emphatically political nature" of the collective's work. He emphasized that the collective did not intervene from "a detached academic observation post" and that this "shocked the academic establishment which had been the custodian of South Asian Studies both in England and India since the nineteenth century" (Guha 2009, 364). This chapter has argued that this stress on the "emphatically political nature" of subaltern studies presents challenges to the configuring of any subaltern geographies project. It has emphasized the importance of attending to specific subaltern trajectories and agency and demonstrated how thinking spatially about subaltern politics can help assert and trace these within broader political relationalities. I have also suggested that reading selected interventions from the subaltern studies oeuvre for their insights on the relations between intersection of space and politics can be both productive and instructive for possible directions for subaltern geographies.

By locating the emergence of the project in relation to political geographies of circulation of dissident left projects in the period after 1956, I have sought to trace some of the productive intersections of subaltern studies and histories from below. Through engaging with Thompson's work and its reception in India I have followed both the ways in which history from below was articulated in various ways with Indian lefts and some of the terms on which history from below was ultimately dislocated by key intellectuals associated with the subaltern studies project. By unsettling the confining nation-centered spatialities of both subaltern studies and histories from below, I have sought to open up different ways of accounting for and engaging with dynamic subaltern spaces of politics.

This move has allowed a reassertion of the importance of subaltern trajectories and agency in ways that nonetheless are shaped by a rupture with some of the spatially circumscribed limits of the collective's work. I have been particularly concerned to challenge some of the refiguring of subaltern politics as an autonomous domain and to open up a more diverse and contested sense of the relationalities of subaltern politics. While Chakrabarty has figured the "subaltern" as a quasi-mythic "ideal figure" who "survives actively, even joyously, on the assumption that the statist instruments of domination will always belong to somebody else and never aspires to them" (2002, 36), this chapter has been informed by an attentiveness to the reassertion of situated subaltern trajectories and interventions. Signaling the situated political trajectories and interventions in claims on the production of place and spatial relations is something that a geographical approach can both draw out of existing subaltern texts and add more explicitly to the debate. It is also an approach that, following Gopal, can challenge the reductive opposition that Spivak makes between "authenticity" and "constitution" in ways that can offer more generative terms of engagement with the dynamic spaces of subaltern politics.

NOTES

This chapter owes much to conversations with Andy Davies and Paul Griffin, to a period as a visiting fellow at the Centre for the Studies of Social Sciences in Kolkata in February 2014, and to a workshop on Transnational Maritime Spaces and Subaltern Maritime Networks held at the center in December 2014. Many thanks are due to Lakshmi Subramanian at the center, in particular, for her hospitality and engagement and to the British Academy for funding the International Partnership and Mobility award that enabled these activities. Some of the archive work in the chapter was supported by a Carnegie Grant on Transnational Politics, Anti-Colonialism and Maritime Labour: The "Global" Indian Seafarer's Strike of 1939. Thanks are also due to the editors and to Sharad Chari for their very helpful comments and support and to the helpful feedback from readers and participants at the Royal Geographical Society—Institute of British Geographers session on subaltern geographies.

1. The Naxalite upsurge refers to the peasant uprising in the Naxalbari area of West Bengal in 1967 from which the broader Naxalite movement, which became directly associated with Maoism, took its name (Menon and Nigam 2007, 115). The Naxalite rebellion and its repression had an important political and intellectual influence on members of the collective, particularly Ranajit Guha, whose decision to work on an "analysis of peasant insurgency" was influenced by engagement with Maoist students (see Amin and Bhadra 1996, 224).

2. This is also achieved by Chibber's lack of engagement with Ranajit Guha's book *Elementary Aspects of Peasant Insurgency*. Thanks to Ashok Kumar for pointing out this omission.

3. There "was more to this than class consciousness alone; otherwise it would not have erupted with such spontaneity. This apparent spontaneity was nothing but a measure of the displacement of class solidarity by ethnic solidarity" (Guha 1983, 170).

4. It is also worth noting that John Saville, Thompson's collaborator on the *Reasoner* and *New Reasoner* and an important figure in history from below in his own right, also had significant connections with Indian radicals. In his autobiography he recalls developing significant engagements and friendships with Indian communists while serving in India during World War II. His memoirs also include a fascinating vignette of being involved in debates on the Royal Indian Naval Mutiny in the Forces Parliament, with fellow Communist Bert Ramelson, and taking part in "vigorous protest at the atrocities that the British Army had inflicted upon the peaceful citizens of Bombay" in the wake of the mutiny (see Saville 2003, 72).

5. The reference to *History Workshop* is excised from the version of the essay published in the volume titled *Dominance without Hegemony*. Interestingly in a fascinating *New Reasoner* essay, published in 1957, John Saville and E. P. Thompson use a detailed engagement with Mill's reaction to the Morant Bay Rebellion as a key example of liberal

anti-imperial opposition, which they use as part of a protest against military brutality by the British army in Cyprus. In the essay, however, Saville and Thompson are silent on the tensions surrounding Mill's writings on India (see Saville and Thompson 1957).

6. Glamorgan Record Office, GB 0214 DNUS.
7. University of Warwick, Modern Records Centre, Mss 175/1/1/4.
8. UK National Archives (hereafter TNA) MT 9/3150.
9. National Archives of South Africa, SAB HEN_2584_474/3/1.
10. TNA MT 9/3150.
11. British Library IOR L/ P&J/ 12/ 630 f.45.
12. *Daily Worker,* November 16, 1939.
13. Glasgow City Archives TD 2020/1/4/3, Glasgow Trades Council minutes for December, 1939.
14. See British Library IOR L/ P&J/12/ 630 for detailed discussion of some of these tensions. British Library IOR India League Activities L/P&J/12/452 notes that both Menon and Surat Ali talked about the disputes at India League meetings such as a conference held by the India League on Sunday, November 12, at the Bengal Indian Restaurant, Percy Street, Tottenham Court Road; the proceedings lasted from 11 am to 4 pm and were chaired by Reginald Bridgeman of the League Against Imperialism.
15. TNA MT 9/3150 .
16. British Library IOR L/ P&J/12/ 630. Interestingly a report of an address by Menon to Glasgow Trades Council at a similar time also makes no mention of the seafarers' strikes, though it is a short report in the GTC minutes. But given that the Trades Council had been active in attempting to support the strike, it might be assumed they would have noted it if he had mentioned it strongly. See Glasgow Trades Council minutes for December, 1939, Glasgow City Archives TD 2020/1/4/3.

REFERENCES

Adams, C., ed. 1987. *Across Seven Seas and Thirteen Rivers: Life Stories of Pioneer Sylheti Settlers in Britain.* London: Thap Books,.
Adi, H., and M. Sherwood. 1995. *The 1945 Manchester Pan-African Congress Revisited.* London: New Beacon Books.
Ahmed, R. 2011. "Networks of Resistance: Krishna Menon and Working-Class South Asians in Inter-War Britain." In *South Asian Resistances in Britain*, edited by R. Ahmed and S. Mukherjeee, 70–87. London: Continuum.
Amin, S. 2003. "De-ghettoising the Histories of the Non-West." In *At Home in Diaspora: South Asian Scholars and the West*, edited by J. Assayag and V. Benei, 91–100. Bloomington: Indiana University Press.
Amin, S., and G. Bhadra 1996. "Ranajit Guha: A Biography." In *Subaltern Studies VIII*, edited by D. Arnold and D. Hardiman, 222–25. New Delhi: Oxford University Press.
Anderson, C. 2012. *Subaltern Lives: Biographies of Colonialism in the Indian Ocean World, 1790–1920.* Cambridge: Cambridge University Press.
Balachandran, G. 2012. *Globalizing Labour? Indian Seafarers and World Shipping, c. 1870– 1945.* Delhi: Oxford University Press.
Ballantyne, T. 2003. "Rereading the Archive and Opening up the Nation-State: Colonial Knowledge in South Asia (and Beyond)." In *After the Imperial Turn: Thinking with*

and through the Nation, edited by A. Burton, 102–20. Durham, N.C.: Duke University Press.
Burton, A., and T. Ballantyne. Eds. 2016. *World Histories from Below: Disruption and Dissent 1750 to the Present*. London: Bloomsbury.
Chakrabarty, D. 1989. *Rethinking Working Class History*. Princeton, N.J.: Princeton University Press.
———. 2000a. *Provincialising Europe: Post-Colonial Thought and Historical Difference*. Princeton, N.J.: Princeton University Press.
———. 2000b. "Universalism and Belonging in the Logic of Capital." *Public Culture* 12, no. 3: 653–78.
———. 2002. *Habitations of Modernity: Essays in the Wake of Subaltern Studies*. Chicago: University of Chicago Press.
———. 2013. "Fifty Years of E. P. Thompson's The Making of the English Working Class." *Economic and Political Weekly*, December 21, 24–26.
Chandavarkar, R. 2000. "The Making of the Working Class: E. P. Thompson and Indian History." In *Mapping Subaltern Studies and the Postcolonial*, edited by V. Chaturverdi, 50–72. London: Verso.
Chari, S. 2004. *Fraternal Capital: Peasant-Workers, Self-Made Men and Globalization in Provincial India*. Stanford, Calif.: Stanford University Press.
———. 2011. "Subalternities That Matter in Times of Crisis." In *The New Companion to Economic Geography*, edited by J. Peck, T. Barnes, and E. Sheppard, 501–14. Chichester: Wiley-Blackwell.
Chatterjee, P. 2004. *The Politics of the Governed*. New York: Columbia University Press.
———. 2009. "Editor's Introduction." In *The Small Voice of History: Collected Essays*, edited by R. Guha, 1–18. New Delhi: Permanent Black.
———. 2011. *Lineages of Political Society*. New York: Columbia University Press.
———. 2012. "After Subaltern Studies." *Economic and Political Weekly* 47, no. 37: 44–49.
———. 2013. "Subaltern Studies and *Capital*." *Economic and Political Weekly* 48, no. 37: 69–75.
———. 2016. "Remembering Asok Sen." *Economic and Political Weekly* 50, no. 6: 30–32. New Delhi: Permanent Black.
Chibber, V. 2013. *Post-Colonial Theory and the Spectre of Capital*. London: Verso.
Choudhury, Y. 1995. *Sons of the Empire: Oral History from the Bangladeshi Seamen Who Served on British Ships during the 1939–1945 War*. Birmingham: Sylheti Social History Group.
Clayton, D. 2010. "The Salty Subaltern: Some Theoretical Ports of Call." Keynote Address, Salt Geographies Conference, October, Glasgow University.
Datta Gupta, S. 2011. "History Re-examined: Anti-imperialism, the Communist Party of India and International Communism." In *John Saville: Commitment and History*, edited by D. Howell, D. Kirby, and K. Morgan, 113–31. London: Lawrence and Wishart.
Davies, A. D. 2013. "Identity and the Assemblages of Protest: The Spatial Politics of the Royal Indian Navy Mutiny, 1946." *Geoforum* 48: 24–32.
Davis, M. 1982. "Nuclear Imperialism and Extended Deterrence." In *Exterminism and Cold War*, edited by E. P. Thompson et al., 35–64. London: Verso.

Featherstone, D. J. 2008. *Resistance, Space and Political Identities: The Making of Counter-Global Networks*. Oxford: Wiley-Blackwell.

———. 2012. *Solidarity: Hidden Histories and Geographies of Internationalism*. London: Zed Books.

———. 2014. "Politics." In *The SAGE Handbook of Human Geography*, vol. 2, edited by R. Lee et al., 522–44. London: Sage.

Featherstone, D. J., and P. Griffin. 2016. "Spatial Relations, Histories from Below and the Makings of Agency: *The Making of the English Working Class at Fifty*." *Progress in Human Geography* 40, no. 3: 375–93.

Ghosh, A. 1992. "The Slave of MS.H." *Subaltern Studies* VII: 159–220.

Gidwani, V. 2008. *Capital Interrupted: Agrarian Development and the Politics of Work in India*. Minneapolis: University of Minnesota Press.

Gilroy, P. 1987. *There Ain't No Black In the Union Jack: The Cultural Politics of Race and Nation*. London: Routledge.

———. 1993. *The Black Atlantic*. London: Verso.

Gopal, P. 2004. "Reading Subaltern History." In *Cambridge Companion to Postcolonial Literary Studies*, edited by Neil Lazarus, 139–61. Cambridge: Cambridge University Press.

G. P. D. [Govind Purushottam Deshpande]. 1988. "E. P. Thompson and Eurocentrism." *Economic and Political Weekly* 23, no. 16: n.p.

Griffin, C. 2008. "Protest Practice and (Tree) Cultures of Conflict: Understanding the Spaces of 'Tree Maiming' in Eighteenth- and Early Nineteenth-Century England." *Transactions of the Institute of British Geographers* 33, no. 1: 91–108.

Guha, R. 1982. "On Some Aspects of the Historiography of Colonial India." In *Subaltern Studies* I, 1–7. Delhi: Oxford University Press.

———. 1983. *Elementary Aspects of Peasant Insurgency in Colonial India*. Oxford: Oxford University Press.

———. 1989. "Dominance without Hegemony and Its Historiography." In *Subaltern Studies* VI, 210–309. Delhi: Oxford University Press.

———. 1997. *Dominance without Hegemony: History and Power in Colonial India*. Cambridge, Mass.: Harvard University Press.

———. 2009. *The Small Voice of History: Collected Essays*. New Delhi: Permanent Black.

Hall, S. 1989. "The 'First' New Left and After: Life and Times." In *Out of Apathy*, edited by Oxford University Socialist Discussion Group, 11–38. London: Verso.

———. 2000. "Conclusion: the Multi-Cultural Question." In *Un/settled Multiculturalisms: Diasporas, Entanglements, Transruptions*, edited by B. Hesse, 209–41. London: Zed.

Hamilton, S. 2011. *The Crisis of Theory: E. P. Thompson, the New Left and British Politics*. Manchester: Manchester University Press.

Hobsbawm, E. J. 1959. *Primitive Rebels*. Manchester: Manchester University Press.

Hobsbawm, E. J., and G. Rudé. 1973. *Captain Swing!* Harmondsworth: Penguin.

Høgsbjerg, C. 2011. "Mariner, Renegade and Castaway: Chris Braithwaite, Seamen's Organizer and Pan-Africanist." *Race and Class* 53: 36–57.

———. 2013. *Mariner, Renegade and Castaway: Chris Braithwaite, Seamen's Organizer and Militant Pan-Africanist*. London: Socialist History Society and Redwords.

Hossain, A. 2013. "The World of the Sylheti Seamen in the Age of Empire, from the Late Eighteenth Century to 1947." *Journal of Global History* 9, no. 3: 425–46.

Hume, M. 2009. *The Politics of Violence: Gender, Conflict and Community in El Salvador.* Chichester: Wiley-Blackwell.

Hyslop, J. 1999. "The Imperial Working Class Makes Itself 'White': White Labourism in Britain, Australia, and South Africa before the First World War." *Journal of Historical Sociology* 12, no. 4: 398–421.

———. 2009a. "Steamship Empire: Asian, African and British Sailors in the Merchant Marine c. 1880–1945." *Journal of Asian and African Studies* 44, no. 1: 49–67.

———. 2009b. "Guns, Drugs and Revolutionary Propaganda: Indian Sailors and Smuggling in the 1920s." *South African Historical Journal* 61, no. 4: 838–46.

Jazeel, T. 2011. "Spatializing Difference beyond Cosmopolitanism: Rethinking Planetary Futures." *Theory Culture and Society* 28, no. 5: 75–97.

———. 2014. "Subaltern Geographies: Geographical Knowledge and Post-colonial strategy." *Singapore Journal of Tropical Geography* 35, no. 1: 88–103.

Joshi, C. 2003. *Lost Worlds: Indian Labour and Its Forgotten Histories.* London: Anthem Press.

Kaiwar, V. 2015. *The Post-colonial Orient: The Politics of Difference and the Project of Provincialising Europe.* Chicago: Haymarket Books.

Kothari, U. 2011. "Contesting Colonial Rule: Politics of Exile in the Indian Ocean." *Geoforum* 43, no. 4: 697–706.

Linebaugh, P., and M. Rediker. 2000. *The Many Headed Hydra: Sailors, Slaves and Commoners and the Hidden History of the Revolutionary Atlantic.* London: Verso.

Massey, D. 2005. *For Space.* London: Sage.

Menon, N., and A. Nigam. 2007. *Power and Contestation: India since 1989.* London: Zed Books.

Mezzadra, S. 2016. "How Many Histories of Labour? Towards a Theory of Post-Colonial Capitalism." Available at http://eipcp.net/transversal/0112/mezzadra/en, accessed June 21, 2016.

Moore, D. S. 1998. "Subaltern Struggle and the Politics of Place: Remapping Resistance in Zimbabwe's Eastern Highlands." *Cultural Anthropology* 13, no. 3: 353–81.

Navickas, K. 2011. "Luddism, Incendiarism and the Defence of Rural 'Task-scapes' in 1812." *Northern History* 48, no. 1: 59–73.

Rabasa, J. 2010. *Without History: Subaltern Studies, the Zapatista Insurgency and the Specter of History.* Pittsburgh: University of Pittsburgh Press.

Raza, A., F. Roy, and B. Zachariah. 2015. "Introduction: The Internationalism of the Moment—South Asia and the Contours of the Interwar World." In *The Internationalist Moment: South Asia, Worlds, and World Views, 1917–39*, edited by A. Raza, F. Roy, and B. Zachariah, xi–xli. New Delhi: Sage India.

Sarkar, S. 1998. *Writing Social History* New Delhi: Oxford University Press.

Satia, P. 2016. "Byron, Gandhi and the Thompsons: The Making of British Social History and Unmaking of Indian History." *History Workshop Journal* 81: 135–70.

Saville, J. 2003. *Memoirs of the Left.* London: Merlin Press.

Scott, D. 2004. *Conscripts of Modernity: The Tragedy of Colonial Enlightenment.* Durham, N.C.: Duke University Press.

Scott, J. 1986. "The Common Wind: Currents of Afro-American Communication in the Era of the Haitian Revolution." Unpublished PhD thesis, Department of History, Duke University.

Sharma et al. 1986. "Cancellation of E. P. Thompson's Visit to India." *Economic and Political Weekly* 21, no. 51: 2204.

Shilliam, R. 2015. *Black Pacific: Anti-Colonial Struggles and Oceanic Connections.* London: Bloomsbury Academic.

Spivak, G. C. 1985. "Subaltern Studies: Deconstructing Historiography." In *Subaltern Studies* IV, edited by R. Guha, 330–62. New Delhi: Oxford University Press.

Subramanian, L. 2016. *The Sovereign and the Pirate: Ordering Maritime Subjects in India's Western Littoral.* New Delhi: Oxford University Press.

Tabili, L. 1994. *"We Ask For British Justice": Workers and Racial Difference in Late Imperial Britain.* Ithaca: Cornell University Press.

Thompson, E. P. 1967. "Time, Work-Discipline, and Industrial Capitalism." *Past and Present* 38: 56–97.

———. 1968. *The Making of the English Working Class.* London: Penguin.

———. 1977. *Whigs and Hunters: The Origins of the Black Act.* London: Peregrine Books.

———. 1978. "Eighteenth-Century English Society: Class struggle without Class." *Social History* 3, no. 2: 133–65.

———. 1980. *Writing by Candlelight.* London: Merlin Press.

———. 1994. *Persons and Polemics.* London: Merlin Press.

———. 2014 [1963]. "Where Are We Now?" In *E. P. Thompson and the Making of the New Left: Essays and Polemics,* edited by C. Winslow, 215–48. London: Lawrence and Wishart.

Thompson, E. P., and J. Saville. 1958–59. "John Stuart Mill and E.O.K.A." *New Reasoner* 7: 1–11.

Ulrich, N. 2013. "Internationalism Radicalism, Local Solidarities: The 1797 Mutinies in Southern African Waters." *International Review of Social History* 58: s21, 61–85.

Visram, A. 2002. *Asians in Britain: 400 Years of History.* London: Pluto Press.

Visweswaran, K. 1996. "Small Speeches, Subaltern Gender: Nationalist Ideology and Its Historiography." In *Subaltern Studies IX,* edited by S. Amin and D. Chakrabarty, 83–125. New Delhi: Oxford University Press.

Pachamama, Subaltern Geographies, and Decolonial Projects in Andean Ecuador

SARAH A. RADCLIFFE

High in the Andes, a simple wedding takes place led by a religious-political authority whose acts reproduce meaningful links between subjects defined by their indigeneity, a politics from below, and the landscape around them. Engaging ethnographically with this event, the chapter examines what we might mean by "subaltern geographies" and what implications it might have for the discipline. Subalternity contains many, often disparate, meanings yet is ineluctably a political category, a way of marking a positionality vis-à-vis a hegemonic state and global power, even as it speaks to the diverse positionings of individuals and collectivities jostling to speak back to power. Drawing on ethnographic co-labor in the present, the chapter describes a wedding organized by and for heterogeneous subjects who come together under the banner of Ecuador's diverse Indigenous nationalities to protest territorial and cultural dispossession and denial of epistemic parity (see also Mamani 2011). In their struggles to imagine and realize nonhegemonic futures, Ecuadorian Indigenous movements have engaged a diversity of imaginative geographies, territorializations, and spatialities. Indigenous civil organizations, often in alliance with diverse social and political actors, have long fought for reductions in uneven development and marginalization, attributed to colonial-modern racism and postcolonial state territorial statehood. Some of these territorializations including countermapping and the legal-cartographic strategy to gain rights to collective territories are documented elsewhere (Bryan 2012; Wainwright and Bryan 2009). Building on these insights, this chapter examines subaltern geographies from two angles: firstly in relation to a politics of Pachamama, and secondly in relation to the production of geographical knowledges outside the academy by Indigenous actors. Pachamama refers to a more-than-human energy-agency that encompasses mountains (such as the site of the wedding described here), rocks, water, and other nonhuman agents. Bringing into focus the more-than-human geographies of Pachamama and the embodied processes of knowledge production, systematization, and practice offers, I suggest, important insights into "subaltern territorialization of space—living it, knowing it, claiming it" (Jazeel and Legg, 6).[1] Subaltern geographies of Pachamama moreover challenge geographical understandings of colonial-modern place, power, and difference.

Let us start at the unfixity of subaltern struggles vis-à-vis dominant power, long acknowledged in the South Asian subaltern studies group and Latin American scholarship. Florencia Mallon paraphrases Ranajit Guha to argue that "subordination is a two-way relationship, involving both dominated and dominant" (Mallon 2000, 1526; see also Sharp et al. 2000). Both authors draw on Antonio Gramsci's insights into how

> subaltern groups attempt to influence "dominant political formations" from the start and . . . this critical engagement was crucial to the transformation of both dominant and subaltern political organizations. In response to pressure from below, dominant groups attempt to enlist the cooperation of subalterns through the formation of new reformist political parties. At the same time, when subalterns struggle politically to create their own increasingly autonomous organizations, they do so in dialogue with, and struggle against, dominant political forms. (Mallon 2000, 1527).

Since the emergence of a national Ecuadorian Indigenous confederation in the mid-1980s, Indigenous politics has sought to reclaim ethnic territories, to have dignified lives in multicultural societies, and to gain parity of recognition for languages and knowledges. As elsewhere in Latin America, non-Indigenous governments introduced neoliberal multiculturalism to enlist Indigenous cooperation. The failures of neoliberalism enlivened autonomous organizations, within and beyond Indigenous populations, leading to the rewriting of the constitution in 2008 to proclaim Ecuador a plurinational state, that is, "a state that merges constitutive sovereignty rooted in the national people (pueblo) and Indigenous plurality and self-determination" (Gustafson 2009, 987; on Bolivia's plurination, see Laing, this volume). In the complex interactions among coloniality-modernity, moves to decolonization, and recolonization (Rivera Cusicanqui 2012), Ecuador's plurinational status has nevertheless not brought about substantive reforms regarding Indigenous autonomous territories, rampant extractivism especially in Indigenous-populated areas, and the criminalization of social protest. It is in precisely this context the Andean wedding took place, in what might be interpreted as a moment of reflection on citizenship, on being Indigenous, and on the utility of classic repertoires of engagement with the state. This generates, I argue, a moment at which more-than-human political subjects have been brought into a subaltern politics. Underlying the wedding's practices and human-socionatural interactions described below were the lineaments of a politics undergoing a process of reconfiguration, a repositioning of Indigenous autonomy vis-à-vis the state.

Indigenous positionings in this sense are as deeply historicized subjects, de-essentialized, crosscut by other relations, and connected to—but not subsumed within—the more-than-human (de la Cadena 2015). Subaltern geographies in this sense speak to the attempts to influence dominant political formations, influence indeed that inscribed a nonhegemonic politico-territorial model of plurinationalism into a postcolonial national constitution (Jazeel 2014; Jazeel and Legg, this volume; also Radcliffe 2012 on Ecuador). Reflecting neither ethnic communalism nor a local interruption to rule, Ecuadorian Indigenous subjects reflect the aporia of the subaltern in relation to the containment of Indigenous populations and territories within "a space of obstruction and foreclosure" (de Jong and Mascat 2016, 718). In this context, a framework to discern and analyze those relations that exist beyond the engagement with the state is required. To understand the forms of knowledge and being through which Kichwa actors in central Ecuador come to terms with and think around the impasse they currently face, this chapter draws on Indigenous theory and modernity-coloniality-decoloniality (MCD) approaches. Indigenous theories of settler colonialism argue that the modular form of the modern nation-state is not merely derivative, as postcolonial theory has argued, but rather is engaged in ongoing epistemic undercutting of the sovereignty of prior peoples (Coulthard 2014; Povinelli 2011; Simpson 2015). These insights provide a series of critical lenses for analyzing the nature of subaltern agency, vis-à-vis the state, when those subalterns are Indigenous. MCD approaches are alert to knowledges produced at the margins of coloniality-modernity, seeing in them the seeds for decolonization. Decolonial analysis refers here to a critique of Western claims to universal knowledge and the identification of diverse forms of knowledge and positions regarding the world that serve to provincialize Western knowledge production. Interpreting specific earth-being subjects in a broader subaltern politics of critique, the chapter also seeks to decolonize what Juanita Sundberg identifies as critical geography's colonial readings of socio-natures (Sundberg 2014). Sundberg argues that posthumanist geography "continuously refers to a foundational ontological split between nature and culture as if it is universal . . . which only serves to perpetuate their presumed universality" (2014, 35). To decolonize geography, Sundberg's distinction between posthumanist theory and Indigenous epistemologies sheds light on Eurocentric ontological violence in scholarship and everyday life. By examining the grounded practices, knowledges, and discourses of Kichwa subjects, this chapter documents how Andean Indigenous political practice is relationally constituted with more-than-human earth-beings.[2] As part of over twenty years' ethnographic work in Ecuador, the chapter works up from subaltern knowledges to deepen geography's insights into Indigenous subaltern agency under colonial modernity and postcolonial sovereignty and also explores how subaltern affiliation with more-than-human agency confronts dominant power.

It all starts with the wedding ceremony for two members of the provincial Indigenous federation, namely twenty-year-old Efrain and Valeria,[3] which was held in Ecuador's central Andes. While the ceremony contained practices associated with the Kichwa Puruhá who comprise the province's demographic majority,[4] and was largely conducted in the Kichwa language,[5] the broader Indigenous—as nondominant—political context for the wedding was just as visible. Wedding sponsors and godparents, the officiating leader, and the discourses utilized through the ceremony carried political resonances that speak to long-standing core disputes over land, territory, citizenship, and rights. Nearly three hundred people, among them senior leaders of provincial Indigenous federations and the Andean Kichwa regional confederation (some traveling from Quito 200 kilometers away), attended the two-hour ceremony and a celebratory meal afterward. The organizations represented on that day have, since 1990, led regular impactful and visible demonstrations against postcolonial regimes of rule. Ecuadorian Indigenous protests have used repertoires familiar to political cultures across the world, including occupations in central squares and in front of parliament, filling streets with large numbers of ordinary citizens, and walking from marginal locations to the capital. With that history at the front of their minds, the group gathered on a high grassy knoll in the bright thin mountain air, where a local *yachaq* (Kichwa, lit., "knowledgeable one") led what he called a "natural ceremony." On our way to the wedding, the *yachaq* explained how the wedding returned to a path trodden by ancestors (*abuelos*, Spanish grandparents) in which the hilltop ceremony engaged Indigenous politics and socio-natures (Radcliffe 2017).[6] Not only in its location was this wedding unlike the spectacular mass weddings led by Bolivia's first Indigenous president. In 2011, President Evo Morales officiated at a mass wedding with 355 Indigenous couples as a means to performatively constitute a decolonized state (Postero 2017). By contrast, the Ecuadorian event described here represents a politics *beyond* the state, which, far from being decolonial, appears to Kichwa people to be *reworking colonialism* in violent and new forms. In this specific moment, subaltern geographies are contestations around ontological fault-lines where the relational dynamic of indigeneity with the nation-state and its interests both encloses and forces new connections in meaning, practice, and imaginations for the future.

As Jazeel and Legg outline in the Introduction to this volume, subaltern analytics elicit responsibility and ethics from the researcher and writer, a point with special force in geography with its long history of upholding coloniality-modernity. Through long-standing engagement with the people described here, this chapter reflects a form of "colabor" in which analysis occurred through sustained conversations with individuals and organizations directly involved in the wedding and associated political actions. As an ethnographer and analyst, my work seeks to "take seriously the epistemic perspective/cosmologies/insights of critical thinkers from the Global South, thinking *from* and *with* subalternized racial/ethnic/sexual spaces and bodies" (Grosfoguel 2007, 212, original emphasis). Participants viewed the wedding as an integral part of making a world for themselves—a subaltern geography. Opening up my analysis to the epistemic implications of this Other way of thinking/doing subaltern geographies was facilitated by engagement with Latin American MCD analysis of the coconstitution of coloniality and modernity and its racial, social, and epistemological violence (Mignolo 2000; Quijano 2000). MCD approaches are highly diverse but focus on seeking a locus of enunciation "with and from a subaltern perspective... reading subalternity as a decolonial critique (... a critique of eurocentrism from subalternized and situated knowledges)" (Grosfoguel 2007, 211). MCD's focus on knowledge production emphasizes how Indigenous and other knowledges have been subordinated under coloniality-modernity yet can generate border thinking outside the parameters of metropolitan knowledge (Mignolo 2000).[7] However, MCD's analytical weakness lies in its lack of detailed attention to people's everyday concerns, with an attendant tendency to sweeping generalizations, decontextualized representations of Indigenous knowledge, and distance from real spaces and subjects (Asher 2013; Rivera 2012), failings this chapter seeks to address.

The South Asian subaltern studies project provided important insights into the subaltern subject for Latin American theorists. Citing Indian scholar Veena Das, Walter Mignolo argues that the subaltern "is not a category but rather a perspective" through which to understand "its contractual relations under colonial rules and the 'forms of domination belonging to the structures of modernity'" (Das 1989, in Mignolo 2000, 188). Whereas Gramsci highlighted class hegemony, subalternity in Latin America points to the racialization of divisions of labor, land, resources, and knowledge through allocating Indians (a colonial category par excellence) and African slaves to distinctive sectors while subordinating, dispossessing, and displacing each group (Kobayashi and de Leeuw 2010). Latin American work also highlights the intersectional and interlocking relations of gender, sexuality, location, and generation (Quijano 2000; Rivera 2010). MCD hence sees in subaltern struggles the seeds of a decolonial project, where decoloniality refers to "long-term processes involving the bureaucratic, cultural, linguistic and psychological divesting of colonial power" (Tuhiwai Smith 2010, 33). Ethnographic decolonial work with subaltern subjects can hence examine the colonial present from diverse perspectives while remaining attuned to the ways in which border knowledges incubate decolonial agendas.

A Wedding and Subaltern Politics

What forms of decolonial praxis must one individually and collectively undertake to subvert the interplay between structure and subjectivity that sustain colonial relations over time?
—Glen Sean Coulthard (2014, 140)

This section contextualizes the wedding ceremony in relation to Ecuadorian Indigenous resistance to marginalization and denial of authority, examining the scope of demands, the repertoires used, and the shifting political cultures through which these subaltern forms of organizing are understood and treated within the postcolonial state.

As noted above, from the 1980s diverse organized Indigenous and racialized groups made demands for land and territory, rights to use language and customary justice systems, and state reform. Through massive protests known as *Levantamientos* (uprisings), Indigenous movements have had an undeniable impact on forms of citizenship and statecraft, not least through small yet significant contributions to the 1998 and 2008 constitutions.[8] Ecuador's highways, roads and urban public squares were sites of successive Levantamientos. Uprisings impacting much of the national territory were held in 1990, 1992, 1994, 2000, 2001, and 2006, and a major March for Life and Water was held in 2012. Given the failure of political parties and widespread disillusionment with the political class, the Levantamientos represented an expression of subaltern discontent, within and beyond the self-identifying and internally heterogeneous Indigenous populations (Clark and Becker 2007; Colloredo-Mansfeld 2009). In addition to bringing grievances into the public sphere, protests reflected and contributed to innovative reinterpretations of history from below and nourished anticolonial intellectuals (Mallon 2000; Rivera and Barragán 1997). In Chimborazo province, the Puruhá coordinated across ethnic, class, and regional divides to bring Levantamientos into being across the country. These histories are held and circulated today in the personal memories of events, song lyrics, radio programs, YouTube uploads, and workshop showings of videos of Levantamientos, all part of a subaltern counterpublic (compare Scott 2013).

This range of political repertoires were, throughout the 1980s, the means for Indigenous subjects to organize events that represented hybrid cultural meanings and performatively practiced indigeneity in ways that slipped away from the normative terms approved by elites and state and toward what became known as cultural recuperation. "Cultural revitalization has been fundamental for the articulation of a new indigeneity that is disentangled from stigma, upon which [Indigenous subalterns] could build a new political identity" (Huarcaya 2015, 821). Festivals, part of the warp and weft of small town and rural life in the Andes, became political. The wedding certainly had a festive aspect, incorporating practices that speak to a politicized version of Indigenous cosmovisions. Just below the hill where the wedding was held stood a small whitewashed chapel. As elsewhere in the Andes, Alajahuan materializes colonial histories and postcolonial hybridity in its landscape. Under Spanish colonialism, chapels and churches were built on top of pre-Conquest religious geographies. Alajahuan hill has a small chapel set over an earth-being in a rock-hewn altar. During the ceremony no reference was made to the Catholic chapel, yet participants' hybrid political and daily cultures meld colonial religiosity *and* anticolonial epistemologies. Andean religious syncretism exemplifies postcolonial hybrids of beliefs and complex life trajectories, which make it difficult and unnecessary analytically to separate "little traditions" of earth-beings and popular ritual from "great traditions" of Catholicism and postcolonial state marriage rites (compare Scott 2013; Lyons 1999; see Laing, this volume). At the end of the "natural" ceremony, a suited man (denoting urban authority) read the couple's full names and communities in Kichwa from a printed paper that the couple then signed. Like the majority of her age cohort (unlike earlier generations of women), the bride could write. Everyone relaxed and chatted, breaking up the circle that had enclosed the ceremony. The *yachaq* took pains to explain that the wedding was neither a Catholic ceremony nor a civil marriage. According to my host and the *yachaq*, the wedding crowd included a rare mix of self-identified evangelicals and self-identified Catholic individuals, a fact that pleased both of them.

Colonial modernity's ongoing undercutting of Indigenous sovereignty contextualizes these processes of resistance, as it works to extinguish Indigenous subjects and knowledges and associate them with the past (not the future). The Ecuadorian postcolonial nation-state has done so by organizing territory in ways that bolster and endorse dominant subjects and their sovereignty claims, while relegating diverse subalterns to history and territorial margins (Povinelli 2011; Viatori 2015).[9] Such colonial imaginative and material geographies were subverted, however, with the foundation of the Pachakutik political party, a coalition of various subaltern and left projects. In Kichwa, "Pachakutik" denotes change, rebirth, transformation, and a world "turning upside down."[10] Kichwa ontology views space-time as a spiral (Universidad Amautay Wasi 2008), in which subaltern interjections seek not to stop history (or return, in most cases, to a pristine past) but to reframe coloniality-modernity and raise the promise of decoloniality. No word exists in Kichwa for forward development; although this is sometimes translated as *ñaupaman* (in the sense of getting ahead), and *ñaupa* also refers to that which is anterior (coming before) (Botero 1990). Indigenous peoples refer to Levantamientos as *pachakutik*, signaling how these protests were not merely about interests determined in postcolonial governance but also contest coloniality-modernity's teleology of progress. The district where the wedding took place is distinctive in Chimborazo province, as its Kichwa-speaking residents maintained active, independent organizations and the district has not experienced endless modernist development projects (Tuaza 2009, 140).

One figure whose position in these political-knowledge projects has gained increasing visibility over recent years is the *yachaq*. Having been collected from another district, the *yachaq* explained on the ride to the wedding the ceremony's role in serving to build what he termed a *"nueva conciencia"* (new consciousness/political enlightenment) around Indigenous identity. Consequently, he continued, the movement carries out new rituals and ceremonies that co-produce a renewed and innovative valuation of Indigenous culture and history. Historically, Indigenous ritual specialists operated alongside small towns' mayors and village leaders to coordinate celebrations,[11] yet the spaces, meanings, and publics for these specialist practices have shifted over time. Male and female *yachaq* are more visible now during demonstrations, carrying out rites that strengthen the combined forces behind the protest and confront the racist and exclusionary spaces they occupy. As elsewhere in the Andes,[12] confederations invite female and male *yachaq* "to perform offerings to the sun, moon, and mountains in exchange for protection and guidance, following a ritual orientation around the four cardinal directions" (Huarcaya 2015, 824). Street marches have become sites for reconfiguring subjectivity, culture, and social relations as political interventions Otherwise. The *yachaq*'s presence at the wedding represents a translocation of such activity rather than an invention or expanded territory. The *yachaq* geographies are made and remade through action and response by subaltern and postcolonial power (Guha, in Mallon 2000), transforming quotidian citizenship acts (public demonstrations) away from urban, primarily white, settler colonial norms into a historically and geographically specific repertoire of practices and meanings, interpreted as a "trajectory from submission to assertiveness" (Huarcaya 2015, 809). The criminalization of public protest in Ecuador since 2008 and the excision of indigeneity as a positive symbol from public culture raise questions about the power relations under which such performances occur.[13]

As an earth-being with considerable power and influence, Alajahuan has great significance for people in a large area around it. Alajahuan hosts Carnival celebrations, drawing participants from far and wide.[14] Across the Andes, mountain earth-beings are attributed with varying degrees of agency and geographies of influence, which creates nested hierarchies of reach. Whereas meaningful and nurturing relations between humans and more-than-human earth-beings are understood to rely on Indigenous practices, the situation regarding land is clearly governed by colonial territorial orders of property, settler statehood, and elite domination of legislative processes (Blomley 2003; Povinelli 2011). Ecuador has one of the most unequal land distributions in Latin America, and Chimborazo province is characteristic with its highly skewed and unequal postcolonial land distribution. Claims for land and territory have lain at the heart of Ecuador's Indigenous movements since the 1960s, reflecting the ongoing dispossession and displacement of smallholder farmers by more powerful actors and structural conditions that prevent secure rural livelihoods. Indigenous groups use cartography to support legal claims through the courts through a legal-cartographic strategy (Wainwright and Bryan 2009). However, such countermapping—maps that make visible an Indigenous presence and political demands—has arguably reached its limit due to the stubborn coloniality of territorial, legal, cultural, and cartographic processes (Bryan 2012; Hale 2011; Radcliffe 2011). Despite challenges from rural movements and international pressure to introduce agrarian reform, hegemonic territorialization combines racialization of labor with spatial displacement to produce inequality (Kobayashi and de Leeuw 2010). Neoliberal multiculturalism saw the state recognize a number of larger ethnic territories (Radcliffe 2010a), yet issues of autonomy, decision making over subsoil resources, and distribution of resources remain touchstones of current politics. As a result, Chimborazo's rural households subsist through farming subfamily plots, migrating off-farm for wages, and selling small amounts of goods. At the meal after the wedding, hundreds of us sat outside on recently ploughed fields and were offered plates of *cuy* (guinea-pig) and *máchica* (barley porridge) soup, foods with cultural-political significance that represent a considerable outlay for the wedding sponsors. Kichwa indigeneity is corporeally inscribed through such food. The female provincial leader described the foods as traditional and healthy; as a women's leader, she knew that Indigenous village women who are the majority of foodstuff producers have actively promoted food sovereignty as part of plurinational agendas.

Echoing South Asian subaltern studies scholars, Bolivian intellectual Silvia Rivera Cusicanqui argues that "the condition of possibility for an Indigenous hegemony is located in the territory of the modern nation—inserted into the contemporary world" and linked into heterogeneous urban spaces (Rivera 2012, 95; also Mamani Ramírez 2011). It is on this basis that Ecuador's diverse Indigenous movements took part in the constituent assembly that was to rewrite the national constitution. During the process, the national Indigenous confederation CONAIE and its allies inserted a proposal for official recognition of the Kichwa and Shuar languages and for Ecuador to be proclaimed a plurinational state (Becker 2010; Jameson 2011). These measures were incorporated into the constitutional text. Since that time, however, the political situation suggests the ongoing undermining of Indigenous subjectivity. The terrain upon which Indigenous subalterns can intervene shifted rapidly under the government of Rafael Correa (2006–17), which promised a "citizens' revolution" and twenty-first-century socialism that proclaims "a plurinational and multicultural state, [with] equal opportunities for our peoples" (Ecuador 2014). Across the country, civic organizations including Indigenous federations protested against government plans for centralized resource management, reform of water resources, and land access. Just over a year later, Indigenous leaders headed an eight-hundred-kilometer march from the southern Amazonian region to Ecuador's capital city, joining forces with crowds of around 200,000 people.

Subaltern Knowledge and Subaltern Intellectuals

If subaltern geographies are to de-essentialize and contextualize marginalized positionalities, the practices and actions of individuals are key. Hence this section describes individual members (not "representative") of Ecuador's Indigenous movement (a *yachaq*, a lawyer, and a female leader) to demonstrate how their processes of political organizing, network creation, and knowledge production contribute to Indigenous geographies that combine political claims through public politics and cosocial reproduction with Pachamama. As self-identifying Indigenous subjects, the leaders' biographies highlight three dimensions of Ecuadorian Indigenous struggles over geography in relation to political-administrative autonomy and customary justice; food sovereignty and justice, and human/more-than-human thriving. Extending subaltern studies' insights into autonomous subaltern organizing, the section draws on MCD theory to explore how Indigenous movement actors are producers of border thinking and epistemologies. Examining the movement's situated production of subaltern geographies highlights how border thinking arises in autonomous, multiple, and interconnected spaces of knowledge production outside state spaces of learning.

Now in his late forties, Faramundo acted as the *yachaq* in the Alajahuan ceremony. The term *yachaq* refers to someone with *yachay*, knowledge and wisdom, whose capacities make them intermediaries and authorities. *Yachaq* work with mountains, mediating between humans and earth-beings, the latter associated with indigeneity and separate from Hispanic social meanings (Lyons 1999, 39, 40).[15] In common with many Ecuadorian Indigenous leaders, Faramundo has pursued a varied trajectory through political organizing and wage earning, tracking back and forth between "mainstream" and "Indigenous" knowledge-producing spaces. Trained initially as a state teacher, he specialized in education management. Working in intercultural bilingual education for the state,[16] he continuously furthered his understanding of political alternatives through popular education at local associations, nongovernmental organizations, and Indigenous federation workshops. Hence while a *yachaq* embodies authority and skill for intermediating with Pachamama, the subaltern geographies producing such responsibility and connections to Pachamama are also institutionalized in subaltern spaces.[17] In other words, the subaltern geographies described in relation to the wedding refer to more than one world and less than two (de la Cadena 2015). Three *yachaq* currently work in Chimborazo province. In some parts of Chimborazo and southern Cañar province, *yachaq* are believed to be born with their abilities and cry in the womb. During our car ride, one leader spoke skeptically of how when Indigenous medicine was finally recognized in the 1998 constitution, there was a sudden boom in "*yachaq*," which cast doubt on their authenticity and formal qualifications. However, as he pointed out, Faramundo took courses in Andean agronomy and medicine at an independent institute in Chimborazo province that previously was affiliated with the Indigenous University in Quito (the latter closed in 2013). The Jatun Yachay Wasi (Kichwa, "Advanced Knowledge Building") describes itself as dedicated to Andean Indigenous knowledges for holistic development in harmony with Pachamama.[18] The institute's 350 students attend classes on a part-time basis, twice a month on Saturday and Sunday.[19] The Jatun Yachay Wasi runs programs on Andean agriculture, Andean construction, and social work in addition to Andean medicine; it is through the latter course that Faramundo trained as a *yachaq*. The course on Andean medicine includes topics of healing, disease prevention, health education, foodstuffs, and historic forms of Andean medicine.

Another figure present at the wedding was Nicodemo, a lawyer trained in mainstream law and an advocate and professional in customary law. Indigenous groups were granted the right to practice customary law in the 1998 constitution. I had met Nicodemo in this capacity previously at workshops to explain the procedures of customary law to rural Kichwa. According to Nicodemo, who hails from an Indigenous nationality in the southern Andes, all Indigenous rights granted by the nation-state are difficult to implement, although he is constantly talking to colleagues about how to best realize their potential. He spoke eloquently on the way to the wedding about how local legal specialists can be trained to take on cases under customary law in coordination with local Indigenous associations, as has already begun with three nationalities. Dressed in distinctive short trousers and a cotton shirt, Nicodemo talks about how Indigenous justice systems comprise a hybrid of human rights, international law, and women's rights and thereby generate judicial pluralism within the national territory. However, his main worry is how customary justice becomes embroiled in colonial-modern forms of distinction that condemn subaltern violence while condoning state violence.

Beatriz was central to my understanding of the wedding and wider subaltern politics. As an elected women's representative for the provincial Indigenous federation, Beatriz highlights the ongoing legacies of colonial exclusion, especially for low-income rural, racialized women. As Andean Indigenous women have documented over recent years, colonial modernity creates interlocking hierarchies of race, gender, class, and sexuality (Choque 1998; Rivera 2010). Like Indigenous female leaders across Ecuador (Radcliffe 2010b), Beatriz pursued education in nonstandard spaces and only completed secondary school in her early thirties, having attended Saturday school for years. Popular education and the radical Catholic church in turn provided networks through which she learnt about grassroots organizing and traveled abroad. As one born and raised in a small village, Beatriz's positionality and forms of theorizing speak to the political organization and ontological questioning traced above. Her political horizon and allies have shifted several times; she retains a commitment to liberation theology but left the church over a priest's rape of an Indigenous young woman. In common with Chimborazo's low-income rural Indigenous women (Radcliffe 2015), she struggles against communal and federation patriarchies to voice unique political perspectives. Beatriz attended the Andean federation women's training center to learn about assertiveness, the Kichwa language, the history of the Kichwa people, anthropology, and project management. Encouraged by a nun to "recover her culture," Beatriz began to wear clothing associated with female indigeneity despite family opposition (compare Radcliffe 2000). Subsequently she moved through a series of increasingly senior roles in the regional church and ethnic federation, consolidating agency in part by producing knowledge linked to subaltern organizing. Viewing embodiment, knowledge, and decoloniality as inseparable, Beatriz completed a thesis at Colta University on healing plants. She also promotes decolonial Indigenous feminism with a parish women's association that seeks Indigenous women's interpretation of a dignified life together with Pachamama. Always wishing to further embody decolonial understandings of the world, she spoke about wanting to train in Andean medicine at "Amautay Wasi."

These leaders—organic intellectuals—represent three facets of Indigenous autonomous organizing for territory and autonomy within a plurination of rights. Between them they combine expertise in border knowledges in building relations with Pachamama, practicing judicial-political power in Indigenous areas, and establishing just relations of social reproduction (gender politics, health systems, and food sovereignty). Kichwa subalterns continuously reflect on and recalibrate the processes of knowledge production by which to understand their autonomous and marginal position. Their life histories contribute to a richer analysis of voice, subjectivity, and positionality with MCD theorization (Asher 2013), which in turn suggest important lessons for the analysis of subaltern geographies. First, territorializations (Jazeel and Legg, this volume) are not merely abstract programs but take embodied, cumulative form in specific subjects. Second, subaltern geographies are in this case actively produced, contemplated, and bound up with complex autonomous institutional and personal trajectories of knowledge production. Subaltern geographies—as a set of imaginaries, as programmatic makings of place and spatial relations, and as a routinized set of practices for their reproduction—are in this case produced by the subalterns in question in spaces and relations that exist autonomously and outside the spaces of mainstream academia. The Andean case modestly suggests thereby that subaltern geographies encompass—and hence need to reflect critically on—the spaces between academia and Other spaces of knowledge production. Decolonial, collaborative, and ethnographic practices of analysis provide important tools in this regard. We now turn to examine the political ontology around which this form of border thinking has been articulated.

Weddings, Pachamama, and Contested Political Ontologies

During the wedding ceremony, people were quiet, whispering and silencing children and dogs although teenage boys disrupted the edges of the crowd. Beatriz, Faramundo, and Nicodemo stood in the center of the four mats decorated with fruit, rose petals, and food, a *cruz andina* (Andean cross) that represents an infinite cosmos and provides a transfer point between human and the more-than-human. The bride's shawl and groom's poncho were placed within the *cruz*, which also contained items permitting the *yachaq* to interact with the *pampa* or landscape and its sentient earth-beings. Surrounded by lit candles, the *yachaq* led interactions with Pachamama by blowing a conch shell and speaking out in every cardinal direction, followed by participants who turned and repeated his words. Indigenous groups were named to each direction, and connections were signaled between Kichwa, Puruhá, and Ecuadorian *runa* (Kichwa, people) with populations across Abya Yala.[20] Later, another leader read the Popol Vuh[21] to evoke Indigenous relationality with the earth and nonhuman agency.

Choosing the site of Alajahuan for the wedding was not coincidental; for Kichwa people the hill is a powerful earth-being or *apu*. Pachamama and mountain earth-beings' agency elicit periodic cycles of human/more-than-human interactions. This section examines what it means for the political event of the wedding to be carried out on—and in interaction with—an earth-being. The section argues that the wedding was not only a sociopolitical choreographing of multiscalar interactions between Indigenous leaders, federation members, and Indigenous society but also a political-ontological practice whereby the *yachaq*, invited authorities, participants, and Alajahuan itself enacted a politics that goes beyond the colonial-modern political sphere. It suggests that in pursuit of greater political autonomy in the current context of criminalization and unforthcoming legal-constitutional reform, the political ontology of Pachamama represents an Other story (see Jazeel and Legg following Guha, this volume).

Pachamama has been invoked in public protests from at least the 1990s in Ecuador and Peru (de la Cadena 2010; Sawyer 2004, 211). Pachamama and its telluric powers inhere not in human subjects but in human relations across an expansive terrain that includes heathlands (*páramo*), mountains, water sources, and rocks. Pachamama and mountain earth-beings have agency regarding human and animal life, requiring periodic cycles of interactions—mediated through socionatural items and embodied gestures—to induct fruitful and sustained relations across forms of sentient being. Human interactions with earth-beings coconstitute life, including animal fertility and the relations through which reproduction can be ordered and balanced. Although such interactions are traced by scholars back to pre-Columbian history, more notable here is their maintenance today by political organizations during struggles with a postcolonial state hegemony. Mountains are not simply benign in relations with humans; they are ambivalent agents capable of harm, discord, and destruction depending on the web of human/more-than-human relations around them (Reinhard 1985, 310). While some mountain earth-beings become the site for punishment for violent landlords after death, they are also associated with possession, animal infertility, and wasting. Mountains can be male or female; spring water on female mountains is symbolically linked to mother's milk (Boelens 2015, 102). Mountain earth-beings also marry: Chimborazo peak is sometimes said to be the husband of (female) volcano Tungurahua (Lyons 1999, 38). Kichwa weddings are often held at the start of the irrigation season, a time when the marriage of apus and Pachamama generates water (Boelens 2015, 102).[22] The wedding ceremony was grounded in established practices common in Indigenous protests described above but was not enacted in a space visible to the national political community.

At a conjuncture when neither constitutional change nor Indigenous movements' legal-cartographic strategies have resulted in significant shifts in power for Indigenous peoples in Ecuador, it is important to pause and ask how the political terrain of positioning, contestation, and authority is being reconfigured in open-ended ways with no clear prospects. The malleability of subaltern claims and priorities hence speaks neither to intrinsic limits within the subaltern category qua political actor nor to the fixity of colonial-modern power but to the contingent articulations of power and difference found in a near-hegemonic situation. Pachamama continues in parallel to, and beyond, the Ecuadorian postcolonial nation-state. Despite the capacity of insurgent diverse subaltern and environmental activism to establish rights *for* Nature/Pachamama in the 2008 constitution, the operability and status of Pachamama rights continue to be foreclosed by dominant epistemic and political economic relations. Accordingly, for the autonomous Indigenous movement, Pachamama retains a radically open possibility whose meanings and agency are carefully made to attach to specific subjects, places, and proposals. Pachamama politics as exhibited at the wedding "are not spectacles geared to achieve the ulterior purposes that our [colonial-modern] categories allow us to imagine (control of resources, political positioning, and so on). They are doing worlds themselves" (Blaser 2013, 558). Pachamama and Alajahuan earth-beings comprise a register of Indigenous struggles, no less or more "authentic" than Levantamientos.

In drawing out the political ontology of which the wedding provides one node we extend and deepen our analytical purchase on the dynamics between the subaltern and hegemony. In its current Andean significance, indigeneity—including, but not reducible to, relations with earth-beings—comprises "a complex formation, the articulation of more than one but less than two, socionatural worlds" (de la Cadena 2010, 347). In this case, Pachamama articulates an Indigenous (earth-)being that is more than the colonial-modern political system—a postconstitutional impasse with multiple fault-lines—and yet is inextricably connected to that same colonial-modern system, being brought into Indigenous autonomous organizing to enhance Indigenous voice and agency. Pachamama then is intrinsically and deeply historical and geographical—a specific being brought into conjunctural political contestations by specific Indigenous actors, using particular combinations of practice, knowledge, and voice, in carefully chosen sites. Thus it is more than one politics but less than two worlds. The wedding and the political ontology of which it comprises one moment of ongoing subaltern organizing represent forms of territorialization of space, living it and claiming it, produced through that partial connection (Strathern 2004). The practices and subjectivities enacted at the wedding denied a separation of nature and politics, of human and more-than-human, and of state governmentality. As noted by anthropologist Marisol de la Cadena, "The appearance of earth beings in social protests may evince a moment of rupture of [colonial-]modern politics ... an insurgence of Indigenous forces and practices with the capacity to significantly disrupt prevalent political formations, and reshuffle hegemonic antagonisms, first and foremost by rendering illegitimate (and thus denaturalizing) the exclusion of Indigenous practices from nation-state institutions" (2010, 336; compare Byrd and Rothberg 2011, 4).

Moreover, the Pachamama politics articulated in Chimborazo addresses Indigenous sovereignty and ongoing survival. Under constraints on organizing, the capacity of the Indigenous movement to provide representation for subaltern subjects becomes central. The wedding ceremony provided a choreographed series of practices and emphasized ties and moral-political injunctions through which seasonal, annual, and generational social reproduction of (Indigenous) people and (human/more-than-human) places were brought into being. As in regular weddings, parental and quasi-parental dynamics informed the corporeal and discursive engagements between the young couple and their parents.[23] Historically in Chimborazo, the surviving parents act as the couple's godparents for the wedding (Botero 1990, 145); by contrast, this event's inclusion of elected provincial and Andean leaders forged quasi-familial ties across wider territories. Marriage godparents have ritual obligations to house the newly married couple until they find their own home and to provide them with the means for conjugal life, including tools and animals, in return for obligations to work harmoniously. Godparent relations in principle inaugurate a series of ties through which to reproduce sociality and space in high-altitude, smallholding farms in poorly provisioned settlements with limited public facilities. The Alajahuan wedding emphasized sociospatial reproduction of *political* communities, with leaders' mantle passed symbolically to younger generations in the Indigenous movement. *Yachaq* Faramundo explained how the couple were embarking on *servinakuy*, when a couple is incorporated into a community and a wider family. Whereas liberal modernity seeks to individuate subjects and provide freedom from attachment (Povinelli 2011), the Alajahuan wedding *reaffirmed* attachments to familial, federation, and more-than-human relations.

According to anthropologist Elizabeth Povinelli, settler colonial states deny first nations' sovereignty in order to thereby establish themselves at the starting point as "originary" settlers—a form of governmentality she calls the "governance of the prior" (Povinelli 2011). Postcolonial governance of the prior inaugurates a territorialization that systematically undercuts Indigenous sovereignty and presence, shaping the scope of Indigenous engagement with the state. Under this form of rule, Indigenous prior inhabitation is unacknowledgable yet continues to haunt postcolonial sovereignty and territory. Despite colonial-modern attempts to banish the prior, a "palpable spectre [continues,] haunting state sovereignty" (Povinelli 2011, 21). In the Andean context, earth-beings are powerful specters as their "presence in politics disavows the separation between nature and humanity" on which liberal politics rests (de la Cadena 2010, 342).[24] Extending subaltern studies into an engagement with Indigenous theory draws attention to the profoundly shifting ground upon which subaltern politics might be founded.

As a riposte to the governance of the prior, the Alajahuan wedding and its political ontology brought Pachamama into subaltern political organizing in ways that fundamentally challenged the governance of the prior. Not only do the wedding's earth-beings reaffirm forms of attachment—federation, more-than-human, familial—but so too Pachamama was invoked at a moment when the dispute over Indigenous sovereignty comprised the crux of tensions between the postcolonial state and Indigenous movements. Indigenous organizations in alliance with environmentalists and diverse others are currently disputing government laws, policies, and interventions that extend and deepen hydrocarbon extraction in Indigenous lands. State rights to subsoil resources trump Indigenous titles every time, paradigmatically illustrating the governance of the prior (compare Laing, this volume). As one part of Indigenous repertoires of protest, the politics of Pachamama stands for what I term a politics of anteriority, namely an insurgent questioning of dominant designations of Indigenous/subaltern as only in the past and the claims of a *living* subaltern (compare de Jong and Mascat 2016, 722). According to this interpretation, the politics of anteriority performs and brings into being Indigenous attachment to and claim over (living) territory, which is positioned as partially connected to the liberal public yet simultaneously constitutes itself as beyond/outside that very public. The epistemologies and practices at the wedding evidence, but by no means designate completely, a politics of anteriority, a leveraging of Pachamama's more-than-human power to push beyond constraints imposed by the governance of the prior. In Chimborazo, earth-beings provincialize the colonial-modern ontology of politics and the hierarchical designation of the subjects who rule, those who are ruled, and those whose political subjectivity is entirely denied. Earth-beings coconstituted with subaltern subjects produce political ethics, forms of mutual aid and livelihoods that speak to political imaginaries and agendas that exceed the political terrain occupied by the postcolonial state and its standard opponents, "an otherness that resists containment" (Prakash 2000, 293).

Conclusion

This chapter has examined the territorializations, claims, and ways of life of Indigenous movements in the Ecuadorian central Andes. Its analytical starting point is situated at the unstable boundary between subaltern political organizations and their practices and a settler postcolonial state. It asks why a wedding should be held outside a church, on a hilltop, with leaders of Indigenous provincial and Andean federations and contextualizes the answers in relation to four registers of subaltern organizing in Chimborazo among Kichwa people. First, it examined the ways in which Indigenous repertoires, spaces, and claims of protest have long articulated claims for territory, land, title, and rights, which have seen partial translation into legislation and political settlements, while closing off wider recognition of plurinational territorial imaginaries and proposals. Second, it explored how these territorializations have increasingly been articulated through public enactment of relations with Pachamama, as occurred in the wedding. Third, by means of short individual biographies, the chapter analyzed the ways in which border thinking around politics occurs across multiple interconnected spaces of systematic knowledge production. And finally, examining the wedding as a political ontology brought into focus how Pachamama politics represents a politics of anteriority that directly engages with postcolonial settler claims to sovereignty.

This decolonial reading of spatialities and political projects highlights the insights from ethnography into subaltern engagements with—and struggles against—colonial modern political power, however partial and compromised those insights might be. Ethnographies of subaltern organizing in the colonial present provide testimony of how diverse subjects engage in ongoing processes of criticizing and theorizing colonial modernity. Ethnographic engagement resituates border knowledges, not as unmoored abstraction but rather as organizational and personal histories of knowledge creation, flexible repertoires of action, and subtle readings and theorization of context, thereby overcoming MCD's tendency to generalized abstractions of subaltern projects as fragmented and inaccessible. Subaltern studies, feminist geography, MCD theorists, and critical geographers all build on an acknowledgment of the loci of enunciation in knowledge production and in political action. Working alongside Indigenous intellectuals and knowledgeable subjects permits—in circumstances of sustained engagement on the one hand, and pragmatic calculations regarding a Western researcher's utility on the other—insights into what would otherwise be largely invisible configurations of subaltern practice. Yet in this exchange, as in others I participate in, the question is not one of metropolitan access followed by theorizing in the name of a scholarly endeavor of canon building. Rather, it is a coproduction—a colabor—of making geographies, making knowledges about/in those geographies, and devising theories to move toward a never-fixed decoloniality. Such ethnographies offer the possibility of deepening critical geography's understandings of subaltern geographies.

Although Ecuador's new constitution reflects vibrant subaltern organizing, it has proven unequal to the task of bringing about structural change in the postcolonial settler nation-state. Plurinationalism and Pachamama have been presented here as repertoires of Andean political action that can be read within the frames of subaltern studies. Yet the combination of Indigenous theory and decolonial more-than-human analysis provide useful grounds to explore the ways in which subaltern organizing in this case bypasses and thereby reveals the empirical and analytical impossibility of containing analysis within the frame of colonial-modern state politics, while at the same time highlighting the paradoxical necessity of reading subaltern geographies precisely in relation to that very same state politics. Exploring the resonances of the Chimborazo wedding suggests that Indigenous movements have mobile terms of reference by which to contest colonial-modern state power. Specifically, the wedding's meanings and practices hint at the ways in which Pachamama politics responds to the historical-geographical configuration of state hegemony founded on settler colonial sovereignty. The Indigenous movement's politics of anteriority necessarily engages with Pachamama as a partially connected ontology whose agency and meanings refer back to the specific articulations of postcolonial state hegemony. Demands for a plurination—sovereignty rooted in indigenous plurality and self-determination—in this sense resonate not merely with a reform process but additionally by ontologically expanding the category of citizen.

NOTES

I am extremely grateful to Penelope Anthias, Álvaro Bello, Tariq Jazeel, Steve Legg, and Sofia Zaragocín for thoughtful and detailed comments on early drafts of the chapter.

1. Indigenous peoples are not automatically subaltern as indigeneity is a field of power that defines subjects and groups in opposition to colonial-modern state power and epistemologies. Indigeneity has uncertain meanings in colonial and postcolonial imaginaries (Byrd and Rothberg 2011, 9; Radcliffe 2015b). In Ecuador being (seen as) Indigenous is strongly associated with racialization, impoverishment, lesser political authority, and prejudged relations with modernity. I use the concept of indigeneity as an analytics to reveal the underside of the postcolonial state, spaces of abandonment, and the fictions of inclusion.

2. "More-than-human" here refers to Andean ethnographies of indigenous cosmopolitics (rather than Actor Network Theory or posthumanism); the term "earth-being" is de la Cadena's (2010).

3. I give individuals pseudonyms and disguise places to respect social realities and political circumstances.

4. Ecuador's coordinated and multistranded Indigenous movement recognizes fourteen ethnocultural groups. The Kichwa nationality includes the Puruhá pueblo, and the majority are bilingual in Kichwa and Spanish.

5. State schooling through much of the twentieth century attempted to literally beat Spanish into Indigenous children.

6. I was invited by a representative of the provincial Indigenous federation, herself a sponsor of the rites; my daughter and I were the only non-Ecuadorians present. My research in the central Andes began nearly twenty years ago; my closer and more sustained interaction with this federation and its leaders began in 2008.

7. MCD identified power relations creating subalternized knowledges *before* Foucault identified the "insurrection of subjugated knowledges" (cited in Mignolo 2000, 21).

8. It is beyond the scope of this chapter to give full justice to the extensive and significant Indigenous revolts and protests that have punctuated colonial and republican history across the Andean countries of Ecuador, Peru, and Bolivia. Needless to say, these histories and other countries have garnered considerable academic attention in history, ethnohistorical studies, and political sciences.

9. Povinelli (2011) argues that these relative positions in space-time play over into the tenses through which subjects are described.

10. Founded in 1996, the party's full name is Movimiento de Unidad Plurinacional Pachakutik—Nuevo País (Pachakutik Movement of Plurinational Unity—New Country (and on an earlier *pachakutik* see Huarcaya 2015, 816).

11. Indigenous authorities known as *curacas* conducted indigenous wedding rites in the northern Andes up until the mid-twentieth century (Korovkin 2001, 47).

12. In Bolivia, public offerings are made to Pachamama in antiprivatization protests (de la Cadena 2010, 337; Perreault 2006).

13. *Non*indigenous subjects also engage in spectacular and affective performances to rework spatialities (Fabricant and Postero 2013; Huarcaya 2015; Schurr 2013).

14. Alajahuan hosts several processions during the year, including Carnival, for residents of nearby towns and villages (Guashpa 2012, 54; and as evidenced by YouTube).

15. Earlier in postcolonial history *curacas* (Kichwa, "Indigenous intermediary") in Chimborazo took the name "mountain" or a specific peak: "the Puruhá *curaca* of Xunxi could have been called by the homonym of the Chimborazo mountain" (Moreno and Borchart 2010, 21). Chimborazo mountain (the province's highest) is today sometimes imagined with European dress and features, reflecting postcolonial embodiments of power.

16. In the mid-1980s, intercultural bilingual education was established in the ministry of education under indigenous management.

17. Indigenous scholar Waskar Ari (2014) discusses the coproduction of Aymara leadership, ritual practices, and strands of organized religion in struggles over land, territory, and autonomy.

18. On Jatun Yachay Wasi, see Instituto Tecnológico Superior Jatun Yachay Wasi, "Informativo," 2018, http://www.jatunyw.edu.ec/, accessed July 25, 2018.

19. Established in 2000, the institute has trained around twenty-five hundred people for public and private hospitals, built community halls, and encouraged a grassroots economy. On Jatun Yachay Wasi's philosophy, see Instituto Tecnológico Superior Jatun Yachay Wasi, "Somos Jatun—Filosofía institucional," 2018, http://www.jatunyw.edu.ec/index.php/intro.

20. Abya Yala is an indigenous name for South America, and this imaginative geography became important in transnational activism for the 500th anniversary of Columbus's arrival in the Americas.

21. The Popol Vuh is a Central American mytho-history, written down in K'ich'e and Spanish in the eighteenth century.

22. Local people collect earth from Alajahuan hill for irrigating (Guashpa 2012, 54).

23. I was told later they gave advice on how to work hard, share food and work, and not be lazy.

24. Likewise this more-than-human politics challenges subaltern studies distinctions between (state/political class) hegemony and subalternity (de la Cadena 2010, 343).

REFERENCES

Ari, Waskar. 2014. *Earth Politics: Religion, Decolonization and Bolivia's Indigenous Intellectuals*. London: Duke University Press.

Asher, K. 2013. "Latin American Decolonial Thought, or Making the Subaltern Speak." *Geography Compass* 7, no. 12: 832–42.

Blaser, Mario. 2013. "Ontological Conflicts and the Stories of People in Spite of Europe." *Current Anthropology* 54, no. 5: 547–68.

Blomley, Nicholas. 2003. "Law, Property, and the Geography of Violence: The Frontier, the Survey, and the Grid." *Annals of the Association of American Geographers* 93, no. 1: 121–41.

Boelens, Rutgerd. 2015. *Water, Power and Identity: The Cultural Politics of Water in the Andes*. London: Routledge.

Botero, L. F. 1990. *Chimborazo de los Indios*. Quito: Abya Yala.

Bryan, Joe. 2012. "Rethinking Territory: Social Justice and Neoliberalism in Latin America's Territorial Turn." *Geography Compass* 6, no. 4: 215–26.

Choque, María Eugenia. 1998. "Colonial Domination and the Subordination of the Indigenous Woman in Bolivia." *Modern Fiction Studies* 44, no. 1: 10–23.

Clark, Kim, and Mark Becker. Eds. 2007. *Indigenous Peoples and State Formation in Modern Ecuador*. Pittsburgh: University of Pittsburgh Press.

Colloredo-Mansfeld, Rudi. 2009. *Fighting Like a Community: Andean Civil Society in an Era of Indian Uprisings*. Chicago: University of Chicago Press.

Coulthard, G. S. 2014. *Red Skin, White Masks: Rejecting the Colonial Politics of Recognition*. Minneapolis: University of Minnesota Press.

Das, Veena. 1989. "Subaltern as Perspective." *Subaltern Studies* 6: 310–24.

de Jong, Sara, and J. Mascat. 2016. "Relocating Subalternity." *Cultural Studies* 30, no. 5: 717–29.

de la Cadena, Marisol. 2010. "Indigenous Cosmopolitics in the Andes: Conceptual Reflections beyond 'Politics.'" *Cultural Anthropology* 25, no. 2: 334–70.

Fabricant, Nicole, and Nancy Postero. 2013. "Contested Bodies, Contested States: Performance, Emotions, and New Forms of Regional Governance in Santa Cruz, Bolivia." *Journal of Latin American and Caribbean Anthropology* 18, no. 2: 187–211.

Grosfoguel, Ramón. 2007. "The Epistemic Decolonial Turn: Beyond Political Economic Paradigms." *Cultural Studies* 21, nos. 2–3: 211–23.

Guashpa, N. C. 2012. "Un centro de interpretación cultural para el centro turístico Pucara Tambo, Parroquia Cacha, Cantón Riobamba, Provincia de Chimborazo. Escuela Superior Politécnica de Chimborazo." Unpublished BA thesis in Ecotourism. Riobamba.

Gustafson, B. 2009. *New Languages of the State: Indigenous Resurgence and the Politics of Knowledge in Bolivia*. Durham, N.C.: Duke University Press.

Huarcaya, S. M. 2015. "Performativity, Performance and Indigenous Activism in Ecuador and the Andes." *Comparative Studies in Society and History* 57, no. 3: 806–837.

Jameson, K. 2011. "The Indigenous Movement in Ecuador: The Struggle for a Plurinational State." *Latin American Perspectives* 38, no. 1: 63–73.

Jazeel, Tariq. 2014. "Subaltern Geographies: Geographical Knowledge and Postcolonial Strategy." *Singapore Journal of Tropical Geography* 35: 88–103.

Kobayashi, Audrey, and Sara de Leeuw. 2010. "Colonialism and Tensioned Landscapes of Indigeneity." In *SAGE Handbook of Social Geographies*, edited by S. J. Smith, R. Pain, S. A. Marston, and J. P. Jones III, 118–38. London: Sage.

Korovkin, Tanya. 2001. "Reinventing the Communal Tradition: Indigenous Peoples, Civil Society and Democratization in Andean Ecuador." *Latin American Research Review* 36, no. 3: 37–67.

Latin American Subaltern Studies Group. 1993. "Founding Statement." *boundary 2* 20, no. 3: 110–21.

Lyons, B. 1999. "Taita Chimborazo and Mama Tungurahua: A Quichua Song, a Fieldwork Story." *Anthropology and Humanism* 24, no. 1: 32–46.

Mallon, Florencia. 2000. "The Promise and Dilemma of Subaltern Studies: Perspectives from Latin American History." In *Postcolonialism: Critical Concepts in Literary and Cultural Studies*, edited by D. Brydon, 1524–53. London: Routledge.

Mamani Ramirez, Pablo. 2011. "Cartographies of Indigenous Power: Identity and Territoriality in Bolivia." In *Remapping Bolivia: Resources, Territory, and Indigeneity in a Plurinational State*, edited by N. Fabricant and B. Gustafson, 30–95. Santa Fe, N.Mex.: School for Advanced Research Press.

Mignolo, Walter. 2000. *Local Histories/Global Designs: Coloniality, Subaltern Knowledges and Border Thinking*. Princeton, N.J.: Princeton University Press.

Moreno, S., and C. Borchart. 2010. "Los Andes ecuatoriales entre la estética y la ciencia: Las catorce láminas relativas al Ecuador en la obra *Vues des Cordillères et Monuments des Peuples Indigènes de l'Amérique* de Alexander von Humboldt." *Internationale Zeitschrift für Humboldt Studien* 20: 42–74.

Perreault, Thomas. 2006. "From the *Guerra Del Agua* to the *Guerra Del Gas*: Resource Governance, Neoliberalism and Popular Protest in Bolivia." *Antipode* 38, no. 1: 150–72.

Postero, Nancy. 2017. *The Indigenous State: Race, Politics and Performance in Plurinational Bolivia*. Berkeley: University of California Press.

Povinelli, Elizabeth. 2005. "A Flight from Freedom." In *Postcolonial Studies and Beyond*, edited by A. Loomba, 145–65. Durham, N.C.: Duke University Press.

———. 2011. *Economies of Abandonment: Social Belonging and Endurance in Late Liberalism.* Durham, N.C.: Duke University Press.

Prakash, Gyan. 2000. "The Impossibility of Subaltern History." *Nepantla: Views from the South* 1, no. 2: 287–93.

Quijano, Aníbal. 2000. "Coloniality of Power." *Nepantla: Views from the South* 1, no. 3: 533–80.

Radcliffe, Sarah A. 2000. "Entangling Resistance, Ethnicity, Gender and Nation in Ecuador." In *Entanglements of Power*, edited by J. Sharp, P. Routledge, C. Philo, and R. Paddison, 164–81. London: Routledge.

———. 2010a. "Re-mapping the Nation: Cartography, Geographical Knowledge and Ecuadorean Multiculturalism." *Journal of Latin American Studies* 42: 293–323.

———. 2010b. "Epílogo: Historias de vida de mujeres indígenas a través de la educación y el liderazgo: Intersecciones de raza, género y locación." In *Celebraciones centenarias y negociaciones por la nación ecuatoriana*, edited by V. Coronel and M. Prieto, 317–48. Quito: FLACSO.

———. 2011. "Third Space, Abstract Space and Coloniality: National and Subaltern Cartography in Ecuador." In *Postcolonial Spaces: The Politics of Place in Contemporary Culture*, edited by A. Teverson and S. Upstone, 129–45. Basingstoke: Palgrave.

———. 2012. "Development for a Postneoliberal Era? *Sumak Kawsay*, Living Well and the Limits to Decolonization in Ecuador." *Geoforum* 43: 240–49.

———. 2015. *Dilemmas of Difference: Indigenous Women and the Limits of Postcolonial Development Policy.* Durham, N.C.: Duke University Press.

———. 2017. "Geography and Indigeneity I: Indigeneity, Coloniality, Knowledge." *Progress in Human Geography* 41, no. 2: 220–29.

Reinhard, J. 1985. "Sacred Mountains: An Ethno-archaeological Study of High Andean Ruins." *Mountain Research and Development* 5, no. 4: 299–317.

Rivera Cusicanqui, Silvia. 2010. "The Notion of 'Rights' and the Paradoxes of Postcolonial Modernity: Indigenous Peoples and Women in Bolivia." *Qui Parle* 18, no. 2: 29–54.

———. 2012. "*Ch'ixinakax utxiwa*: A Reflection on the Practices and Discourses of Decolonization." *South Atlantic Quarterly* 111, no. 1: 95–109.

Rivera Cusicanqui, Silvia, and Rosaria Barragán. Eds. 1997. *Debates postcoloniales: Una introducción a los estudios de la subalternidad.* La Paz: Sephis/Aruwiyri.

Schurr, Carolin. 2013. *Performing Politics, Making Space: A Visual Ethnography of Political Change in Ecuador.* Stuttgart: Franz Steiner Verlag.

Scott, James C. 2013. *Decoding Subaltern Politics: Ideology, Disguise and Resistance in Agrarian Politics.* London: Routledge.

Sharp, Joanne, P. Routledge, C. Philo, and R. Paddison. Eds. 2000. *Entanglements of Power: Geographies of Domination/Resistance.* London: Routledge.

Simpson, Audra. 2014. *Mohawk Interruptus.* Durham, N.C.: Duke University Press.

Strathern, Marilyn. 2004. *Partial Connections.* New York: AltaMira.

Sundberg, Juanita. 2014. "Decolonizing Posthumanist Geographies." *Cultural Geographies* 21, no. 1: 33–47.

Tuaza, Luis Alberto. 2009. "Cansancio organizativo." In *Repensando los movimientos indígenas*, edited by C. Martínez Novo, 123–43. Quito: FLACSO.

Tuhiwai Smith, Linda. 2010. *Decolonizing Methodologies: Research and Indigenous Peoples*. 2nd ed. London: Zed Books.
Universidad Intercultural Amautay Wasi. 2008. *Sumak yachaypi, alli kawsaypipash yachakuna/Aprender en la sabaduría y el buen vivir*. Quito: UNESCO.
Viatori, M. 2015. "Rift, Rupture and the Temporal Politics of Race in Ecuador." *History and Anthropology* 26, no. 2: 187–205.
Wainwright, Joel, and Joe Bryan. 2009. "Cartography, Territory, Property: Postcolonial Reflections on Indigenous Counter-mapping in Nicaragua and Belize." *Cultural Geographies* 16: 153–78.

Time, Space, and the Subaltern

The Matter of Labor in Delhi's Grey Economy

VINAY GIDWANI AND SUNIL KUMAR

Madanpur Khadar is a large resettlement colony in Delhi's southeast fringe, wedged between the states of Uttar Pradesh and Haryana, partially abutting the Yamuna River. Its original residents were relocated here in 2000–2001 after being evicted from slums in Gautam Nagar, Gautampuri Phase II of Yamuna Pushta, Nehru Place, Raj Nagar, East of Kailash, Alaknanda, Hanuman Camp, and VP Singh Colony (Hazards Centre 2007; Jagori 2009). Since then a steady influx of renters has added to the settlement's population. The tightly packed streets and impossibly narrow lanes of the jhuggi-jhopari (JJ) colony at Madanpur Khadar resemble the morphology of other such habitations.[1] Single rooms in exposed-brick tenements, stacked one atop another as owners and slumlords strive to garnish maximum rent from desperately tiny plots, are the modal form of housing. Open drainage that attracts flies, pools of water that offer fertile breeding ground for mosquitoes, scattered piles of garbage with packs of stray dogs, and severe lack of toilet facilities—aspects that are typically associated with poor working-class settlements in media reports—are routine features of life in many quarters of Madanpur Khadar.[2] A 2010 study on child-related health issues conducted by a network of nongovernmental organizations (NGOs) found that 20 percent of children in Madanpur Khadar were suffering from severe malnutrition; diarrhea, typhoid, and respiratory ailments were commonplace.[3] By April, when the heat mounts and power outages limit the use of fans, the conditions in JJ colonies become furnace-like; a lassitude descends on humans and animals alike, and even the surviving plants sag.

The stain of poverty and ill health and the sheer rigor of daily existence in settlements like Madanpur Khadar are impossible to ignore. But these challenges can obscure the importance of places like Madanpur Khadar to the city's economy. Madanpur Khadar is a diverse economic center, one of many that collectively forms the vital human infrastructure that keeps Delhi humming.[4] Madanpur Khadar's residents work as cleaners, sweepers, office helpers, and laborers; and large numbers of the colony's women are employed as domestic workers in adjacent upper-middle-class neighborhoods such as Sarita Vihar. Madanpur Khadar is also a multiform waste hub, which, like tens of other waste hubs scattered across and around Delhi—some specializing in a single waste product, others more flexible in character—daily process thousands of tons of detritus and discards whose accumulation would render urban existence as we know it impossible.

Delhi's waste hubs and the pathways of people, objects, information, and money that connect them are the city's lymphatic system, sequestering its waste and inoculating it from lasting damage. The intricate yet undervalued operations, until a moment of breakdown, of this sprawling waste infrastructure—from waste hubs to municipal landfills to sewage pipelines—hinges on the toil, ingenuity, practical knowledge, and risk taking of several hundred thousand workers, small entrepreneurs, and petty government functionaries. This labor—which I have elsewhere characterized as "infrastructural" (Gidwani and Maringanti 2016), mobilizing the double meaning of that adjective, "below" and "beyond," to underscore its subordination in academic and policy imaginations to "formal-sector" activities—recuperates and returns to the present matter that has outlived its time and place and that, left untreated, would erode the frail certitudes of city life. Thus, the urban experience and the viability of its sociospatial processes hinges on a continuous whittling away, even reversal, of the "chronography of things" as they pass from the domain of "use-time" to "waste-time," reinvesting objects with new functions and social use-values (Viney 2014, 5, 7). And yet, residents of places like Madanpur Khadar have an anxious existence within the city's aesthetic and political imaginary: their dwellings and livelihoods are continuously in jeopardy of disruption or dislocation to make way for "development" (Bhan 2016; Ghertner 2015; Nigam 2011; Sharan 2014; Srivastava 2014; Sundaram 2010,).

This constitutive injustice of the contemporary city is at the heart of my chapter. Drawing on ethnographic research of Delhi's informal waste economies, I connect the "stuff" of waste matter, labor, value, time, and geography to the ethical-political question of "the subaltern." The structural forces that condition the life-worlds of Madanpur Khadar's waste workers and traders—many precariously employed, some less so (as a relative location without stable identity, "being-subaltern" is profoundly geographical, always a question of "where and in relation to who")—provide the site at which I bring subaltern studies and political economy into engagement with the partisan aim of generating a counternarrative: the rudiments of a subaltern spatial history of the city that can upend elite imaginaries by showing how the devalorized labor of workers and small-time entrepreneurs in places like Madanpur Khadar sustain the temporal illusions that underwrite metropolitan modernity in Delhi and beyond.

Subaltern Urbanism

The term "subalternity" and its variant "subaltern" have become a staple of critical scholarship in numerous fields, including urban geography and urban studies (see, for instance, Bayat 2000; Chattopadhyay 2012; Harrison 2010; Ismail 2013; Legg 2016; Mukhopadhyay, Zerah, and Denis 2012; Ranganathan 2014; Roy 2011; Schindler 2014; Sheppard et al. 2013). While these terms frequently function as empirical placeholders for the "urban poor" (and otherwise vulnerable populations), they also evoke the original twofold thrust—epistemological and ethical-political—of the categories. On the epistemological front, the categories catalyze attention on how "subalternity" as a state of being subaltern is produced by a geographically and historically variable combination of forces, directive (ideological) and dominating (coercive), with certain accompanying subject-effects that are more or less prone to slippage during a recurring process of interpellation (see Gidwani 2008). In short, the object of inquiry is the subject who comes to "know" itself in particular ways and is thereby enabled to act (or desist) as the "author of its initiatives"—that is, the double sense of "subject" (*in subjection to* and *subject of*) Louis Althusser postulates in his essay on ideological state apparatuses (Althusser 1971).

Gayatri Chakravorty Spivak, whose writings—particularly her 1988 chapter "Can the Subaltern Speak?"—have acquired canonical status in the field of subaltern studies, builds on Louis Althusser and Jacques Derrida among others in mounting a vigorous critique of empiricist epistemologies of presence, arguing that even the most well-intended of efforts ultimately constitutes "the Other as the Self's shadow." The subaltern's singularity (an ethical site but also one of epistemic alterity to sanctioned forms of knowing) is domesticated by rendering it a particular instance of a general scheme. One common sleight of hand is to "explain" the specifics of the subaltern's world by inserting her into a spatio-temporal metanarrative of progress, staging her in a time and place that is upstream of the "present" (Fabian 1983; see also Massey 2005, 68–70; Spivak 1999). The "present" here operates as metonym for a range of normative locations: modern, civilized, secular, political, industrialized, developed, and urban being the most common. The phenomenological variant, which claims hermeneutic understanding of the subaltern's life-world, is the second and philosophically more refined sleight of hand, a recent and influential exemplar being Dipesh Chakrabarty, who creatively extends Heidegger to discuss dwelling within capitalist modernity (Chakrabarty 2000, 180). In their place Spivak enjoins a methodological strategy of "reading": a radical practice, which can unravel the *text*ile weave of an empiricism that claims access to subaltern consciousness or authentic being. Her stark and simple injunction to intellectuals in the First and Third World: "To confront them [subaltern Others] is not to represent them (*vertreten*) but to learn to represent (*darstellen*) ourselves" (Spivak 1988, 288–89).[5]

The central premise of Spivak's writings on the subaltern is unmistakable. He who represents and she who is represented (I use these pronouns merely to underscore the asymmetry and paternalism that Spivak urges constant vigilance against) are in a double bind: an *aporia* (Greek, *a + poros* = nonpassage) that both must confront, but especially those who are structurally positioned to represent and, therefore, act as representatives. There is no outside the ethics and politics of representation. Stephen Morton (2007) notes that Spivak's strident arguments have been a source of frustration for left academics (such as Hallward 2002) who surmise that the subaltern for Spivak is "altogether-beyond-relation," indeed "theoretically untouchable," hence outside the ambit of collective political action or counterhegemonic mobilization (as anticipated, for instance, by Antonio Gramsci, the original theorist of the subaltern condition). However, here it might be said that Spivak's critics fail to recognize how her thinking around the subaltern has shifted over the years. Thus, in "Scattered Speculations on the Subaltern and the Popular," Spivak characterizes the subaltern as "removed from all lines of social mobility" (2005, 475). Drawing on this essay, Morton remarks:

> Indeed, it is this "lack of access to mobility" that Spivak calls a "version of singularity." ... If the singularity of the subaltern is defined by its lack of access to mobility, the possibility of a broader political movement that includes the subaltern needs to take the singular social position of the subaltern into account rather than simply co-opting the subaltern into its hegemonic struggle. ... Spivak's engagement with the ethical dimension of deconstruction is precisely concerned with the ethical limitations of rational political programmes, such as nationalism or Marxism, which have at times failed to do justice to the singularity of subaltern constituencies by subsuming these constituencies within the hegemonic logic of these ... programmes. (Morton 2007, 66–67)

Madanpur Khadar's waste economy is illustrative here. It is not unusual to find waste pickers who currently occupy the lowest rungs of waste value chains and dream of owning a business, however small. Predictably, capital sustains itself by recruiting bearers of its drive to accumulation from the ranks of the proletariat and semiproletariat. The lesson for critics of contemporary urbanization is that urban subalterns frequently view capitalist enterprise with a great deal more ambivalence. Waste pickers experience capitalism's injustices—drudgery, exploitation, punishment—intimately, every day. They can deliver razor-sharp critiques of it. Yet they also find in its solvent energies opportunities to dislodge sedimented social orders and fabricate a life that is more. To operate a petty scrap-trader's *dukaan* (shop-cum-storehouse, typically all in a single room) is to possess an engine of arbitrage: the node where "raw" waste is purchased, segregated, and stored, before being channeled into secondary circuits of value.

Vigilance against the temptation to insert subaltern constituencies cut off from "lines of mobility" into the temporal grid of the intellectual's political ideology is also evident in Kalyan Sanyal's (ultimately problematic)[6] effort to theorize the "need economy" as a space governed by an economic logic that is different from the capitalist logic of the "accumulation economy"—a separation that foreshadows Sanyal's political break with "class essentialism." Sanyal writes:

> The need economy . . . is a space in which the distinction between capital and labor is, in most cases, blurred. The small entrepreneur in the informal sector may be an employer of a few wage-workers, and seen from the perspective of class politics, it is an exploitative class process as surplus value is extracted from wage labor in the form of profit. However, productivity is so low owing to low level of technology and other resource constraints that wages and profits taken together allow for a very low level of income and consumption for both the producer and the appropriator of surplus labor. Anti-capitalist politics in this case will be bent on pitting the workers against the "capitalist employer" and is thus likely to subvert the very conditions of existence of the enterprise. Thus the politics that is effective in the interior of capital and its accumulation-economy can be totally counter-productive in the need economy. (Sanyal 2007, 260)

While Spivak and Sanyal both, in contrasting ways, problematize the temporal politics of representation that sustain modernity's certitudes, neither, ironically, is attentive to the textures of time and matter that are effaced in order for working bodies to be represented as objects of disdain by advocates of urban modernity—as bodies that occupy an anachronistic (hence: inferior) time-space and deter the march of "development." I discuss the implications of this claim next, demonstrating in the process how subaltern studies and political economy can be conjoined to read the conditions of possibility of urban modernity differently.

Labor, Time, and Matter

It is not impossible to imagine how time itself is transacted in waste hubs like Madanpur Khadar: past for future, life for death. Waste is both matter out of place (Douglas 2002) and matter out of time (Thompson 1979; Viney 2014). It is matter, organic and inorganic, sometimes simple in form and content but at other times complex, even unwieldy, which has exited the utility-space that once ordered its existence. What makes it dangerous is its capacity to linger, momentarily or obdurately, often for years, alive with potential for reorganizing ecosystems, tiny and vast, human and beyond. This spatiotemporal potential presents a danger to human life possibilities unless impounded; yet it can also be the source of new life possibilities when, for instance, waste processors alter undesired matter into reusable forms. In this respect, waste has no invariant attributes; it is use- and exchange-value in waiting, whether or not it reenters those orbits. Such reentry may require transformation of form or content, or both; but arbitrage, a movement of objects in space or time without substantial alteration, may equally suffice.

No mode of reentry, however, is possible without application of labor, and it is here that life is swapped for slow death. On the one side, waste matter is given a new lease on life, urban ecosystems that otherwise might reel from its build-up are reprieved and repaired, and various fractions of capital—petty and large, informal and formal—are revivified as waste, now invested with use-value, is able, again, to don the garb of commodity. Hodges (2013, 114) discerningly remarks: "As 'waste,' garbage retains its 'backwardness' and serves a marker of the past. It is both the end of one story (or 'chain') of value and a problem in need of a solution. Stemming from this, the formal design of the legislation and regulations reproduces this organic temporality of garbage through a regulatory apparatus of waste management. Yet as 'scrap'—licit, illegible, and illegal—garbage is the beginning of another story. In this telling, garbage is the future."

But there is, of course, the other side to this story. Labor in the course of transporting or transforming waste matter earns a money wage, allowing it to reproduce its "life-activity"; but this renewal of "living immediate labour" (Marx 2010a, 220) comes at a steep price, the inexorable depletion of labor's capacity to renew itself as a result of repeated exposure to the physical and biochemical hazards associated with waste-related work. Labor is unique in that respect within classical political economy's holy trinity: while land and capital can be amassed and hoarded, for some duration, without peril, labor's "life-activity" cannot. Its biological survival is intimately conjoined with time. To replenish its physical and imaginative capacity it needs time to rest, to devote to activities that rebuff the summons of utility and instrumental reason. This understanding, that politics is about the production of space *and* time—indeed, about the *body* in space and time—pulses through Henri Lefebvre's declarative essay "The Right to the City." In it, Lefebvre calls for a transformation where the city's inhabitants are no longer alienated from its spaces and practices, characterizing it as a "cry and a demand" for a "renewed *right to urban life*" (Lefebvre 1996, 158; italics in the original). "Social needs," he asserts, "have an anthropological foundation. Opposed and complimentary, they include the need for security and opening, the need for certainty and adventure, that of organization of work and of play, the needs for the predictable and the unpredictable, of similarity and difference, of isolation and encounter, exchange and investments, of independence (even solitude) and communication, of immediate and long-term prospects. *The human being has the need to accumulate energies and to spend them, even waste them in play*" (Lefebvre 1996, 147; my italics).

However, when capital comes to shape social relations, labor finds it must allow capital to commandeer its labor-time in order to exist. Workers who own no other means of production other than their labor-power can ill-afford to idle time, wittingly in play or unwittingly in the anxiety-inducing embrace of the "reserve army." As Marx observes, "Labour itself is productive only as absorbed into capital, only where capital constitutes the basis of production and the capitalist is therefore the commander of production" (Marx 2010a, 234). Hence, the willingness of workers in Madanpur Khadar to forge a dalliance with forms of waste matter that pose jeopardy: knowing well that the longer this dalliance, the shorter their lease on life, as daily wear and tear, accidents, and chronic exposure to toxins truncate their bodies' capacities to regenerate. By the same token, because labor is the "*general possibility* of wealth"—"the living source of value"—capital not only strives to regulate labor's spatiotemporal practices, including time for "leisure" but also, to the extent possible, passes on the costs of labor's upkeep to it. Indeed, how capital repeatedly denudes labor's capacities to "be human" is a refrain across Marx's corpus of writings, but perhaps nowhere as powerfully as in his "Outlines of the Critique of Political Economy" (Rough Draft of 1857–58), *Grundrisse*, which underwrites his defining work, *Das Kapital*. At the nub of this theft of labor's capacity—its lease on life—is the relationship of labor to time, as illustrated by Marx's barbs at bourgeois political economy in the Chapter on Capital:

> The workers should save enough in times of good business to be able to more or less live in bad times, to endure SHORT TIME or the reduction of wages, etc. (The wage would then fall still lower.) It really amounts to the demand that they should always make do with a minimum of pleasures of life and make crises easier, etc., for the capitalists; that they should consider themselves as pure laboring machines, and pay as much as possible of their WEAR AND TEAR themselves. (Marx 2010a, 216)

And shortly thereafter:

> The capitalist desires nothing more than that the worker should *expend his dosages of life power as much as possible without interruption*. (Marx 2010a, 220; italics in the original)

However, the daily grind and hazards associated with waste work ensure that waste pickers age prematurely, their bodies depleted of "life power."[7] Few are able to work into the fifties. Nusrat Begum, a resident of Madanpur Khadar, says she is from Dhubri district, in the northeastern state of Assam.[8] She has been in Delhi for nine to ten years and in this line of work from the time she arrived. Her husband, who she guesses is in his forties, has fallen ill and is unable to pick waste these days. She notes that he keeps falling ill: "When he gets sick, he gets some treatment here [in the city], but if the illness persists he returns to the village for treatment" ("*Bimaar hone par yahaan thoda bahut ilaaj karaate hain, theek nahin hone par ve gaon chale jaate hain ilaaj karaane ke liye*") (interview notes, October 2014). Marx's brutal analysis of pauperism, the "lowest sediment of the relative surplus population," in volume 1 of *Capital* seems to foreshadow the fate of Nusrat Begum's ailing husband. There, Marx writes that in the "sphere of pauperism" dwell, among others, "the demoralised and ragged, and those unable to work, chiefly people who succumb to their incapacity for adaptation, due to the division of labour; people who have passed the normal age of the labourer; the victims of industry, whose number increases with the increase of dangerous machinery, of mines, chemical works, &c, the mutilated, the sickly, the widows, &c" (Marx 2010b, 638). He then goes on to famously declare:

> Pauperism is the hospital of the active labour army and the dead weight of the industrial reserve army. Its production is included in that of the relative surplus population, its necessity in theirs; along with the surplus population, pauperism forms a condition of capitalist production, and of the capitalist development of wealth. It enters into the *faux frais* [overhead costs] of capitalist production; but capital knows how to throw these, for the most part, from its own shoulders on to those of the working class and the lower middle class. (Marx 2010b, 638).

Nusrat's children don't attend school: they also pick waste, partly to compensate for their father's illness. But Nusrat's unrequited aspirations for her children are apparent when she bitterly remarks: "*Agar ma-baap koode mein rahenge to bacche is se door kaise reh sakte hain?*" ("If the parents live amid garbage can the children stay away from it?") (interview notes, October 2014). Her comment mobilizes the double sense of the word *kooda*. She implies that her children's trajectories can't be otherwise given that *kooda* (waste) is both a source of the parents' livelihood and the squalor or filth that marks their lives. Nusrat's existence is a blunt reminder that women carry the double burden of production and reproduction. Their labor time is never done. After she has finished sorting the day's waste, Nusrat turns her attention to household chores such as cooking the evening meal. Nusrat says that her bones ache and her back constantly hurts; she is unable to sleep at night. "Thus: the raw material is consumed by being changed, formed by labour, and the instrument of labour is consumed by being used up in this process, worn out," Marx writes, in the Chapter on Capital in *Grundrisse*. "On the other hand, labour is likewise consumed by being employed, set in motion and so a definite quantity of the muscular strength, etc., of the worker is spent, whereby he exhausts himself" (Marx 2010a, 226). These observations encapsulate Nusrat's austere life, which, along with the lives of so many others in the waste economy, underwrites the city's very possibility.

Given capital's vast and ingenious apparatuses to capture living labor, it is easy to overlook the "small arms fire" (Scott 1985, 22) that workers continuously unleash in an effort to wrest a modicum of control over time and space. Mohammad Ashraf, a homeless day laborer who is the protagonist in Aman Sethi's nonfiction account *A Free Man* (2012), has made a living as a butcher and tailor and sold lemons and lottery tickets; but in another life he could well have been a philosopher. His musings reveal the struggle and, poignantly, the solitude of poverty. Marx observes that "the worker is . . . formally posited as a person who is something for himself apart from his labour, and who alienates what expresses his life [*Lebensäusserung*] only as a means for his own life" (Marx 2010a, 218). As if offering a counterpoint to this, Ashraf at one point defiantly remarks: "Azadi is the freedom to tell the *maalik* [boss] to fuck off when you want to. The *maalik* owns our work. He does not own us" (Sethi 2012, 19). Thus, Ashraf asserts his autonomy by striving for jobs that allow "the perfect balance of *kamai* and *azadi*"—wages and freedom. He rejects the self-abnegation required to save; shunning the future, he freely spends the little money he earns on beedis, boiled eggs, and glassfuls of illicit booze. Ashraf's life is a series of repeating presents. While such militant embrace of immediacy is not the modal ethos of waste workers in Madanpur Khadar (and, for that matter, workers who toil in other waste hubs I have visited in Delhi), it is not uncommon to meet individuals who gave up waged factory work to enter the hardscrabble world of waste picking because they resented being bossed around and wanted more control of their own time, even if their newfound livelihood is recurrently abhorrent and unstable.[9] This desire for autonomy from oversight has global cognates: illustratively, the French sociologist Robert Castel (2003) has documented that wage labor was associated with indignity for a very long time in Western societies, where it was viewed as a sign of compulsion and site of dependency rather than freedom.

Grey Waste Economies

According to Naveen Kumar, who runs a small teashop in Madanpur Khadar and doubles up as a petty scrap dealer, approximately 3,000 households in the JJ (jhuggi-jhopari, a planning category that refers to a small, roughly built home or shelter) colony rely on waste work. The bulk of them, like Nusrat Begum, have come to Delhi from Assam, but there are also large numbers from West Bengal and Uttar Pradesh. Naveen operates a 300-square-foot *godown* (warehouse) to store the scrap and claims there are tens of such warehouses in the area. To build a *godown*, the police demand an initial payment of INR 20,000 to 30,000 ($300 to $450), with a monthly cess of INR 500 thereafter. The next challenge for the small-time scrap operator is inventory management in the face of intense competition. Time is key. He (or, very occasionally, she) must establish a supply chain that brings him a regular inflow of scrap. He orchestrates this through interlocking arrangements with waste pickers: in return for petty loans, a place to rest, and camaraderie, an anonymous transaction is transformed into something more personal, even a patron-client relation. This thwarts the predatory competition that might otherwise imperil the scrap dealer's survival (and with it, his costly investment of toil and savings) and lays the foundations of an enterprise that is robust enough to endure—at least in the short term—the press of market fluctuations and extra-economic forces (Gidwani 2015).

While the small scrap traders/warehouse owners who contract with waste pickers can be characterized as merchant or petty-industrial capitalists, the vast majority are waste pickers risen from the ranks, who have managed, through toil, savings, loans, family help, occasional strong-arming, well-directed graft to petty police and municipal staff, and a cultivated knowledge of trading networks, to elevate themselves within the city's waste economies. Climbing up and consolidating oneself in the value chain is taxing. Madanpur Khadar's scrap traders customarily arrange accommodation for waste pickers in proximity to their *godowns* in return for first rights of purchase of their daily haul of recyclables; other owners, who are unable to provide accommodation, secure the labor of waste pickers by paying them advances of INR 50,000 to 100,000 ($750 to $1,500). For this higher advance payment, the expectation is that the waste picker will bring *kabaad* (scrap) worth INR 1,000 ($15) on a daily basis. While scrap dealers sometimes try to pay their regulars lower prices for items, stiff competition from rivals limits the effectiveness of this tactic. This is clear from the manner in which advances are treated. There is no daily deduction from the payment for recyclables sold to the scrap dealer; and it is commonplace for waste pickers to shift allegiance to another warehouse when its owner pays them a larger advance, which in turn is used to pay back the first dealer his original advance without interest. Naveen Kumar complained that, in spite of money advances, waste pickers surreptitiously sell a portion of their daily haul to other buyers. But the pendulum can also swing the other way: according to Nusrat Begum, now that her husband is ill, their *thekedaar* (the trader to whom they are contracted to sell) is only paying half-price for items and deducting the other half for rent and electricity.

Shashank *thekedaar* (contractor) runs a large warehouse, which employs roughly fifty men, primarily Muslims and SCs, from eastern Uttar Pradesh according to one of the workers. They collect and process the *kabaad*—dry, largely paper, waste—that Shashank sources from around the city. Most of the workers, thirty-five of them, live in the 2,000-square-feet compound, which houses two pressing machines that transform sheets of paper into tightly packed bundles (figure 1). The workers have no fixed work hours; whenever a delivery arrives they are put to work. Their tasks range from unloading the trucks that deliver scrap paper to operating the pressing machines to, once again, loading trucks that come to fetch the bundled paper. Some of the workers say they have been working at Shashank's warehouse for six to seven years. They earn between INR 6,000–7,000 ($90–$105) per month but are neither paid overtime nor have

FIGURE 1. Worker operating a pressing machine. (Photograph by Sunil Kumar)

any days off. Workers are expected to learn on the job how to operate the pressing machines; no formal instruction is provided. Labor regulations and work safety protocols are absent, and workers seemed unaware of (or were possibly indifferent to) legal protections that apply to them. Inability to work due to illness or family obligations results in loss of pay. In the law's gaze, Shashank *thekedaar*'s workers don't exist: there is no record of their hiring, no labor register is maintained, the warehouse operates under the radar with the complicity of police and municipal staff, and, as such, workers have no basis to mount complaints.

While a majority of waste pickers who reside in Madanpur Khadar obtain the recyclables that sustain their livelihoods from door-to-door collection of municipal waste in neighborhoods and apartment blocks that adjoin this settlement, a sizable minority earns its living from biomedical waste. There are about ten warehouses that handle hospital waste, which arrives from various medical facilities around Delhi in large black polythene bags. The most common items are white and glossy paper, cardboard, file folders, and used tissue paper. A *godown* owned by a man locals call "Rameez" also receives hospital waste in red and yellow polythene bags containing discarded medicines, injections, needles, bottles, rubber items, and so on (figure 2).

We were told by an informant who knows the business that hospitals, which

FIGURE 2. Hospital waste in Madanpur Khadar. (Photograph by Sunil Kumar)

are required by the government to follow prescribed guidelines for the disposal of biomedical waste, bid the task out to private companies.[10] But instead of destroying this waste, some of it unsafe (such as infected needles, soiled rubber gloves, used urine bags, prescription-only painkillers), as per prescribed procedures, a few companies illicitly convey the items in closed trucks to warehouses such as Rameez's. Rameez, we learned, has an annual contract (*theka*) with two companies (or possibly a subset of their employees: we were unable to verify), paying out INR 9 lakhs ($14,000) to one and INR 10 lakhs ($15,000) to another for first rights to their biomedical garbage. Rameez in turn sells this hospital scrap to smaller warehouse owners in Madanpur Khadar, where the items are first cleaned in hot water. The metal caps of medicine bottles are sold to aluminum scrap dealers, the bottles themselves (depending on their material) to plastic or glass scrap dealers, and the syringes to plastic scrap traders. Puran, a local scrap dealer who does not deal in hospital waste, tells us that the hospital waste often contains packaged medicines that are yet to reach their expiration date; these are sold to shopkeepers who visit the *godowns* expressly for this purpose. Unused liquids in glass or plastic bottles are poured into a can, which is then buried underground; capsules and tablets are sealed in polythene bags and similarly buried.

Kartar works in a small warehouse owned by a person named Binod. He hails from Rohtak district in Haryana and has been handling hospital waste for twenty years. He earns a monthly salary of INR 7,500 ($115). According to him, the stench from the hospital waste is so overpowering that new workers have great difficulty adjusting. Many leave. I have repeatedly underscored that a city's upkeep pivots on jobs that are regarded by its well-to-do residents as banal and dirty—clearing garbage, sweeping streets, cleaning toilets, unclogging sewers, processing various forms of waste, operating a small butcher shop, being a roadside hair stylist, washing people's laundry, running a tire repair shop, or vending food. Each of these demands a sensory resilience (visual, aural, olfactory, and tactile) that is extraordinary. Indeed, that which bourgeois senses condemn as "filthy" or "revolting" is very often the normal order of things for the city's underclasses" (Gidwani 2015).[11] Women are a common sight in the warehouses; they can be seen sorting the waste, the lower part of their faces covered by the *pallu* (trailing end) of their saris or a *chunni* (stole) to ward off the stench. Some of them are provided gloves, ostensibly as a safety measure, harvested from the discards they handle. But most workers work without gloves or masks. The supervisor at one of the *godowns* told us that workers are administered a tetanus injection—he was unable to name the medication—every six months and that each injection costs the *maalik* (owner) INR 3,000 ($50). The majority of workers at the *godowns*, thanks to the extended kin and social networks that lubricate pathways of migration from rural to urban areas, are from adjoining districts of Bengal.[12] Their monthly pay ranges from INR 3,500 to 6,500 ($55 to $100). Some live on the premises, others in hutments adjoining the warehouses. The women tend to be daily wagers; they are paid INR 150 ($2.50) and hired as needed.

Lessons from Dalit Studies

As the foregoing discussion shows, there is a persistent, if unsteady, relationship between low-caste status and the handling of waste matter (see, for example, Gill 2010, chap. 6; Prashad 2000), with those who handle organic or wet waste matter (household garbage, slaughterhouse waste, sewage, biomedical waste, human waste) liable to be regarded as more "unclean"—hence, more lowly in the caste order—than those who work with dry waste matter (paper, metal, and plastic "scrap," glass, e-waste).[13] Such caste assignments extend to *mussulmans* (Muslims), who have come to dominate specific circuits and segments within Delhi's informal waste economies.[14] In trying to understand the implications for urban political economy and subaltern studies of this recursive relationship between these bodies and the matter that is the object of their toil, I have found highly suggestive an "Indian Debate on Experience and Theory," the subtitle of the book *The Cracked Mirror*, which takes the form of a conversation between two leading intellectuals, Gopal Guru (a political scientist) and Sundar Sarukkai (a philosopher) (Guru and Sarukkai 2012). The authors venture a provisional and radical thesis: to reclaim the lived experience of the Dalit—of pain, suffering, humiliation—as singular and inassimilable, as well as the grounds for a new, universal social theory that "connects the ideas of social location, an angularity of vision, and perception or experience of that society" (Kaviraj 2013, 382). Their mandate resonates, in one register, with Lukacs's provocative analysis in *History and Class Consciousness* (1922) of proletarian experience and the revolutionary theory and praxis that it incubates (allowing the proletariat alone to become the privileged agent of History); or Fanon's call for "a new humanism" in *The Wretched of the Earth* (1963) and, more vividly, his bitter disagreement with his friend, Jean-Paul Sartre, in *White Skin, Black Masks* (1952) over the latter's glib extrapolation of the (European) "dialectic," so entirely impervious, in spite or perhaps because of his Marxism, to the lived experience of the black man.

But no matter how abject the black person's condition, Guru is surely right to point out that untouchability is a unique fact of Indian society in the way it has spatiotemporalized the Dalit body, prescribed its movements, symbolically and physically regulated Dalit life, and strived to impoverish the "feel" for thinking that would challenge "theoretical Brahminism";[15] and that while it is instructive to draw comparisons between caste violence against Dalits with black people's experience of racism (as Dalit scholars frequently do), we mustn't lose sight of their respective singularities. As Sudipta Kaviraj observes in his instructive review of *The Cracked Mirror*, untouchability "has no equivalent in European social history, so the theory of a European social structure could not explain it" (Kaviraj 2013, 381). Thus, *The Cracked Mirror* not only signifies the inability of existing (European) social theory to mirror Dalit experience, it also signifies the inability of Dalits to mirror—to systematically reflect, "know," conceptualize, intensify, and theorize—their singular experience as the grounds for a new universal as a result of pervasive, long-standing institutional exclusion and derision that (till the present day) continues to crush the confidence of aspiring Dalit scholars.

While Fanon in *Black Skins, White Masks*, with subversive fidelity to Hegel, sought the restoration of "a world of reciprocal recognitions" (Fanon 2008, 193), Guru and Sarukkai are more circumspect. In a fascinating chapter, "The Phenomenology of Untouchability," which draws on Indian Nyaya-Vaisesika philosophical and Western phenomenological traditions, Sarukkai argues that *"the real site of untouchability is the person who refuses to touch the untouchable"* (2012, 186; original italics), namely, Brahmins, who have cleverly outsourced their "not wanting to be touched" to Dalits who must then carry the burden of not touching. This inhuman configuring then circumscribes where Dalits can be and how and what activities they must undertake—manual scavenging, the clearing of animal carcasses, curing of hides, street sweeping, sewer work, garbage collection, and waste picking—in order to find means of existence. The Dalit body that defiles and matter that defiles—caste society's detritus and excrement—are, thus, ontologically joined. Omprakash Valmiki, a Dalit from the untouchable Chuhra caste, describing his childhood in a village in Uttar Pradesh, powerfully underscores this ontological coupling. "Untouchability was so rampant," he writes, "that while it was considered all right to touch dogs and cats or cows and buffaloes, if one [a higher-caste person] happened to touch a Chuhra, one got contaminated or polluted. The Chuhras were not seen as human. They were simply things for use. Their utility lasted until the work was done. Use them and then throw them away" (2003, 2).

How does all this pertain to the urban informal economy and its vast flotilla of waste workers? I want to propose that Guru and Sarukkai's debate on Dalit embodiment in *The Cracked Mirror* is suggestive for how we might think about the thick entanglements of matter and bodies as they circumscribe the life-worlds and time-space mobility of Dalit and non-Dalit waste workers who labor in the grey nooks and crannies of the urban economy.[16] Many of these workers, particularly those from the lower castes, come to the city to escape the inherited burden of caste. *But caste frequently gets a new lease on life in cities by virtue of the matter workers are compelled to handle. The contemporary city propelled by its "world-class" imaginary produces new relations of untouchability and exclusion.* The segregated worlds of urban labor can be stark: so much so that while many workers will trace a circuitous arc of doing odd jobs in multiple cities prior to their arrival in Delhi, they will also describe—particularly women—a painfully restricted existence in the city, often confined to one rigidly demarcated portion of their place of work and habitation. The gradient that arrays the city's working classes on an aspirational slope—but that nevertheless divides them sharply—can be precipitously shallow. Minute class differences and associated perceptions of social status can quickly subsume caste affiliations.

Take the case of Dulichand Colony, which abuts three warehouses that process hospital waste. Many residents here, like Madanpur Khadar's waste workers, labor in the city's informal economy with little to no job security. But they have not the slightest sympathy for the laborers who handle biomedical scrap. In fact, we were told by waste workers that Dulichand Colony's inhabitants have repeatedly complained at the local police *thana* (substation) about the unsanitary conditions that prevail in these places of business. They blame a proliferation of skin ailments among residents to environmental contamination from the waste, noting that the area becomes almost impassable during the monsoons. Protests by Dulichand Colony's residents led to a onetime closure of the warehouses, but after a few days they were up and running again. The residents accuse the owner who leases his land to the warehouses of indifference to their plight: he lives far away, comes once in a while to collect rent, gets his money and doesn't even have to step out of his car to do it, and drives away. It is clear to them as well that the local police and municipal staff are also complicit, getting a cut from the warehouse owners to turn a blind eye.

Henri Lefebvre, who Guru repeatedly invokes in *The Cracked Mirror*, writes that every "social space . . . once duly demarcated and oriented, implies a superimposition of certain relations upon networks of named places," that is, a toponymy encompassing accessible routes, boundaries, and forbidden territories; places of abode; and junction points that are places of passage and encounter (1991, 193). Waste picking offers a telling illustration. The routes a waste picker treads and the places she frequents in her daily quest for the scrap that sustains her life in the city is closely tied to place of dwelling. Uproot her dwelling and you undercut, perhaps uproot, her source of livelihood. It is easy to overlook how vitally informal economies depend upon "a feel for space that is prior to the thought of space . . . [and] how it is to this reassuring notion of space that one applies the stamp of one's will and volition" (Wakankar 2013, 405). Furthermore, the lived experience of space is always bodily as Lefebvre notes in dense but vivid prose: "Space—*my* space—is not," he writes, "the context of which I constitute 'textuality': instead, it is first of all *my body*, and then it is my body's counterpart or 'other', its mirror-image or shadow: it is the shifting intersection between that which touches, penetrates, threatens or benefits my body on the one hand, and all other bodies on the other" (Lefebvre 1991, 184). Thus, the path and waypoints the waste picker traverses, where she sorts the putrid results of her daily toil (gleaning discards with salvage value from a sometimes amorphous mass of rotting food, oozing diapers, bloody tampons, or even infected syringes), and whom she sells to, are activities that pivot on the bodily "feel" for space. Space can be friendly, hostile, or humiliating—with crucial implications for one's capacity to use space for movement, for a body to become. In *Metaphysics*, Aristotle defines becoming as "the active exercise of something's being able to be otherwise" (Kosman 2013, 70), an ontological supposition that, journeying through the ages, finds its imprint in Hobbes, when he characterizes liberty as the absence of external impediments to motion (also see Kotef 2015).[17] But perhaps in addition we ought also to emphasize how the freedom (or unfreedom) of becoming-being hinges on the wherewithal to *stop* when and where necessary: thus, for waste pickers and small-time scrap dealers, the ability to segregate and store recyclables (Chintan 2003), to rest and rejuvenate without fear of being asked to move, is as essential to their existence in the city as the obverse capacity for movement.

As such, one lesson to embrace from Dalit scholarship—black and feminist scholarship also treads this ground—is that while the subjective experience of devaluation, suffering, and humiliation will always remain, in some final sense, inaccessible (I can't inhabit the sufferer's body, just as I can't plumb an authentic subaltern "consciousness" were it ever so available), a structural analysis of the conditions in which certain bodies are devalued, even as others are valorized, *is* possible—so long as I am vigilant, as Spivak urges, to how my "interests" as a theorist normatively inform the itinerary I ascribe to subaltern individuals and the narrative I build on that basis. In this space of intersubjectivity, perhaps, lies the kernel of the new universal that Guru and Sarukkai seek, a new universal that can enliven our understanding of how bodies comport and interact in cities.

Conclusion

On Monday, July 11, 2016, four members of a Dalit family who were skinning a dead cow were stripped and beaten with iron rods and sticks by a group of self-proclaimed *gau rakshaks* (cow protectors) in Mota Samadhiyala village, near Una town, in the Gir Somnath district of Gujarat. The upper-caste *gau rakshaks* accused the Dalit youths of slaughtering the cow, even as the latter tried to explain that they had transported the carcass from a nearby village. The incident, which was captured on film and uploaded to the Internet, went viral, sparking furor nationwide. In Gujarat, thousands of angry Dalits took a pledge not to lift carcasses. Their pledge, which underscored the expectation, still entrenched, of caste Hindus that Dalits will perform the "unclean" task of disposing dead animals, rejects this caste privilege and the ontological joining of "defiled" matter and bodies that is its founding warrant. It also demonstrates how seven decades after independence, scores of Dalits are compelled to survive by forms of labor that society stigmatizes and that are regarded as degrading. But the content of the pledge also has profound symbolic import. It recalls one of Babasaheb Ambedkar's fiery speeches in which he issued a caustic rebuke to caste Hindus: "I asked them," he says in that speech, "'You take the milk from the cows and buffaloes and when they are dead you expect us to remove the dead bodies. Why? If you carry the dead bodies of your mothers to cremate, why do you not carry the dead bodies of your "mother-cows" yourself?'" (Ambedkar 1969, 143).

The parallels to waste removal in metropolises like Delhi by workers who are frequently low-caste, Dalit or not, are unmistakable if imperfect. Imagine if the workers and petty entrepreneurs who comprise the human infrastructure of waste remediation in Delhi were to call a mass strike. Imagine if the landfills were to close, the sewers were to overrun, and the garbage was to accumulate, causing a proliferation of sights, odors, and ooze, ordinarily hidden or confined and on which depend the certitudes of modern life. At such times, the fragility of "civil society"—of life, liberty, and property, and the sanitized sensorium in which these are ensconced—stands exposed and tremulous (as the inhabitants of Beirut, Naples, and New York, among others, can vouchsafe). The architectonics, aesthetics, and economics of contemporary cities pivot on the daily infrastructural work of repair and reproduction that is undertaken by subaltern populations, including waste workers, whose labors and whose claims to a dignified existence are persistently devalued. Their labor transforms matter—via a set of intricate transactions in time and space—from waste to forms that can once more inhabit the universe of value, thereby renewing the ecological and economic conditions of possibility of the polis. Their life-dissipating labor is the constituent power that keeps cities alive, and yet it is unjustly devalorized: this simple point has been the chapter's partisan summons.

In bringing "the subaltern question" to the city, endowing the work of waste with an ethical-political charge, I have allusively and analytically stitched together an array of conceptual objects: labor, value, time, waste matter, and geography.

In trying to remedy perceived omissions in subaltern studies scholarship, I have turned to Marxist and, then, to Dalit scholarship. The latter in particular has allowed me to foreground how the capacity for mobility and stoppage—or, rendered geographically, spaces of movement and places of rest that are secure and not unstable—are vital dimensions of urban existence that are differentially distributed across bodies. That is to say, time-space is "lived" in vastly different ways by different bodies with profound implications for their survival and reproduction. Dalit scholarship, I argue, also enjoins us to think more insistently about the "sensorium" that workers in the informal economy (are forced to) inhabit. And here, it provides an important complement to Jacques Ranciere's now familiar thesis that every governing order (liberal or otherwise) produces a "distribution of the sensible" that regulates the "visible" and the "sayable," and that this same operation effects a partition between those who can "*partake*" in the order and those who may not. In Ranciere's words: "The people is a supplementary existence that inscribes the count of the uncounted, or part of those who have no part—that is, in the last instance, the equality of speaking beings without which inequality itself is inconceivable" (2010, 33). Dalit scholarship adds the insights that, like caste, any social system of belonging or inclusion is perforce supplemented by an "outside": it is regulated by far more than normative prescriptions (do's, what's proper) and proscriptions (don'ts, what's improper) in the realms of the "visible" and the "sayable."[18] The aural, the olfactory, the gustatory, and the (un)touchable are also implicated. A social order is a moral order and a sensory order.

In spite of widespread acknowledgment of the importance of informal economies—or as I now prefer to call them, grey economies, which straddle the licit and the illicit—to urban livelihoods, far more study is required of their material imbrications and how their survival pivots on a capacity for movement and rest in time-space. If space is intimately bound to the body's senses, it is also intimately bound to the body's rhythms and the textures of time that infuse space—implicated in the routines, flows, and interactions of social and economic life. Lefebvre, again, writes evocatively in this regard: "The body does not fall under the sway of analytical thought and its separation of the cyclical from the linear," he says. "The unity which that reflection is at such pains to decode finds refuge in the cryptic opacity which is the great secret of the body. For the body indeed unites cyclical and linear, combining the cycles of time, need and desire with the linearities of gesture, perambulation, prehension and the manipulation of things—the handling of both material and abstract tools" (Lefebvre 1991, 203).

The complex of practices and plural entanglements in times of workers' bodies are evident from my illustrations of their life-worlds in Madanpur Khadar, a multispectrum waste hub in southeast Delhi. As several scholars have ably documented, the local state actively participates in the production of urban space and its conditions of access for subaltern populations in cities like Delhi. The eviction of waste pickers from slum settlements, their fraught relocation to JJ colonies, sealing drives[19] targeting scrap dealers' establishments in middle-class residential neighborhoods, corporate privatization of waste management, and periodic attempts by politicians to stir moral panic over growing criminality in Indian cities (blamed on lumpen elements like waste pickers, specially undocumented "Bangladeshis" who have entered this and other manual trades) are all tendencies that are abetted by the ruling classes. In effect a milieu has arisen, a "distribution of the sensible" in the fuller sense suggested by Dalit scholarship, where waste recyclers in the grey economy, although growing in numbers, have been relegated to an ever-diminishing part in the new city order. This repartitioning via rules, regulations, ordinances, directives, edicts, and imperatives—the polychrome attires of law as sovereign power—can be properly regarded as a "chronopolitics" that devalorizes the time practices of the urban poor (for further details, see Gidwani and Reddy [2011]; also Sharma [2014], chap. 1). It is in this sense that we can think of the urban order—who may properly belong to the city, and who may not—as a moral *and* sensory order.

To wit, the state in its amoebic instantiations has power to abet or disrupt the architectonics of informal waste economies by altering the conditions of access to time-space at any and every point along waste commodity chains: waste pickers may be evicted from settlements by municipal slum demolition drives, their bicycles or painstakingly sorted recyclables may be impounded by policemen for a perceived slight or failure to grease the right palms, cycle rickshaws may be banned from plying certain thoroughfares by city ordinances that are hard to fathom and harder still to revoke, scrap dealers' shops in residential areas may be shielded or sealed for nonconformity with zoning codes or complaints from RWAs enforced under arcane "nuisance" laws, and warehouses and reprocessing units may be allowed to operate unhindered or shut or asked to relocate under court-directed antipollution directives. Informal recycling economies in Delhi and other Indian cities have borne the brunt of each. But let's be clear. The fact that law in its many guises can be deployed in the name of the sovereign, minor or majestic, neither foreordains it will be nor that it will be applied uniformly. Power, more effective when it is unpredictable, preserves the constitutive injustice that founds the polis.[20]

NOTES

Thanks to workers and traders in Madanpur Khadar who opened a window into their lives; and to Sarah Hodges, Tariq Jazeel, and Stephen Legg, whose hard-nosed questions and perceptive suggestions on a draft have pressed us to do better even as we have willfully ignored their tougher criticisms for want of time and insight.

    1. The official taxonomy of settlement types in Delhi can be confusing; Bhan (2016, 48–74) provides a useful overview of settlement types and their histories. Jhuggi-jhopari (JJ) settlements included JJ clusters as well as JJ resettlement colonies. In general, the appellation JJ refers to settlements "that have not been declared slums by notification under the Slum Areas Act and that are imagined to retain the physical fragility and deprivation of the slum . . . [although] there are no strict metrics of infrastructural services, income or spatial layouts, for example, to determine whether a settlement is or is not a JJ cluster" (Bhan 2016, 71). Layouts, infrastructure, population density, and housing quality can differ considerably from one JJ colony to another (CPR 2015).

    2. Infrastructure provision can vary between different settlement types (for instance, "JJ clusters" versus "unauthorized colonies"); between similar settlement types (for instance, "JJ resettlement colonies" in different parts of the city); and even within a settlement type (thus, across different blocks in Madanpur Khadar).

    3. Srinand Jha, "Delhi's Irony: Urban Poverty," *Hindustan Times*, April 7, 2012.

    4. Gidwani and Maringanti (2016) discuss the parallel case of Bholakpur, a multispectrum waste hub in Hyderabad in south India.

    5. In her writings on education Spivak enjoins educators "to learn to learn from below," a remark that I find in kinship with the foregoing injunction—and consonant with the ethical imperative that guides her critiques.

    6. See Gidwani and Wainwright (2014) for a sympathetic critique of Sanyal's arguments.

    7. Labor studies scholars have long documented the precarious and exploitative employment conditions that workers endure. For example, Werner (2016) in her instructive ethnographic political economy of uneven development in the Caribbean recounts the story of José, a thirty-eight-year-old garment factory operator, who is thrown out of his job. "I was there for seventeen years," José tells Werner. "They took my youth, my strength, everything. It's like [sugar] cane. You take the juice and you're left with the pulp" (Werner 2016, 97).

    8. Interviews in Madanpur Khadar were conducted in October 2014. Names of all informants have been altered.

    9. I have heard from numerous workers who are otherwise habituated to the textures and smells of the waste matter they encounter that the sense of disgust never com-

pletely dissipates. Certain articles—such as pus-ridden cotton wool and bandages, used syringes, tampons streaked with menstrual blood, and casually discarded diapers—have an "infectious materiality" that arouses revulsion in even the most hard-bitten waste workers.

10. Sarah Hodges (2013, 112) notes: "Like other nations' biomedical waste measures, India's regulations require hospitals to guard against the health risks that medical garbage presents. Hospitals must segregate waste before passing it on to specialist haulers, and haulers must deliver it to dedicated common treatment facilities (CTFs). Finally, the CTFs must autoclave (steam-clean), shred, and then incinerate and/or bury the waste. These regulations design pathways through which the detritus of everyday healthcare travels from "cradle" to "grave." But as she proceeds to discuss in her insightful analysis of the afterlives of biomedical waste in Chennai, these prescribed pathways are replete with leakages. This is in no small part because, as per Hodges's characterization, "The rules are framed as though biomedical waste has no resale value. The pre-existing regime of value for used, discarded medical plastics has thrived in the rules' regulatory blind spots. In short, the CTF itself has come to function not as a waste graveyard, but as a wholesale market for scrap dealers" (Hodges 2013, 116).

11. "Thus man is affirmed in the objective world not only in the act of thinking, but with *all* his senses" (Marx 1988, 108, italics in the original).

12. Over time these pathways lead to the commonly observed phenomenon of labor market segmentation in cities, where certain occupations come to be dominated by certain caste, ethno-religious, and/or regional groups (waste pickers from Bengal, plumbers from Odisha, auto mechanics from Punjab, maids from Jharkhand, security guards from Rajasthan, drivers from Himachal Pradesh, and so on). The formation of these niches and flux over time warrants further investigation.

13. Sarah Hodges, personal communication, points out that the terms "waste" and "scrap," although sometimes used interchangeably, have different valences. Most simply, "waste" includes things that are nonutilitarian (e.g., nuclear waste or toxic industrial effluents), whereas "scrap" suggests already a market valuation. But as I have stated in the text, waste has no immutable attributes: "it is use- and exchange-value in waiting, whether or not it re-enters those orbits" and that "such re-entry may require transformation of form or content, or both." In short, changes in knowledge, social-historical conditions, and technologies can make into "scrap" matter that was previously considered without use- or exchange-value. I would insist, as such, that "scrap" be considered a subset of "waste" matter.

14. It is difficult to ascertain caste identity of waste workers from surnames, and lower-caste migrants who have come to the city from villages or small towns partly or primarily to escape the strictures and stigma of social assignation by birth are understandably reticent around questions of caste (see, e.g., Valmiki 2003). Furthermore, as is well-known, caste hierarchies traverse religion: Hindus and Muslims can both share low-caste status. Gill (2010, 119n20) offers a corroborating account from her research in Delhi's plastics waste sector.

15. Guru (2002) castigates the social sciences in India for producing a cultural hierarchy of "theoretical Brahmins" and "empirical Shudras." The resonances with postcolonial scholarship are evident, as Guru bluntly rebukes the naturalized relations of power between the dominant and dominated or, to summon another familiar binary, the

North (metropole, site of accumulation, place of canonical knowledge, radiant center of universality) and the South (margins, site of raw materials, home to disqualified knowledges, abode of the particular and the marginal), operating at various geographic scales of analysis.

16. On these points, see Sarah Hodges (forthcoming).

17. "LIBERTY, or FREEDOM, signifieth (properly) the absence of opposition (by opposition, I mean external impediments of motion) and may be applied no less to irrational and inanimate creatures than to rational. For whatsoever is so tied or environed as it cannot move but within a certain space, which space is determined by the opposition to some external body, we say it hath not liberty to go further" (Hobbes 1994, 136).

18. A comparable yet ultimately different uptake of the "supplement" than that discussed in both Ranciere and Guru occurs in Etienne Balibar's essay "Racism and Nationalism." There, Balibar declares that "racism is not an expression of nationalism, but a supplement of nationalism or more precisely a supplement internal to nationalism" (1991, 54). In positing racism as a supplement, Balibar wants to emphasize that it is always in excess, always indispensable, and yet always still insufficient to the constitution of a community of belonging that flies under the flag of nationalism.

19. "Sealing" refers to the closure of a business by city authorities for failure to conform to existing laws and regulations (such as pollution ordinances, zoning prescriptions, tax violations, etc.).

20. Hence Roy's (2009) generative observation that governance in cities often operates through "unmapping."

REFERENCES

Althusser, L. 1971. *Lenin and Philosophy and Other Essays*. Translated by Ben Brewster. New York: Monthly Review Press.
Ambedkar, B. R. 1969. *Thus Spoke Ambedkar: Selected Speeches*. Vol. 2. Edited by B. Das. Jullundur, India: Bheem Patrika Publications.
Balibar, E. 1991. "Racism and Nationalism." In *Race, Nation, Class: Ambiguous Identities*, E. Balibar and I. Wallerstein, 37–68. London: Verso.
Bayat, A. 2000. "From 'Dangerous Classes' to 'Quiet Rebels': Politics of the Urban Subaltern in the Global South." *International Sociology* 15, no. 3: 533–57.
Bhan, G. 2016. *In the Public's Interest: Evictions, Citizenship and Inequality in Contemporary Delhi*. Delhi: Orient Blackswan.
Castel, R. 2003. *From Manual Workers to Wage Labor*. Translated by Richard Boyd. New Brunswick, N.J.: Transactions Publishers.
Centre for Policy Research. 2015. "*Categorisation of Settlement in Delhi*, CPR Policy Brief." Centre for Policy Research, New Delhi. Available at http://cprindia.org/sites/default/files/policy-briefs/Categorisation-of-Settlement-in-Delhi.pdf.
Chakrabarty, D. 2000. *Provincializing Europe: Postcolonial Thought and Historical Difference*. Princeton, N.J.: Princeton University Press.
Chattopadhyay, S. 2012. "Urbanism, Colonialism, and Subalternity." In *Urban Theory beyond the West: A World of Cities*, edited by T. Edensor and M. Jayne, 75–92. London: Routledge.
Chintan. 2003. *Space for Waste*. New Delhi: Chintan Environmental Research and Action Group.

Douglas, M. 2002 [1966]. *Purity and Danger: An Analysis of Concepts of Pollution and Taboo*. London: Routledge.

Fabian, J. 1983. *Time and the Other: How Anthropology Makes Its Object*. New York: Columbia University Press.

Fanon, F. 2008 [1952]. *Black Skin, White Masks*. Translated by Richard Philcox. New York: Grove Press.

Ghertner, A. 2015. *Rule by Aesthetics: World-Class City Making in Delhi*. Delhi: Oxford University Press.

Gidwani, V. 2008. Capitalism's Anxious Whole: Fear, Capture and Escape in the *Grundrisse*, *Antipode* 40, no. 5 (November): 857–78.

———. 2015. "The Work of Waste: Inside India's Infra-Economy." *Transactions of the Institute of British Geographers* 40, no. 4: 575–95.

Gidwani, V., and A. Maringanti. 2016. "The Waste-Value Dialectic: Lumpen Urbanization in Contemporary India." *Comparative Studies of South Asia, Africa and the Middle East* 36, no. 1: 112–33.

Gidwani, V., and R. N. Reddy. 2011. "The Afterlives of Waste: Notes from India for a Minor History of Capitalist Surplus." *Antipode* 43, no. 4 (November): 1625–58.

Gidwani, V., and J. Wainwright. 2014. "Capital, Not-Capital, and Development: After Kalyan Sanyal." *Economic & Political Weekly* 49, no. 34 (August): 40–47.

Gill, K. 2010. *Of Poverty and Plastic: Scavenging and Scrap Trading Entrepreneurs in India's Urban Informal Sector*. Delhi: Oxford University Press.

Guru, G. 2002. "How Egalitarian Are the Social Sciences in India?" *Economic and Political Weekly* 37, no. 51: 5003–9.

Guru, G., and S. Sarukkai. 2012. *The Cracked Mirror: An Indian Debate on Experience and Theory*. Delhi: Oxford University Press.

Hallward, P. 2002. *Absolutely Postcolonial: Writing between the Singular and the Specific*. Manchester: Manchester University Press.

Harrison, L. 2010. "Subaltern City, Subaltern Citizens: New Orleans, Urban Identity, and People of African Descent." In *Subaltern Citizens and Their Histories: Investigations from India and the USA*, edited by G. Pandey, 109–24. New York: Routledge.

Hazards Centre. 2007. *A Fact-finding Report on the Eviction and Resettlement Process in Delhi*. Compiled by D. Leena and S. Chotani. New Delhi: Hazards Centre.

Hobbes, T. 1994 [1668]. *Leviathan*. Edited by E. Curley. Indianapolis: Hackett.

Hodges, S. 2013. "Medical Garbage and the Making of Neo-Liberalism in India." *Economic & Political Weekly* 48 (November 30): 112–19.

———. Forthcoming. "Plastic History, Caste and the Government of Things in Modern India." In *South Asian Governmentalities: Michel Foucault and the Question of Postcolonial Orderings*, edited by S. Legg and D. Heath. Delhi: Cambridge University Press.

Ismail, S. 2013. "Urban Subalterns in the Arab Revolutions: Cairo and Damascus in Comparative Perspective." *Comparative Studies in Society and History* 55, no. 4: 865–94.

Jagori. 2009. *Making Delhi a Safer Place for Youth in a Resettlement Colony: Madanpur Khadar, Delhi*. New Delhi: JAGORI.

Kaviraj, S. 2013. "Why Is the Mirror Cracked?" *Comparative Studies of South Asia, Africa and the Middle East* 33, no. 3: 380–90.

Kosman, A. 2013. *The Activity of Being: An Essay on Aristotle's Ontology*. Cambridge, Mass.: Harvard University Press.

Kotef, H. 2015. *Movement and the Ordering of Freedom: On Liberal Governances of Mobility*. Durham, N.C.: Duke University Press.

Lefebvre, H. 1991. *The Production of Space*. Translated by D. Nicholson-Smith. Oxford: Blackwell.

Legg, Stephen. 2016. "Empirical and Analytical Subaltern Space: Ashrams, Brothels, and Trafficking in Colonial Delhi." *Cultural Studies* 30, no. 5: 793–815.

Marx, K. 1988 [1844]. *Economic and Philosophic Manuscripts of 1844*, Translated by M. Milligan. Buffalo, N.Y.: Prometheus.

———. 2010a. *Marx & Engels Collected Works*. Vol. 28, *Marx 1857–61*. London: Lawrence and Wishart Electric Book.

———. 2010b. *Marx & Engels Collected Works*. Vol. 35, *Karl Marx—Capital Volume 1*. London: Lawrence and Wishart Electric Book.

Massey, D. 2005. *For Space*. London: Sage.

Morton, S. 2007. *Gayatri Spivak: Ethics, Subalternity, and the Critique of Postcolonial Reason*. Cambridge, Mass.: Polity Press.

Mukhopadhyay, P., M-H. Zerah, and E. Denis. 2012. "Subaltern Urbanization in India." *Economic and Political Weekly* 47, no. 30: 52–62.

Nigam, A. 2011. *Desire Named Development*. Delhi: Penguin.

Prashad, V. 2000. *Untouchable Freedom: A Social History of a Dalit Community*. Delhi: Oxford University Press.

Ranciere, J. 2010. "Ten Theses on Politics." In *Dissensus: On Politics and Aesthetics*, edited by S. Corcoran, 27–44. London: Bloomsbury.

Ranganathan, M. 2014. "Paying for Pipes, Claiming Citizenship: Political Agency and Water Reforms at the Periphery." *International Journal of Urban and Regional Research* 38, no. 2: 590–608.

Roy, A. 2009. "Why India Cannot Plan Its Cities." *Planning Theory* 8, no. 1: 76–87.

———. 2011. "Slumdog Cities: Rethinking Subaltern Urbanism." *International Journal of Urban and Regional Research* 35, no. 2: 223–38.

Sanyal, K. 2007. *Rethinking Capitalist Development: Primitive Accumulation, Governmentality & Post-colonial Capitalism*. New Delhi: Routledge.

Schindler, S. 2014. "Understanding Urban Processes in Flint, Michigan: Approaching 'Subaltern Urbanism' Inductively." *International Journal of Urban and Regional Research* 38, no. 3: 791–804.

Scott, J. C. 1985. *Weapons of the Weak: Everyday Forms of Peasant Resistance*. New Haven, Conn.: Yale University Press.

Sethi, A. 2012. *A Free Man: A True Story of Life and Death in Delhi*. New York: W. W. Norton.

Sharan, A. 2014. *In the City, Out of Place: Nuisance, Pollution and Dwelling in Delhi, c. 1850–2000*. Delhi: Oxford University Press.

Sharma, S. 2014. *In the Meantime: Temporality and Cultural Politics*. Durham, N.C.: Duke University Press.

Sheppard, E., H. Leitner, and A. Maringanti. 2013. "Provincializing Global Urbanism: A Manifesto." *Urban Geography* 34, no. 7: 893–900.

Spivak, G. C. 1988. "Can the Subaltern Speak?" In *Marxism and the Interpretation of Culture*, edited by C. Nelson and L. Grossberg, 271–313. Urbana: University of Illinois Press.

———. 1999. "History." In *A Critique of Postcolonial Reason: Toward a History of the Vanishing Present*, 198–311. Cambridge, Mass.: Harvard University Press.

———. 2005. "Scattered Speculations on the Subaltern and the Popular." *Postcolonial Studies* 8, no. 4: 475–86.

Srivastava, Sanjay. 2014. *Entangled Urbanism: Slum, Gated Community, and Shopping Mall in Delhi and Gurgaon*. Delhi: Oxford University Press.

Sundaram, R. 2010. *Pirate Modernity: Delhi's Media Urbanism*. Delhi: Oxford University Press.

Thompson, M. 1979. *Rubbish Theory: The Creation and Destruction of Value*. Oxford: Oxford University Press.

Valmiki, O. 2003. *Joothan: A Dalit's Life*. New York: Columbia University Press.

Viney, W. 2014. *Waste: A Philosophy of Things*. London: Bloomsbury Academic.

Vishwanathan, S. 2014. "Rethinking Waste: Time, Obsolescence, Diversity and Democracy." In *Arts and Aesthetics in a Globalizing World*, edited by R. Kaur and P. Dave-Mukherji, 99–118. London: Bloomsbury.

Wakankar, M. 2013. "Topics of the New Dalit Critique." *Comparative Studies of South Asia, Africa and the Middle East* 33, no. 3: 403–8.

Werner, Marion. 2016. *Global Displacements: The Making of Uneven Development in the Caribbean*. Malden, Mass,: Wiley-Blackwell.

Subaltern Geographies in the Plurinational State of Bolivia

The TIPNIS Conflict

ANNA F. LAING

> Thanks be to the Bolivian people! Once more, we are here in front of the cathedral of Santísima Trinidad to remind them that on this day, 21 years ago, we set out to demand indigenous territories from the government.
> —Ernesto Noe, August 15, 2011

Following this speech by the Mojeño leader, around eight hundred indigenous peoples departed from Trinidad in the Amazonian region of Bolivia on the Eighth Indigenous March named "for the Defence of the TIPNIS, for Life, for Dignity and for the Rights of Indigenous Peoples."[1] The marchers were resisting the government's plans to build a road through the Isiboro Sécure National Park and Indigenous Territory (TIPNIS; Territorio Indígena y Parque Nacional Isiboro Sécure), which carries the dual status of a national park and legally recognized territory communally titled to the Mojeño-Trinitario, Yuracaré, and Chimane peoples. Significantly, this infrastructure would open up the park to the exploration and exploitation of hydrocarbons. Two decades after the 1990 March for Territory and Dignity led by Ernesto Noe, which resulted in the legal recognition of four indigenous territories including the TIPNIS, the lowland indigenous movement—spearheaded by CIDOB (Indigenous Confederation of the Bolivian East, Chaco and Amazon; Confederacíon Indígena del Oriente, Chaco y Amazonía de Bolivia)—was retracing its steps toward the seat of government in La Paz (approximately six hundred kilometers). This time the marchers were defending their constitutional right to free, prior, and informed consultation, which had been neglected by the very government responsible for establishing the new constitution and refounding Bolivia as a "plurinational" state in 2009. The conflict revealed a paradox: that despite the MAS (Movimiento al Socialismo; Movement toward Socialism) administration's avowed goals of decolonizing the nation-state and incorporating indigenous populations more comprehensively into decision-making practices of the state, "the sense remains that resource extraction blessed by the government trumps all other considerations"

(Bebbington, Humphreys Bebbington, and Bury 2010, 313). Within this chapter, I contend that there is a persistent logic of "coloniality" embedded within the MAS's self-styled "indigenous" state. Yet indigenous movements continue their decolonial efforts through demands for self-determination, which would entail the delinking of state machinery from its colonial foundation.

This chapter explores the resisted, contested, and negotiated configurations of the Bolivian decolonial path by bringing into conversation scholarship by the modernity-coloniality-decoloniality (MCD) (see Escobar 2007; Mignolo 2007a) project in Latin America and South Asian subaltern studies. MCD proponents have challenged postcolonial theorists for presenting a postmodern reading of subalternity, which Ramón Grosfoguel contends "represents a Eurocentric critique of eurocentricism" (2007, 211; also see Mignolo 2000). Instead, MCD scholars marshal a decolonial reading of subalternity, which critiques Eurocentrism *from* and *with* subalternized knowledges. Postcolonial thinkers, such as Edward Said, Gayatri Spivak, and Homi Bhabha, are questioned for grounding their work in the poststructuralism of Foucault, Lacan, and Derrida. Walter Mignolo argues that they present "a project of scholarly transformation within the academy" (2007b, 452) that remains internal to Europe. Instead, decoloniality is understood as a project of *desprendimiento* (Quijano 1992) or "delinking" (Mignolo 2007b) from contemporary legacies of coloniality. This includes coloniality of power (Quijano 1992, 2000), knowledge (see Lander 2000), and being (Maldonado-Torres 2007). Delinking starts from "other sources" (Mignolo 2007b, 452), such as the activism and scholarship of Mahatma Gandhi, Aimé Césaire, and Frantz Fanon, to name a few examples. This politico-epistemic move is crucial for displacing Eurocentric knowledge and bringing subaltern epistemologies into the fold. To be sure, this is a move I seek to pursue in this chapter by drawing on ethnographic engagement with indigenous movements in defense of the TIPNIS from September 2011 to June 2012, including six weeks on the Ninth Indigenous March (a second march in defense of the TIPNIS).

That said, I work from a position that does not reject postcolonial critiques from the West in their entirety, in part since there is no "outside" of modernity that can be recovered simply by focusing on marginalized and silenced voices in the Global South. To do so risks a romanticism and essentialism of identitarian politics, particularly in regards to race and ethnicity. In reference to indigenous peoples, Sarah Radcliffe recognizes that "the emancipatory valence of indigeneity is neither natural nor automatic" (2017, 223) but rather relational. Indeed, this can be seen in the Bolivian case where there has been a substantial resignification of indigenous identity politics over time. Kiran Asher also points out that the collective evades the problem of representation and falls into the trap of "making the subaltern speak" (2013, 832). With this in mind, I agree with Asher that bringing Gayatri Spivak (1987, 1990, 2014) into conversation with the MCD project would add conceptual rigor. More recently, Spivak conceptualizes subalternity as "the idea of no access to the structures of citizenship, the structures of the state" (2014, 10). Although indigenous peoples are recognized as constitutional citizens of Bolivia and given rights as collective subjects, the government has established certain limits and sanctions—a distinction between de jure and de facto political power—that constitutes a "domestication" of decolonial trajectories (Garcés 2011, 46). Using Spivak's interpretation of the problem of representation, one may argue that factions of the indigenous populations are unable to "speak" since they have not had their constitutional rights to self-determination (and free, prior, and informed consent) respected and complied with. The TIPNIS protesters pushed at these limits and sought, as María Saldaña-Portillo remarks in reference to indigenous Mexicans, a shift from "the position of the subaltern who evades representation . . . to the position of constitutional subject: the Indian as citizen as Indian" (2001, 412). Fundamentally, I argue that the TIPNIS protesters were enacting a decolonial move aimed at transcending their own subalternity. Subalternization can therefore be understood as a relational process constantly reworked through the spatial dynamics of cultural hegemony (Rabasa 2010).

This chapter will first outline the antecedents to the TIPNIS conflict, indicating some of the contradictions embedded within the MAS's decolonial project. I then discuss processes of coloniality within the state, including the government's use of police intervention in the Eighth March and the use of a development narrative based on ideas of progress, modernity, and assimilation. This section is followed by an examination of the ways in which the TIPNIS struggle has mobilized subaltern memories of a collective "colonial wound" (Mignolo 2005, 95). Although not widely chronicled by scholars of the conflict, I argue that analyses of colonial legacies are vital since they shape subaltern resistance in the present. Finally, I document the ways in which the lowland indigenous movement has resisted contemporary processes of colonial subjugation, namely through the use of nonviolent protest marches to assert their right to be represented in the public sphere.

The Plurinational State: A Decolonial Move?

In 2006, Evo Morales became president of Bolivia with 54 percent of the votes. The MAS, the party behind the so-called social-movement state (Gustafson 2009a, 255), had its roots in the Unity Pact, a national alliance among the country's five principal peasant and indigenous grassroots movements, including the two indigenous organizations of the lowlands and highlands: CIDOB and CONAMAQ (National Council of Ayllus and Markas of Qollasuyu; Consejo Nacional de Ayllus y Markas del Qullasuyo). Despite fragmentary objectives, the pact had a united vision to "refound" the country "through the participation of indigenous peoples as *peoples* (pueblos)" (Garcés 2011, 50). That is to say, the intention was to foreground collective—rather than individual—subjects of decision making within state structures. This conceptualization of governance was articulated through the demand for a Constituent Assembly that aimed to transcend the colonial legacy of liberal democracy that accompanies the ideology of the modern nation-state. For some, this shift constitutes a decolonial transition (see Escobar 2010).

The decolonial project was substantiated through the 2009 constitution that renamed the "Republic" the "Plurinational State of Bolivia" in recognition of the nearly two-thirds of the population who self-identified as indigenous in the 2001 national census (INE/UMPA 2003, 157). While there are many plurinational and pluricultural states, Latin American nationalisms—as elsewhere—have fictionalized idealistic visions of an "imagined community" based on ethnolinguistic homogeneity (see Anderson 1991). The Bolivian government has departed from this inherited colonial model, however, by reimagining "a state that merges constitutive sovereignty rooted in the national people (*pueblo*) and indigenous plurality and self-determination" (Gustafson 2009b, 987). The constitution rebalances democratic norms by acknowledging communitarian forms of decision making practiced by indigenous peoples, alongside individual citizenship regimes. In this way, state structures have incorporated what David Slater has called "demo-diversity," democracy that "emerges from indigenous roots" (2013, 75). This departure from the liberal democratic framing of state-society relations in Bolivia, as well as in other Latin American countries, has caused scholars to speculate on whether there has been a "post-liberal" shift in civilian regimes (Nolte and Schilling Vacaflor 2012; Yashar 2005).

Further, the constitution expressly grants indigenous autonomy and territorial self-determination. Under Article 403, indigenous peoples inhabiting Original Indigenous and Peasant Territories (Territorios Indígena Originario Campesino; TIOCs) have

> the right to land; to the use and exclusive exploitation of renewable natural resources under conditions determined by law; to prior and informed consultation; to participation in the benefits of the exploitation of the non-renewable natural resources that are found in their territory; the authority to apply their own norms, administered by their structures of representation; and to define their development in accordance with their own cultural criteria and principles of harmonious coexistence with nature. (Gobierno de Bolivia 2009, 148).

These land titling efforts reflect a broader "territorial turn" in Latin America, where there has been significant state recognition of communal indigenous property and land rights (see Bryan 2012; Offen 2003). Indeed, "politico-territorial autonomy" has been the long-standing articulating demand of indigenous movements across Latin America (Díaz Polanco 1997).

Plurinationalism marks a transformative moment since previous governments have failed to assimilate the indigenous masses to the nation-state (Rivera Cusicanqui 1987). The 1952 National Revolution, in which workers and peasants overthrew the entrenched oligarchy of tin barons and landholders, resulted in the granting of universal suffrage and instigated agrarian reform that redistributed land to peasant laborers (see Dunkerley 1984). Nonetheless, class-based interests superseded ethnic demands and indigenous movements were "considered to be an obstacle to the sovereignty of the State" (Rivera Cusicanqui 1987, 93). The COB (Central Obrera Boliviana), Bolivia's chief trade union confederation, took a central role in state politics and formed the backbone of working-class resistance (Crabtree 2005; Dunkerley 1984). What prevailed was a nationalist "ideology of *mestizaje*—the mixture of indigenous and nonindigenous—[which] was paired with the extension of individual citizenship rights to newly designated campesinos [peasant farmers] who, it was imagined, would set aside their collective cultural investments in keeping with the expectations of modernity" (Albro 2010, 74). The "Indian question" was addressed through acculturation and civilization, rather than recognizing indigenous cosmologies within the nation-state (Malloy 1970). Thus, decolonial visions of communal representation and territorial self-determination were sidelined in the interest of promoting a homogenous nationalism.

Furthermore, the 1952 revolution had a very different impact in the Amazonian tropics of Bolivia, sparking what James Jones has referred to as the "colonization of the Oriente" (1984, 71). Under the land reform decree, lowland indigenous peoples were referred to as "in a savage state and with a primitive organization" and denied full-fledged citizen status (cited in Jones 1984, 76). Although the law was later changed, the view that the lowlands was *tierras baldías* (public or vacant lands) served to awaken investors to the opportunity of obtaining land titles, with the Amazonian region becoming a new frontier for development and expansion (Jones 1984; Lehm Ardaya 1999). In the area around the TIPNIS, this colonization continued with the migration of Andean peasants to the south of the park after the closure of state mines under the neoliberal reforms of the 1980s. The cultivation of coca has been the predominant livelihood of these migrants, converting the Chapare province into the biggest coca-producing area of Bolivia, with the *cocalero* (coca-grower) movement becoming a formidable political force (Healy 1991; Paz 2012). Since the 1990s a significant ethnicization of national politics served to unite peasant and indigenous factions, however (see Postero 2007; Van Cott 2005). Most notably, various social movements and trade unions came together in popular resistance during the Water and Gas Wars.[2] These groups lent their support to the MAS, which showed a marked ability to subsume heterogeneous identities under an "indigenous nationalism" that crosscut class and ethnicity (Stefanoni 2006, 37). Indeed, for Vice President García Linera, "Evo symbolizes the breaking of an imaginary and horizon of possibilities restricted to the subalternity of the indigenous" (cited in Svampa and Stefanoni 2007, 147).

Tensions between the government's self-styled "indigenous" state and indigenous movements remain, however. Most notably, land and resource conflicts have been a key feature of the MAS's three administration periods. There are two interconnected grounds for this contestation. Firstly, the MAS has significantly departed from the Unity Pact's decolonial agenda on several fronts. For instance, the pact proposed that indigenous peoples be granted veto power on the exploitation of nonrenewable resources within their territories, but this was redacted from the final version of the constitution; indigenous autonomy status is difficult to achieve due to restrictive administrative requirements; free and prior consultation processes with indigenous communities are not binding; and indigenous deputies of the Plurinational Legislative Assembly are elected by majority, rather than through the procedures of indigenous communities (see Garcés 2011; Tockman and Cameron 2014).

Secondly, state-led neo-extractivism has severely threatened indigenous autonomy and territorial self-determination (see Bebbington 2009; Bebbington and Bury 2013). In 2006, the MAS initiated a "nationalization" of the country's hydrocarbon industry, increasing state funds from USD$287 million in 2004 to USD$1.572 billion by 2007 (Kaup 2010, 129). The government has used these revenues to enact social welfare programmes, dramatically reducing absolute poverty rates from 60 percent in 2006 to 30 percent by 2011 (Kohl and Farthing 2012, 231). Resource extraction is integral to the country's economic development plan, not least as 55 percent of Bolivia's territory is of potential hydrocarbon interest (Bebbington 2009, 14). This has respatializing effects since the exploration and exploitation of subsoil resources has expanded into new frontiers in the Amazonian region, an area inhabited by many indigenous communities (Bebbington and Bury 2013). Moreover, the constitution acts to undermine indigenous rights to territorial self-determination as it declares hydrocarbons to be under the ownership of the state (Gobierno de Bolivia 2009, Art. 359: I).

Does the Plurinational State of Bolivia constitute a decolonial move? The incorporation of precolonial nations and their epistemologies within the legal structures of government represents a distinct departure from previous formulations of state, nation, and society. In many ways, then, the plurinational project can be understood as a push to fulfill the "uncompleted revolution" (Malloy 1970) of 1952. It is also noteworthy that the MAS has made concrete steps toward political and economic parity for many sectors of society, especially peasant and urban indigenous populations who form the majority of citizens who identified as "indigenous" in the 2001 census (INE/UMPA 2003). Nonetheless, subaltern studies theorists in Latin America have critiqued *both* neoliberal governmentality *and* more progressive ideologies on the left, for reproducing colonial legacies of modernity (Rodríguez 2001). Indeed, plurinationalism has not been fully embraced by the nationalist left (on Ecuador, see Radcliffe 2012). Aníbal Quijano reflects that the vision of socialist revolution as "control of the state and as state control of labor/resources/product" is a "Eurocentric mirage" and that true decolonialism would require a "socialization of power" (2000, 572) to all societal sectors. As the Bolivian writer Rafael Bautista concludes, "To decolonise the state means dismantling the structural and conceptual content of its colonial constitution" (2010, 10). This change would involve not only the recognition, but also the practical application, of state mechanisms to integrate the respective forms of decision making carried out by ethnic nations. Without this, the MAS can no longer act as the articulator at an organizational level of indigenous demands (Tapia 2011, 41). The degree to which the plurinational state is inherently a decolonial move is therefore limited in part, as it fails to fully embrace the alternative spatio-political imaginaries of subalternized indigenous sectors.

Progressive Neo-Extractivism, Coloniality, and the TIPNIS

The TIPNIS conflict exemplifies these challenges for the plurinational project. The TIPNIS (an area of over 1.2 million hectares) sits on the border area between the departments of Beni and Cochabamba. This biologically diverse region was recognized as a national park in 1965 at a time when conservation was deemed important due to threats from increasing land colonization in the Amazonian region as a result of the 1953 agrarian reform law (Paz 2012). The park is home to sixty-nine communities and was legally recognized as an indigenous territory in 1990 as a result of the historic march led by CIDOB. The legal titling was made more concrete through a process of *saneamiento de tierras* (land cleansing), and in 1997 the indigenous communities were granted a TCO (Tierras Comunitarias de Origen; First Nations or "Original" Communal Lands) title. At this time, a *línea roja* (red line) was established separating the TCO from a colonized area to the south of the national park, known as Polygon 7, that is predominantly inhabited by coca-growers (see map 1). The TIPNIS has been under threat despite this dual protection status, not only as a result of the proposed road but also due to interrelated processes, namely the expansion of coca growing and oil and gas extraction (McNeish 2013). Notably, the road would open up access to natural resources with concessions granted for hydrocarbon exploration in 25.5 percent of the TIPNIS (CEDLA 2012; see map 1). Further, the conflict has pitted highland peasants and lowland indigenous peoples against one another, since many Andean migrants and coca-growers living adjacent to the park have supported the road (Fabricant and Postero 2015). Significantly, this sector is a key base of support for Morales, who made his name as the charismatic leader of the *cocalero* movement.

Government discourse proclaimed the necessity of the road for the integra-

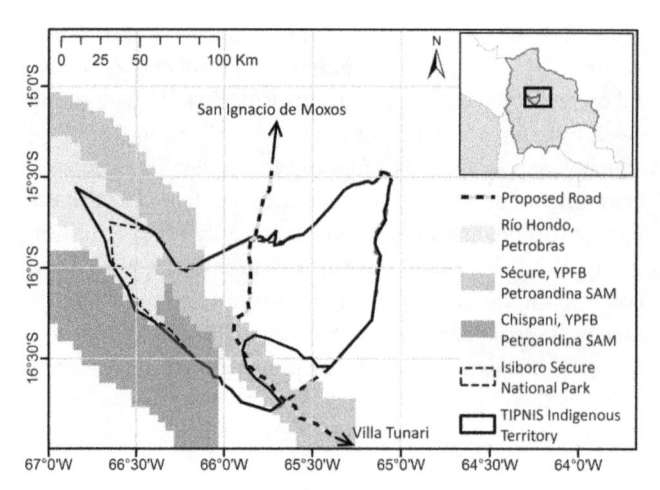

MAP 1. Hydrocarbon Concessions in the TIPNIS.

tion of the eastern and western regions of Bolivia. The development agenda was rationalized through a discourse of "modernity" and "progress" that echoed the assimilationist logic of the government after the 1952 national revolution (Laing 2015; Sanjinés 2013). In reference to the TIPNIS conflict, Luis Tapia writes that "the idea of the lowlands as a space of colonization corresponds to the lack of recognition of the existence of other peoples and their territories" (2012, 271). Tellingly, after the lowland indigenous movement announced that it was going to organize a protest march resisting the construction of the road, the president declared, "whether they want it or not, we are going to build this road" (Los Tiempos 2011, n.p.). "Progressive neo-extractivism" (Gudynas 2009, 188) evidently supplanted indigenous autonomy and territorial self-determination.

These tensions came to the fore on September 25, 2011, when the TIPNIS conflict was catapulted into national and international media attention following police intervention on a protest march. Using tear gas, rubber bullets, and batons, a group of approximately five hundred federal police entered the marchers' campsite at Chaparina and escorted them onto waiting buses to transport them to nearby towns with the aim of transferring the detainees back to their territories in military planes. Roughly a hundred people were injured and two women suffered miscarriages. As television footage of the police violence emerged, vigils sprang up in Bolivia's main plazas and there were several protests against the government intervention. Interior minister Sacha Llorenti was forced to resign over accusations that he issued the police order. After five days the marchers regrouped and continued their journey to La Paz, where they were greeted by tens of thousands of supporters on October 19. Due to national pressure, the government canceled the road contract under *Ley Corta* (Short Law)

No. 180, which was promulgated on October 24. The government's use of force marked a fundamental crisis in the hegemony of the MAS to act as a "social-movement state" (Gustafson 2009a, 255). John-Andrew McNeish suggests that it "sparked both a national political crisis and debate about the validity of the government's credentials as a progressive government that supports indigenous rights" (2013, 221).

On February 1, 2012, the road project was back on the agenda again, however, after the promulgation of Law No. 222 as a result of pressure from a countermarch by TIPNIS highway supporters. The countermarch was instigated by the Indigenous Council of the South (CONISUR; Consejo Indígena del Sur), representing coca-growers and inhabitants of the southernmost part of the national park, located outside of the indigenous titled territory. The new law reopened the possibility of the road subject to a consultation with the sixty-nine TIPNIS communities. The prior consultation process (widely referred to as the "postconsultation") was carried out between July and December 2012 with the final report suggesting that 80 percent of the communities agreed to advance proposals for the road (TSE 2012). However, the consultation included eighteen communities of coca-growing peasants and a further eleven communities boycotted the consultations (TSE 2012). Furthermore, an independent "verification commission" carried out by human rights organizations and the Catholic Church concluded that the consultation did not adhere to the respective organizational structures of indigenous communities and therefore failed to meet legal structures respecting the cultural diversity and world-visions of ethnic nations (FIDH-APDHB 2013). Even where communities agreed to the proposal of the road, it has been suggested that the consultation process was manipulated since the wording focused on whether communities wanted Law No. 180—the act that canceled the road project—to be restored. This was a double-edged sword, however, since it also described the TIPNIS as an "intangible" (untouchable) zone, which would prohibit the inhabitants of the park from using its natural resources for wealth production. The process of building consent was also marked by gift giving since the inception of the road project. For instance, the leader of the Ninth March, Bertha Vejarano, stated that she had seen the government "taking them [TIPNIS communities] gifts, buying their conscience. The government uses them, convinces them to say 'yes to the road,' by taking them things that are not worth it. Taking them motors and cell phones" (personal interview, May 15, 2012).[3]

The communities of the TIPNIS do not oppose development per se, however. For instance, the platform of demands of the Ninth March included calls for the implementation of community development models in line with the world-visions and self-determination of indigenous peoples, the recognition of community organizations as actors in the mineral and hydrocarbon sectors, and the right for communities to benefit from the revenues created through extractive industries (personal field-notes, May 20, 2012). Rather, indigenous communities seek representation in state decision-making processes through their respective organizational forms as outlined in the constitution. For instance, for the indigenous leader and former president of CONAMAQ Rafael Quispe, the significance of prior consultation is more than just a legislative framework, since it "is a mechanism for other rights, such as self-determination, autonomy, [and] self-governance and that is important for us. It is one of the safeguards for protecting indigenous peoples" (personal interview, April 29, 2012). Further still, when asked whether the communities would have accepted the road project had they been consulted, the president of Sécure Sub-Central (one of two organizing bodies within the TIPNIS), Emilio Noza Yuco, affirmed that "the communities would always accept a prior consultation process before approving a project. But now, they feel they have been humiliated, sidelined by the government" (personal interview, May 9, 2012). Fundamentally, then, resistance to the road was also a call for greater self-determination over decisions affecting communally owned indigenous territories. In the next section, I demonstrate that the indigenous protest was shaped by collective memories of a "colonial wound" (Mignolo 2005, 95) resulting from a long history of settler colonialism into indigenous lands. In turn, these memories were mobilized to fashion a subaltern version of the past to suit the political needs of the present.

Mobilizing Subaltern Pasts toward Decolonial Futures

Intellectual engagement with the TIPNIS conflict has predominantly circulated around the extent to which Bolivia can now be conceived of as a "post-neoliberal" state. Though pertinent, these discussions have not engaged fully with the historical experiences of colonial territorialization and ensuing anticolonial resistance in the Amazonian regions.[4] This is not surprising given that popularized chronicles of Bolivia have focused on the history of the Andean region, which "has left a lasting mark on internal cultural politics and academic frameworks and continues to influence policy-making" (Fabricant 2012, 22). Here, I attempt to address this gap in the literature by using ethnographic engagement with the TIPNIS protest marches to illuminate the ways that "long memories" have served to instill "people with a sense of continuity, the inevitability of resistance, and the legitimacy of struggle" (Kohl and Farthing 2011, 196). Specifically, I focus on the ways that place-based millenarian movements *en busca de la Loma Santa* (in search of the Holy Hill) have been rearticulated in pan-indigenous movements for the recognition of indigenous territory in lowland Bolivia.

The millenarian movements in search of the *Loma Santa* were a series of migrations by the Mojeño peoples lasting between the 1880s and the 1990s from ex-Jesuit settlements in the department of Beni into the surrounding forests, including the area of the TIPNIS. The migrations sought a religious space—the Holy Hill—free from the strictures of (post)colonial domination. Movements sought a place of retreat away from the *carayana* populations (*carayana* is a lowland indigenous term for white people or outsiders, see Lehm Ardaya 1999; Riester and Fischerman 1976). The arrival of the Jesuit missionaries into Beni between 1684 and 1767 had an immense impact on indigenous society and culture (Riester and Fischerman 1976). The Jesuits rounded up local riverine communities into sixteen *reducciones* (centralized settlements) across the plains of the Moxos region in order to spread Christianity, civilize indigenous peoples, and consolidate tax collection (Chávez Suárez 1986). The Jesuits laid the first territorial foundations of the colonial state in the remote "frontier" regions of the Amazonian lowlands. Kevin Healy remarks that, prior to the Jesuit missions, "ancestor worship, devotion to forest spirits, and jaguar cults flourished in a society closed off from the world" (2001, 363). Later, the reductions were taken over by secular officials who forced many indigenous inhabitants into service during the rubber boom of the late nineteenth century. The dire working conditions resulted in deaths and consequent hostility toward the *carayana* traders (Riester and Fischerman 1976; Van Valen 2013).

It is in this context of sociocultural change that in 1842 a series of migrations started to occur "in which people were pushed by liberal reforms, labor demands associated with the rubber boom, and floods, and pulled by the prospect of rich, higher lands which were distant from the authorities" (Van Valen 2013, 107). In 1887, these scattered migrations became a unitary movement under the leadership of an Itonama shaman named Andrés Guayocho. The leader guided migrations from Trinidad into the forests to the west of the Mamoré River in the united belief that a paradise on earth existed there that would grant the indigenous peoples freedom to live according to their respective world-visions. Guayocho considered himself to be a messiah and savior of the Mojeño peoples from *carayanas*, whom he considered a damned race that were spreading evil into the land (Lehm Ardaya 1999; Riester and Fischerman 1976). Zulema Lehm Ardaya thus describes the *Loma Santa* as "a sacred space of abundance and free from the socio-cultural pressures that diverse actors of national society exerted on them" (1999, 9). The shaman leader combined the Christian faith brought by the Jesuits with local ancestral customs and "articulated a millenarian ideology" to give "supranatural sanction to the abandonment of Trinidad" (Van Valen 2013, 120). In doing so, he articulated legends of a Christian "promised land" alongside precolonial spiritual beliefs, such as the practice of channeling deceased people and the use of jaguar and caiman worship.

The movement in search of the *Loma Santa* has been resurrected in later migrations lasting until the 1990s (see Cortés Rodríguez 1987; Lehm Ardaya 1999; Querejazu Lewis 2008). Many of these migrations settled in the adjoining forests next to the Sécure and Isiboro rivers (Querejazu Lewis 2008). For example, the TIPNIS communities of San Lorenzo, Trinidadcito, and Santa Rosario were founded as part of these relocations. These waves occurred due to increasing colonization of lands as a result of the promulgation of the Law of Barren Lands in 1905 that opened the lowland regions to foreign investment; the collapse of the rubber trade (around 1910–20) that led to a rise in cattle ranching, which required larger tracts of land; the 1953 agrarian reform law that encouraged the resettlement of peasant sectors, also known as *colonos* (colonizers), into the Chapare region; and the granting of "public" lands to a government-supported oligarchy during the military dictatorship period of the 1960s and 1970s (see Healy 2001; Jones 1984; Lehm Ardaya 1999; Querejazu Lewis 2008). Deborah Yashar notes that between the 1960s and the 1980s "indigenous communities in the Beni confronted the ongoing threat of loggers, cattle ranchers, and *colonos* who occupied tracts of land considered by Amazonian Indians as open space for working, hunting, and residing" (2005, 206).

Oral testimonies and collective memories of the movements in search of the *Loma Santa* informed the political repertoires and cultural terrains of resistance during the TIPNIS conflict. Emilio Noza Yuco, the president of Sécure Sub-Central, explained that Mojeño-Trinitario peoples "always had a religious vision that supposedly they knew biblically, that God had a place prepared for them" as a result of being "completely enslaved by the Spanish, the Jesuits and by everything" (personal interview, May 9, 2012). Beliefs of the *Loma Santa* were significant to the marches as many of the indigenous protesters were descendants of the second generation of the later 1950s–1980s migrations. In an interview with an indigenous protester from a community located on the banks of the River Sécure, he talked of the migrations in the 1950s and sketched a map to show the places the communities had settled. He explained that the Mojeño ethnic nation in Trinidad "had made a belief of a symbiosis between the Catholic religion and our beliefs" and that his "ancestors believed that by looking again for the *Loma Santa*, they would find a place where everyone would be at peace" (personal interview, March 19, 2012). Indigenous marchers similarly practiced spiritual, ritual, and festive components that amalgamated pre-Hispanic customs of the Mojeño peoples with the religious aspects inherited from the Jesuits. Indeed, Catholic beliefs and practices were part of the routine activities of the Ninth March. For example, we took mass and observed prayers at the beginning of the marching day, and the march was led by two symbolic mascots of the Catholic faith: the Virgin Mary and a wooden cross that read "Mojeño Cross: Permanent Mission." The participants interviewed on the Ninth March gained courage from their faith and often described themselves as the *hijos de dios* (children of God). Emilio Noza Yuco stated that "all the people who are here today, they believe that this is a test from God, that if they love their territory, they will have to defend it" (personal interview, May 9, 2012). This relationship between precolonial identities of the indigenous peoples and colonial properties of the Western world is not deemed contradictory, however, and the integration of Christian symbols and concepts into millenarian movements is a common trait across the Amazonian region (Brown 1994). This element of indigenous movements does not signify acculturation as there are "robust efforts to wrestle control of Christianity from whites while reshaping it to meet the spiritual needs of Indian peoples" (Brown 1994, 299).

As demonstrated, the internal dynamics and motivations of the marches in defense of the TIPNIS were inflected with a millenarian element that predates the more recent rise of indigenous rights politics in Latin America.[5] Unlike in the past, retreat into the remote areas of the Amazon Basin can no longer secure politico-territorial autonomy since private enterprises, coca-growing, and state-led extractivism have encroached into indigenous lands. Thus, indigenous movements have called for state recognition of territorial self-determination, alongside greater involvement in government decision-making structures, as a way to protect their ways of living and respective world-visions. I would therefore echo Wendy Wolford's observation that "the critical study of resistance requires an analysis of the ways different historical-cultural frameworks shape the decision to mobilize in particular people and places" (2004, 421). Crucially, these frameworks played a role in guiding the spatial politics employed by the lowland indigenous movement, an idea that I unpack in the next section.

Spatial Politics of the Indigenous Marches

Since the inception in 1982 of CIDOB—the umbrella organization of the lowland indigenous movement—the concept of "territory" has become "an icon of indigenous-state relations" (Postero 2007, 49). Specifically, CIDOB has called for a degree of autonomy and self-determination over the governance of land and resources within ancestral territories, alongside greater participation in state institutions through their respective organizational forms (Yashar 2005). The plurinational agenda has been at the heart of these decolonial struggles, and CIDOB therefore aligned itself to the MAS government through the Unity Pact. Yet the pact's indigenous and peasant members have long held contrasting views on key issues such as the nature of national development, the extent of land redistribution, the meaning and limits of political autonomy, and the social control of the state (Garcés 2011). Tensions ran high when defining the organizational structure of the Constituent Assembly, for example, as the law established that representation would be through political parties, "thus failing to acknowledge the demand of the indigenous organizations (many of them with limited regional presence) for representation as collective subjects" (Regalsky 2010, 46). As such, CIDOB representatives increasingly questioned the extent to which the MAS was fulfilling its promises of decolonizing Bolivia.

Consequently, in late 2011—when the TIPNIS conflict was at its peak—the two indigenous movements of the lowlands and highlands abandoned the Unity Pact. Juan José Sardina, a leader from the highland indigenous organization CONAMAQ, explained that they had chosen to leave the Unity Pact as they "were simply being used by the president for electoral spoils" (personal interview, June 17, 2012). Rosa Chao, a regional leader of CIDOB, stated that Morales had treated the lowland Amazonian peoples "as if we are *entenados* [stepchildren or illegitimate children, i.e., looked down upon]." She explained, "We had a dream that we [indigenous peoples] would be inside the parliament, with a minister, a vice-minister, deputies and senators. We are in the process, as at least now we have seven deputies. But for us, it [Bolivia] is not yet a plurinational state. It will be called 'plurinational' when we are represented by the ministries, vice-ministries and the mayors" (personal interview, January 20, 2012). Thus, the Morales administration was conceived to be continuing to subalternize indigenous populations by limiting access to the structures of citizenship and the state (see Spivak 2014, 10). Following this view, the MAS could be said to be creating a respatialized internal colonialism that positions peasants and coca-growers as the dominant sector and the lowland indigenous as subordinate (Laing 2012).

Resultantly, CIDOB decided to reestablish more traditional forms of rebellious practice in order to make demands on the state. After the announcement of Law No. 222, CIDOB set in motion the Ninth March named "for the Defence of Life and Dignity, Indigenous Territories, Natural Resources, Biodiversity, the Environment, Protected Areas, Compliance with the State Constitution and Respect for Democracy" between April 27 and June 27, 2012. The marches in defense of the TIPNIS were attempts to visibly reappropriate urban public spaces and articulate indigenous subjects as equal citizens of the nation-state. In her work with the Landless Peasants Movement in Bolivia, Nicole Fabricant states that indigenous marches are "about the use of the body—specifically, indigenous bodies moving visibly through national space." This tool of political action requires "sacrifice and determination, pushing the body through a severe regime of pain in order to gain legislative rights to land, resources, and alternative ways of living" (2012, 136). These embodied performances challenged the spatial segregation of indigenous peoples into enclosed rural areas, which the MAS had attempted to reinforce during the police intervention at Chaparina aimed at transferring the indigenous protesters back to their territories. The marchers were therefore problematizing the nature of indigenous territories as an "ethno-environmental fix," which Penelope Anthias and Sarah Radcliffe argue has "inevitably de-politicized and de-historized the realities of postcolonial territoriality" (2015, 262).

Indigenous protesters on the Eighth and Ninth Marches walked through metropolitan centers, including the towns of Trinidad, San Ignacio de Moxos, and San Borja. These spaces hold colonial significance as they were founded as Jesuit settlements in the seventeenth century. Additionally, the marchers occupied sites of symbolic importance in La Paz, namely Plaza Murillo (the political center, location of the Presidential Palace) and Plaza San Francisco (the religious center, location of the Catholic Basilica). The marches in defense of the TIPNIS fundamentally challenged the ideology of the MAS as a social-movement state that represented indigenous peoples. For example, as the indigenous protesters entered Plaza Murillo on the Eighth March they chanted, "*¿si este no es el pueblo, el pueblo dónde está?*" (if this is not the people, where are the people?) (personal field-notes, October 19, 2011). An illustrative space was the city of San Ignacio de Moxos, a hub of political support for the MAS. During the Ninth March, the inhabitants of the city prohibited the marchers from passing through the central plaza. A meeting was convoked to discuss whether the marchers should force their way through the town, with one community leader of the TIPNIS asking, "Are we not Bolivians as well?" (personal field-notes, May 7, 2012). In the end the marchers decided to reroute around the outskirts of the town for fears of violent confrontations. Below is an extract from my field diary from that day:

> I woke early to the noise of people packing up, alerting me to the fact that we were definitely marching today. We headed from El Algodonal towards San Ignacio de Moxos at around 8 am. I was a little scared this morning after hearing that drunken locals had been circling our campsite on motorbikes through the night and threatening to hurt people. Even the researchers from the NGO Fundación Tierra [Land Foundation] had their car graffitied with the word *traidor* [traitor] outside of their hotel in the town. We approached with some trepidation and were met with around 1,000 of the city's inhabitants lined up along the roadside chanting and shouting derogatory racial abuse against the marchers, calling them *monos* [monkeys] and yelling, "*caminen como perros, como lo que son*" [walk like dogs, as what you are]. (field journal extract, May 8, 2012)

In this instance, the language and practices of some residents of San Ignacio de Moxos negated the marchers' right to occupy these public metropolitan spaces as Bolivian citizens. This likening of the indigenous marchers to animals reified subordinate representations of the marchers. This echoes the concept of "coloniality of being" put forward by Nelson Maldonado-Torres (2007), in which subaltern subjects are dehumanized through the lived experiences of coloniality. Such antagonism was the cause of much concern for the marchers. The next day at a camp meeting in Puerto San Borja, Bertha Vejarano gave an emotionally charged speech in which she declared, "They cannot deny our rights, as Bolivians, as citizens! We don't even have the right to enter or move freely through the streets on public roads" (personal field-notes, May 9, 2012). Although the state and affiliated sectors attempted to control public sites within metropolitan areas, protesters on the Eighth and Ninth Marches actively resisted these practices and sought to reappropriate these spaces and give them new meaning.

Moreover, the resignification of public spaces was integral for gaining recognition and solidarity from other sectors of national society. The cultural expression of resistance and collective memories, or the "geopoetics of resistance" (Routledge 2000, 375), formed part of this political terrain. For instance, a song titled "Coraje" (Courage) was the anthem of the Eighth and Ninth Marches. Originally written by the activist songwriter Luis Rico for the 1990 March for Territory and Dignity, the song was resurrected for the Eighth and Ninth Marches and functioned as a multisensory register of subaltern politics, made up of sound (voices and guitars), bodies (dividing and blocking public space and joining in the performances), and representational objects (national, regional, and indigenous flags alongside indigenous symbols such as the Amazonian Patujú flower).

> ¡Coraje!
>
> Vengo desde la selva, el bosque chimán,
> Donde niño y serpiente tienen su hogar,
> Vengo desde la tierra que ya no está,
> Donde antes se vivía en libertad.
> Vengo a decirles que allá siembran dolor,
> El que depreda, mata y corta la flor,
> El que mancha los ríos, el talador.
>
> CHORUS:
> ¡Coraje, coraje!
> La unión hace la fuerza,
> Y un corazón Americano,
> Crece a la luz del sol.
>
> Les traigo en las palabras el corazón,
> Desde la Amazonía Yuracaré,
> Les traemos la esperanza, la fe y la razón,
> Que cargan en sus espaldas hombre y mujer.
> La furia y la codicia del carayana,
> Está sembrando envidia y desolación,
> Y eso es lo que me duele en el corazón.
>
> Chorus
>
> Unidos los Movima y los Sirionó,
> Mojeños la esperanza, razón y fe,
> En contra el carayana depredador.

Luchando en el Isiboro y el Sécure,
Por eso el territorio y la dignidad,
Nos venimos buscando al caminar,
De los hermanos la solidaridad.

Courage!

I come from the jungle, the Chimane forest,
Where child and snake have their home.
I come from the land that is no longer there,
Where once one lived in freedom.
I come to tell you that pain is sown there,
He who destroys, kills, and decimates the flora,
He who defiles the rivers, the logger.

CHORUS:
Courage! Courage!
Unity is strength,
And an American heart,
Grows to the light of the sun.

I bring to you the heart in words,
From the Yuracaré Amazon.
We bring you the hope, faith and reason,
Which men and women shoulder.
The fury and greed of the *carayana*,
Are sowing envy and desolation,
And that is what pains my heart.

Chorus

United the Movima and the Sirionó,
Mojeños, the hope, reason and faith,
Against the destroyer *carayana*.
Fighting in the Isiboro and the Sécure,
For territory and dignity.
We are searching while walking,
The solidarity of brothers.

Reproduced with permission of Luis Rico

The song gained notoriety through performances in a number of public spaces as a tool to articulate the collective demands of the indigenous movement to wider sectors of civil society. For example, Luis Rico and Nazareth Flores, one of the indigenous leaders of the movement, sang the anthem when the marchers entered Plaza San Francisco on the Eighth March. Their moving rendition swept through the crowd and invigorated the marchers after a seven-hour descent into the capital city. The music was especially poignant when the soft dynamics and slow tempo of the verses were juxtaposed with the gradual crescendo of the chorus and the impassioned call for "coraje" (courage) as hundreds of *paceños* (residents of La Paz) joined in. Nazareth had captured media attention because of her emotional oral testimony of the events at Chaparina when she was gassed, had her hands tied, and was thrown onto a truck resulting in a miscarriage. The crowd was stirred when she changed the last line of the song, "*de los hermanos la solidaridad*" (the solidarity of brothers) to "*de los hermanos paceños dignidad*" (the dignity of *paceño* brothers). In this moment the song developed what Michelle Bigenho has described in her work on Bolivian music as "experiential authenticity" or the shared experience of an embodied practice and sonorous performance that acts to create a common bond (2002, 17–18). The song played an integral role in gaining visibility (and audibility) for the demands of the lowland indigenous movement and in providing a cultural expression of urban solidarity. Crucially, the song also expresses collective histories of colonial subjugation in the lowland Amazonian region. The song refers in various ways to the "*carayana*," identified here as a destroyer, killer, defiler, and greedy logger. The colonial agent is positioned as the common enemy to the lowland indigenous peoples, thus serving to consolidate collective action around a shared sense of place-based history.

As demonstrated, the spatial politics of the TIPNIS marches resisted normative imaginaries of the "ethno-environmental fix" (Anthias and Radcliffe 2015, 262) by articulating *national-public* space as *indigenous* space. In doing so, the marchers sought to strengthen "*interculturalidad*" (interculturality)—a project to rebuild society based on communication, interaction, and dialogue between different ethnicities and cultures—that has been part of the political discourse of indigenous movements since the 1990s (see Andolina, Laurie, and Radcliffe 2009; Gustafson 2002). Subaltern agency is therefore key to deepening the meaning and concrete significance of decolonization in Bolivia.

Conclusion

This chapter has brought conceptualizations of "subalternity" into dialogue with scholarship by the MCD project in Latin America. I have articulated a relational understanding of subalternity based on access to citizenship and state structures. Through ethnographic engagement with the marches in defense of the TIPNIS, I have brought a methodological focus to subaltern epistemologies and modes of representation as a "way of intervening in the present on the side of the subaltern" (Beverley 2001, 49). Specifically, I have demonstrated the limits of the plurinational project in Bolivia. While there has been a reconfiguration of the coloniality of power, empowering certain peasant and indigenous populations, a national development model based on state-led neo-extractivism has sidelined more radical demands for indigenous autonomy and territorial self-determination. In this vein, Amazonian indigenous communities continue to undergo a process of subalternization as they are denied full access to the machinery of the state. Indeed, almost six years to the day after indigenous marchers set out on the first protest march in defense of the TIPNIS, the Bolivian government announced Law No. 969 on August 13, 2017, nullifying the park's status as "untouchable," effectively paving the way for the road to be built.

Yet subaltern agency has also been critical to the decolonial project of plurinationalism, which has been recrafted through practices of domination and resistance in the past and present. In particular, histories of (post)colonial subordination of lowland indigenous peoples have served to instill collective spatial imaginaries of territoriality, governance, and nationhood. These subaltern geographies have shaped resistance to the government-backed road project alongside attempts to make space for lowland indigenous peoples in the imaginary of the nation-state. The TIPNIS struggle has strengthened and given new meanings to the project of "interculturality" (see Walsh 2009), further disrupting the hegemonic political order and its associated spatio-political structures. Indeed, this decolonial trajectory is apparent through CIDOB's contemporary slogan, "*Bolivia nunca más sin los pueblos indígenas*" (Bolivia never again without the indigenous peoples).

More broadly, this analysis speaks to wider debates on whether decolonization can ever be fulfilled within the confines of the colonial apparatus of the modern nation-state. As in Ecuador (see Radcliffe, this volume), the incorporation of indigenous subaltern agendas into the national constitution has not achieved de facto decolonization. Indeed, MCD proponents have highlighted the need for a programmatic delinking from contemporary legacies of coloniality. Rather, they argue, decolonial thinking must be fostered from the sites of colonial difference. Analytical treatment of subaltern geographies therefore requires a commitment to receptivity and (un)learning *from* and *with* the spaces of what Mignolo calls "epistemic disobedience" (2011, 139).

NOTES

1. Cited in Fundación Tierra (2012).

2. It is outside the scope of this chapter to discuss the complex configuration of these indigenous-peasant alliances (see Crabtree 2005; Perreault 2006).

3. In this chapter I use the real names of well-known representatives but omit other names to protect confidentiality. Unless otherwise stated, all translations from interviews or non-English texts are my own.

4. See Sanjinés (2013) for a notable exception.

5. For an overview of multiculturalism and indigenous rights within Latin America, see Sieder (2002).

REFERENCES

Albro, R. 2010. "Confounding Cultural Citizenship and Constitutional Reform in Bolivia." *Latin American Perspectives* 37, no. 3: 71–90.

Anderson, B. 1991. *Imagined Communities: Reflections on the Origins and Spread of Nationalism.* New York: Verso.

Andolina, R., N. Laurie, and S. A. Radcliffe. 2009. *Indigenous Development in the Andes: Culture, Power, and Transnationalism.* Durham, N.C.: Duke University Press.

Anthias, P., and S. A. Radcliffe. 2015. "The Ethno-Environmental Fix and Its Limits: Indigenous Land Titling and the Production of Not-Quite-Neoliberal Natures in Bolivia." *Geoforum* 64: 257–69.

Asher, K. 2013. "Latin American Decolonial Thought, or Making the Subaltern Speak." *Geography Compass* 7, no. 12: 832–42.

Bautista, R. 2010. "Qué significa el estado plurinacional?" *Bolivian Research Review* 8, no. 2: 1–26.

Bebbington, A. 2009. "The New Extraction: Rewriting the Political Ecology of the Andes?" *NACLA Report on the Americas* 42, no. 5: 12–20.

Bebbington, A., and J. Bury. Eds. 2013. *Subterranean Struggles: New Dynamics of Mining, Oil, and Gas in Latin America.* Austin: University of Texas Press.

Bebbington, A., D. Humphreys Bebbington, and J. Bury. 2010. "Federating and Defending: Water, Territory and Extraction in the Andes." In *Out of the Mainstream: Water Rights, Politics and Identity,* edited by R. Boelens, D. Getches, and A. Guevara-Gil, 307–28. Washington, D.C.: Earthscan.

Beverley, J. 2001. "The Im/possibility of Politics: Subalternity, Modernity, Hegemony." In *The Latin American Subaltern Studies Reader,* edited by I. Rodríguez, 47–63. Durham, N.C.: Duke University Press.

Bigenho, M. 2002. *Sounding Indigenous: Authenticity in Bolivian Music Performance.* New York: Palgrave Macmillan.

Brown, M. F. 1994. "Beyond Resistance: Comparative Study of Utopian Renewal in Amazonia." In *Amazonian Indians: From Prehistory to the Present: Anthropological Perspectives,* edited by A. Roosevelt, 287–313. Tucson: University of Arizona Press.

Bryan, J. 2012. "Rethinking Territory: Social Justice and Neoliberalism in Latin America's Territorial Turn." *Geography Compass* 6, no. 4: 215–26.

CEDLA (Centro de Estudios para el Desarrollo Laboral y Agrario). 2012. *Análisis y debate sobre el conflicto del Isiboro Sécure. Tipnis: derechos indígenas, consulta, coca y petróleo.* Year 2: Issue 4. La Paz: Plataforma Energética.

Chávez Suárez, J. 1986. *Historia de Moxos.* 2nd ed. La Paz: Don Bosco.

Cortés Rodríguez, J. 1987. "Diagnóstico sobre las Poblaciones Mojeñas en Busca de la Loma Santa." In *Anales de la Reunión Annual de Ethnología,* 91–104. La Paz: Museo Nacional de Etnografía y Folklore.

Crabtree, J. 2005. *Patterns of Protest: Politics and Social Movements in Bolivia.* London: Latin America Bureau.

Díaz Polanco, H. 1997. *Indigenous Peoples in Latin America: The Quest for Self-Determination.* Boulder, Col.: Westview Press.

Dunkerley, J. 1984. *Rebellion in the Veins: Political Struggle in Bolivia, 1952–82.* London: Verso.

Escobar, A. 2007. "Worlds and Knowledges Otherwise: The Latin American Modernity/Coloniality Research Program." *Cultural Studies* 21, nos. 2–3): 179–210.

———. 2010. "Latin America at a Crossroads: Alternative Modernizations, Post-Liberalism, or Post-Development?" *Cultural Studies* 24, no. 1: 1–65.

Fabricant, N. 2012. *Mobilizing Bolivia's Displaced: Indigenous Politics and the Struggle over Land.* Chapel Hill: University of North Carolina Press.

Fabricant, N., and N. Postero. 2015. "Sacrificing Indigenous Bodies and Lands: The Political-Economic History of Lowland Bolivia in Light of the Recent TIPNIS Debate." *Journal of Latin American and Caribbean Anthropology* 20, no. 3: 452–72.

FIDH (Federación Internacional de Derechos Humanos) –APDHB (Asamblea Permanente de los Derechos Humanos de Bolivia). 2013. *Bolivia: Informe de Verificación de la Consulta Realizada en el Territorio Indígena Parque Nacional Isiboro-Sécure.* Available at http://fidh.org/IMG/pdf/bolivie609esp2013.pdf, accessed April 13, 2013.

Fundación Tierra. 2012. *Marcha indígena por el TIPNIS: La lucha en defensa de los territorios.* La Paz: Fundación Tierra.

Garcés, F. 2011. "The Domestication of Indigenous Autonomies in Bolivia: From the Pact of Unity to the New Constitution." In *Remapping Bolivia: Resources, Territory, and Indigeneity in a Plurinational State,* edited by N. Fabricant and B. Gustafson, 46–67. Santa Fe, N. Mex.: SAR Press.

Gobierno de Bolivia. 2009. *Constitución política del estado.* La Paz: Presidencia de la República.

Grosfoguel, R. 2007. "The Epistemic Decolonial Turn: Beyond Political-Economy Paradigms." *Cultural Studies* 21, nos. 2–3: 211–23.

Gudynas, E. 2009. "Diez tesis urgentes sobre el nuevo extractivismo. Contextos y demandas bajo el progresismo sudamericano actual." In *Extractivismo, política y sociedad,* edited by CAAP/CLAES, 187–225. Quito: CAAP/CLAES.

Gustafson, B. 2002. "Paradoxes of Liberal Indigenism: Indigenous Movements, State Processes, and Intercultural Reform in Bolivia." In *The Politics of Ethnicity: Indigenous Peoples in Latin American States,* edited by D. Maybury-Lewis, 267–306. Cambridge, Mass.: Harvard University Press.

———. 2009a. *New Languages of the State: Indigenous Resurgence and the Politics of Knowledge in Bolivia.* Durham, N.C.: Duke University Press.

———. 2009b. "Manipulating Cartographies: Plurinationalism, Autonomy, and Indigenous Resurgence in Bolivia." *Anthropological Quarterly* 82, no. 4: 985–1016.

Healy, K. 1991. "Political Ascent of Bolivia's Peasant Coca Leaf Producers." *Journal of Interamerican Studies and World Affairs* 33, no. 1: 87–121.

———. 2001. *Llamas, Weavings, and Organic Chocolate: Multicultural Grassroots Development in the Andes and Amazon of Bolivia.* Notre Dame, Ind.: University of Notre Dame Press.

INE/UMPA. 2003. *Bolivia: Características sociodemográficas de la población.* La Paz: INE.

Jones, J. C. 1984. "Native Peoples of Lowland Bolivia." In *Frontier Expansion in Amazonia,* edited by M. Schmink and C. H. Wood, 62–82. Gainesville: University Press of Florida.

Kaup, B. Z. 2010. "A Neoliberal Nationalization?: The Constraints on Natural-Gas-Led Development in Bolivia." *Latin American Perspectives* 37, no. 3: 123–38.

Kohl, B., and L. Farthing (with F. Muruchi). 2011. *From the Mines to the Streets: A Bolivian Activist's Life.* Austin: University of Texas Press.

———. 2012. "Material Constraints to Popular Imaginaries: The Extractive Economy and Resource Nationalism in Bolivia." *Political Geography* 31, no. 4: 225–35.

Laing, A. F. 2012. "Beyond the Zeitgeist of 'Post-Neoliberal' Theory in Latin America: The Politics of Anti-Colonial Struggles in Bolivia." *Antipode* 44, no. 4: 1051–54.

———. 2015. "Territory, Resistance and Struggles for the Plurinational State: The Spatial Politics of the TIPNIS Conflict." Unpublished Ph.D thesis, University of Glasgow.

Lander, E. Ed. 2000. *La colonialidad del saber: Eurocentrismo y ciencas sociales. Perspectivas latinoamericanas.* Buenos Aires: Consejo Latinoamericano de Ciencas Sociales.

Lehm Ardaya, Z. 1999. *Milenarismo y Movimientos en la Amazonia Boliviana: La Busqueda de la Loma Santa y La Marcha Indigena por el Territorio y la Dignidad* APCOB-CIDDEBENI. Santa Cruz de la Sierra: Oxfam America.

Los Tiempos. 2011. *Evo: Quieran o no, vamos a construir la carretera Villa Tunari-San Ignacio de Moxos* (June 29, 2011). Available at: http://www.lostiempos.com/diario/actualidad/economia/20110629/evo-quieran-o-no-vamos-a-construir-la-carretera-villa-tunari-san-ignacio_131792_266957.html, accessed October 30, 2012.

Maldonado-Torres, N. 2007. "On the Coloniality of Being: Contributions to the Development of a Concept." *Cultural Studies* 21, nos. 2–3: 240–70.

Malloy, J. M. 1970. *Bolivia: The Uncompleted Revolution.* Pittsburgh: University of Pittsburgh Press.

McNeish, J.-A. 2013. "Extraction, Protest and Indigeneity in Bolivia: The TIPNIS Effect." *Latin American and Caribbean Ethnic Studies* 8, no. 2: 221–42.

Mignolo, W. D. 2000. *Local Histories/Global Designs: Coloniality, Subaltern Knowledges, and Border Thinking.* Princeton, N.J.: Princeton University Press.

———. 2005. *The Idea of Latin America.* Malden: Blackwell.

———. 2007a. "Introduction: Coloniality of Power and De-colonial Thinking." *Cultural Studies* 21, nos. 2–3: 155–67.

———. 2007b. "Delinking: The Rhetoric of Modernity, the Logic of Coloniality and the Grammar of De-coloniality." *Cultural Studies* 21, nos. 2–3: 449–514.

———. 2011. *The Darker Side of Western Modernity: Global Futures, Decolonial Options.* Durham, N.C.: Duke University Press.

Nolte, D., and A. Schilling-Vacaflor. Eds. 2012. *New Constitutionalism in Latin America: Promises and Practices.* Farnham: Ashgate.

Offen, K. H. 2003. "The Territorial Turn: Making Black Territories in Pacific Colombia." *Journal of Latin American Geography* 2, no. 1: 43–73.

Paz, S. 2012. "La marcha indígena del 'TIPNIS' en Bolivia y su relación con los modelos extractivos de America del Sur." *GEOgraphia* 13, no. 26: 7–36.

Perreault, T. 2006. "From the Guerra Del Agua to the Guerra Del Gas: Resource Governance, Neoliberalism and Popular Protest in Bolivia." *Antipode* 38, no. 1: 150–72.

Postero, N. 2007. *Now We Are Citizens: Indigenous Politics in Postmulticultural Bolivia.* Stanford, Calif.: Stanford University Press.

Querejazu Lewis, R. 2008. *Trayectoria Histórica y Cultural de los Trinitarios.* Cochabamba: Swedish International Development Cooperation Agency—Instituto de Investigaciones de Arquitectura—UMSS.

Quijano, A. 1992. "Colonialidad y Racionalidad/Modernidad." *Perú Indígena* 29: 11–29.

———. 2000. "Coloniality of Power, Eurocentrism and Latin America." *Nepantla* 1, no. 3: 533–80.

Rabasa, J. 2010. *Without History: Subaltern Studies, The Zapatista Insurgency, and the Specter of History.* Pittsburgh: Pittsburgh University Press.

Radcliffe, S. A. 2012. "Development for a Postneoliberal Era? Sumak Kawsay, Living Well and the Limits to Decolonisation in Ecuador." *Geoforum* 43, no. 2: 240–49.

———. 2017. "Geography and Indigeneity I: Indigeneity, Coloniality and Knowledge." *Progress in Human Geography* 41, no. 2: 220–29.

Regalsky, P. 2010. "Political Processes and the Reconfiguration of the State in Bolivia." *Latin American Perspectives* 37, no. 3: 35–50.

Riester, J., and B. Fischerman. 1976. *En busca de la Loma Santa.* La Paz: Los Amigos del Libro.

Rivera Cusicanqui, S. 1987. *Oppressed but Not Defeated: Peasant Struggles among the Aymara and Qhechwa in Bolivia, 1900–1980.* Geneva: United Nations Research Institute for Social Development.

Rodríguez, I. Ed. 2001. *The Latin American Subaltern Studies Reader.* Durham, N.C.: Duke University Press.

Routledge, P. 2000. "Geopoetics of Resistance: India's Baliapal Movement." *Alternatives: Global, Local, Political* 25, no. 3: 375–89.

Saldaña-Portillo, J. 2001. "Who's the Indian in Aztlán? Re-writing Mestizaje, Indianism, and Chicanismo from the Lacandón." In *The Latin American Subaltern Studies Reader*, edited by I. Rodríguez, 402–23. Durham, N.C.: Duke University Press.

Sanjinés C. J. 2013. *Embers of the Past: Essays in Times of Decolonization.* Durham, N.C.: Duke University Press.

Sieder, R. Ed. 2002. *Multiculturalism in Latin America: Indigenous Rights, Diversity and Democracy.* New York: Palgrave Macmillan.

Slater, D. 2013. "Space, Democracy and Difference: For a Post-Colonial Perspective." In *Spatial Politics: Essays for Doreen Massey*, edited by D. Featherstone and J. Painter, 70–84. Malden: Wiley-Blackwell.

Spivak, G. C. 1987. *In Other Worlds: Essays in Cultural Politics.* London: Methuen.

———. 1990. *The Post-Colonial Critic: Interviews, Strategies, Dialogues.* Edited by S. Harasym. New York: Routledge.

———. 2014. "Scattered Speculations on Geography." *Antipode* 46, no. 1: 1–12.

Stefanoni, P. 2006. "El nacionalismo indígena en el poder." *Observatorio Social de America Latina* 19: 37–44.

Svampa, M., and P. Stefanoni. 2007. "Entrevista a Álvaro García Linera: 'Evo simboliza el quiebre de un imaginario restringido a la subalternidad de los indígenas.'" *Observatorio Social de América Latina* 22: 143–64.

Tapia, L. 2011. *El estado de derecho como tiranía.* La Paz: CIDES/UMSA.

———. 2012. "Los pueblos de tierras bajas como minoría plural consistente." In *La victoria indígena del TIPNIS*, edited by R. Bautista, M. Chávez, P. Chávez, S. Paz, R. Prada, and L. Tapia, 253–95. La Paz: Autodeterminación.

Tockman, J., and J. Cameron. 2014. "Indigenous Autonomy and the Contradictions of Plurinationalism in Bolivia." *Latin American Politics and Society* 56, no. 3: 46–69.

TSE (Tribunal Supremo Electoral). 2012. *Informe de observación acompañamiento de la consulta previa, libre e informada a los pueblos indígenas del Territorio Indígena y Parque Nacional Isiboro Sécure (TIPNIS)*. La Paz: SIFDE.

Van Cott, D. L. 2005. *From Movements to Parties in Latin America: The Evolution of Ethnic Politics*. New York: Cambridge University Press.

Van Valen, G. 2013. *Indigenous Agency in the Amazon: The Mojos in Liberal and Rubber-Boom Bolivia, 1842–1932*. Tucson: University of Arizona Press.

Walsh, C. 2009. *Interculturalidad, estado, sociedad: Luchas (de)coloniales de nuestra época*. Quito: Universidad Andina Simón Bolívar.

Wolford, W. 2004. "This Land Is Ours Now: Spatial Imaginaries and the Struggle for Land in Brazil." *Annals of the Association of American Geographers* 94, no. 2: 409–24.

Yashar, D. J. 2005. *Contesting Citizenship in Latin America: The Rise of Indigenous Movements and the Postliberal Challenge*. New York: Cambridge University Press.

Subaltern Sea?

Indian Ocean Errantry against Subalternization

SHARAD CHARI

Oceanic accounts:

> Man is a terrestrial, a groundling. He lives, moves and walks on the firmly-grounded Earth. It is his standpoint and his base. . . . And since we found out that our earth is spherically shaped, we have been speaking quite naturally of the "terrestrial sphere" or of the "terrestrial globe." To imagine a "maritime globe" would seem strange, indeed.
>
> —Carl Schmitt (1997, 1)

> For us, and without exception, and no matter how much distance we may keep, the abyss is also a projection of a perspective into the unknown. Beyond its chasm we gamble on the unknown. We take sides in this game of the world. . . . And despite our consenting to all the indisputable technologies; despite seeing the political leap that must be managed, the horror of hunger and ignorance, torture and massacre to be conquered, the full load of knowledge to be tamed, the weight of every piece of machinery that we shall finally control, and the exhausting flashes as we pass from one era to another—from forest to city, from story to computer—at the bow there is still something we now share: this murmur, cloud or rain or peaceful smoke. We know ourselves as part and as crowd, in an unknown that does not terrify. We cry our cry of poetry. Our boats are open, and we sail them for everyone.
>
> —Édouard Glissant (1997, 8–9)

> Maritime history is not simply the story of landed society gone to sea. Which is to say: we need to learn to see the world's seas and oceans as real places, where a great deal of history has been made, and indeed is still being made. Many maritime historians continue to see the oceans as unreal places, as voids between the real spaces, which are inevitably lands or nations. So maritime history has exhibited—and continues to exhibit—what, for lack of a better term, I will call terracentric bias.
>
> —Marcus Rediker (2004, 198)

> The fear of, and desire for, métissage is inscribed in the history of human societies.... [W]hat has remained constant has been a suspicion about the loyalty of the métis because of their "division."... To compound the difficulty, it is clear that the "West" is now not really disturbed with the addition of the métis voice to the choir of the postcolonial world.... Global capitalism can absorb métissage as another commodity.... Thinking métissage, I argue, requires accepting a genealogy and a heritage. In other words, the recognition of a past of rape, violence, slavery, and the recognition of our own complicity with the wicked ways of the world. No projection onto the Other, no denial of one's complicity.... To acknowledge the primal scene is to accept that one was born of sexual intercourse between a man and a woman and in the colony between white and black parents, whether the sexual intercourse was violent or loving. It signifies the rejection of the colonial family romance.
>
> —Françoise Vergès (1999, 10–11)

This chapter is an exercise in intellectual errantry, to borrow Glissant's sense of a journeying of thought in an open boat, a "gamble on the unknown," and a refusal of Carl Schmitt's insistence that "man" is "a groundling." These quotations are not quite moorings but provocations as I approach what are, for me, as yet uncharted seas. As Glissant's (1997, 1) epigraph puts it, "Thinking thought usually amounts to withdrawing into a dimensionless place in which the idea of thought alone persists. But thought in reality spaces itself out into the world." We might expect this "spacing of thought" by the theorist of antillanité to be a tradition of geo-graphy or Earth-writing, self-consciously emerging from the Caribbean islands and from the critical traditions of the ocean "whose time is marked by these balls and chains gone green" (Glissant 1997, 6). However, as the text proceeds, Glissant's geographical praxis is less about Caribbean difference than about speaking through its entangled, creole multilingualism to the world as a whole; as he puts it, "Poetry's circulation and its action no longer conjecture a given people but the evolution of the planet Earth" (Glissant 1997, 32).

I read Glissant's enigmatic provocation in marked contrast to that *ur*-text of the oceanic humanities, Braudel's (1978) *The Mediterranean and the Mediterranean World in the Age of Philip II*, a sweeping account of the "collective destinies" of "the Mediterranean world," in the age of a king, no less. In his incisive review of this text, Rancière (1994, 23) responds sharply thus: "The new history cannot simply receive its new object from the death of kings." In contrast to his expansive gaze on the Mediterranean as world-making, grounded and ungrounded, as it were, by sovereignty, Glissant's Caribbean is "a sea that diffracts," propelling his "errantry" (Glissant 1997, 32). While one might misread errantry as a call for unbridled voluntarism, I pose it as a resolute break with what McKittrick (2013, 8) calls the fatal repetition of "plantation futures" that neurotically reproduce "black geographies as dead spaces of absolute otherness." Rather, errantry is a global call for intellectual marronage that refuses the normativization of sovereign power/knowledge. Or, contra Schmitt, we had better imagine a maritime globe or face the consequences.

Consider this maritime globe on a planet whose surface is overwhelmingly oceanic and that might have more aptly been called "Ocean" (Helmreich 2009, 3). Marcus Rediker, historian of the Trans-Atlantic slave trade, poses the challenge as thinking beyond "terracentrism," for which the ocean is simply a "void" or "unreal space" and maritime history "simply the story of landed society gone to sea" (Rediker 2004, 198). Indeed, Rediker and Linebaugh's magisterial (2000) work of connective histories of dispossession, commoning, and revolution across the Atlantic accomplishes exactly what Rediker (2004, 198) calls "a people's history of the sea." This is the perfect point to consider subalternity and the sea, as Indian subaltern studies had emerged precisely from a critical engagement with the historiographic praxis of Marxist social history that Rediker and Linebaugh share. All these historians self-consciously broke from a more party-line, Marxist-nationalist social history, framed differently in different national academic formations. In the case of several of the Indian historians across the United Kingdom and India, this break was so charged that it has often been recalled as absolute. I suggest that the retrospective refusal of the baggage of Marxist social history by some of the progenitors of Indian subaltern studies is not only inaccurate but also analytically uncreative. The specter that haunts subalternity, as an analytical and political project, is Marxist social history as an optic for diagnosis of past and present struggles against the many-headed hydra of modern social domination. And specters, we know from Shakespeare, Derrida, or Morrison, cannot be so hastily exorcized as some, notably Marx himself, may have wished (Chari 2017). But let us consider Rediker's "people's history of the sea" a bit more carefully for what exactly the phrase "of the sea" might mean.

Certainly, if the ocean "is also a projection," as Glissant puts it, Rediker (2004) makes it his task to account for histories and legacies of the enslaved and resistant Atlantic submerged by dominant historical narratives. In other words, the ocean calls for attentiveness to mediation, concealment, and haunting rather than an uncritical affirmation of transparency. We might think with the analogy that light does not travel easily through the ocean beyond 200 meters. How might we think about the watery depths other than as a metaphor of material or spatial transcendence? What else might the oceans provoke for a productive revision of the concept of subalternity beyond the presumption of transparency in popular thought and action? Indeed, is there any value to calling a sea "subaltern," and specifically to calling the Indian Ocean a "subaltern sea"? Consider Benton's (2005, 2009) response to Linebaugh and Rediker (2000): when we rethink their Atlantic history in relation to the Indian Ocean, the figure of the pirate does not so easily signify subaltern resistance to sovereignty and capital. Rather, Benton argues, pirates traversing these oceans sought as often to exploit enduring legal ambiguities in European and Mughal imperial sovereignties over oceanic space.

More pointedly, Vine's (2009) careful study of Chagossian dispossession in the making of the U.S. military base at Diego Garcia attests to the Indian Ocean as an exemplary space of imperial sovereignty today, in which the constitution of resistant subaltern will remains frustrated but not defeated. Vine's ethnographic praxis points precisely to a way beyond the debate between Linebaugh and Rediker on the one hand and Benton on the other, or indeed to Schmitt and Glissant as I have posed them in counterpoint. Vine refuses to represent the Chagossian independence movement as stranded in the poorer quarters of urban Mauritius, a kind of shipwreck of twentieth-century anticolonial nationalism. In the wake of multifaceted dispossession, Chagossian determination to continue to imagine and organize subaltern political will points precisely beyond an area-studies argument about a region or population that is more subaltern than others. As the Chagossian call for repatriation questions the broader basis of our imperial moment, Chagossian subaltern will exemplifies a mode of political errantry, or oceanic critique, that refuses their conditions of subalternization and the broader imperial forces that support it.

This chapter is an experiment in journeying through a wide and growing field of oceanic studies and offers some thoughts on subalternity and geography (Earth-writing, ocean-writing, world-writing.) In the next section, I turn to a set of insights, putatively from the Indian Ocean, to reflect on the possibilities of thinking from this particular "people's ocean" with implications for rethinking subalternity more generally. Shifting from primarily historical work, I ask in the subsequent section how we might reconsider "the sea itself" through the critique of terracentrism as conceived through the ontological or posthuman turn in anthropology and geography. The subsequent section revisits these concerns through an important recent work of oceanic political ecology focused on the Bay of Bengal. I conclude, as much as any experiment in errantry can, with a set of provocations for the recomposition of a subaltern studies project of the future as proposed through these thoughts, grounded as they are in specific works from "the subaltern sea." But what, more precisely, do we make of the idea of the Indian Ocean as a "subaltern sea" (Hofmeyr 2015)?

We cannot approach this question without considering the insights emerging from the Caribbean. As Rediker (2004, 201) recalls, Linebaugh and Rediker (2000) had built on prior scholarship, including, crucially, the important doctoral dissertation of Julius Sherrard Scott on the interracial circulation of knowledge of the Haitian Revolution in the Caribbean and beyond (J. S. Scott 1986). As he puts it in a published chapter of his dissertation, J. S. Scott's (2010, 73) insight is about how "the constant shifting stream of itinerant seafaring folk provided the masterless underground in the colonies with a crucial transatlantic connection." J. S. Scott points us to the subaltern production of sociocultural infrastructure, a work simultaneously of labor and of theory. The layering of citation and circulation from the action and intellection of seafarers, through J. S. Scott and his academic interlocutors, is important in itself as part of the praxis that the ocean calls forth to the hidebound locational obstinacy of scholarship that purports to be "from" any particular place, let alone from the strange hybrids of priestly and corporate power that are the elite universities of our time.

Perhaps the most powerful artifact of the intellectual and practical circulation in this "masterless underground" is a text that emerged in conversation with the papers that were the precursor of Linebaugh and Rediker (2000), but with a different "transcultural" archive, Paul Gilroy's (1993) *The Black Atlantic: Modernity and Double Consciousness*. As an interconnected set, the works of J. S. Scott, Rediker, Linebaugh, and Gilroy, along with others they draw from and inspire, demonstrate an errantry that refuses a sharp break between social history and subaltern studies and between institutionalized and popular praxis. Indeed, the diagnosis of subaltern praxis as always both action and intellection, a point that I owe to Dilip Menon, need not be at odds with what Rediker calls "a people's history of the sea," precisely if it takes Rancière's critique of Braudel seriously. Indeed Rediker's (2004) most exciting errantry emerges when he thinks about what kinds of "geographical knowledge" might be just beyond our groundling fields of vision. How might we (geographers of various stripes) yet account for Earth-writing that "spaces itself out into the world," we might add with Marx's political hope, "in order to change it" (see, for instance, Featherstone 2008)? In light of the idea of the anthropocene, we might adapt this hope into something like "in order not to destroy the world as concertedly," even if "we" are not yet the benign universal subject that Dipesh Chakrabarty (2009, 221–22) evokes so eloquently. We might call this necessary subject of the future a "species-for-itself-and-others." Rather than consigning our seafaring forebears to a submerged past, might we engage their presence in a call for solidarity with future inhabitants of our planet who will inherit the Earth we write into being?

To be clear, such a relentlessly anti-essentialist and hopefully planetary point of departure makes it logically impossible to resurrect the subaltern as the subject of radical and emplaced otherness, which was at a preoccupation of many of the historians of subaltern studies, despite critiques by Gayatri Spivak (for instance in Spivak 1988) and others inside/outside subaltern studies. Neither will it be possible to reproduce Chakrabarty's (2000) recasting of entangled and contradictory processes into the History 1 of capitalist and Enlightenment rationality as separable from the History 2 of dwelling. From the perspective of the critical traditions of the Black Atlantic, dualist formulations like this are doomed to replicate plantation futures.

Rather, I suggest that we approach subalternity through Barnor Hesse's (2011, 58) call to address "creolization repressed in the modern institution and representation of the political," which I adapt into the political-economic. Capitalism always already differentiates people and places in hierarchical ways, drawing on prior forms of quasi-racial authority. Cedric Robinson's (2000) theorization of "racial capitalism" makes this explicit. Henri Lefebvre (1991, 395–96)—no great thinker on racism or colonialism—nevertheless has useful things to add to this formulation in arguing that "the enigma of the body—its secret at once banal and profound—is its ability, beyond 'subject' and 'object' to produce differences 'unconsciously' out of repetitions" and that "just like the fleshy body of the living being, the spatial body of society and the social body of needs ... cannot live ... without creating differences." Capitalist "abstract space" attempts to reduce this production of embodied difference to "induced differences" that are "prefabricated" and essentially "redundant," but Lefebvre sees this as in a sense futile, as many forms of "differential space" proliferate to prefigure a possible socialist future, as Antonio Gramsci (1971, 229–39, 265) might put it. From the perspective of colonial capitalism and its aftermath, this embodied and sociospatial difference-making is unavoidable, even when specifically colonized bodies are subject to neglect, shaming, intervention, or abandonment (Legg 2014). But what I want to suggest, particularly with the Antilles and the Southern African Indian Ocean in mind, is that "creolization" or "métissage" marks the proliferation of embodied difference at the heart of the banal operations of colonial and postcolonial capitalism everywhere. The repression of creolization, in Hesse's formulation, means that mixture is often named in violently narrow and exclusionary ways, if it is named at all.

The passage from Françoise Vergès (1999, 10–11) with which I begin reframes this problematic in an explicitly postcolonial and racial (and sexual) capitalist frame to show how the production of embodied difference, crystallized in métissage, becomes a perennial site of loathing and longing, of suspicion and repression. Vergès's critical move is to refuse the capture and commodification of difference, while attending to a different mode of attending to the past by acknowledging the ghostly presence of psychic, social, and sexual entanglement. Vergès has carried out this task in a series of curatorial projects, including one that sought to disinter the many ghosts of slavery within the national patrimony of the Louvre; and another on the history of La Réunion, or Reunion Island, which offered a museum with no objects for people who could not leave a trace. Too threatening for establishment histories, neither project in fact survives.

Vergès's perspective emerges from her own fraught engagement with the island of her origins, La Réunion, which is, like Glissant's Martinique, trapped in a long embrace with La Mère-Patrie, as she puts it, the French "metropole" as "a character mixing the feminine and the masculine: the castrating and protective mother" of a child allegedly entranced by this "the colonial family romance" for its eternally belated promise of republican ideals (Vergès 1999, 5). In Vergès's formulation, métissage provides a means of accepting a genealogy while rejecting the violent intimacy at the scene of the crime. These thinkers from La Réunion and Martinique, both overseas departments of France in very different but interconnected oceans, think against very specific and intertwined "plantation futures." Yet both have a way of speaking universally about that which endures and survives colonialism and racial capitalism.

Vergès provides a way of approaching the African Indian Ocean as a fertile intellectual field that connects the Caribbean, the Black Atlantic, and indeed the Mediterranean, through islands and continental littorals and through sociocultural processes premised on what Schmitt (1997, 1) proposes is impossible—that we can indeed imagine a "maritime globe." In the following section, I turn to an important symposium of historians engaged with literary and sociocultural dynamics of the Indian Ocean, who debate various ways in which they might rethink praxis through archives linked to the Indian Ocean and with implications for the future of the "subaltern" concept.

"Indian Ocean as Method": Infrastructures of Conscription and Movement

The title of Antoinette Burton's (2013, 498) introduction, "Indian Ocean as Method," is a provocation drawn from Kuan-Hsing Chen's (2010) *Asia as Method*, which proposes as "an intercultural space" a regionalism shaped by broader forces that enable both "the exuberant possibilities of permeability and porousness, on the one hand, and the machinery of imperial-nation state power, on the other." Madhavi Kale's (2013, 531) response points out that Chen builds on Mizoguchi Yuzo's 1989 *China as Method*, via a 1960 lecture from Tekeuchi Yoshima, which argued for an inter-Asian mode of comparative reflection. The multiple citations gesture to East Asian critique of "Europe" as the means of comparison but also to the wider history of praxis that I have suggested are called forth by Caribbean social and intellectual history. While these are important gestures beyond Euro-American self-obsession, also in postcolonial studies, the question remains: What precisely might "Indian Ocean as method" offer to the project of recasting subaltern geographies?

In a thoughtful contribution, Isabel Hofmeyr (2013, 510) reads several aspects of Indian Ocean concern as emergent in the notoriously inward-looking South African academy, alongside renewed interest in "forms of transoceanic 'citizenship' and belonging, which nationalism obscures." Elsewhere, my own work engages this methodological nationalism of South African scholarship by considering the praxis of people racialized as "Indian" and "Coloured" through the repression of creole Indian Ocean pasts (Chari 2014). From quite a different direction, Christopher J. Lee's (2013) paper for the collection poses the Indian Ocean "as a theater of the Cold War," in which he suggests that "the central continuity between the premodern and modern eras has been the rich set of resources found across the region and the environmental factors that seasonal weather patterns and enabling waterways—the Persian Gulf and Red Sea, as well as the Indian Ocean itself—presented for facilitating migration and commerce"; and, he goes on, "while the technology of modern transport has circumvented remaining environmental limitations, these elements continue to be significant, providing wealth and ongoing incentives for political control" (Lee 2013, 527). This attentiveness to what I would call the political ecology of Indian Ocean infrastructure ought to be a key aspect of explanation of the "subaltern sea" that reconnects questions of subjectivity with their material and ecological integuments. In the next section, I turn to important scholarship on the Bay of Bengal by Sunil Amrith that bridges Hofmeyr's and Lee's insights by showing how the political-ecological basis of transoceanic and regional subaltern belonging has been eroded, quite literally, by postcolonial nationalism and development.

The paper that address "subalternity" most squarely, although conventionally given its focus on individual subjectivity, is Clare Anderson's (2013, 504) on "subaltern biography" and, she clarifies, "with subalternity a process rather than a fixed category of identity." Anderson draws on the resources of her own monograph, Anderson (2012), as well as Engseng Ho's (2006) foundational historical ethnography of the Hadrami diaspora from the Middle East to Indonesia, Marina Carter and Khal Torabully's (2002) work on "coolitude" as a parallel to Negritude, and Vergès's (1999) on La Réunion. Anderson offers insights for historical research through family and community genealogies to address problems of narrative silencing in official archives. In her response, Kale (2013, 532) proposes that "the multi-sited archival research and multi-citational apparatus" in Anderson's attention to "subaltern lives" may be "the kernel of what thinking the Indian Ocean world as method" might mean. Kale's (2013, 533) interest is in the way in which what Sanjay Subrahmanyam (2005) calls "connected histories" of the Indian Ocean are "brought into conversation at specific conjunctures, however evanescently or transiently by bodies . . . in motion, willingly and otherwise."

I would like to push these insights a bit farther, by returning to Anderson (2012) and to the human-geographic (or human-oceanographic) conditions of possibilities that have propelled people into variously forced movements to then enable such historiographic "conversations." At the heart of Anderson's and Kale's insights lies something of relevance to the question of "subaltern geographies," not just as sites of abjection or withholding of cultural difference but, rather, of the geographical infrastructure that makes particular forms of subalternity possible. One of the virtues of Anderson's *Subaltern Lives* is that it shifts attention from the Indian Ocean as a gulag archipelago, stretching from Robben Island to the Andaman Islands, to focus on the contingencies of convict transport and experience across colonies and penal settlements (Anderson

2012). Anderson shows in great detail how forced movement through imperial conscription networks is often disabling but sometimes enabling of some room for maneuver and representation, as well as of interaction with far-flung kin through epistolary cultures and petitions to multiple, linked authorities. These insights are part of a broader postnational turn in colonial and imperial history, through which Anderson calls effective attention to the Indian Ocean as a set of linked "spaces of governance, mobility and experience" (Anderson 2012, 9). The "subaltern" in the title of this book points to marginal biographies but also to a method of reading the infrastructural supports for convict experience and movement, legible in fits and starts through dispersed archival fragments. But biographies always also imply geographies as their conditions of material and lived possibility, and Anderson might also have named her book the title of this collection to point to the specificity of the Indian Ocean as infrastructure.

One of the insights of recent historical scholarship on the maritime infrastructure of the Indian Ocean in the heyday of British colonialism is its contradictoriness, and its various openings for "appropriation" by maritime labor, as Ravi Ahuja (2009, 33) puts it. Radhika Singha makes a compelling parallel argument for the mobility of "pauper pilgrims" on Hajj through the fissures of colonial governmentality (Singha 2009). What is striking in these and other studies in a British colonial frame is the focus on instability, disorder, and movement—for instance, in the essays in Tambe and Fischer-Tiné (2009)—but rarely with an attention to the recompositions that the Francophone literature directly names "creolization" or "mettisage." This is precisely Hofmeyr's argument about rethinking subalternity from the Indian Ocean as a product of what she terms "conscripted creolization" forged through the lives of motley peoples thrown together through nonlinear trajectories of unfree labor (personal communication, Johannesburg, April 2016.) Hofmeyr poses this as the distinguishing feature of debates about the Indian Ocean, which distinguish this from other oceanic epistemes like the "Black Atlantic." I find this to be a powerful argument, but it does not do adequate justice to thinking beyond a landed history gone to sea by attending to the sea as the sea. I turn in the following section to the materiality of the sea as considered through some works that are either inspired by or that have been part of the ontological turn in geography and anthropology, as one albeit insufficient way of engaging the materiality of maritime infrastructure, before turning to insights from an important environmental history of the Bay of Bengal.

The Sea Itself

I detect, among some oceanographers, a claim that thinking from southern oceans—with their greater proportion of seawater and ice—might be needed to upend the northern assumptions built into many wave models and to account for intensified ocean storms, massive coral and mangrove depletion, and sea-ice breakup: southern-sea processes with planetary effects.

—Stefan Helmreich (2014, 269)

There is a set of scholarly work I cannot actually follow fully here, but I mark them as routes not taken. The first is this remarkably creative provocation from anthropologist Stefan Helmreich (2014, 269), who calls for a southern oceanography attentive to "southern sea processes with planetary effects." My absolutely rudimentary understanding of oceanography aside, it is certainly plausible that a "southern theory of the ocean" might gain from the insights of the dissident oceanographers Helmreich refers to, who point to the importance of thinking beyond the sea as the statistical ocean of wave science, the Eurocentric view also critiqued by Steinberg (2001). Helmreich's work is often folded into what is called the "ontological turn" in anthropology, which spans linked but varied insights on Amerindian or indigenous cosmologies, posthuman and multispecies ethnography, affect and vital materiality, and science and technology studies (STS). This research includes some very useful work pertinent to understanding ontological multiplicity pertinent to human interaction with oceans, for instance in Anne Salmond's (2014) work on rights to water in Aotearoa / New Zealand, and of course Helmreich's work with experts in marine biology and microbial oceanography.

In a gloss on various strands of the ontological turn, in Chari (2017), I find some of this work useful for showing how socially constructed difference and contradiction may point to deeper forms of ontological instability or of haunting of the ontic by what we presume to be its ontology. One of the main arguments among ontological anthropologists is that they claim to refuse our Western metaphysics of mononature and multiculture for an engagement with what they call "multinaturalism." I am agnostic on this point. I find convincing John Kelly's (2014, 265) generous suggestion that the ontological turn may be less interesting for its revival of cultural relativism in ontological (or multinatural) garb than for "a better theorization and understanding of situations" implicit in Haraway's (1991) notion of "situated knowledges." We are back, in other words, to geo-graphy, to world-, Earth-, and ocean-writing as representational practice, to knowledges not just mired in but as constitutive of geographical situatedness.

Here, I draw attention to Helmreich's (2014, 272) attentiveness to what historian of science Paul Edwards (2010) calls "data friction," as the northern hemispheric presumptions of oceanographic expertise rub against other human-natural processes. Helmreich (2014, 276) notes a set of macro differences of southern hemispheric oceans, such as that they have more ice and cover a larger uninterrupted surface area, which means more solar radiation and swell and less atmospheric particulate plant matter. For two intriguing approaches to a conception of oceanic subalternity engaged with oceanographic processes, Charne Lavery's (2016) current work on writing the deep ocean thinks with "companion species" beyond the limits of human experience through insights from astrobiology, and Meg Samuelson (2016) has been arguing suggestively about the difference of Indian Ocean waves and shorelines as experienced by surfers "searching for stoke."

A geographer who does engage oceans through the ontological turn, at some length, is Philip Steinberg. In a recent essay, Steinberg and Peters (2015, 247–48) "turn to the ocean itself: to its three-dimensional and turbulent materiality . . . to explore how thinking with the sea can assist in reconceptualizing our geographical understandings"; and what they offer is that "the sea's material and phenomenological distinctiveness can facilitate the reimagining and reenlivening of a world ever on the move." The essay is in many ways a series of provocations, and it concludes by analogy with James C. Scott's (2011) work on highland Asia as a space of political evasion—a work indebted to the Black radical tradition for its engagement with forms of marronage—to ask, quite obliquely, "might the ocean, when understood through a 'wet ontology,' generate a 'wet' politics" (Steinberg and Peters 2015, 260). At its best, the ontological turn in anthropology has often driven scholars to better ethnography. The parallel with the ontological turn in geography is not quite as clear. When they turn to the oceans, ontological geographers' distance from proletarian and Black politics makes their insights less politically satisfying, and this is a shame, given the wealth of insight that is to be gained from thinking with maritime networks precisely to reimagine subaltern politics (Featherstone, this volume). Without engagement with actual archives, practices, languages, or poetics, let alone more prosaically anthropocentric racial/sexual/class struggles, the ontological turn offers a flight from the postcolonial hope for a subaltern politics. As an alternative, I turn to an important text that considers the efficacy of sociocultural and natural processes in the subregion of the Bay of Bengal in more prosaic historical terms, but with clearer use-value and a more challenging politics for fragile futures.

An Intellectual and Political Ecology of the Sea

Sunil Amrith's (2013, 1–2) beautifully written environmental history of the Bay of Bengal connects natural history to the "people's sea." He shows how the material infrastructure of life shifts from a "maritime highway between India and China, navigable by mastery of its regularly reversing monsoon winds," to a new regime linking steamships powered by fossil fuels, plantation production fueled by indentured labor, and "imperial laws that both uprooted and immobilized people" in new ways (Amrith 2013, 1–2). In the aftermath of the Great Depression and World War II, and during the period of decline of the British Empire, Amrith shows how the regional political ecology of the Bay of Bengal entered a period of fragmentation of politics, popular mobility, trade, imagination, movement, and livelihood. The era of nation-states and intensified development ushered a new phase of despoliation and destruction of the highly populated littoral of the Bay, "the front line of Asia's experience of climate change" (Amrith 2013, 5). Alongside this increasingly vulnerable ecology, Amrith's historical geography points to the strained, or indeed destroyed, networks of interaction and exchange that are increasingly necessary for remediation.

In Amrith's (2013, 4–5) deft hands, the Bay matters in concrete ways through the effects of industrialization in its littoral hinterlands, as it continues to be a key site of Indian and Chinese interest as well as "a frontline of Asia's experience of climate change: its densely populated coastal zone . . . home to nearly half a billion people." The deep ocean and the movement of undersea tectonic plates is vital here, though not necessarily in the ways that the ontological turn might propose. Amrith (2013, 10) reminds us of the planetary significance of the undersea earthquake in December 2004 that led to the devastating tsunami across various shores. Another major oceanographic process with fundamental sociocultural consequences is, of course, the monsoon. "The monsoon sustains life on the Bay," argues Amrith, but he cautions that while "they appear to be outside history . . . the monsoons have changed; they change constantly" (2013, 12). And then there is the dramatically changing shape of the Bay of Bengal, its changing coastlines and shorelines, and the acceleration of change in the heated, fish-depleted, much-trashed sea of the second half of the twentieth century (2013, 30).

The sea itself is consequential in Amrith's environmental history of a much-peopled sea, but equally exciting is his use of sources and his fluid narrative style in constructing a compelling account of a changing oceanic region, all the while keeping in mind that "the Indian Ocean was 'global' long before the Atlantic" (2013, 26). Rather than celebrate the recovery of subaltern lives across "the Bay," what is useful in Amrith's account is his concern with shifting forms of socionatural infrastructure in the passing of a particular set of "crossings." As the Bay fragments in the era of postcolonial nationalism, with a sharper political division between South Asia and Southeast Asia, Amrith (2013, 260) aptly argues that this launches "the final enclosure of the Bay—the treatment of the sea as an extension of national territory—[which] facilitated its overexploitation as a resource." In what seems a familiar oceanic account of plastic detritus on the sea's surfaces, "dead zones," depleted fish stocks, eroding coastlines, and destroyed mangroves, Amrith writes passionately in defense of the "climate refugees" on the edges of the Bay.

Amrith's conclusion is a call to value regional conceptualization even as the region has fallen on difficult times, and here we return to what I have suggested is an attention to regional sociocultural, material, and environmental infrastructure that marks the differences of life on the Bay of Bengal in various ways. The traces of these regional sociocultural and material processes are left in various ways in various places, sometimes evident in agrarian ecologies and sometimes in the built environment or in ritual practices. For instance, Amrith (2013, 89) finds offerings in shops along the passage to the main shrine in the Tamil town of Nagore with images of ships, which are meant to be used in prayer for voyages across the Bay of Bengal. Elsewhere around the Bay, Amrith finds shrines called Nagore Durgah, tied to their Tamil counterpart, in Penang and Singapore, and he has oral evidence of similar shrines across Burma, Ceylon, Indonesia, and Vietnam. Against official doctrines of tolerance, Amrith finds evidence of syncretic public cultures in which wide-ranging solidarities come to view. New modes of circulation, particularly through print capitalism, provided the infrastructure for debate about nationalism, reform, revolt, war, and anticolonial struggle across plantations, villages, towns, and cities of a Bay on the verge of a new age. A conjuncture of revolutionary upheaval, British colonial conquest, interconnection through steam navigation, and the shocks of World War II "marked the Bay's rise and fall as a region at the heart of empires and global capitalism" (Amrith 2013, 210).

Amrith concludes with an argument that can be read as fundamentally about geographical change and about the importance of reconstituting subaltern political will: "The rising waters of the Bay are due to global causes, but it is at the level of the region that their effects will be felt. The region has the cultural resources to generate a new ethic of hospitality and aid to strangers: a store of collective memories, intercultural understandings, and stories that allow the imagination of solidarities over long distances" (Amrith 2013, 275). Rather than (ontologically or ontically) separating the sea from its denizens or nature from history, I read Amrith as calling for geo-graphia, Earth-writing, and world-writing fueled by the poetics of syncretism, a specific kind of pan-Asian métissage foundational to the social ecology of the Bay of Bengal. What is more, the political lesson he draws out so powerfully, on the importance of new articulations of "the Bay," will be important for any future "human oceanography."

Errantry and the Subaltern Sea

Where aporias of understanding occur in the research imagination, the work of teasing out subaltern geographies must desist from the knee-jerk reaction to fill those gaps with the radiant light of sovereign and familiar Euro-American concept-metaphors.
    —Tariq Jazeel (2014, 99)

What I suggest is that thinking with the Indian Ocean offers precisely such an aporetic opportunity, but I would add to Jazeel's caution above that we should not be satisfied with a Euro-American concept-metaphor of "aporia" as any consolation. Indeed, Indian subaltern studies carried the hope that subalternity stands for the unknowable, aporetic, or uncontaminated space of dwelling; these are presumptions that an oceanic perspective cannot support. We might, instead, consider journeying through the material and intellectual archives that a region or spatial process offers so as to think with the propositions that emerge from geo-graphy as errantry. Neither unbound voluntarism nor rigid conformity to the "radiant light" of Euro-American expectation, as Jazeel puts it, the dialectical errantry of the Black radical tradition speaks to deepening socioecological precariousness on land and sea. In geography, David Featherstone has championed precisely such a dialectical spatial praxis that connects distanced struggles and political imaginations. In Featherstone's contribution to this volume, thinking with subaltern geographies pushes well beyond a sign of the emplaced small voices of history and beyond "the spatially circumscribed limits of the [subaltern studies] collective's work." In the spirit of Antonio Gramsci, Featherstone's work relentlessly refocuses our attention on the spatial integuments of insurgent political will across oceanic space-times. And it is important to note in our age that these integuments are materially complex and fragile articulations of capital and nature, past and future, across diverse sociocultural environs. The human oceanography of the Indian Ocean only makes this explicit.

The Indian Ocean is a vast region, and I make no claims as a neophyte in this field to sum it up or to offer a rejoinder to the varied insights of its many scholars. However, I offer a few thoughts from some errantry in the Southern African Indian Ocean. I recently attended a conference on ports and logistics in Saint-Denis, the capital of La Réunion. The conference was a kind of marketplace of port operators, shippers, and merchants of various kinds of port equipment—from the latest in surveillance technology to determine human or nonhuman contraband in shipping containers to enormous gantry cranes to keep up with the giganticism of container shipping. One of the concerns of the Port of Réunion was to try to project this island, after all a department of France in the Indian Ocean, as the obvious place for transhipment to Europe. What remained unsaid was that precisely as a part of France, Le Port (the Port of Réunion) is in fact an extremely expensive port in this part of the world and its size and significance has never been particularly important in the global scheme of shipping, even when compared with neighboring Mauritius. A second concern in the self-presentations of port operators from La Réunion, Mauritius, and Madagascar was that they might find themselves capturing a larger share of trade given the slowing of growth on the African continent in relation to the ports of Durban, Maputo, and Mombassa. Deep-sea port projects, and the maritime and logistical technology that goes into their construction, are a massive investment in the built environment of a future that may or may not come to be. From what I call the "Southern African Indian Ocean," the conference was a kind of theater of competition and fantasy projection among regional ports as well as an attempt at collective boosterism for the region as a whole as an intermediary point in the traffic in commodities across East Asia, South Africa, and Brazil.

As an excursion from the event, delegates were taken along the road that hugs the steep volcanic mountain that drops directly into the depths of the Indian Ocean between Saint-Denis and Le Port. As we drove on the edge of the island, we looked out at the rough and foreboding waters as we were told of periodic cyclones and rock falls that make the road inoperative. As a consequence, the Prefecture of Réunion, in partnership with the French government and a large number of French contractors, had begun building a massive road on pillars out in the ocean. At 1.4 billion euros/kilometer, this oceanic highway would perhaps be the most expensive road in the galaxy. I narrated details of my site visit to a key intellectual and poet from La Réunion, Jean-Claude Carpanin Marimoutou, who asked me how much of the road I had actually seen. I thought about it and responded, "One pillar, or perhaps two halves." "Exactly," he replied. Whether he meant that the road was an absolute impossibility or a perpetual drain on public funds, it is clear that Marimoutou was singularly unimpressed by this feat of engineering.

While this capitalist fix to oceanic infrastructure may be a boon to contractors, it is not the kind of geo-graphia that might support an incipient collective subaltern political will. Marimoutou posed to me a set of concerns that are of a piece with Amrith's arguments about the intellectual and political life of the Bay of Bengal—that there was at once a significant regional circulation of intellectual and cultural resources across the neighboring Francophone islands of Réunion, Mauritius, and Madagascar. Now, he laments, these exchanges have become largely matters of business and of generic commodities, of cranes and kitsch. The possibility of new forms of regional intellectual and cultural exchange remain as key here as it is in the Bay of Bengal, or indeed in the circulations in the Antilles, which became the point of departure for the great subaltern political-cultural archive of the Black Atlantic. As island nations face the social and political consequences of climate change, we might find new ways in which their denizens consider regional and oceanic rearticulations of subaltern political will.

Conclusion

I have made the case for thinking of subalternity in "the subaltern sea" as not just (but also) a project of engaging with a multiplicity of subaltern subjects and their possibilities of regional hospitality, as Amrith (2013) puts it, but also of the material, political-economic, ecological, multispecies, and infrastructural integument of subalternity that thinking oceanically makes manifest. To return to Gramsci, progenitor of this still arcane concept, the project of subalternity cannot be a celebration of fragmentation, marginality, or the small voice of history but rather, in his terms, a proposition for the reconstitution of political will. Precisely after the disasters of twentieth-century state socialisms, the question of subalternity returns to us as our collective political project of the future. As Chakrabarty (2009) puts it, we need not have a name for this collective agent. The subaltern, the multitude, the proletariat, or the human were always only placeholders, but the praxis of solidarity remains absolutely necessary. What maritime infrastructure like the oceanic road to the port of La Réunion recalls attention to are the massive interests of corporate and state power in the oceans as conduits for the world's commodities as well as untapped sites of mineral and energy exploration. Against this inevitability, oceanic errantry calls attention to the many points at which people question these currents, gathering the intellectual and cultural resources necessary to build the subaltern political will for the future. The lessons of the Antilles and the Bay of Bengal are never far from the contemporary Southern African Indian Ocean.

One of the unfortunate consequences of the academic disciplining of South Asian subaltern studies in Anglo-Americo-Australian postcolonial studies has been its deracination from the political struggles that were its forebears, however we might trace them. Indeed, there are multiple and changing origin stories to be had, and that is beside the point. I have, after all, sought to articulate the historical geography of Indian Ocean subalternity in the Antilles, in the lost intellectual histories of seafarers, in the spectral archive of the Black Atlantic, in the intellectual and political ecology of the Bay of Bengal, and in the contemporary struggles for Chagossian spatial justice. The disciplining of "subalternity" in academia has also come with an allergy to making audaciously universal claims. This takes me back to the creative insights of Isabel Hofmeyr, to whom I am indebted for provoking us with the thought that the Indian Ocean is a subaltern sea. Hofmeyr (2010, 722) poses transoceanic forms in Indian Ocean circulation as pointing to "a historically deep archive of competing universalism." This is a qualitatively different argument from the quest to rescue subaltern subjects from archival obscurity. Like Glissant, Hofmeyr presumes that these "competing universalisms" are not located in multicultural (or indeed, for ontologists, multinatural) difference but that they are also forms of situated knowledge.

This returns us to the variously written, read, and lived archives of this ocean, largely in the southern hemisphere, its interactions premised on deep and non-linear histories of metissage, unfreedom, and uncertain futurity. What I reserve from Amrith, Glissant, Vergès, Gilroy, Vine, and others considered here is the necessity for cultural-intellectual interaction as the medium for imagining a different relationship to the future other than of gulag archipelagos, despoiled island ecologies, abandoned precarious peoples, and oceans of trash. These are the material cultures through which our oceanic world might yet be rewritten. The search for "subaltern geographies" need not be trapped in an ever-receding past. Rather, this experiment in errantry asks how we might discern residual and emergent forms of Earth-writing and world-writing: of geo-graphy for our uncertain collective and planetary future.

NOTES

I am grateful for comments on this paper from David Featherstone, Isabel Hofmeyr, Tariq Jazeel, Stephen Legg, Meg Samuelson, and an anonymous referee. All errors of commission or omission are solely mine. I am grateful to the National Institute for Humanities and Social Sciences, South Africa, for research support.

REFERENCES

Ahuja, Ravi. 2009. "Networks of Subordination—Networks of the Subordinated: The Ordered Spaces of South Asian Maritime Labour in an Age of Imperialism (c. 1890–1946)." In *The Limits of British Colonial Control in South Asia: Spaces of Disorder in the Indian Ocean Region*, edited by Ashwini Tambe and Harald Fischer-Tine, 13–48. London: Routledge.

Amrith, Sunil. 2013. *Crossing the Bay of Bengal: The Furies of Nature and the Fortunes of Migrants*. Cambridge, Mass.: Harvard University Press.

Anderson, Clare. 2012. *Subaltern Lives: Biographies of Colonialism in the Indian Ocean World, 1790–1920*. Cambridge: Cambridge University Press.

———. 2013. "Subaltern Lives: History, Identity and Memory in the Indian Ocean World." *History Compass* 11, no. 7: 503–7.

Benton, Lauren. 2005. "Legal Spaces of Empire: Piracy and the Origins of Ocean Regionalism." *Comparative Studies in Society and History* 47, no. 4: 700–24.

———. 2009. *A Search for Sovereignty: Law and Geography in European Empires*. Cambridge: Cambridge University Press.

Braudel, Fernand. 1978 [1949]. *The Mediterranean and the Mediterranean World in the Age of Philip II*. London: William Collins Sons.

Burton, Antoinette, Madhavi Kale, Isabel Hofmeyr, Clare Anderson, Christopher J. Lee, and Nile Green. 2013. "Sea Tracks and Trails: Indian Ocean Worlds as Method." *History Compass* 11, no. 7: 497–502.

Carter, Marina, and Torabully Khal. 2002. *Coolitude: An Anthology of the Indian Labour Diaspora*. London: Anthem Press.

Chakrabarty, Dipesh. 2000. *Provincializing Europe*. Princeton, N.J.: Princeton University Press.

———. 2009. "The Climate of History: Four Theses." *Critical Inquiry* 35: 197–222.

Chari, Sharad. 2014. "An 'Indian commons' in Durban? Limits to Mutuality, or the City to Come." *Anthropology Southern Africa*, 37, nos. 3–4: 149–59.

———. 2017. "The Blues and the Damned: (Black) Life-That-Survives Capitalism and Biopolitics." *Contemporary African Studies* 9, no. 2: 152–73.

Chen, Kuan-Hsing. 2010. *Asia as Method: Toward Deimperialization*. Durham, N.C.: Duke University Press.

Edwards, Paul. 2010. *A Vast Machine: Computer Models, Climate Data, and the Politics of Global Warming*. Cambridge, Mass.: MIT Press.

Featherstone, D. J. 2008. *Resistance, Space and Political Identities: The Making of Counter-Global Networks*. Oxford: Wiley-Blackwell.

Gilroy, Paul. 1993. *The Black Atlantic: Modernity and Double Consciousness*. London: Verso.

Glissant, Édouard. 1997 [1990]. *Poetics of Relation*. Translated by Betsy Wing. Ann Arbor: University of Michigan Press.

Gramsci, Antonio. 1971. *Selections from the Prison Notebooks*. Translated and edited by Quintin Hoare and Geoffrey Nowell Smith. New York: International Publishers.

Green, Nile. 2013. "Maritime Worlds and Global History: Comparing the Mediterranean and Indian Ocean through Barcelona and Bombay." *History Compass* 11, no. 7: 513–23.

Haraway, Donna. 1991. *Simians, Cyborgs and Women: The Reinvention of Nature*. New York: Routledge.

Helmreich, Stefan. 2009. *Alien Ocean: Anthropological Voyages in Microbial Seas*. Los Angeles: University of California Press.

———. 2014. "Waves: An Anthropology of Scientific Things." *JAU: Journal of Ethnographic Theory* 4, no. 3: 265–84.

Hesse, Barnor. 2011. "Symptomatically Black: A Creolization of the Political." In *The Creolization of Theory*, edited by F. Lionnet and S. Shih, 37–61. Durham, N.C.: Duke University Press.

Ho, Engseng. 2006. *The Graves of Tarim: Genealogy and Mobility across the Indian Ocean*. Berkeley: University of California Press.

Hofmeyr, Isabel. 2010. "Universalizing the Indian Ocean." *Publications of the Modern Language Association of America (PMLA)* 125, no. 3: 721–29.

———. 2013. "South Africa's Indian Ocean—Notes from Johannesburg." *History Compass* 11, no. 7: 508–12.

———. 2015. "Styling Multilateralism: Indian Ocean Cultural Futures." *Journal of the Indian Ocean Region* 11, no. 1: 1–12.

Jazeel, Tariq. 2014 "Subaltern Geographies: Geographical Knowledge and Postcolonial Strategy." *Singapore Journal of Tropical Geography* 35: 88–103.

Kale, Madhavi. 2013. "Response to the Forum." *History Compass* 11, no. 7: 531–35.

Kelly, John D. 2014. "Introduction: The Ontological Turn in French Philosophical Anthropology." *Journal of Ethnographic Theory* 4, no. 1: 259–69.

Lavery, Charne. 2016. "Indian Ocean Depths." Paper presented at Indian Ocean Energies, WiSER, University of the Witwatersrand, Johannesburg, July 4.

Lee, Christopher J. 2013. "The Indian Ocean during the Cold War: Thinking through a Critical Geography." *History Compass* 11, no. 7: 524–30.

Lefebvre, Henri. 1991. *The Production of Space*. Oxford: Blackwell.

Legg, Stephen. 2014. *Prostitution and the Ends of Empire: Scale, Governmentalities, and Interwar India*. Durham, N.C.: Duke University Press.

Linebaugh, Peter, and Marcus Rediker. 2000. *The Many-Headed Hydra: Sailors, Slaves, Commoners and the Hidden History of the Revolutionary Atlantic*. Boston: Beacon Press.

McKittrick, Katherine. 2013. "Plantation Futures." *Small Axe* 17, no. 3: 1–15.

Rancière, Jacques. 1994. *The Names of History: On the Poetics of Knowledge*. Minneapolis: University of Minnesota Press.

Rediker, Marcus. 2004. "Toward a People's History of the Sea." In *Maritime Empires: British Imperial Maritime Trade in the Nineteenth Century*, edited by David Killingray, Margarette Lincoln, and Nigel Rigby, 195–206. Woodbridge: Boydell Press.

Robinson, Cedric J. 2000 [1983]. *Black Marxism: The Making of the Black Radical Tradition*. Chapel Hill: University of North Carolina Press.

Salmond, Anne. 2014. "Tears of Rangi: Water, Power, and People in New Zealand." *HAU: Journal of Ethnographic Theory* 4, no. 3: 285–309.

Samuelson, Meg. 2016 "Indian Ocean Surf Zones and the Search for Stoke: Surfaris, Offshoring and the Shore-Break." Paper presented at Indian Ocean Energies, WiSER, University of the Witwatersrand, Johannesburg, July 4.

Schmitt, Carl. 1997 [1954]. *Land and Sea*. Washington, D.C.: Plutarch Press.

Scott, James C. 2011. *The Art of Not Being Governed: An Anarchist History of Upland South-East Asia*. New Haven, Conn.: Yale University Press.

Scott, Julius Sherrard. 1986. "The Common Wind: Currents of Afro-American Communication in the Era of the Haitian Revolution." PhD diss., Duke University.

———. 2010 [1986]. "Negroes in Foreign Bottoms: Sailors, Slaves and Communication. Reprint of Chapter 2 of Scott (1986)." In *Origins of the Black Atlantic*, edited by Laurent Dubois and Julius Sherrard Scott, 69–98. New York: Routledge.

Singha, Radhika. 2009. "Passport, Ticket, and India-Rubber Stamp: 'The Problem of the Pauper Pilgrim' in Colonial India c. 1882–1925." In *The Limits of British Colonial Control in South Asia: Spaces of Disorder in the Indian Ocean Region*, edited by Aswhini Tambe and Harald Fischer-Tine, 49–83. London: Routledge.

Spivak, Gayatri Chakravarti. 1988. "Can the Subaltern Speak?" In *Marxism and the Interpretation of Culture*, edited by Lawrence Grossberg and Cary Nelson, 271–313. Urbana: University of Illinois Press.

Steinberg, Philip. 2001. *The Social Construction of the Ocean*. Cambridge: Cambridge University Press.

Steinberg, Philip, and Kimberley Peters. 2015. "Wet Ontologies, Fluid Spaces: Giving Depth to Volume through Oceanic Thinking." *Environment and Planning D: Society and Space* 33: 247–64.

Subrahmanyam, Sanjay. 2005. *Explorations in Connected History: From the Tagus to the Ganges*. Oxford: Oxford University Press.

Tambe, Ashwini, and Harald Fischer-Tine. 2009. *The Limits of British Colonial Control in South Asia: Spaces of Disorder in the Indian Ocean Region*. London: Routledge.

Vergès, Françoise. 1999. *Monsters and Revolutionaries: Colonial Family Romance and Metissage*. Durham, N.C.: Duke University Press.

Vine, David. 2009. *Island of Shame: The Secret History of the U.S. Military Base on Diego Garcia*. Princeton, N.J.: Princeton University Press.

Urban Fragments

A Subaltern Studies Imagination

COLIN MCFARLANE

In this chapter I argue that the idea of the "fragment" in subaltern studies offers useful resources for how we understand the making of urban knowledge and theory. While there is a productive history of attempts to use subaltern studies in urban research (e.g., Chattopadhyay 2012; Robinson 2006; Roy 2011), there has been little consideration of what the idea of the fragment might offer. Instead, most discussion has remained focused on the category of "subaltern," related to but not equivalent to the idea of the fragment. This, I hope to show, is a missed opportunity for urban research. I will argue that there are useful conceptual guides in what I call a "subaltern studies imagination" of the fragment for how we think about the project of urban theory and knowledge-making.

I begin by exploring the broad influence of subaltern studies on urban studies and then highlight three issues as especially important: the subaltern as *a relation to "popular" political struggle*; subaltern as simultaneously *an epistemology of the urban subject and ethical challenge of representation*; and subaltern as *a name for the limits of urban theory* rather than spaces of urban marginality alone. Second, I examine how the fragment is understood in subaltern studies accounts. And third, I compare this with how the fragment is often understood in urban studies. The chapter ends with a consideration of what a subaltern studies imagination of the fragment might offer urban research.

Subaltern Studies and Urban Studies

Subaltern studies, like urban studies, is a theoretically diverse set of debates (Chaturvedi 2012). Indeed, the lack of any clear "subaltern theory," as Vivek Chibber (2013) among others has argued, has often been viewed as a weakness in prominent critiques of the literature. While subaltern studies has always been focused on some key categories—such as the problem of how to identify and understand different forms of agency, subject position, and hegemony historically—theoretically this body of work increasingly diversified over time, taking it beyond its Gramscian and economic focus to include various strands of poststructuralist and cultural theory, in some cases as an explicitly Marxist project and in others as a decisive break from Marxism. This theoretical multiplicity echoes the proliferation of approaches in urban studies and has itself shaped the patchwork take-up of subaltern studies in urban studies research, in which the key influences have probably been Dipesh Chakrabarty's writings on provincialization, Partha Chatterjee's writings on political society, and Gayatri Spivak's conception of the subaltern.

Subaltern studies has had an influence on urban studies in two broad ways: first, as part of a wider influence of postcolonial thought on research (e.g., Bunnell and Maringanti 2010; Robinson 2006; Sidaway et al. 2014); and, second, as a more specific attempt to work with particular subaltern studies theorists or conceptualizations (e.g., Chattopadhyay 2012; Gidwani 2008, 2012; Roy 2011). Three uses stand out: subaltern as *a relation to "popular" political struggle*; subaltern as simultaneously *an epistemology of the urban subject and ethical challenge of representation*; and subaltern as *a name for the limits of urban theory* rather than spaces of urban marginality alone.

For Swati Chattopadhyay (2012, 251–52), in her reconceptualization of infrastructure in relation to contemporary urbanism in India, subaltern practices exist on the "edges of visibility," beyond definition and representation and in excess of authority, but can become "popular" and visible to state and capital as they become agents of social change. She draws on a rich array of routes through which this might take place, from familiar cultural practices like cricket and puja festivals or more explicitly political cultural acts like political graffiti or some forms of vehicular art. These practices can take ordinary spaces such as streets, neighborhoods, walls, or trucks and turn them, temporarily, into "spatial fragments" that belong "neither to the everyday nor to the exceptional . . . [they are] created out of a series of conjunctures, of bodies and objects, movements and views, noise and warmth, walls and roads, events and memories" (Chattopadhyay 2012, 119). For Chattopadhyay, in the spaces and switches between subaltern and popular, facilitated in part by these processes of urban fragment-making, lie a reconceptualization of infrastructure—as vital infrastructures of urban change—and a challenge to how urban theory might "unlearn the city" (Chattopadhyay 2012, 252).

Vinay Gidwani (2008, 2009, 2013; this volume) has reflected on the appeal of "subaltern" in his work, and he usefully identifies two senses that are deeply entwined: the *epistemological* and the *ethical*. Epistemologically, his work has examined how the subaltern subject, for example in relation to his work on urban waste and livelihoods, is "enabled to act (or desist) as the 'author of its initiatives'—that is, the double sense of 'subject' (*in subjection to* and *subject of*)" (this volume; Gidwani and Reddy 2011). Ethically, and here Gidwani chimes with a wider sense in which subaltern debates have impacted methodological and representational concerns in urban studies, Spivak's argument that to confront the subaltern is both to represent others and to represent ourselves is vital. This, as Gidwani (this volume) writes, creates a "double bind" or "nonpassage": "He who represents and she who is represented (I use these pronouns merely to underscore the asymmetry and paternalism that Spivak urges constant vigilance against) are in a double bind: an *aporia* (Greek, *a + poros* = nonpassage) that both must confront, but especially those who are structurally positioned to represent (and therefore, act as representatives)" (and see Jazeel 2014, 2016; Jazeel and McFarlane 2010).

Ananya Roy (2011), also drawing on Spivak, makes a different argument. While Roy (2011, 235) is sympathetic to research that locates the subaltern in the urban slum of the megacity, she looks to shift subaltern urbanism beyond forms of thinking that "assign unique political agency to the mass of urban subalterns." The subaltern, she argues, is not located in any pregiven territory, nor simply to be found in politically subversive practices. Writing against what she calls "ontological and topological readings of the subaltern," for Roy the subaltern is a more generalized category that "marks the limits of archival and ethnographic recognition" (2011, 231). Roy seeks to expand the realm of what she calls "subaltern urbanism" by, for example, examining how practices too often attributed to the slum alone, such as informal patterns of urban inhabitation, are also to be found in state planning processes.

These three senses of the subaltern in urban studies—as a political struggle, as an epistemic and ethical challenge of researching urban space and subjects, and as a limit point not just of a group or a space but of urban theory more generally—mirror wider debates in the social sciences and humanities around how to define, conceptualize, research, and think politically about what has long been a slippery and daunting concept. Each of the accounts work with distinct definitions of the subaltern, but at least two crosscutting issues emerge: first, a concern with the importance of representation, including who does the representation as much as who/what is being represented; and, second, a concern with what those representations might mean for how we understand contemporary urbanism. There has, however, been less consideration of what the notion of the "fragment" in subaltern studies might mean for urban studies.

What I take from these accounts is less a concern with pinpointing the specificity of the subaltern and more a challenge for how we encounter and conceptualize urban multiplicity and difference. In particular, there is value for urban studies in what I am calling here a "subaltern studies imagination," that is, a focus on different ways of being, thinking, acting, producing knowledge, and making spaces that lead us to critically reflect on how "the urban" is represented and understood in urban studies. This imagination is alert to the challenge of the subaltern—to that which is barely visible and which exists beyond dominant forms of knowing urbanism—but it seeks a wider canvas that exceeds the subaltern itself. It takes the concern with how we represent to include the kinds of status we in urban studies grant to marginalized urban spaces more generally, spaces that are themselves not necessarily subaltern but are nonetheless undervalued in the challenges they bring to mainstream urban theory. A subaltern studies imagination, as I will argue, brings an analytical strategy to these fragments, which includes an approach to how we think about the relation between the general and the particular, the continuous and the episodic, and to both the content and the style of abstraction that we put to work.

Subaltern Studies and the Fragment

The "fragment" plays an important role in subaltern studies. Fragments of knowledge are fundamental to the subaltern studies project because they present tantalizing clues to other histories and to new forms of conceptualization and methodology, often hinted at in archival research but speaking to a different way of conceiving some of the basic categories of historical investigation, including agency, struggle, insurgency, consciousness, politics, class, even history itself. At stake in attending to fragments is not empirical variation alone, but new "vantage points." As Vinayak Chaturvedi (2012, x) has argued, in the early work of subaltern studies, for instance in the work of Ranajit Guha, Partha Chatterjee, Dipesh Chakrabarty, and David Arnold, there was a belief in the early work that "meticulous thick descriptions of insurgency could disclose the otherwise concealed political character of peasant consciousness by reconstructing the vantage point, the spontaneous ideology of the peasant rebel." The aim is not to uncover an "authentic" peasant consciousness—there isn't one—but instead to try to understand multiple and sometimes incommensurable ways of being, perceiving, and becoming political that open out to other histories, entangled though they were with histories of the state, capital, and colonial modernity.

Partha Chatterjee (1993), for example, uses the idea of "fragment" in *The Nation and Its Fragments* as a shorthand for forms of difference and resistance in Bengal that cannot be adequately understood within mainstream representations of nationalism. Conventional accounts of the struggle for Indian independence and the formation of the modern nation either excluded or actively subordinated fragments around caste, gender, and religion (especially Islam), missing the ways in which anticolonial projects often operated with referent points outside of largely European understandings of categories like "nation," "modern," and "community." Gyanendra Pandey (2006), in *Routine Violence: Nations, Fragments, Histories*, focuses on more contemporary versions of Indian nationalism to show how nationalist discourse can be used to spark violence against minority groups. Pandey shows, for example, how minority groups are recovered as the targets of incorporation, including Dalits, who are incorporated in ways that reproduce caste hierarchy rather than in ways that seek to challenge it. As Pandey (1991, 559) elsewhere wrote: "The 'fragments' of Indian society—the smaller religious and caste communities, tribal sections, industrial workers, activist women's groups, all of which might be said to represent 'minority' cultures and practices—have been expected to fall in line with the 'mainstream' (Brahmanical Hindu, consumerist) national culture." It is these minority groups that constitute the fragments in Pandey's critique of Hindu nationalism, and in this sense there is a broad similarity between Chatterjee's and Pandey's accounts of how certain discourses of nationalism can serve variously to exclude and subordinate particular ways of knowing or forms of identity.

A fragment is marked out as such in these accounts by Chatterjee and Pandey in two broad ways. First, because of its position to or within a wider set of political, social, and cultural power relations, fragments emerge in the making of dominant national cultures and can therefore shift over time depending on how that process changes. Second, the fragment can be a form of expression, whether a piece of drama, a collection of poems, or a political protest, that presents clues to a different way of understanding history, the nation, the community, or citizenship. Both these conceptions of the fragment are often found together in subaltern studies work and they are of course closely interrelated.

Dipesh Chakrabarty (2002) locates subaltern struggle in relation to the "fragmentary and episodic," rather than the pregiven abstractions of the general and continuous routinely put to work by historians. Antonio Gramsci (1971) is an important influence on Chakrabarty here. For Gramsci the aim was for the subaltern, working with the revolutionary intellectual, to transcend subalternity by becoming a unified political force that can better understand and challenge power and the state. For Chakrabarty, however, it is important analytically and politically to stay with those forms of subaltern struggle that do not coalesce into a cohesive force—this, after all, is partly what marks those struggles out as subaltern. "Can we imagine another moment of subaltern history," writes Chakrabarty (2002, 34–35), "where we stay—permanently, not simply as a matter of political tactics—with what is fragmentary and episodic, precisely because that which is fragmentary and episodic does not, cannot, dream of the whole called the state and therefore must be suggestive of knowledge-forms that are not tied to the will that produces the state?"

Notice here that Chakrabarty connects "fragment" and "whole." But it is a whole, for subaltern political agitators at least, that remains obscured. Subaltern struggle cannot "dream of the whole," and so they are fragments in two senses:

first, in their status as marginalized or silenced forms of knowledge and episodic political action on the edges of conventional historical archives; and second, because they are animated not by critique of a conventional political whole, where the state in particular is vital, but by different centers of gravity. The "knowledge-forms" of subaltern struggle cannot dream the whole because they operate with a different referent point to struggles that focus on the state. There may be other wholes at work in these imaginaries, but for Chakrabarty (2002, 274), it is important analytically to stay with the fragment without recourse to the whole. In this sense he wants to push the notion of fragment to disrupt commonplace conceptions of both the fragment and the whole: "Not 'fragmentary' in the sense of fragments that refer to an implicit whole but fragments that challenge not only the idea of wholeness but the very idea of the 'fragment' itself," because if the fragment is not framed as part of a whole then it needs to be understood differently, as an abstraction that challenges, contests, and pushes different theoretical positions. Similarly, for Gyanendra Pandey (2006, 296), the fragment is not just "a 'bit'—the dictionary's 'piece broken off'—of a preconstituted whole."

But there is a third sense in which Chakrabarty uses "fragment": as an orientation toward the social world as beyond any one system of representation. For Chakrabarty, fragments are provocations that demand recognition that the world is more than simply "plural" but "so plural as to be impossible of description in any one system of representation." Instead, the challenge is to "learn from the subaltern"—or, as we might put it here, to *learn from the fragment*: "To go to the subaltern in order to learn to be radically 'fragmentary' and 'episodic' is to move away from the monomania of the imagination that operates within the gesture that the knowing, judging, willing subject always already knows what is good for everybody, ahead of any investigation" (Chakrabarty 2002, 275). The fact that Chakrabarty's fragments are episodic brings an important temporal dimension to his critique of singular systems of representation. The systems of representation he critiques are not just spatially and socially encompassing in their claims to see the world and its future but temporally encompassing too: they are driven by an arc of history telling at the level of the broad sweep, the large-scale shift, and are ill equipped to see episodic actions, despite the fact these episodic actions recur over time.

The claim from Chakrabarty is that thinking of politics in relation to the fragment provides a suggestive lure to other ways of thinking about the political. The fragment here is no mere side story to the grand arc of political struggle. In fact, the fragment calls into question the grand arc of politics, which Chakrabarty locates here as a narrow representation of the political that links it to conceptions of unified state-focused struggle. The fragment then is both an empirical operator and a conceptual operator. It is empirical because it refers to particular kinds of episodic struggle that reflect different ways of knowing and practicing politics from accounts focused on unified struggle that questions and seeks to transform the state ("the whole"); and it is conceptual because the fragment is used both to ask us to avoid the risk of incorporating difference too quickly within existing conceptual formulations of the political and as a basis to open out other ways of conceptualizing political knowledge, practice, and thinking.

Chakrabarty has lots of examples in mind. He mentions for instance Gyan Prakash's (1990) book on bonded labor in Bihar, *Bonded Histories: Genealogies of Labour Servitude in Colonial India*, and uses it to argue that some peasant knowledge-forms in colonial India understood power not in relation to the state, labor, and class struggle but to ghosts and spirit cults. However, such accounts tend to be understood through the prism of a system of representation that takes the modern subject and political struggle as an implicit framing device, meaning that peasant knowledge-forms and (episodic) political action always remain analytically and politically subordinate to the modern. The scope for peasant knowledge-forms to enter into and dominate the nature of the modern as knowledge, practice, and politics are unimaginable in these systems. We might think of these accounts as traces, as Chakrabarty (1996, 60) does in his argument that histories of heterogeneous subaltern labor can only be located in narratives of capitalist transition as a Derridean trace "that constantly challenges from within capital's and commodity's—and by implication History's—claim to unity and universality" (see Derrida 1976, 1981). As with a trace, a fragment both contains the marker of that which it is not, an absent presence that influences but does not delimit its form, and points to the gap between the representable and the nonrepresentable (Napolitano 2015). But, more than a trace, Chakrabarty (2002) positions fragments signaling more than absence. Fragments play a vital role in the generation of new ways of seeing history and the agents of change. And fragments lure attention by saying something new and/or neglected outside the usual optics of seeing history. Similarly, for Gyan Pandey (2006, 66–67), the fragment has the potential to act as "a 'disturbance,' a contradiction ... in the self-representation of that particular totality and those who uncritically uphold it." The fragment is "an appeal": to an alternative possibility or perspective, a marker of the "fragility and instability of the 'givens'" (Pandy 2006, 66–67).

The subaltern nature of any act, group, individual, or space is an empirical question and cannot be defined in advance other than to say that it is that which, as Roy (2011, 231) has put it, drawing on Spivak, exists beyond recognition and identification and "marks the silences of our archives and annals." Of course, the tendency to equate the subaltern with a more generalized conception of the marginalized has been one of the flashpoints of debate around the use and potential of the subaltern category. Rather than conflate the two, fragment is a wider category that names a series of socially marginalized spaces that may or may not be subaltern and that are both increasingly important to the constitution of urban life yet often unaccounted for in the run of most urban studies debates.

Here an important lesson from subaltern studies lies in the risk of celebrating the fragment. The fragment may well be an analytically disruptive force, but this does not mean that the fragment itself constitutes an emancipatory space. The aim cannot surely be then to align with efforts to incorporate subalternity within existing dominant frames of, for instance, the entrepreneurial citizen (see, e.g., Ananya Roy [2010] on microcredit, subjectivity, and "poverty capital") or, for example, in efforts to incorporate immigrant groups into dominant visions of nationality with their associated codes, sensibilities, and ways of being (e.g., Bagelman 2013; Darling 2014; and see Spivak 1993). Such fragments, either on their own terms or in dialectic relation with dominant forms of power and representation, should not be romanticized. And yet, an important lesson from subaltern studies here is that we cannot simply step around the problem of incorporation, because it lurks always in the background as part of the politics of representation, as a delicate line and inescapable dialectical tension between, and comprehending the significance of, a fragment and its incorporation within existing frames.

Having examined some of the ways in which the fragment is used in subaltern studies, I will now examine its potential in urban research. In order to do that, we need to foreground how the fragment is currently understood in urban research in order to identify points of critical dialogue for future research.

The Fragment in Urban Studies

In contemporary urban research, the fragment is put to work in a range of ways. It is used in a general sense to describe urban *process and form*, where fragmentation is the process, linked to capitalist urbanization, and fragment is the form. Here, we see fragmentation and fragment used in relation to a wider family of terms, not least "splintering," linked to Graham and Marvin's (2001) defining image of urbanism but also in relation to a variety of other forms, from gated enclaves and gentrified neighborhoods to different forms of sociospatial polarization and postjustice urbanism, as well as historical processes linked to colonial forms of *cordon sanitaire* and "archipelago" or "medieval" urbanism (e.g., AlSayyad and Roy 2006; Bakker 2003; Caldiera 2000; Kooy and Bakker 2008; Lees et al. 2008; Macleod and McFarlane 2014; McFarlane 2008; Mitchell 2001; Smith 1996). In each of these accounts, there is a specific relation between fragmentation, fragment, and whole at work. In general terms, however, the tendency is to link fragmentation and the whole through processes of capitalist urbanization. Henri Lefebvre (2003, 1991) provides perhaps the most compelling example in this tradition. For example, in both *The Production of Space* and *The Urban Revolution*, capitalist urbanization is explicitly conceived as a whole—a whole that not only is productive of the fragmentation of urban space but also *actively requires* the fragmentation of urban space in order to sustain itself (for instance in terms of the geographical placing of labor or the targeting of specific spaces in the city for accumulation and speculation).

In these urban accounts, the fragment and the whole are thought and related in radically different ways to those of Chakrabarty. These accounts tend to position the fragment as a product of the whole, where the whole is a system of representation linked to capitalist modernization, and in particular to categories of class, labor, land, and infrastructure. The key spheres through which the urban is understood to become fragmented in these accounts include neoliberalism, gentrification, the proliferation (or resurgence) of gated communities, the commodification of public space, and the deepening of class inequalities. I do not, to be clear, raise this point as a criticism of this work. This literature is vital analytically and politically. But it is important to note that this is quite a particular way of seeing fragments and their production, which emerges from quite a narrow range of systems of representation, despite the differences between the accounts above. Thus the question that Chakrabarty asks us to raise: What does this stop us from seeing?

In this context, there is an important connection between Chakrabarty's conception of the fragment and some strands of urban studies. Consider this claim from Edgar Pieterse (2011, n.p.), writing about cities in Africa, where he pronounces a certain faith in spaces, often at the margins not of everyday life in urban Africa but of urban theory: "I have no doubt that the street, the slum, the waste dump, the taxi rank, the mosque and church will become the catalysts of an unanticipated African urbanism" (and see Rokem et al. 2017). By "catalyst," I take it that Pieterse is referring both to progressive forms of politics in African cities and to new ways of conceptualizing African cities outside the usual referent points (accounts, for instance, of the state and policy). To take another example, writing about urban wastepickers in municipal garbage grounds in India, Vinay Gidwani (2013, 774) suggests that theory could be enriched by attending more closely to the life-worlds of wastepickers and their interconnections to spatially distanciated relations of capital, labor, and urbanism. In such spaces there may be sources for new ways of thinking about urbanism and political change that we might think of, to use a phrase of Gidwani's, as a "conjuring of the positive": "I take this conjuring of the positive from what has been cast aside—marginalized, remaindered, and stigmatized—as the primary intellectual and political task of the postcolonial scholar as archivist of the city."

There are a lot of different social forms being highlighted here—taxi ranks, garbage grounds, mosques, informal settlements, streets, and so on. Some of these have long played a prominent role in the history of mainstream urban theory, especially the street but also, in quite different forms and registers, the "slum" (or "ghetto," "informal settlement," etc.). I am not claiming that these are all "fragments." Instead, I argue that it is useful to keep ahold of a "subaltern studies imagination" (I will explain this term in the next section) of the fragment as a marker of the edges of how cities and the urban are understood and represented—ways of living, being, imagining, and making the city that have been at the margins or even invisible to much of urban studies and that may point to new kinds of knowledge. The fragment, in this analysis, acts as a kind of lure—an invitation to pause and stay with difference.

If this is in part about immersion in difference, there is of course a history of doing this in urban thought. We might think, for example, of Walter Benjamin's literary form of connecting fragments of text, of abandoned or usually ignored parts of the city, and of assembling them in montage. *The Arcades Project*—a form that has had widespread influences in spatial and urban thinking (e.g., Buck-Morss 1989; Pred 2000; Swanton 2010)—is a strategy of "blind immersion in the particular" (Tiedemann 2008, 247–48), and a "blasting apart of pragmatic historicism—grounded, as this always is, on the premise of a continuous and homogenous temporality" (Eiland and McLaughlin 2003, xi). The question, one that Benjamin repeatedly examined in his writing and in his reflections on how he wrote, is whether and how fragments on the margins of urban studies may provoke new ways of conceptualizing urban space, urban politics, or urban knowledge. We cannot know the answer to such a question in advance: the force of the fragment, from a subaltern studies imagination, is to ask the question again and again and to look for where the question pushes us as we conduct urban research.

The challenge goes to the heart of long-standing debate in urban studies about how we should understand particular cases of difference in relation to the wider whole. So, in the Lefebvrian tradition, the insistence is that analytically and politically urban scholars must shift from narrating fragmentation to critically engaging with the whole, even if the whole cannot be understood without understanding fragmentation. Here, it is never enough just to document fragments, which analytically take the form of "end products" (quite different from the Gramscian promise of subaltern fragments that might take on a unified force, where fragments are a starting point and not an end point). Instead, fragments need to be understood as both spatial *products* in cities and *processes* of fragmentation historically shaped through capitalist urbanization (the whole). Fragments, here, do not lose their specificity—it would be impossible to read Lefebvre, for instance, and conclude that he bypasses the specificity of fragments as products—but they are always being analytically resolved into a larger whole. How might this approach sit with the kind of work that would seek to stay with the fragments as provocations to different kinds of thinking?

There is no single answer here. But in some quarters of urban studies, there is at least a degree of caution in finding "catalysts" (to use Pieterse's term) in spaces often marginal to critical urban thinking—often spaces in the Global South. In an intervention in the *International Journal of Urban and Regional Research*, Michael Storper and Allen Scott (2014, 12–13) address this directly. They assert that urban studies needs to "guard against over-hasty impulses to take certain dramatic or peculiar instances of urban development (e.g., the crumbling infrastructure and violence of Kinshasa, the extensive slums of Mumbai, or the current financial collapse of Southern European cities) as *prima facie* evidence that a reformulation of theory is required." Now, as a general intellectual strategy, it is of course important to take heed of what Storper and Scott are saying here. It would be wrong, in any context (not just in relation to fragments of space in Southern Europe, Africa, or South Asia!), to make "over-hasty" claims about needing to reformulate theory. It would be difficult to find any critical urban researcher who would disagree with that.

However, it is worth paying attention to the language used by Storper and Scott here and what it reveals about the power to represent and to act as representative. "Guard against"—who should do the guarding? Who gets to say they are guardians? "Peculiar instances"—peculiar to whom? From which location is some urbanism deemed odd and others, implicitly, familiar? A central contribution of subaltern studies is precisely to draw attention to the privilege and power relations of location and authorship (*author*ity). This is precisely the kind of thinking—where "thinking" is both conceptualization and the institutional infrastructures of privilege and location that structure it—that Chakrabarty calls into question in his claims around the fragment. Might it be possible that the very capacity to define "peculiar" instances as peculiar is precisely what the fragment as a conceptual provocation seeks to question? Might it be that what we need to "guard against," to use Storper and Scott's term, is not impulses to theorize from the (presumably rather weird) urbanisms of, say, Bombay's slums but the claims by self-appointed guardians for what constitutes normal and peculiar urbanisms? Might it also be possible that one of the imperatives of subaltern studies is precisely to trouble that divide between "conceptual" and "empirical," not to attempt to naively bypass that divide but to transgress it by identifying how empirical particularities may also act conceptually, as provocations?

From this perspective, it seems, there are too many fragments. Weird fragments of slums and infrastructure in cities away from the Euro-American heartlands (see also Robinson 2006; and in fact the whole postcolonial project, e.g., Roy 2015) and fragments of theory itself—postcolonial this, poststructural that. Scott and Storper (2015, 3) worry over what they call a "sense of fragmentation" in urban studies. They bemoan an "ever-widening discontinuity and disjuncture in the conceptual frameworks, questions and methodologies that dominate research." They go on to say there is no "general concept of the urban and urbanization," no "shared vocabulary" to reveal its "inner logic" (Scott and Storper 2015, 3–4). Fragments, whether they are empirical realities, conceptual provocations, or theoretical insights that differ from the historical theorizations we've inherited in urban studies, pose a challenge to urban studies. But the solution cannot be a drive to consensus about what the urban is. The fact that there are radical differences around what the urban or urbanization or the city is, or about how to theorize and research it, is not a crisis to fret over and to resolve through the formulations of disciplinary grandees. Instead, it is something to embrace.

Rather than attempting to resolve how can we find an "inner logic," we might more productively reflect on what is at stake in different characterizations of fragments and wholes and to critically debate the stakes of different claims about fragments in their different forms (empirical, conceptual, theoretical). This I think is the spirit with which subaltern studies embraces—again, in often hotly contested debate—the fragment. The fragment operates here in a double sense. It is a thing in the world, but it is also a provocation to how we understand knowledge, politics, history, or space. As a shorthand, I will refer to this sense of the fragment as a "subaltern studies imagination."

Urban Fragments and the Subaltern Studies Imagination

In archival research, "locating" evidence of subalternity is to find a glimpse of those without identity, in the sense that they or their ways of knowing and being can only be noticed rather than understood by mainstream forms of conceptualizing or mainstream regimes of political power (Jazeel 2014, 2016; Legg forthcoming). If in archival research the fragment—subaltern or not—appears as a clue in state archival documents, or as a description of a space that is beyond regulation and recognition, in urban research the fragment appears in different ways. For example, it may appear as a form of politics that offers a challenge, yet to be realized, to existing debates on urban politics or as a way of expressing the significance of political struggle that jars with existing ways of explaining the nature of struggle. Some urban research will seek out urban fragments, subaltern or otherwise, and some will stumble across them; some accounts will seek to incorporate the fragment into a whole of some form, while others will seek to find in the fragment itself an insight into a whole, and others still will seek to stay with the fragment without speaking to something "bigger."

A fragment, in this reading, may be a marginalized space or group that is regularly identifiable but has not yet been taken seriously as a challenge to conventional ways of conceptualizing and researching. The figure of the "peasant," in the historical archive, *may* appear to the researcher as a subaltern fragment in the sense that elements of that figure require different forms of conceptualization and thinking, for instance in the importance of spirituality to conceptions of the political in colonial India and the intersections between those conceptions and particular notions of "modernity" (e.g., Chakrabarty 2002; Chatterjee 1993, 2004, 2011; Shah 2010). But it may also appear as a nonsubaltern fragment in the sense that it is identified, partially understood, and debated but not granted the level of appreciation that does justice to it in the production of historical scholarship. The fact that subaltern studies scholars, and those influenced by them, have moved between these positions in their different definitions of "subaltern" is partly why the term has become so uncertain.

As Spivak (2005) has argued, the subaltern is difficult to discern in dominant ways of knowing because such forms of knowing are themselves constituted by nonrecognition: it is not simply that they don't record the subaltern, but that they are structured as a way of seeing and knowing that makes them unable to recognize and record the subaltern. A fragment may take this form, but it does not *only* refer to that which is beyond recognition. Some fragments are easily identifiable as such, and some—subaltern fragments—are merely detectable by existing approaches but cannot be identified and understood. Importantly, however, *both* kinds of fragments may require in different ways new forms of theorization, whether in radically translating existing conceptions or developing new forms of conceptualization and methodology. For example, understandings of the production of infrastructure in various parts of the urban Global South have challenged urban researchers to rethink the basis upon which infrastructure becomes politicized, especially in delinking politicization from narratives of privatization and breakdown, but these are not on the whole subaltern fragments (e.g., Chattopadhyay 2012; Graham and McFarlane 2014; Kooy and Bakker 2008; McFarlane 2011; Simone 2009, 2014).

The fragment is not the same as the particular, but names what is abstracted from the particular. The fragment then speaks in different ways beyond the particular: whether in the hands of Lefebvre (as part of a whole), Benjamin (as revelatory of a wider truth), or Chakrabarty (as a critique of what the whole stops us seeing and as a generative space of new ways of knowing or conceiving politics, history, etc.). In other words, the fragment is related in different ways to the idea of the whole, which is first and foremost a question of how the fragment functions as an abstraction. Given this location to the whole, the forming of the fragment as an abstraction is a process that occurs within certain power relations. The fragment takes on its identity *as* a fragment by virtue of how it is placed either within or apart from the whole, and the act of shifting the fragment beyond mere empirical particularity through abstraction is then an act of critique of how the whole is understood.

Abstraction entails establishing a connection or rapport across different cases, comparatively or through a revelatory insight or provocative juxtaposition that is not carried through into a formal comparison. Drawing on Isobel Stengers (2008), Derek McCormack (2012) shows how some forms of abstraction operate not simply as generalizations but as lures that draw attention to something that matters. He calls for "greater attention to the generative role that abstraction plays in disclosing and giving consistency to different kinds of worlds" (McCormack 2012, 727).

In beginning to develop a subaltern studies imagination of urban fragments, this question of abstraction-as-lure is useful. A critical sense that there is something important not being seen and said, or being actively prevented from being seen and said by histories of representation and power, is at the heart of the subaltern project. It is in this sense that a lure to something that seems to matter operates as a useful analytical strategy of the fragment. The spaces that Pieterse signposts as potential "catalysts" to a different urban knowledge—the slum, the taxi rank, the mosque, the garbage ground, and so on—are fragments in a conceptual rather than strictly empirical sense in that they act as lures to something that matters. Why lures? Because they have yet to be adequately appreciated in the histories of urban thought. But the lure to spaces marginal to theory need not be the spaces of the impoverished and dispossessed or, in Chakrabarty's terms, "episodic" fragments. Fragments have, then, no pregiven geography. They may be found in the contemporary city or in the archive, and while in much of my discussion in this chapter I have mentioned cities in South Asia or Africa, fragments may be found in all sorts of cities across the Global South and North. What marks out a fragment as such is its marginal relation to how the city is understood; the marginal relation is also a relation of power, given that the focus of attention in any disciplinary endeavor reflects particular ways of seeing and narrativizing the world.

A subaltern studies imagination rejects the idea that research can or should be judged in relation to a narrow range of abstractions of generalization, universalism, and particularism, where "higher-level" forms of abstraction are privileged as more powerful. It does not predetermine the potential "reach" of a fragment. Reaching out beyond empirical cases, the fragment is an uncertain, searching, and challenging provocation that may form new abstractions and ways of seeing. In other words, insight into the whole may come as much from fragments as from well-heeled generalizations.

In a subaltern studies imagination of the fragment, marginal spaces are cast not as peculiarities but as challenges to existing forms of conceptualization and methodology: Do we need to translate, rethink, or generate anew existing conceptualizations or methodological approaches to better understand this fragment? Theoretical pluralism is not an unfortunate outcome of this process but a necessary one: it reflects the multiplicity and often jarringly incommensurable nature of an urban world, not a crisis in consensus or an inability to identify generalized processes. A subaltern studies imagination is not a position that is against generalization. Generalization is another form of abstraction, based on identifying logics, processes, or forms that translate and reshape across space and that have a certain degree of irrefutable, evidential basis. The form of abstraction relevant to the fragment is different in that it seeks to take the messages from an empirical moment to speak out, as a process of dialogic translation, from an empirical moment to other logics, forms, and processes in different parts of the urban world. Here, abstraction is that which exceeds the particular but which is not necessarily "general." A subaltern studies imagination of abstraction entails a certain style or atmosphere of urban studies—a generative openness to the epistemic and methodological challenge and possibilities of marginal spaces; a recognition that urban multiplicity, translation, and incommensurability necessitates theoretical experimentation and difference; and a recognition of the need for generalization but with a desire to stay with and listen to the fragment longer than we might otherwise have done.

Conclusion

In this chapter I have sought to extend the dialogue between subaltern studies and urban studies through the idea of the fragment. While the fragment is important in different ways to both sets of debates, there has been little consideration of what a subaltern studies imagination of the fragment might bring to urban research. This is not a straightforward conversation. Identifying fragments in archival research, for instance, is not the same process as identifying fragments in urban space, not least because urban space continually presents multiple prompts that compete for our attention and that challenge our systems of representation. There is, of course, a great deal more thinking to do to arrive at new ways of conceiving and researching fragments. What I have attempted is to point out that subaltern studies offers some useful resources here, and these resources challenge some traditions of thinking and researching fragment-whole relations in urban studies while providing useful development in others. To ignore the possibilities of a subaltern studies imagination of the fragment, as part of a wider effort to think fragments and their relations to urban knowledge, would be a missed opportunity for urban researchers.

As a starting point, two steps are especially important in bringing a subaltern studies imagination to urban fragments. The first is the recognition that constructions of the urban whole involve a set of power relations that can exclude, subordinate, or otherwise transform fragments. A key insight of the critical work on nationalism, history, and fragments in India from scholars like Partha Chatterjee and Gyanendra Pandey is that fragments are produced as such because of conceptual power relations. These relations entail ways of seeing that exclude other knowledge-forms (such as those around spirituality), actively subordinate other ways of being and knowing through incorporation (e.g., of Dalits), or serve to justify different forms of violence (e.g., against Muslims). The first step then is one of recognition that fragments are produced as fragments because of systems of representation that are also systems of power, and it is for this reason that slums for instance not only remain relatively marginal to the construction of most urban theory but in some, albeit rare, cases are perceived as "peculiar."

The second step relates to the potential of the fragment as an abstraction, that is, as more than just the empirical particularity that constructions of the whole may imply. Here, the fragment is a form of experimentation, where experimentation derives from speculating rather than incorporating. There are different ways in which we might begin to explore analytical strategies for thinking about the fragment. For example, in montage the analytical strategy is one of juxtaposition of different renderings of urban life, as in the work of Walter Benjamin. Or, as a lure, the fragment is an invitation to speculative thought, requiring a pause to dwell with something that appears to offer something that matters for how we represent the urban world but that lies at the edges of those ways of representing. A research agenda around urban fragments would require an elaboration of these and other forms of analytical strategies. What I hope to have opened out here is the productive contribution that subaltern studies can make to this effort. Such fragments have the potential to act as moments of disruption; knowledge-forms that take the shape of an event that challenges understanding and theory and that potentially goes further in translating existing knowledge or prompting new ways of knowing urbanism.

In closing, I want to highlight two other issues that are important to a research agenda of urban fragments: first, on the implications for the imaginary of urban studies as a field; and, second, for the role of translation and incommensurability in urban theorization. First, from the perspective of the subaltern studies imagination of the fragment outlined here, urban studies is not a field to be narrowed around shared definitions, vocabularies, and inner logics. It is an expanding set of conceptual fragments, some articulate and some contradicting one another. It is an urban studies, then, without a consensus on what urbanism is, or on what urban politics is, or on what urban space is—an urban studies, in short, inherently open, experimental, and generative around the very question of "*what is*." Or, as AbdouMaliq Simone (2011, 356) has put it in a different context, an urban studies centered—or, perhaps more accurately, decentered—on how "the acknowledgement of multiple realities—visible and invisible—means that the urban is always 'slipping away' from us, always also somewhere else than where we expect it to be." This does not mean, of course, that it is not possible to make general claims about what cities are today or how urbanism operates, about why urbanism takes the shape it does, or around how we might respond. However, it does mean that not only are these questions understood in a context of radical openness to revision through fragments but also fragments themselves are at least as important, if not more so, than the generalities and systematizations through which urbanism is often understood.

Second, and following this, the mode of theorization of urban fragments is attuned to notions of translation and incommensurability. As Roy (2011) has argued, it is important that marginalized or subaltern spaces are not theorized simply within preconceived parameters, such as the informal settlement or the megacity, given that such moves reinstate the false notion of the slum or the megacity as possessing unique forms of urbanism. Fragments need not be restricted to what Roy calls the "habitus of the dispossessed" but may provide pointers, as they are translated in the process of abstraction, to better understand urban practices in quite different domains—from planning and the state to the operations of global movements and markets (and, conversely, see Simone [2009, 2014] on redeploying grammars of financial capital for understanding ordinary urban spaces). For example, improvised forms of politics, housing, or infrastructure in informal settlements in Mumbai may help to clarify the nature of improvised economies and housing left in the wake of austerity urbanism in Western cities; shed new light on the long histories of experimental urban squatting witnessed in Amsterdam, Berlin, or Copenhagen; provide resources for understanding the calculations that increasingly constitute the everyday lives of British families dependent on urban food banks; or develop better understandings of new ways of organizing relatively wealthy neighborhoods in Mumbai and elsewhere (e.g., see Lisa Björkman, forthcoming, on water in Mumbai). In each of these moves, the translation of fragments as they are abstracted from particular empirical contexts is a vital process, requiring care and focus on what, if anything, a fragment may offer for understanding quite different places and processes.

By incommensurability, I am referring not just to the sense that urban politics or cultures might take radically different forms in different parts of the world but to the sense that there is no one particular way of thinking about the nature of urbanism, the city, urbanization, urban politics, urban space, and so on. Neither fragments themselves, nor ways of thinking about them, are homogeneous. All knowledge of the urban, and the locations from which knowledge is produced and the routes through which it is composed, however revelatory and important, is provisional and limited. This is not, again, to reject the need for grand narratives or generalizations. Generalized abstractions, such as the increasingly global nature of processes like neoliberalism in the shaping of cities, are not just inevitable but essential. They help us to locate resonances in processes shaping urban space and politics, identify shifts in multiple locations, and provide framings through which to build comparative research. They can also, of course, stifle the capacity of other explanations or concepts to survive and thrive. Neoliberalism is particularly adept at this precisely because of the hybrid, contingent, and changing form—it can gather just too much up into its explanatory frame. But as Dipesh Chakrabarty has argued (2002), it surely cannot be the business of theorists to seek out grounds to *reject* such macrological explanations of globality but instead to look *for the grounds upon which we can accept them* in any particular context (i.e., around whether and how, and through which translations, we might put them to use). This means acknowledging that however global its reach, and despite the fact that neoliberalism could hardly be described as a fragment, it is nonetheless limited: its operation in some contexts may be one of translation through different fragments, while in others it may be incommensurable with other fragments that are more important in producing and contesting urban space (Bunnell 2013; Parnell and Robinson 2012). As Spivak (1993, 60) has put it, this entails saying an "impossible 'no' to a structure [of explanation], which one critiques, yet inhabits intimately."

REFERENCES

AlSayyad, N., and A. Roy. 2006. "Medieval Modernity: On Citizenship and Urbanism in a Global Era." *Space and Polity* 10, no. 1: 1–20.
Amin, A. 2013. "The Urban Condition: A Challenge to Social Science." *Public Culture* 25, no. 2: 201–8.
Bagelman, J. J. 2013. "Sanctuary: A Politics of Ease?" *Alternatives: Global, Local, Political* 38: 49–62.
Bakker, K. 2003. "Archipelagos and Networks: Urbanisation and Water Privatisation in the South." *Geographical Journal* 169, no. 4: 328–41.
Benjamin, W. 2003. *The Arcades Project*. Translated by Howard Eiland and Kevin McLaughlin. Cambridge, Mass.: Harvard University Press.
Björkman, L. Forthcoming. *Pipe Politics: Mumbai's Contested Waters*. Durham, N.C.: Duke University Press.
Brenner, N. 2013. "Theses on Urbanization." *Public Culture* 25, no. 1: 85–114.
Brenner, N., and C. Schmid. 2012. "Planetary Urbanization." In *Urban Constellations*, edited by M. Gandy, 10–13. Berlin: Jovis.
Buck-Morss, S. 1989. *The Dialectics of Seeing: Walter Benjamin and the Arcades Project*. Cambridge, Mass.: MIT Press.
Bunnell, T. 2015. "Antecedent Cities and Inter-referencing Effects: Learning from and Extending beyond Critiques of Neoliberalisation." *Urban Studies* 52, no. 11: 1983–2000.
Bunnell, T., and A. Maringanti. 2010. "Practising Urban Regional Research beyond Metrocentricity." *International Journal of Urban and Regional Research* 34: 415–20.
Caldeira, T. 2000. *City of Walls: Crime, Segregation, and Citizenship in Sao Paulo*. Berkeley: University of California Press.
Chakrabarty, D. 1996. "Marxism after Marx: History, Subalternity and Difference." In *Marxism beyond Marxism*, edited by S. Makdisi, C. Casarino, and R. E. Karle, 55–70. New York: Routledge.

———. 2002. *Habitations of Modernity: Essays in the Wake of Subaltern Studies*. Chicago: University of Chicago Press.

Chatterjee, P. 1993. *The Nation and Its Fragments: Colonial and Postcolonial Histories*. Princeton, N.J.: Princeton University Press.

———. 2004. *The Politics of the Governed: Popular Politics in Most of the World*. New York: Columbia University Press.

———. 2011. *Lineages of Political Society: Studies in Postcolonial Democracy*. New York: Columbia University Press.

———. 2013. "Subaltern Studies and *Capital*." *Economic and Political Weekly* 48, no. 37: 69–75.

Chattopadhyay, S. 2012. *Unlearning the City: Infrastructure in a New Optical Field*. Minneapolis: University of Minnesota Press.

Chaturvedi, V. Ed. 2012. *Mapping Subaltern Studies and the Postcolonial*. London: Verso.

Chibber, V. 2013. *Postcolonial Theory and the Specter of Capital*. London: Verso.

Darling, J. 2014. "Asylum and the Post-Political: Domopolitics, Depoliticisation and Acts of Citizenship." *Antipode* 46, no. 1: 72–91.

Derrida, J. 1976. *Of Grammatology*. Translated by Gayatri Chakravorty Spivak. Baltimore, Md.: Johns Hopkins University Press.

———. 1981. *Positions*. Translated by Alan Bass. Chicago: University of Chicago Press.

Dikeç, M. 2005. "Space, Politics and the Political." *Environment and Planning D: Society and Space* 23: 171–88.

Eiland, H., and K. McLaughlin. Eds. 2003. "Translator's Foreword." In W. Benjamin, *The Arcades Project* (2003), edited by H. Eiland and K. McLaughlin, ix–2. Cambridge, Mass.: Harvard University Press.

Featherstone, D. J. 2008. *Resistance, Space and Political Identities: The Making of Counter-Global Networks*. Oxford: Wiley-Blackwell.

———. 2009. "Counter-Insurgency, Subalternity and Spatial Relations: Interrogating Court Martial Narratives of the Nore Mutiny of 1797." *South African Historical Journal* 61, no. 4: 765–86.

———. 2012. "Chapter 23: Politics." In *The SAGE Handbook of Human Geography*, edited by Roger Lee and Noel Castree, 522–43. London: Sage.

Gidwani, V. 2008. "Capitalism's Anxious Whole: Fear, Capture and Escape in the *Grundrisse*." *Antipode* 40, no. 5: 857–78.

———. 2009. "Subalternity." In *International Encyclopedia of Human Geography*, edited by Rob Kitchin and Nigel Thrift, 65–71. London: Elsevier.

———. 2013. "Six Theses on Waste, Value and Commons." *Social and Cultural Geography* 14, no. 7: 773–83.

Gidwani, V., and R. N. Reddy. 2011. "The Afterlives of Waste: Notes from India for a Minor History of Capitalist Surplus." *Antipode* 43, no. 4 (November): 1625–58.

Graham, S., and S. Marvin. 2001. *Splintering Urbanism: Networked Infrastructures, Technological Mobilities and the Urban Condition*. Oxford: Blackwell.

Graham, S., and C. McFarlane. Eds. 2014. *Infrastructural Lives: Urban Infrastructure in Context*. London: Routledge-Earthscan.

Gramsci, A. 1971. *Selections from Prison Notebooks*. London: Lawrence and Wishart.

Harvey, D. 1993. "Social Justice, Postmodernism, and the City." *International Journal of Urban and Regional Research* 16: 588–601.

Jacobs, J. M. 2012. "Urban Geography I: Still Thinking Cities Relationally I." *Progress in Human Geography* 36, no. 3: 412–22.
Jazeel, T. 2014. "Subaltern Geographies: Geographical Knowledge and Postcolonial Strategy." *Singapore Journal of Tropical Geography* 35, no. 1: 88–103.
———. 2016. "Between Area and Discipline: Progress, Knowledge Production and the Geographies of Geography." *Progress in Human Geography* 40, no. 5: 649–67.
Jazeel, T., and C. McFarlane. 2010. "The Limits of Responsibility: A Postcolonial Politics of Academic Knowledge Production." *Transactions of the Institute of British Geographers* 35, no. 1: 109–24.
Kaviraj, S. 1997. "Filth and the Public Sphere: Concepts and Practices about Space in Calcutta." *Public Culture* 10, no. 1: 83–113.
Kooy, M., and K. Bakker. 2008. "Technologies of Government: Constituting Subjectivities, Spaces, and Infrastructures in Colonial and Contemporary Jakarta." *International Journal of Urban and Regional Research* 32: 375–91.
Lees, L., T. Slater, and E. Wyly. 2008. *Gentrification*. New York: Routledge.
McCormack, D. P. 2012. "Geography and Abstraction: Towards an Affirmative Critique." *Progress in Human Geography* 36, no. 6: 715–34.
McFarlane, C., and G. MacLeod. 2014. "Grammars of Urban Injustice." *Antipode* 46, no. 4: 857–73.
Merrifield, A. 2013. "The Urban Question under Planetary Urbanization." *International Journal of Urban and Regional Research* 37, no. 3: 909–22.
———. 2014. *The New Urban Question*. London: Pluto Press.
Mitchell, D. 2001. "Postmodern Geographical Praxis? The Postmodern Impulse and the War against Homeless People in the 'Post-Justice' City." In *Postmodern Geography: Theory and Praxis*, edited by C. Minca, 57–92. Oxford: Blackwell.
Napolitano, V. 2015. "Anthropology and Traces." *Anthropological Theory* 15, no. 1: 47–67.
Pandey, G. 1991. "In Defence of the Fragment: Writing about Hindu-Muslim Riots in India Today." *Economic and Political Weekly* (March): 559–72.
———. 2006. *Routine Violence: Nations, Fragments, Histories*. Stanford, Calif.: Stanford University Press.
Pieterse, E. 2011. "Rethinking African Urbanism from the Slum." LSE Cities, http://lsecities.net/media/objects/articles/rethinking-african-urbanism-from-the-slum/en-gb/, accessed July 2014.
Pred, A. 2000. *Even in Sweden: Racisms, Racialized Spaces, and the Popular Geographical Imagination*. Berkeley: University of California Press.
Robinson, J. 2006. *Ordinary Cities: Between Modernity and Development*. London: Routledge.
———. 2011. "Cities in a World of Cities: The Comparative Gesture." *International Journal of Urban and Regional Research* 35: 1–23.
Rokem, J., S. Fregonese, A. Ramadan, A. Pascucci, G. Rosen, I. Charney, T. F. Paasche, and J. Sidaway. 2017. "Interventions in Urban Geopolitics." *Political Geography* 61: 253–62.
Roy, A. 2010. *Poverty Capital: Microfinance and the Making of Development*. New York: Routledge.
———. 2011. "Slumdog Cities: Rethinking Subaltern Urbanism." *International Journal of Urban and Regional Research* 35: 223–38.

Scott, A. J., and M. Storper. 2014. "In the Nature of Cities: The Scope and Limits of Urban Theory." *International Journal of Urban and Regional Research* 39, no. 1: 1–15.

Shah, A. 2010. *In the Shadows of the State: Indigenous Politics, Environmentalism, and Insurgency in Jharkhand, India*. Durham, N.C.: Duke University Press.

Sidaway, J. D., C. Y. Woon, and J. M. Jacobs. 2014. "Planetary Postcolonialism." *Singapore Journal of Tropical Geography* 35, no. 1: 4–21.

Simone, A. 2009. *City Life from Jakarta to Dakar: Movements at the Crossroads*. London: Routledge.

———. 2011. "The Surfacing of Urban Life." *City* 15, nos. 3–4: 355–64.

———. 2014. *Jakarta, Drawing the City Near*. Minneapolis: University of Minnesota Press.

Smith, N. 1996. *The New Urban Frontier: Gentrification and the Revanchist City*. London: Routledge.

Spivak, G. S. 1993. *Outside in the Teaching Machine*. New York: Routledge.

———. 2005. "Scattered Speculations on the Subaltern and the Popular." *Postcolonial Studies* 8, no. 4: 483.

Stengers, I. 2008. "A Constructivist Reading of Process and Reality." *Theory, Culture and Society* 25, no. 4.: 91–110.

Swanton, D. 2010. "Flesh, Metal, Road: Tracing the Machinic Geographies of Race." *Environment and Planning D: Society and Space* 28, no. 3: 447–66.

Swyngedouw, E. 2011. "Interrogating Post-Democratization: Reclaiming Egalitarian Political Spaces." *Political Geography* 30, no. 7: 370–80.

Tiedemann, R. 2008. "Additional Notes." In T. Adorno (2008), *Lectures on Negative Dialectics: Fragments of a Lecture Course, 1965/66*, edited by Rolf Tiedemann, translated by Rodney Livingstone, 178–82. Cambridge, Mass.: Polity Press .

Young, I. M. 1990. *Justice and the Politics of Difference*. Princeton, N.J.: Princeton University Press.

CONTRIBUTORS

David Arnold, Emeritus Professor of History at the University of Warwick, has written widely on science, technology, medicine, and the environment in relation to modern India. A member of the original Subaltern Studies Collective, his work has engaged with many aspects of subaltern life. Recent publications include *Everyday Technology: Machines and the Making of India's Modernity* (2013) and *Toxic Histories: Poison and Pollution in Modern India* (2016).

Sharad Chari is at the Department of Geography at the University of California, Berkeley, and is affiliated to WiSER at the University of the Witwatersrand. He is the author of *Fraternal Capital* (2004) and is completing a book called *Apartheid Remains* on the remains of racial capitalism and struggle in South Africa. His current interests are in black Marxism, oceanic studies, and geography as a form of writing.

David Featherstone is Senior Lecturer in Human Geography at the University of Glasgow. His research focuses on the relations between space and politics and the formation of transnational solidarities, and he has a long-standing interest in the relations between subaltern studies and histories from below. He is the author of *Resistance, Space and Political Identities: The Making of Counter-Global Networks* (2008) and *Solidarity: Hidden Histories and Geographies of Internationalism* (2012), and he is a member of the editorial collective of *Soundings: A Journal Politics of Culture*.

Vinay Gidwani studies the entanglements of labor and ecology in agrarian and urban settings as well as capitalist transformations of these. He focuses on questions of waste and value; the cultural politics and geographies of work; the more-than-human constitution of social relations; and emergent terrains of poverty, injustice, stigma, and struggle. His ongoing research, employing oral histories, is on the life-worlds of informal-sector workers in India's cities.

Tariq Jazeel teaches Human Geography at University College London. His research interests are positioned at the intersections of critical geography, postcolonial theory, and South Asian studies. His work focuses on aesthetic and cultural constitutions of space and the political as well as the postcolonial politics of geographical knowledge production. He is the author of *Sacred Modernity: Nature, Environment and the Postcolonial Geographies of Sri Lankan Nationhood* (2013) and coeditor of *Spatialising Politics: Culture and Geography in Postcolonial Sri Lanka* (2009).

Mukul Kumar is a PhD candidate in the Department of City and Regional Planning at the University of California, Berkeley. His current research examines the politics of land, energy, and development in India.

Sunil Kumar is a Delhi-based social and political activist and an independent writer and researcher.

Anna F. Laing is Lecturer in International Development and Geography at the University of Sussex. Her chapter is based on her doctoral research, which explored the spatial politics of left-indigenous movements during the TIPNIS conflict, Bolivia. Her wider academic interests include the geographies of social movements, the political ecology of resource governance, critical development studies, subaltern studies and decolonial perspectives, climate justice, and food sovereignty movements.

Stephen Legg is Professor of Historical Geography at the University of Nottingham. His research focuses on interwar India, exploring the geographies of colonialism and nationalism at the scales of the city, the state, and the imperial-international. He is the author of *Spaces of Colonialism: Delhi's Urban Geographies* (2007) and *Prostitution and the Ends of Empire: Scale, Governmentalities and Interwar India* (2014) and the coeditor, with Deana Heath, of *South Asian Governmentalities: Michel Foucault and the Question of Postcolonial Orderings* (in press).

Colin McFarlane is Professor of Urban Geography at Durham University, UK. His work focuses on the making, experience, and politics of urban life and their relation to urban knowledge, infrastructure, and informalities. This has involved research across Mumbai, Kampala, Berlin, and Cape Town. He is author of *Learning the City: Knowledge and Translocal Assemblage* (2011) and coeditor of *Infrastructural Lives: Urban Infrastructure in Context* (2014, with Steve Graham), *Urban Navigations: Politics, Space, and the City* (2011, with Jonathan Anjaria), and *Urban Informalities: Reflections on the Formal and Informal* (2012, with Michael Waibel).

Sarah A. Radcliffe is based at the Department of Geography, University of Cambridge. Her research focuses on the sociospatial dynamics of rule and resistance in the Andes, especially in relation to colonial-modern intersectionality. She has published widely on these themes including discussions of development, social movements, and governance and in *Dilemmas of Difference: Indigenous Women and the Limits of Postcolonial Development Policy* (2015).

Ananya Roy is Professor of Urban Planning, Social Welfare, and Geography and inaugural Director of the Institute on Inequality and Democracy at the University of California, Los Angeles. Her most recent research is concerned with the urban land question and imaginations of abolition, reconstruction, and redistribution.

Jo Sharp is Professor of Geography at the University of Glasgow. Her research interests are in the intersections of feminist, postcolonial, and political geographies. Her publications include: *Geographies of Postcolonialism: Spaces of Power and Representation* (2009), *The Ashgate Research Companion to Critical Geopolitics* (coedited with Klaus Dodds and Merje Kuus, 2013), *Geopolitics: An Introductory Reader* (with Jason Dittmer, 2014), and *The Wiley-Blackwell Companion to Political Geography* (with John Agnew, Virginie Mamadouh, and Anna Secor, 2015).

INDEX

1857 uprising (India), 7, 37

Abstraction, 38, 71, 135, 213–15, 222–26
Agency: Indigenous, 121, 133, 136; more-than-human, 119, 121, 126, 131–32, 136; peasant, 4, 6, 98; philosophical, 7, 12–16, 103–6, 211; political, 74, 75, 89, 95, 108, 212; political society and, 21
Agriculture, 9, 40, 44, 129
Ali, Surat, 110, 111, 114n14
Althusser, 9, 13, 28, 144
Amazonian region and peoples, 127, 167, 171–73, 176–80, 182–85
Ambiguity, 6, 9, 37, 46, 49, 69
Anticolonialism, 46, 108, 110–11, 124, 213
Archive: colonial, 4, 17–18, 26–27; historical narratives and, 14, 38, 63–64; transcultural, 195, 197–98, 204, 206
Autonomy: Indigenous, 127–28, 130–31, 170, 172, 176, 179; theoretical, 9–10, 12, 20–21, 51, 104

Bay of Bengal, 194, 198, 199, 201–3, 205–6
Bengal, 5, 26, 38, 58–71, 98–100, 213
Bolivia, 23, 120, 122, 127, 167–85

Caste, 23–24, 42–46, 49–51, 154–56, 158–59, 213–14
Chakrabarty, Dipesh: on class, 103–4, 108; on Eurocentrism, 17–19, 66; on urban theory, 25–26, 37–38, 214–16, 218, 227
Chatterjee, Partha: on autonomy, 9–11, 105–6; on particularism, 18, 68–69, 213–14; on political society, 20–21, 58, 60–61
cidob (Indigenous Confederation of the Bolivian East, Chaco and Amazon), 167, 169, 173, 179–80, 185
City, 36–53, 142–43, 156–60, 181, 218–19, 226
Civil society, 13, 18, 20, 94, 101, 158, 183
Colonialism: coloniality and, 19, 23, 120–25, 168–69, 181, 185; discourses of, 10, 63, 196–97; geography and, 3, 70, 121–22, 124
Communalism: religious groupings, 7, 37, 40, 44, 51; shared ownings, 72, 78, 130, 170–71, 173
Congress, Indian National, 7, 100, 111
Conrad, Joseph, 1–2
Consciousness: peasant, 7–8, 37, 40, 71; political, 96–99, 103, 113n3, 155; sovereign, 11–14
Cosmopolitanism, 24–25, 137n2

Daily Worker, 110, 114n12
Dalit, 24, 154–60, 214, 225
Decoloniality, 19, 23, 121–23, 125, 130, 168
Decolonization, 77, 84, 120–21, 184–85
Decolonizing, 121–22, 180
Deconstruction, 13, 15–16, 61–62, 98, 104, 145
Development, 78–79, 125, 169–72, 174–75, 220
Difference: historical, 5, 59, 61; political, 96–97, 103; representation of, 14–18, 23–25, 192; rule of, 20, 213

Earth-being, 121, 124–26, 128, 131–32, 134–35
East, 2, 8, 70, 77
Elite, 6–11, 20–21, 51–53, 76, 78–80, 90
Enlightenment, 18, 85, 125, 195
Epistemology: disruption of, 4, 15, 84, 144; of fragments and otherness, 19, 22, 199, 210–12, 224; Indigenous, 121–24, 128, 132, 172, 184–85; of property, 58–63, 65–66, 71
Ethnicity: collaborations, 6–7, 37, 98, 105, 124, 127; conflict among, 19, 171; postcolonial categories of, 23, 120–22
Ethnography, 122, 135, 200–201
Eurocentrism, 4, 17–19, 25, 58, 83, 102, 121, 123, 168, 173, 200
Europe: history writing in, 102, 105, 168; political economic theory and, 59, 62, 65, 70; provincializing of, 17–18, 83, 87, 89–90, 155, 213

235

Feminism, 5, 12, 26, 130, 135, 157, 196
Foucault, Michel, 9, 13, 15, 19–20, 39, 137n7, 168
Fragment, 17, 76, 135, 199, 206, 210–27

Gandhi, Mohandas Karamchand, 9, 38, 52, 99, 102, 168
Gender, 8, 15, 76, 123, 129–30, 213
Generalization, 123, 135, 212, 216, 223–24, 226
Geographical imagination, 2–4, 6–7, 17, 74–79, 90, 138n20
Geography: decolonizing, 121–22; discipline of, 1, 3–5, 17, 19, 21–28, 135; political, 59, 75; subaltern, 53, 136, 204
Geopolitics, 19, 24–25, 74–78, 90
Gopal, Priya, 98–99, 108, 113
Governmentality, 18–21, 39, 60, 133–34, 172, 199
Gramsci, Antonio: influence on subaltern scholarship, 120, 123, 145, 206, 214, 219; influence on Subaltern Studies Collective, 4, 51, 94, 96, 101, 112
Guha, Ranajit, 1–14, 37–39, 48–50, 58–68, 96–98, 100–104; *A Rule of Property for Bengal*, 5, 26, 58–67, 70–71

Heart of Darkness (Conrad), 1–2
Hegemony: domination and, 51–52, 98, 102, 123, 132, 136; political society and, 19–20, 39
Hindu, 38, 42, 51, 158, 162n14, 214
Historiography: colonial and imperial, 9, 63, 70, 103; elite, 18, 20, 58–59, 69; subaltern, 13, 61, 98

Imperialism: interpretations of, 8–9, 15, 102, 199; practices of, 26–27, 82, 89, 194, 197, 201
Incommensurability, 26, 213, 223–27
Indian National Congress, 7, 100, 111
Indigenous, 19, 23, 26, 119–36, 150, 167–85
Infrastructure: human, 158, 195, 197–99; transport, 167, 201–3, 205–6; urban, 142–43, 161n1, 211, 220, 222, 226
Insurgency, 5–6, 14, 36–37, 40, 58, 68
Islam. *See* Muslims

Land: disputes, 23, 40, 122–24, 126–27, 170–73, 177–81; ownership, 58–61, 63–71, 218
Landscape, 24, 41, 62, 119, 124, 131
Language, 11, 66, 74, 124, 130, 181

Latin America, 19, 123, 168, 170, 179, 184
Liberal governance, 23, 61, 99, 134, 170, 177
Liberal historiography, 59, 66, 69, 70–71
Liberalism, 71, 72n6

Maritime labor, 110, 199
Marx, Karl, 13, 19, 147–50, 162n11
Marxism, 88, 100, 104, 145, 155; Marxian analysis, 25, 40, 88–90, 159, 193; Marxian historiography, 13, 59, 63, 66, 69, 96
Massey, Doreen, 103, 144
Memory, 11
Menon, Krishna, 100, 110–11, 113, 114n16
Mignolo, Walter, 19, 123, 137, 168–69, 176, 185
Mononature, 200
Muslims, 7, 51, 111, 151, 154, 162, 225

Nation: building, 74–75, 84–87; ethnic, 175, 178; Indian, 39, 53, 162n10; island, 205; modern, 127; partition of, 7–8, 11
Nationalism: anti-/post-colonial, 194, 198, 202–3; Indian, 2, 213–14, 222, 224; Latin American, 170–71; mentioned, 77–78, 145, 163n18, 197–98
nation-state: modern, 121–22, 170; postcolonial, 124, 132–33, 136
Nature, 24, 121–22, 132–34, 170, 180
Neocolonialism, 3, 13, 74, 78–79, 88, 90
Network: Actor Network Theory, 137n2; maritime, 107, 113n, 201–2; subaltern, 22; mentioned, 2–3, 7–8, 11–12, 16, 24, 76, 100, 128–29, 142, 151, 154, 157, 199
networking, 7, 11, 108
New Left, 96, 100

O'Hanlon, Rosalind, 13
Orientalism, 1, 3, 11, 20, 70, 76–77

Pachakutik political party, 125
Pachamama, 23, 119–20, 128–36, 137n12
Particular, 61–63, 76, 144, 163, 219–20, 222–26
Partition, 8, 159–60
Peasant: agency/consciousness, 4–6, 12–14, 213; insurgency/revolt/uprising, 9–10, 58–60, 68, 100, 113n1; Landless Peasant Movement, 180, 216, 221; movement, 96
Permanent Settlement, 58–68
plague, 2, 42–43, 45–46, 49–52, 75
Plurinationalism, 121, 130, 135–36; constitution, 23; state, 120–21, 127, 167, 169–72;

mentioned, 127, 135, 137n10, 169–73, 179–80, 184–85
Political ontology, 33, 130–35
Political society, 9, 20–21, 211
Politics of anteriority, 134–36
Postcolonialism: geography and, 3; history of, 90; states and, 81, 124–25, 132, 134–36; studies/theory of, 1, 3, 14, 65, 71n3, 94, 96, 121, 168, 206
Poststructuralism, 13, 15, 28, 168, 211, 220
Precolonialism, 37, 172
Pre-political, 4, 96–98
Property, 5, 26, 58–72, 126, 158, 170
Protest: Indigenous, 122, 132, 176; political, 214; subaltern, 50–51, 106; mentioned, 44–45, 49–53, 85–86, 113, 114n5, 119–20, 124–27, 131–35, 137n8, 156, 169, 174, 185
Protestors: Indigenous protestors, 180–82; mentioned, 53, 178–80

Relationalities, 25, 95, 104, 112, 131
Rent, 61, 67–69, 72, 142, 151, 157
Representation: misrepresentation, 16; politics of, 3, 14, 17, 19, 74, 145–46; representational practice, 200; spaces of representation, 2, 13
Resistance: domination and, 24, 76, 185; geopoetics of, 182; Indigenous, 123; subaltern, 179, 193
Revenue, 59, 61, 64–69, 172, 175
Revolutionary, 69, 107, 155, 203, 214
riots, 38, 44, 50–52, 105
Rule of Property for Bengal, A (Guha), 5, 26, 58–67, 70–71
rumor, 12, 37, 50

Said, Edward, 1–3, 10, 20, 28, 70, 168
Sartori, Andrew, 60, 68–69, 71
Scale, 6, 8–12, 76, 163, 215
Seafarers' strikes, 113
Self-determination, 120, 136, 168–76, 179
Silence, 1, 3, 26–27, 74, 168, 215–16
Sovereignty: Indigenous, 125, 127–28, 130, 133–34; postcolonial, 121, 134; sovereign power, 8, 20, 160, 193; sovereign subjects, 10, 13, 203; mentioned, 6, 8, 12, 18, 120–21, 125, 134, 135, 136, 170–71, 192–94
Space: city/urban, 41, 127, 161, 212–13, 218–19, 224–26; colonized, 3; conceptual, 13, 38, 53; disciplinary, 36, 47; public, 38, 180, 182–84, 218; religious/sacred, 177; subaltern space / space of subalternity, 3–4, 13, 19, 95, 106, 112, 128, 226
Speech, 16, 158, 167, 181
Spivak, Gayatri Chakravorty, 22, 27, 113, 161n5, 195; changing views over time, 144–46; deconstructionism of, 13–19, 98–99, 168–69; epistemology and, 222, 227; Guha's *A Rule of Property for Bengal* and, 60, 62, 66, 70; representation in, problems of, 13–19, 60, 158, 168–69, 211–12, 216–17; on value, 66
State: colonial, 7, 49, 69, 134, 177; Indian, 9; plurinational, 120, 127, 167–77, 180; postcolonial, 76, 81, 124–25, 132, 134–36; statehood, 119; Tanzanian, 90
Street life, 38, 44, 49, 53
Strikes: Indian Seafarer's strike of 1939, 95, 110–11; mentioned, 44–46, 49, 51, 108–11, 114n16, 158
Subaltern agency, 4, 5, 16, 20–21, 95, 99, 103–4, 106, 108, 121, 184, 185
Subalternity: analytical, 27; empirical, 23, 27; oceanic, 201, 206; spaces of, 106; urban, 36–37, 39–40, 42–43, 46
Subaltern knowledge, 121, 128
Subaltern Studies Collective, 1–2, 4–5, 10, 17–19, 21, 28, 95, 101, 204
Subaltern Studies imagination, 206, 210, 212–13, 219, 221, 223–25
Subject: versus citizen, 60, 68; collective, 169, 179; ideological, 20; versus object, 16–17; sovereign, 11, 13; subaltern, 12–13, 15, 17, 26, 98, 123, 133, 135, 181, 211; universal, 195, 205

Territoriality, 6–8, 37, 49, 180, 185
Territorializations, 6, 119–20, 127, 130, 133–35, 176
Territory: Indigenous, 167, 176; national, 124, 129, 202
Theory: communist, 78; cultural, 211; Indigenous, 121, 134; literary, 5, 13; postcolonial, 3–5, 65, 70, 71n3, 121; posthumanist, 121; urban, 25, 210–13, 218–20, 223
Thompson, E. P., 97–102, 106, 113–14n5
tipnis (Territorio Indígena y Parque Nacional Isiboro), 167–69, 171, 173–81, 184–85
Translation, 3, 65–67, 135, 185n3, 224, 225–27
Transmission, 6, 37, 49–50

Universality, 18, 103, 206, 223; of history, 66, 105; of knowledge, 5, 121; of subject, 195; of

Universality (*continued*)
suffrage, 171; mentioned, 18, 25–26, 58–59, 61, 63–70, 72n7, 81, 102–5, 108, 121, 155, 158, 163n15, 197, 216
Urban fragments, 210, 221, 223–26
Urban geography, 25–26, 144
Urban politics, 219, 221, 225–26
Urban research, 210, 217, 219–22, 224
Urban turn, 39

Value: communal, 78; exchange, 147, 162n13; intellectual, 6; surplus, 146–47; theories of, 60, 67; traditional, 80; use, 143, 201
Violence: caste, 155; epistemological, 123; ontological, 121; police, 174; popular, 97; state, 129; subaltern, 7, 129

Worker: agency, 4; *Daily Worker*, 110, 114n12; domestic, 143

GEOGRAPHIES OF JUSTICE AND SOCIAL TRANSFORMATION

1. *Social Justice and the City,* rev. ed.
   BY DAVID HARVEY
2. *Begging as a Path to Progress: Indigenous Women and Children and the Struggle for Ecuador's Urban Spaces*
   BY KATE SWANSON
3. *Making the San Fernando Valley: Rural Landscapes, Urban Development, and White Privilege*
   BY LAURA R. BARRACLOUGH
4. *Company Towns in the Americas: Landscape, Power, and Working-Class Communities*
   EDITED BY OLIVER J. DINIUS AND ANGELA VERGARA
5. *Tremé: Race and Place in a New Orleans Neighborhood*
   BY MICHAEL E. CRUTCHER JR.
6. *Bloomberg's New York: Class and Governance in the Luxury City*
   BY JULIAN BRASH
7. *Roppongi Crossing: The Demise of a Tokyo Nightclub District and the Reshaping of a Global City*
   BY ROMAN ADRIAN CYBRIWSKY
8. *Fitzgerald: Geography of a Revolution*
   BY WILLIAM BUNGE
9. *Accumulating Insecurity: Violence and Dispossession in the Making of Everyday Life*
   EDITED BY SHELLEY FELDMAN, CHARLES GEISLER, AND GAYATRI A. MENON
10. *They Saved the Crops: Labor, Landscape, and the Struggle over Industrial Farming in Bracero-Era California*
    BY DON MITCHELL
11. *Faith Based: Religious Neoliberalism and the Politics of Welfare in the United States*
    BY JASON HACKWORTH
12. *Fields and Streams: Stream Restoration, Neoliberalism, and the Future of Environmental Science*
    BY REBECCA LAVE
13. *Black, White, and Green: Farmers Markets, Race, and the Green Economy*
    BY ALISON HOPE ALKON
14. *Beyond Walls and Cages: Prisons, Borders, and Global Crisis*
    EDITED BY JENNA M. LOYD, MATT MITCHELSON, AND ANDREW BURRIDGE
15. *Silent Violence: Food, Famine, and Peasantry in Northern Nigeria*
    BY MICHAEL J. WATTS
16. *Development, Security, and Aid: Geopolitics and Geoeconomics at the U.S. Agency for International Development*
    BY JAMEY ESSEX
17. *Properties of Violence: Law and Land-Grant Struggle in Northern New Mexico*
    BY DAVID CORREIA
18. *Geographical Diversions: Tibetan Trade, Global Transactions*
    BY TINA HARRIS
19. *The Politics of the Encounter: Urban Theory and Protest under Planetary Urbanization*
    BY ANDY MERRIFIELD
20. *Rethinking the South African Crisis: Nationalism, Populism, Hegemony*
    BY GILLIAN HART
21. *The Empires' Edge: Militarization, Resistance, and Transcending Hegemony in the Pacific*
    BY SASHA DAVIS
22. *Pain, Pride, and Politics: Social Movement Activism and the Sri Lankan Tamil Diaspora in Canada*
    BY AMARNATH AMARASINGAM
23. *Selling the Serengeti: The Cultural Politics of Safari Tourism*
    BY BENJAMIN GARDNER

24. *Territories of Poverty: Rethinking North and South*
    EDITED BY ANANYA ROY AND EMMA SHAW CRANE
25. *Precarious Worlds: Contested Geographies of Social Reproduction*
    EDITED BY KATIE MEEHAN AND KENDRA STRAUSS
26. *Spaces of Danger: Culture and Power in the Everyday*
    EDITED BY HEATHER MERRILL AND LISA M. HOFFMAN
27. *Shadows of a Sunbelt City: The Environment, Racism, and the Knowledge Economy in Austin*
    BY ELIOT M. TRETTER
28. *Beyond the Kale: Urban Agriculture and Social Justice Activism in New York City*
    BY KRISTIN REYNOLDS AND NEVIN COHEN
29. *Calculating Property Relations: Chicago's Wartime Industrial Mobilization, 1940–1950*
    BY ROBERT LEWIS
30. *In the Public's Interest: Evictions, Citizenship, and Inequality in Contemporary Delhi*
    BY GAUTAM BHAN
31. *The Carpetbaggers of Kabul and Other American-Afghan Entanglements: Intimate Development, Geopolitics, and the Currency of Gender and Grief*
    BY JENNIFER L. FLURI AND RACHEL LEHR
32. *Masculinities and Markets: Raced and Gendered Urban Politics in Milwaukee*
    BY BRENDA PARKER
33. *We Want Land to Live: Making Political Space for Food Sovereignty*
    BY AMY TRAUGER
34. *The Long War: CENTCOM, Grand Strategy, and Global Security*
    BY JOHN MORRISSEY
35. *Development Drowned and Reborn: The Blues and Bourbon Restorations in Post-Katrina New Orleans*
    BY CLYDE WOODS
    EDITED BY JORDAN T. CAMP AND LAURA PULIDO
36. *The Priority of Injustice: Locating Democracy in Critical Theory*
    BY CLIVE BARNETT
37. *Spaces of Capital / Spaces of Resistance: Mexico and the Global Political Economy*
    BY CHRIS HESKETH
38. *Revolting New York: How 400 Years of Riot, Rebellion, Uprising, and Revolution Shaped a City*
    GENERAL EDITORS: NEIL SMITH AND DON MITCHELL
    EDITORS: ERIN SIODMAK, JENJOY ROYBAL, MARNIE BRADY, AND BRENDAN O'MALLEY
39. *Relational Poverty Politics: Forms, Struggles, and Possibilities*
    EDITED BY VICTORIA LAWSON AND SARAH ELWOOD
40. *Rights in Transit: Public Transportation and the Right to the City in California's East Bay*
    BY KAFUI ABLODE ATTOH
41. *Open Borders: In Defense of Free Movement*
    EDITED BY REECE JONES
42. *Subaltern Geographies*
    EDITED BY TARIQ JAZEEL AND STEPHEN LEGG

CPSIA information can be obtained
at www.ICGtesting.com
Printed in the USA
LVHW092347250820
664211LV00006B/488

9 780820 354880